Madeline McDowell Breckinridge

Topics in Kentucky History
James C. Klotter, Series Editor

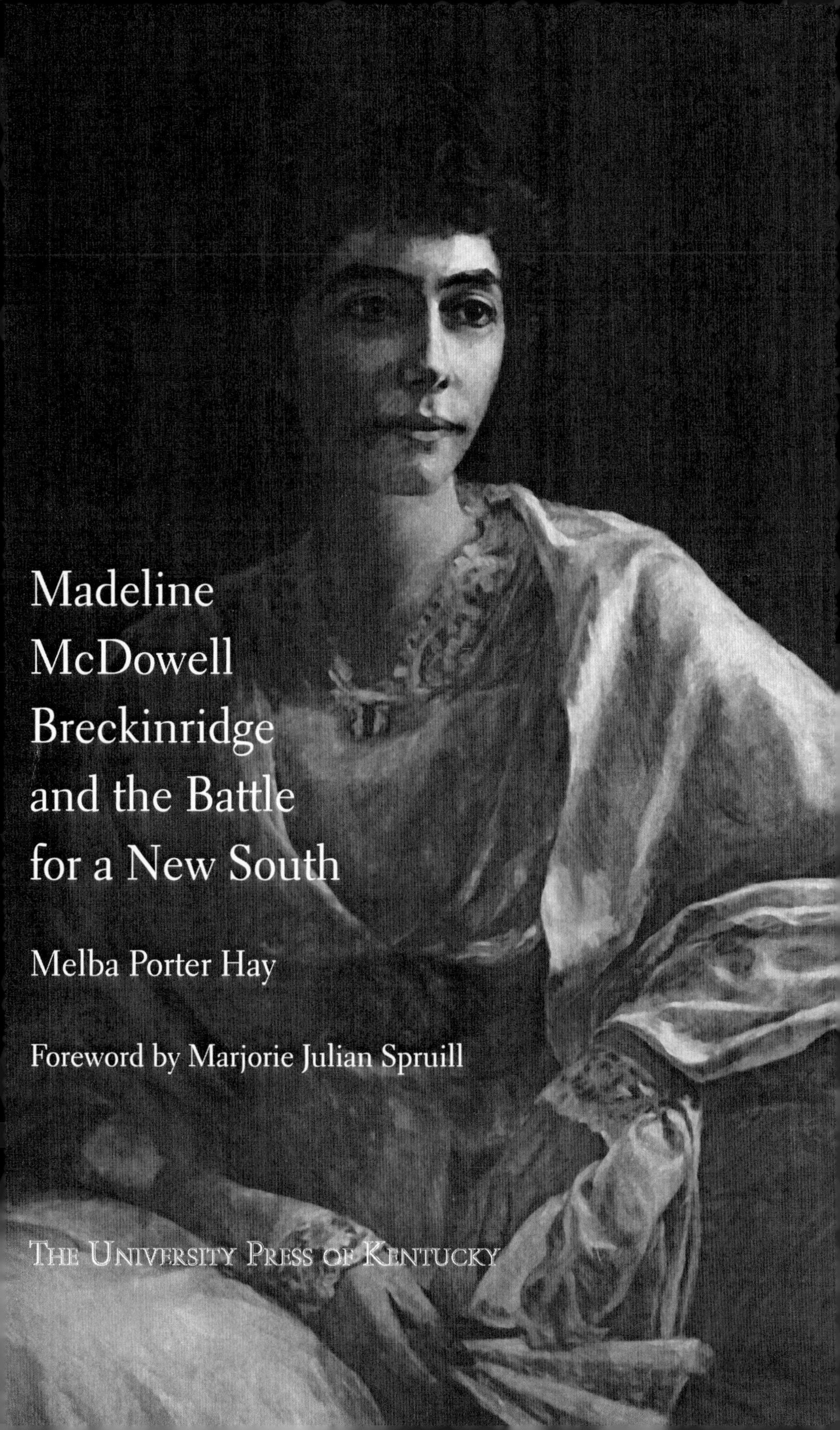

Madeline McDowell Breckinridge and the Battle for a New South

Melba Porter Hay

Foreword by Marjorie Julian Spruill

The University Press of Kentucky

Scholarly publisher for the Commonwealth,
serving Bellarmine University, Berea College, Centre College of Kentucky, Eastern Kentucky University, The Filson Historical Society, Georgetown College, Kentucky Historical Society, Kentucky State University, Morehead State University, Murray State University, Northern Kentucky University, Transylvania University, University of Kentucky, University of Louisville, and Western Kentucky University.

Editorial and Sales Offices: The University Press of Kentucky
663 South Limestone Street, Lexington, Kentucky 40508-4008
www.kentuckypress.com

13 12 11 10 09   5 4 3 2 1

Library of Congress Cataloging-in-Publication Data

Hay, Melba Porter, 1949–
Madeline McDowell Breckinridge and the battle for a new south / Melba Porter Hay ; foreword by Marjorie J. Spruill.
p. cm.
Includes bibliographical references and index.
ISBN 978-0-8131-2532-9 (hardcover : alk. paper)
1. Breckinridge, Madeline McDowell, 1872–1920. 2. Women—United States—Biography. 3. Women's rights—United States—Biography. 4. Women—Suffrage. 5. Women—United States—History. I. Title.
HQ1413.B74A3 2009
324.6'23092—dc22
[B]   2008045793

This book is printed on acid-free recycled paper meeting the requirements of the American National Standard for Permanence in Paper for Printed Library Materials.

Manufactured in the United States of America.

Member of the Association of
American University Presses

In memory of my parents,
Clyde and Bobbie Porter

Contents

Illustrations

Foreword

Madeline McDowell Breckinridge is one of the most important figures in the history of Kentucky as well as a major figure in the interconnected histories of the Progressive Era and the woman suffrage movement in the United States. She contributed to the enactment of Progressive reforms and the success of woman suffrage at every level: local, state, and national. As she rose to become a member of the boards of the National Conference of Social Work, the National Child Labor Committee, and the National American Woman Suffrage Association, she applied ideas gleaned from her successes in Kentucky. Conversely, she brought to her beloved Kentucky ideas she acquired from her association with national and international experts and activists.

As historian Melba Porter Hay tells us, "Madge" was an extraordinary woman from an extraordinary family who married into another such family. The descendant of Henry Clay and Judge Samuel McDowell, she was the daughter of privilege. She was, however, brought up in the tradition of her distinguished ancestors to believe that from great privilege comes great responsibility. In addition, her personal struggle against tuberculosis led her from a carefree girlhood into a life of service to others. With her marriage to Desha Breckinridge, she gained a husband whom she persuaded to support her causes and a newspaper through which to promote them. She also acquired a sister-in-law, Sophonisba Breckinridge, through whom she developed strong connections with leading social scientists at the University of Chicago and with settlement house workers, including the celebrated Jane Addams.

Like Addams, Madeline Breckinridge exemplifies the generation of women who, in the Progressive Era, applied new research by social scientists in attempts to interrupt the cycle of poverty, seeking to resolve rather than ameliorate social problems. In the process, Breckinridge and her contemporaries bridged the gap between private charities and the emerging field of social work. Working through the Lexington Civic League, the Associated Charities, and other organizations, Breckinridge made tremendous contributions to her community and her state, particularly to children and the poor, white and black. Being particularly devoted to children, she worked to get them out of the workplace and into school, sought to provide them with quality education and safe places to play, and advocated judicial reforms to insure that young people who made mistakes got second chances through juvenile justice programs. Her own suffering made her especially devoted to improving public health, and she supported many health-related causes, from provision of pure water and milk to the prevention and cure of tuberculosis—the disease that ravaged her own family.

Madeline McDowell Breckinridge's sense of justice and her desire to enhance women's power to support Progressive reforms led her to become an advocate of woman suffrage. Building upon the work of Laura Clay, the founder of the Kentucky Equal Rights Association, she applied her organizational and oratorical talents to advance the cause in her state; as a result, Kentucky was one of four—and only four—southern states to ratify the Nineteenth Amendment. Breckinridge, an ardent proponent of woman suffrage by either state or federal action, rose to national prominence in the movement and did much to further the cause. As Second Vice President of the National American Woman Suffrage Association (NAWSA), she helped bring other southern women to join national suffragists in the final battle for the federal woman suffrage amendment—action that placed her in direct opposition to Laura Clay who, despite decades of commitment to woman suffrage, opposed the federal amendment as a violation of states' rights. Few realize, however, the extent or significance of Breckinridge's contributions to the movement or the fact that she nearly became the national president of the NAWSA.

With the publication of this book, this admirable and influential figure has finally received the recognition she deserves. Scholars interested in the history of Kentucky, Progressivism, and woman suffrage will find Hay's meticulously researched, richly detailed biography invaluable, yet the author tells this compelling story in such a way that it achieves a much wider appeal. Breckinridge's story is a deeply personal and inspirational account of an extraordinary woman whose advantages and adversities led her to seize new opportunities for women and to do extraordinary things. She built a legacy of civic justice and equality that still resonates today.

Marjorie Julian Spruill
The University of South Carolina

Acknowledgments

Since I began this project more than thirty-five years ago, I have incurred more debts than can possibly be acknowledged. It began in 1972 in a graduate history seminar after Professor Richard Lowitt suggested Madeline McDowell Breckinridge as a possible topic for a paper. I quickly became enthralled by the subject—her personality, the scope of her career, and her influence on Kentucky and the woman's rights movement—and decided to make her life my dissertation topic. Two years later Professor Charles P. Roland agreed to be my dissertation director, and to him I owe a huge debt for sharing his expertise in southern history, writing, and editing.

I soon came to see that studying Breckinridge's life would involve extensive research not only into her papers and the voluminous collection created by the Breckinridge family, but also into many years of the *Lexington Herald*, the newspaper edited by her husband. On my first trip to the Library of Congress in 1976 I would have found myself totally at sea in the gigantic, then-unprocessed Breckinridge Family Papers had it not been for the advice of James C. Klotter, biographer of the Breckinridge family and the only researcher to have extensively mined that collection. As a graduate school friend, later my boss at the Kentucky Historical Society, Kentucky's state historian, and the general editor of the series in which this book appears, Jim has played an influential role in bringing this project to fruition, and I thank him for his advice and encouragement and for freely sharing his extensive knowledge of the Breckinridges and Kentucky history. Likewise, Thomas H. Appleton Jr. has supported this project from its inception. From the days we scanned newspapers on microfilm in the Margaret I. King Library at the University of Kentucky while researching our dissertations to the years we worked together at the Kentucky Historical Society to his proofing of the final draft of this manuscript, his assistance has proved invaluable.

I must also thank many of my colleagues at *The Papers of Henry Clay* documentary editing project and at the Kentucky Historical Society who provided information and help along the way. At *The Papers of Henry Clay* these included the late Anna B. Perry, Carol Reardon, the late Robert Seager II, Mackelene Smith, Margaret Spratt, Kenneth H. Williams, and Richard E. Winslow III, and at the Kentucky Historical Society Gretchen Haney, Anne McDonald, Thomas E. Stephens, and Mary E. Winter. I owe special thanks to Lynne Hollingsworth and Charlene Smith of KHS, who helped with last-minute fact-checking on legislative matters.

Staff at the University of Kentucky Special Collections, including William J. Marshall, Claire McCann, Frank Stanger, and Jason Flahardy, often went above and beyond the call of duty in assisting me. I want to express my gratitude to them especially for allowing access immediately to the collection of the Henry Clay Memorial Foundation when it was transferred to Special Collections after being uncovered in the early 1990s during renovation of Ashland, the Henry Clay Estate. These papers shed significant light on the early life of Madeline McDowell, answering questions that had long proved a puzzle and furnishing a very different perspective on her personality from those papers at the Library of Congress. Staffs at the Filson Historical Society, the Library of Congress, and the University of Chicago's Regenstein Library also gave valuable assistance. Author Berry Craig generously shared his research on nineteenth-century prosthetics and early orthopedic surgery. My lifelong friend Janella Garner Peters critiqued several chapters and transcribed a number of Desha Breckinridge's letters written in his atrocious scrawl—noting that as a nurse she had read much worse physicians' handwriting! Eric Brooks, curator at Ashland, supplied photos from the collection still at the mansion, and Paul E. Fuller and Melanie B. Goan both read the finished manuscript and gave insightful suggestions. I am also grateful for the assistance provided by the staff of the University Press of Kentucky and copy editor Robin DuBlanc. Of course, any errors that remain are solely my responsibility.

The greatest acknowledgment goes to my family. My parents, the late Clyde and Bobbie Porter, supported me throughout my education, constantly encouraged me, and financed my research expeditions. My husband, Charles C. Hay III, has endured both the writing of the dissertation and the rewriting for this edition. He has read the entire manuscript, made important suggestions, and cheered me on for more than thirty years.

Chapter 1

"One great honored name" 1872–1889

Sitting back from a road that winds through the heart of the Bluegrass between Frankfort and Georgetown rests a large two-story house surrounded by trees, with rolling fields on all sides. Stone gates on the edge of the highway read "Woodlake." In this calm, serene setting in Franklin County, Kentucky, Madeline McDowell was born on May 20, 1872. She was originally named Magdalen after her father's sister Magdalen Harvey McDowell, but her name was later changed to the French form, Madeline. The sixth and next to the youngest child of Henry Clay McDowell and Anne Clay McDowell, she soon acquired the nickname Madge. Four brothers—Henry Clay Jr., William Adair, Thomas Clay, and Ballard—and two sisters—Nanette, called "Nettie," and Julia—completed this close-knit family. The McDowell name itself carried with it a legacy of wealth, power, and pride in its heritage.[1]

While the circumstances of a person's birth do not necessarily determine that person's fate, in Madge McDowell's case they certainly had a great influence. Her family, with its long history of accomplishment and prominence, its political, social, and business ties, and its wealth, played a major role in the development of her personality, her opportunities, and her achievements. From early childhood her parents impressed upon her a sense of heritage that was to stamp an indelible imprint upon her character. She was a member of that privileged segment of Bluegrass society described by author and family friend James Lane Allen as "a landed aristocracy" in which "family names come down from generation to generation" and where "one great honored name will do nearly as much in Kentucky as in England to keep a family in peculiar respect." [2]

Actually, Madge's family was composed of several "great honored"

Woodlake, Franklin County, Kentucky. Courtesy of Special Collections and Digital Programs, Margaret I. King Library, University of Kentucky, Lexington.

names. On her father's side she descended from the McDowells, famous for their achievements in politics and medicine, while her mother was the granddaughter of Henry Clay, Speaker of the House, secretary of state, U.S. senator, and ofttime presidential candidate. "There was no Kentucky of which she was not a part," her sister-in-law accurately noted.[3]

Beginning in early childhood Madge developed a sense of family history and a desire to match her ancestors in terms of community service, a sentiment strongly encouraged by her father. She heard from both father and mother stories of what the McDowells and Clays had accomplished in Kentucky's early history. Perhaps recalling this early training, she once stated: "To me the inspiration of the past seems to call to the inspiration of the future. I think every Kentuckian may pronounce with the English poet that invocation to the

> Spirits of old that bore me,
> And set me meek of mind,
> Between great deeds before me
> And deeds as great behind!"[4]

To understand Madge and the influence her heritage exerted on her life and career, it is necessary to know at least the brief outline of her family history. To such a family genealogy was important, and the McDowells especially were fully committed to maintaining an awareness of it in their descendants. They were originally the McDougals from Scotland of the Duke of Argyle's clan. They immigrated first to Ireland and then to Pennsylvania, where Madge's great-great-grandfather Samuel was born in 1735. He married Mary McClung in 1754 and moved to present-day Mercer County, Kentucky, in 1784. For his service in the French and Indian War, the Virginia House of Burgesses awarded him a large tract of land in Fayette County, which at that time constituted one-third of the "District of Kentucky." During the American Revolution he served as a colonel in a regiment of volunteers from Augusta County, Virginia, and after the war he was appointed surveyor of public lands in Fayette County. In 1783 he sat as one of three justices in the first district court held in Kentucky and three years later was one of the judges who presided over the first county court held in the Kentucky District of Virginia. He then became a leader in Kentucky's effort to separate from Virginia. After presiding over most of the ten Danville conventions that led to statehood, Samuel was appointed by President George Washington as a United States judge for the new commonwealth.[5]

One of Samuel McDowell's sons, known as Judge Samuel McDowell of Mercer, married Anna Irvine. He appeared to have a great political future in store, but he died at an early age before attaining high office. His fourth son, William Adair McDowell, was born in 1795 and graduated from the University of Pennsylvania Medical School. For a time he lived with and assisted his uncle, Dr. Ephraim McDowell, the pioneer of abdominal surgery, who practiced in Danville, Kentucky. William, too, appeared destined for a brief life when he contracted tuberculosis while enrolled in medical school. The disease had reached an advanced stage before he decided on a regimen of diet and exercise to invigorate himself. He recovered and in 1843 published a book called *A Demonstration of the Curability of Pulmonary Consumption in All Its Stages*. Although the cure rate for his method of treating tuberculosis exceeded other methods then in use, many of his colleagues in the medical profession proclaimed him a charlatan and denounced his treatment. In time, however, the treatment—which consisted of four meals a day of rich, easily digestible foods, outdoor air, carefully regulated exercise, and iron tonics—became the basic "rest cure" mode of treatment that was used until the discovery of streptomycin in 1944. Yet unlike his famous uncle, who is widely known as the father of abdominal surgery, William received little credit for developing a new treatment, and his name is rarely, if ever, mentioned in studies concerning the search for a cure for tuberculosis. After practicing medicine for nine years in Louisville, he fell victim to a stroke. It is possible that the diet to treat consumption, which emphasized highly fat, rich foods, contributed to his early demise.[6]

Madge's father, Henry Clay McDowell, son of William Adair McDowell and Maria Hawkins Harvey, was born in 1832 in Fincastle, Botetourt County, Virginia. In 1838 the family moved to Louisville, where Henry later attended law school at the University of Louisville and practiced the profession with his brother-in-law, Bland Ballard. As a young man he was described as "well-proportioned and vigorous, black haired and dark eyed, graceful in carriage and manners." In later years he presented a very distinguished-looking visage, with silver beard and hair. He ultimately became an extremely successful businessman and horse breeder. One of the founders and controlling officers of the Kentucky Trotting-Horse Breeders' Association, president of the Lexington & Eastern Railroad, and a leader in developing the eastern mountain region of Kentucky during the boom period of the 1880s, he speculated heavily in land and mineral deposits in Big Stone Gap, Virginia. In addition, he owned extensive real estate in Louisville and several other cities. He became a noted philanthropist, and it is from him that Madge acquired her strong sense of noblesse oblige.[7]

In 1856, nineteen-year-old Anne, or Nannie, as the family called her, recorded in her diary that Henry had found a ring hidden in her birthday cake, apparently a sign that the two would make a match. Her uncle, she noted with embarrassment, "insisted upon calling [it] . . . the 'bride's cake.'" The next year she did indeed become the bride.[8]

Nannie had been orphaned in February 1847 at the age of ten, when her father, Henry Clay Jr., was killed in the battle of Buena Vista in the Mexican War. Her mother, Julia Prather Clay, had died in 1840, and from that time on Nannie and her brothers, Thomas and Henry, had lived with various relatives. Before departing for the Mexican War, Henry Jr. placed Nannie and Thomas in Louisville with his cousin, Nanette Price Smith, and her husband, Thomas, and left Henry in the care of his brother James Clay in Lexington. After their father's death, Nannie, lamenting that "now we are poor little orphans indeed," wrote her brother Henry, begging him to come to Louisville. However, she seems to have been quite happy, as she grew very attached to the Smiths, calling Nannette "Mother" and Thomas Smith "Uncle Smith."[9]

In appearance Nannie strongly resembled her grandfather Henry Clay with his long Roman nose and piercing eyes. Though not beautiful by any standard, photographs show her in later years to be a dignified-looking woman. The tranquil life that she and Henry undoubtedly hoped for after their marriage was soon interrupted by the Civil War, causing them to become one of the many sharply divided families in the commonwealth. Henry Clay McDowell, one of the first Kentuckians to join the Union army, eventually rose to the rank of major under General A. McDowell McCook in the Army of the Cumberland, while Nannie's two brothers served on opposite sides in the war, Thomas for the Confederacy and Henry for the Union. Her Clay uncles and cousins were also sharply divided.

It was a traumatic time for everyone, made particularly difficult when Thomas Clay was captured and held prisoner. In March 1862, Henry McDowell wrote his wife that he did not think he could or should seek a parole and exchange for Thomas, noting that it had been especially painful for Thomas's brother, Henry, to think "that any engagement might bring him in contact with his brother." It was a relief to both Henrys to know they would not be facing Thomas in battle. Apparently they soon received word that Thomas was ill, and less than a month later McDowell wrote his wife that Henry, too, was sick and would be going home on a twenty-day leave. Henry eventually recovered and distinguished himself in the bloody battle of Shiloh, only to die later that year from fever. While a prisoner of war Thomas wrote his sister of his relief in learning that she still cared for him despite their differences over the war. Thomas later received a parole and rejoined the Confederate troops. Then, in 1863, he, too, succumbed to fever. In October 1862, Henry McDowell left active duty to become a federal marshal in Kentucky. He would keep his pro-Union, Republican Party sentiments throughout his life, a fact that influenced his daughter greatly in her adult years.[10]

Following the war, the McDowells finally settled down at Woodlake for a seemingly idyllic existence. The older children doted on Madge and Ballard, the two youngest, who both enjoyed playing on the farm and riding the pony, "Cigarette." Madge was very close to her father and delighted in being with him. It was later said of her: "Memory will bring to different hearts different pictures of her; a child, all eyes and legs, climbing upon her father's horse to ride with him over the farm, seeking and giving companionship to him to whom difference of age made no difference; a girl, with eyes that still seemed bigger than her body, and long legs below her skirts, who romped with boy and girl, and led in chase and in study at the old schoolhouse, and over the hills around the pond on the Woodlake Farm."[11]

Henry McDowell's sister, Magdalen, often brought some excitement to the family with her visits. Aunt Mag, as she was affectionately called, was an unusual woman for her day. In an era where women generally married and reared a family, Mag inherited enough money and property from her parents to be financially independent. Although she had a number of suitors, she never married. She studied painting in New York City, acquired numerous patents for inventions, and became an amateur architect. To be sure, she always had the security of knowing she could fall back on her devoted brother, who stood ready to lend financial support whenever she needed it. Still, Henry worried about his sister's health and feared that life in New York City was "bound to savor somewhat of Bohemianism." For those reasons, he urged her to make her home at Woodlake, which she eventually did. Mag and her namesake became devoted to each other, so Madge had this unusual woman as a role model from her earliest childhood. Later, Josephine Clay, wife of her mother's uncle John Morrison Clay, would provide another strong female role model with her successful horse-breeding and racing enterprise, a business that usually excluded women during the Victorian era.[12]

The McDowell coffers expanded with the purchases of lots in Chicago in 1868 for $4,000 and ownership of property in the heart of downtown Louisville. Some of the documents describing these transactions are signed by Henry Clay McDowell as "trustee for Anne C. McDowell" and probably represent property she inherited from her mother's family, the Prathers, who were among Louisville's wealthiest citizens.[13]

Yet in the midst of this pleasant life, tragedy struck. In November 1881, four-year-old Ballard died at Woodlake. According to one account, Ballard had left the breakfast table and gone upstairs to retrieve something from the mantle above the fireplace when his clothes ignited. Hearing his screams, the family rushed upstairs, but by the time they reached him, he was badly burned. He lingered until 4:30 in the afternoon in great pain, saying frequently, "Kiss me, mamma."[14]

Madeline and Julia McDowell (standing and kneeling) with two friends at Woodlake, ca. 1880. Courtesy of Special Collections and Digital Programs, Margaret I. King Library, University of Kentucky, Lexington.

It was a devastating blow to the family. A friend wrote Aunt Mag, "The baby, the darling pet of the family, taken off in such a manner. What will they do?" The answer perhaps was to move, get away from the place with all the memories, for the next spring Henry McDowell purchased Ashland, the Henry Clay estate in Lexington, and moved his family there. Was it because of Ballard's death and the unhappy memories? Although no explicit statement has been found to that effect, it seems a likely reason, since McDowell received a less-than-desirable price for the Woodlake property. The main part of the farm, 430 acres, sold at auction for $70.25 an acre and another 153.5 acres at $45.80. This was a very low, disappointing price. The eldest son, Henry McDowell Jr., had grave misgivings about selling Woodlake but ultimately felt it was a good decision, noting that his mother seemed more cheerful at Ashland than she had in months. This lends support to the theory that the move was designed at least in part to get away from tragic memories of Ballard's death. Henry Jr. finally decided that it was "glorious to think that we are going to be at Ashland," persuading himself that he was "wild to live" there. His brother Will, however, was not thrilled with either the price or the purchaser of Woodlake. After the move, family friends in Frankfort continued to put fresh flowers on Ballard's grave, and Aunt Mag began to paint his portrait from memory, since no photograph existed.[15]

After Henry Clay's death in 1852, his Ashland estate had been purchased by his son James, who tore down the house and rebuilt on the same foundation. The property eventually passed from the hands of the Clays, and not until the McDowells moved there in 1882 did a descendant of the Great Compromiser again own it. They immediately began to renovate the house in the Victorian style, creating such havoc in the process that Mrs. McDowell lamented about the "noise and dirt" it produced. Soon the home became a mecca for admirers of Clay. Few well-known people visited the Bluegrass without experiencing the McDowells' lavish entertainment. Writers such as Thomas Nelson Page and John Fox Jr. became frequent guests, and poet and painter Robert Burns Wilson wrote a sonnet titled "Evening at Ashland," presenting Madge with two copies. The guest book, which has Wilson's handwritten poem glued inside, is replete with names of foreign guests from far and wide, even the director of the Imperial stud farm in Tokyo.[16]

Madge was ten when her family moved to Lexington. She seems to have already developed a sense of responsibility and a desire to be of service to others. According to one story, while they still lived at Woodlake her brother was asked to run an errand. "What," he asked, "is Madge dead?"[17]

On arriving in Lexington, Madge entered Mrs. Higgins' School. Sessions were longer and the school more demanding than had been the case at the country school at Woodlake, so she entered behind her grade, but an old school chum remembered that in "a very short time . . . she caught up with and passed us all and we were simply running to keep up with her." In those days she wore her hair loose, and her dark eyes were "the biggest part of her face." One composition she wrote, called "The Story of a Pair of Old Shoes," was so vivid and appealing it reduced everyone, including the teacher, to tears. Even then Madge displayed an interest in beautiful and exact speech. One of her friends said: "I can see her now when she said to me once, 'Mattie says sometimes when she means some time, and sometime when she means sometimes. It sounds very queer to me.'"[18]

By all accounts Madge's success in school continued unabated. She took first place in composition in 1885, causing Mrs. Higgins to bring a book back from London for her as a reward. Evidently, the teacher had

Madeline McDowell, aged fourteen, after she cut her hair. Courtesy of Special Collections and Digital Programs, Margaret I. King Library, University of Kentucky, Lexington.

overestimated her student's scholarly leanings, however, for Madge noted, "I am afraid I like the binding better than the inside for it is 'rather deep.'" The book, by John Ruskin, caused her to form "one positive conclusion and, that, that Ruskin is mightily—excuse the expression—conceited." A report card from Mrs. Higgins' School in 1887 shows an average slightly above 97; only deportment fell below 95, with a score of 93. The next year at Miss Butler's Day School, her deportment was rated "excellent," and she had an average of 99 with a standing of "1st rank." Perhaps the same precociousness that resulted in a 93 in deportment caused her in 1886 to cut her hair very short, much to the consternation of her family. She, however, felt it was "perfectly splendid[;] every time I get very warm I just go and dip my head in the bowl."[19]

Besides school, her childhood and early girlhood were filled with hours of dancing, playing tennis, and riding, and she excelled at all of these. Her father recognized her daring and tried to limit her activities. After participating in a rabbit hunt one day, she recorded in her diary that she did not take any jumps, because "Papa had told me not to take any risks and I did not want to have rabbit hunts proscribed in the beginning as coon hunts have already." Her health appeared good, as her absence rate at school was low, and her sister Nettie wrote Aunt Mag in 1885 that, although Madge had suffered a bout of dyspepsia, she had nearly recovered and "is as tall as I am." She added: "She thinks she is taller, but I do not think so."[20]

Because of the McDowells' many Louisville connections, Madge visited there frequently. On virtually every visit to Louisville she received many invitations to tennis and card parties, the theater, and a variety of other social activities. While she was on one such trip in early 1889, the *Louisville Courier-Journal* ran a story on the Clay family that included a photograph of Madge and her cousin Ida Clay, granddaughter of James B. Clay. In referring to the McDowells and their life at Ashland, the paper noted that they were "surrounded by all the refinements and luxuries that wealth bestows. They entertain with simple elegance and large hearted hospitality." Madge's take on the article was somewhat different. She wrote her mother: "I'm sure Papa will be filled with remorse, when he sees the picture of me and Ida, for it has undoubtedly ruined our prospects in life—We look like the advertisement for some cosmetic; I, before and Ida, after, where her disposition is somewhat spoiled by the taking of it."[21]

During the 1880s Madge's brothers were growing up, going away to school, and attempting to establish careers. Henry Jr. and Will attended Yale, where Henry roomed with Billy Bristow of New York City, son of the wealthy and politically powerful lawyer, railroad entrepreneur, and former U.S. secretary of the treasury, Benjamin F. Bristow. The Bristows and McDowells were already good friends, dating from the days when Bristow and Henry Clay McDowell had been two of the leading Unionists and Republicans in Kentucky. Henry Jr. remarked that having Billy as a roommate considerably increased his own invitations to social events. After graduating from Yale, Henry Jr. went to law school at the University of Virginia, where his brother Tom briefly joined him as an undergraduate. Various family members lamented the difficulty Tom had in school, especially in spelling and reading. It seems likely that he had a learning disability, perhaps dyslexia, for, despite having a tutor and writing four or five pages a day, which Henry corrected and Tom then recopied, he continued to have difficulty. Henry also attempted to interest his brother in reading by persuading him to try *The Count of Monte Cristo,* but from November 1884 to February 1885, he only read forty-six pages, prompting Henry to write their mother that Tom did much better in boxing than reading. By 1885 Tom had left Virginia to study at a school in Yarnallton, Kentucky.[22]

An article appearing in a Chicago newspaper in the early 1880s described the Ashland estate and the lavish entertainment provided there in glowing terms. It also reported that Henry Clay McDowell served as president of the Lexington & Eastern Railroad, which ran from Lexington to Jackson, Kentucky, and would soon extend to the seaboard. It predicted that McDowell would shortly "become a very wealthy man." Although by ordinary standards the McDowells were already wealthy, much of that wealth lay in real estate, including extensive property in downtown Louisville, and at times they were short of cash. This was exacerbated during the 1880s as they sought to pay the mortgage on Ashland, which had not been covered by the low price received for the Woodlake property. Also, having several children in school at the same time, helping them to start their careers, buying houses for them, and assisting other family members, such as Aunt Mag and Henry's brother W. P. McDowell, placed a burden on the family's finances. Major McDowell seems to have been very generous with his children, since Will indicated his allowance for a year at Yale was $1,500.[23]

More important, however, Henry McDowell made a large number of

Henry Clay McDowell Sr. with horses being trained on his Ashland estate. Courtesy of Special Collections and Digital Programs, Margaret I. King Library, University of Kentucky, Lexington.

unfortunate speculative investments in eastern Kentucky and western Virginia during the land and mineral boom there in the 1880s. He, his cousin Rogers Clark Ballard Thruston, and John Fox Sr. were among those investing heavily in the region with the hope of developing the area's coal, timber, and iron deposits and building railroads and towns. Great plans were drawn for Middlesborough, Kentucky, in the extreme southeastern part of the state, and Big Stone Gap in western Virginia.[24]

Yet even before he invested so heavily in the mountains, there were indications that McDowell had some financial problems. In an 1883 catalog he advertised forty-seven trotting horses for sale, which produced a sizeable income. But two years later, circumstances forced him to sell his prize trotting horse, King Rene, for $15,000. Though the horse had brought an excellent price, Tom McDowell lamented the loss of the animal to his father but agreed that the transaction was preferable to selling any of the family's real estate.[25]

Yet these events did not prevent McDowell from helping incorporate the Goff Land Company in 1887 with a capital of $50,000 for the purpose of buying, leasing, holding, selling, and trading in land, timber, and mineral rights at Big Stone Gap. Two months later McDowell became a partner in the $250,000 Dictator Cannel Coal Company, which was designed for the same purpose as the Goff Land Company, except that it would engage in coal mining and other manufacturing. By 1890 he was also chairman of the Big Stone Gap Improvement Company and president of the South Appalachian Land Company. The former planned to build two great blast furnaces with a capacity of one hundred tons of steel per day. The company had let contracts for a street railroad, and Tompson-Houston Light Company of Boston was to put in a large electricity plant. A waterworks was under way, and plans had been drawn for a $150,000 hotel in Big Stone Gap with three hundred rooms. In addition, there were hopes of building a great interstate railroad tunnel system through Big Black Mountain on the east and Pine Mountain on the west for the sum of $2.5 million. During this boom the price of lots in Big Stone Gap jumped overnight from $50 to $1,000. The Mountain Park Association was formed to purchase three thousand acres at the intersection of Stone and Powell Mountains for use as a game preserve. It was to have a Swiss-style clubhouse that was expected to draw tourists from all over America. Henry McDowell Jr., who had been practicing law in St. Paul, Minnesota, returned home to go to work for the Big Stone Gap Improvement Company. His brother Will also moved to Big Stone Gap, where he opened a bank. Aunt Mag even considered building a house there. This town's growth was typical of that which occurred throughout the Appalachian region during the period 1889 to 1893. When financial panic hit in 1893, the bottom fell out of all these investments, and the boomtowns, including Big Stone Gap, virtually dried up. The only people ultimately profiting from the phenomenon were those who had sold land to the developers at extremely high prices.[26]

Meanwhile, as Madge grew up she tried to decide where to pursue an education. At this stage of life she appeared destined for the traditional role assigned to women in the Victorian era. Often called the Cult of True Womanhood, this role demanded that women be pious, pure, submissive, and completely immersed in domesticity. The True Woman guarded her family's morals and exercised her influence indirectly by passing her values to the next generation. Viewed as too frail and innocent to participate in the rough-and-tumble world of business and politics, the True Woman achieved fulfillment by dedicated performance of her duties as wife and mother and thus needed training only in those domestic pursuits.[27]

Yet the post–Civil War era had brought new educational opportunities for females: several women's colleges opened and a number of male colleges and universities became coeducational. In perhaps the first indication that she would not follow the traditional role expected of her, Madge apparently considered attending one of the new women's colleges. In April 1889 she acquired a prospectus for Harvard University's "Examinations for Women," which entitled admission to Smith, Vassar, Bryn Mawr, or Wellesley. She finally decided on Miss Porter's School in Farmington, Connecticut. This exclusive girls' school offered a rigorous course of study that included Latin, German, and science as well as the arts, exceeding the traditional curriculum of many girls' schools. Why she made this choice is a mystery. Although she came from a fairly wealthy family, most of her classmates had far more money. Nevertheless, she loved Miss Porter's and made lifelong friends there. In later years these connections would prove to be an asset as she called upon her school chums for contributions to various causes.[28]

Before leaving home, Madge held a number of social events. On July 16 she hosted a large party, described effusively the following day in the *Lexington Leader:*

> If the ghost of Henry Clay meditatively paces the halls of his former home at Ashland, where the elegant residence of Major H. P. [*sic*] McDowell now stands, and if he was out on his accustomed rounds last night, he witnessed a sight that was well calculated to make his blood run faster through his shadowy veins and make his spiritual features light up with pleasure. He would have seen the broad, ancestral halls illuminated by the brilliance of many lights, in the glare of which scores of beautiful girls and manly young fellows walked and talked. . . . And with the discretion that tradition grants to ghosts—and the ghost of Henry Clay, in particular . . . he would have known that all this gaiety was the outcome of invitations issued by one of his direct descendants, a young lady whom he might well have been proud of, had he lived until today.

> For Miss Madge McDowell proved herself an excellent hostess last night, although the task was an arduous one.

The newspaper continued by extolling Julia McDowell, who had assisted her sister in entertaining, and further noted: "Ashland is a place that is not surpassed by any residence in Lexington for its facilities for party-giving." The largest "crowd of the season" attended this ball, which included a band and a "super-excellent" supper produced by a Louisville caterer. On July 26 the *Leader* noted that Madge would give a tea and tennis party on the following day. In contrast to the ball, this would be "an informal affair."[29]

Madge's father, vacationing on the Yellowstone River in North Dakota (where he ran into Republican friend Theodore Roosevelt), wrote his daughter, advising her to take French, German, music, and English literature, as well as to exercise regularly. He was pleased for her to enter Miss Porter's but seemed sad to have her away from home. He noted, however, that she would make "some most desirable acquaintances" there. In October he took her to Chicago for a visit, and from there she traveled by train to New York. Madge enjoyed her visit to Chicago, where she gave away so many photographs of Ashland she had to write her mother for more. On the train to Chicago, she and her father ran into old friends John Fox Jr., whose novel *Little Shepherd of Kingdom Come* would sell more than one million copies in 1903, and Robert Burns Wilson, who was to become known particularly for his poem "Remember the *Maine*" as well as for his portrait and landscape paintings. When they arrived in New York City, Madge stayed with the family of one of her closest friends, Marion Houston, daughter of James Buchanan Houston, and had lunch with Mrs. Benjamin Bristow. These were two families she visited frequently during her stay at Miss Porter's.[30]

Arriving at Miss Porter's on October 9, she resided in the house of a Miss Hillard. Classes started two days later with Madge taking the subjects her father had advised except for general, rather than English, literature. She believed she "played awfully" for the music teacher and was not particularly thrilled that the evenings were to be devoted to "fancy work." Describing the meals at the school, she reported with enthusiasm that dessert was served for dinner every day, but she seemed puzzled that no butter accompanied their meals except on Sunday. During this time she apparently was in the best of health. After being there a couple of weeks

Miss Porter's School in Farmington, Connecticut. Courtesy of Special Collections and Digital Programs, Margaret I. King Library, University of Kentucky, Lexington.

she was chagrined to find her weight up to 121 pounds, noting that everyone said students got fat at Farmington. She vowed to maintain 121 as her limit, because if she gained more, her clothes would no longer fit.[31]

During her time in Farmington, Madge sometimes saw a friend from Lexington, Ralph Shaw, then a student at Yale. He came to Miss Porter's occasionally on Sundays and took her for long walks. She wrote home frequently for items to be sent to her and, like most young girls, was very concerned about clothes. She felt "very elegant" going to church in her new brown dress and described her new tam as "a perfect beauty." Before Christmas she planned to travel to the Bristows' to await her father, who was to accompany her home. She suggested that for Christmas she would like a tennis outfit and a new purse, "as the clasp of mine is beginning to look rather brassy." At the last minute her father became ill, and she telegraphed Ralph Shaw to ask him to travel home with her on the train. She was so inspired by the looming vacation that she skipped her music practice, which she continued to dislike.[32]

The carefree time at Miss Porter's must have passed quickly. In the spring Madge began to make plans to meet her parents for Easter break in Washington, DC. She eagerly sent a list of things she wanted her mother to bring, including summer clothes and her silver picture frame, but added items to be sent to Farmington immediately—corset laces, white ribbon, kid gloves, stockings, and shoes. Her feet had grown and her old shoes were too small. Also, she added a request familiar to all parents of children away at school—she would like to receive a check. Music continued to be her least-favorite activity, but she played "a little baby piece" in the spring concert. She also informed her mother that she would be in a tableau, but all she knew about it was that she would be draped in ten yards of white cheesecloth.[33]

The girls at Miss Porter's became very excited when, during the spring, a center page of the *Yale Record* was devoted to sketches of Farmington. They ordered several copies, but Madge noted, "There is great trepidation . . . as to what Miss Porter will think of it, if she happens to get hold of it."[34]

The elder McDowells delayed their trip to Washington, but on April 1, Madge set out with a group from Farmington and had a "delightful trip." On her return she had a new roommate, one who practiced music three and a half hours a day. "I am almost afraid to tell you that for fear you will think I ought to do it too," she wrote her father. Rather, she found the newly repaired tennis courts too inviting to spend much time practicing the piano. In fact, tennis was so important that in April Mrs. McDowell purchased a blue-and-white-striped flannel tennis suit and cap for her daughter's eighteenth birthday.[35]

In May Madge journeyed to New York City to visit her first roommate, Mrs. Bristow, and the Houstons. She found her former roommate's friends stylish but not pretty and rather stiff. School continued to be fun. On one occasion she was invited to tea at Miss Porter's. Expecting the event "to be pretty bad," she, in fact, enjoyed it "immensely."[36]

The climate in Connecticut was considerably harsher than in Kentucky, prompting Madge to wear her flannels until the middle of May, although she had always assumed "that when I had the managing of it myself I should take it off about the first of April." By the time of her birthday she sent her flannels and sealskin coat home and requested that lighter-weight clothes be mailed, including "my blue cheesecloth and my blue gingham." Ever interested in clothes, she also expressed a desire for another gingham to wear with an Irish lace collar. When her birthday box arrived she found everything she had requested except her ribbons and sashes and more than she had expected otherwise. The box included a $5 gold piece and a bangle bracelet from Julia, the tennis suit, various jams, and other items she had requested. One of her chief pleasures at the time was enjoying the newly ripened strawberries, which they had almost every day at Farmington, and she even attended a strawberry festival at the town hall because she wanted strawberry ice cream. During the spring she took part in the tennis tournament. In short, her life as reflected in letters home was that of a bright, happy, carefree young girl.[37]

When the term ended in the summer at Miss Porter's, Madge returned to Lexington, apparently undecided whether to go back to Farmington in the fall. One friend, Grace Otis, wrote from the school telling Madge how much she was missed and saying that she herself would not return for the fall session unless Madge did, too. On the other hand, Aunt Mag urged her to go on a trip abroad—something she also wanted to do—rather than to Miss Porter's. For whatever reason, Madge did not go back to Connecticut for the fall term. Her sister-in-law later explained that Major McDowell had not wanted his daughter separated too long "from the community in which she expected to live out her life." The sister-in-law also mentioned that fear for Madge's health kept her from pursuing further education away from home, but it seems unlikely this influenced the decision, for there is no evidence that she was anything less than perfectly healthy at this time. Indeed, her tennis playing and other outdoor pursuits, plus her weight gain after arriving at Farmington, indicate that she was neither frail nor delicate.[38]

It is more likely that family finances played a role in Madge's failure to continue at the expensive school. Investments in various businesses associated with the development of Big Stone Gap had depleted Major McDowell's coffers, and the whole endeavor was in great financial trouble by late 1890. Also, the expense of maintaining the high standard of living to which they were accustomed and assisting the older children were major drains on his finances.[39]

At any rate, Madge enrolled at the State College (Agricultural and Mechanical College of Kentucky), now the University of Kentucky, where she studied part-time from 1890 to 1894, though she never earned a degree. Although it was not obvious at the time, Madge's return to Lexington marked the end of one phase of her life and the beginning of another. The friends she had made at Miss Porter's, however, would have a lasting influence. She had made social contacts and formed deep friendships with girls from some of the wealthiest families in the country. She would not forget them, and they would not forget her.[40]

By the time she turned eighteen, then, in 1890, little in Madge McDowell's life suggested that she would differ from others of her class and status in society. With some variations, she seemed a typical young Victorian southern belle, enjoying dancing, tennis, clothes, books, and more. Yet that surface image hid much, and her life would soon change—and change dramatically.

Chapter 2

"A thunder-bolt out of a clear sky" 1890–1896

Back in Lexington in the summer of 1890, eighteen-year-old Madge McDowell resumed her active social life. She suffered a near-serious mishap in her cart when the pony Cigarette ran away with her. Her brother had envisioned her driving into town "in her glory all summer," but that expectation vanished after Cigarette's "foolishness."[1]

Then, during the Christmas season, Madge's life changed forever. What occurred did not seem significant at first. It appeared she had merely sprained her ankle. Accounts vary in referring to a "foot" or an "ankle" problem. One would-be suitor commiserated that it "must have been a severe strain to have sent you to bed so long after the hurt," but he continued facetiously that he had cured Madge's cousin Fanny Ballard of a painful problem by providing her with "some of the trashiest books printed in modern time." He noted, however, that Fanny "did not twist her ankle while in the midst of a whirling waltz and while at the same time looking over her left shoulder at the best looking man in the room who didn't dance. She was not wearing shoes with heels four inches high." Whether he was describing an actual account of the event or was simply teasing her with a scenario he imagined remains uncertain. Whatever the case, before long the problem had become chronic. At the end of January 1891 Henry Clay McDowell wrote his son that "we are all well, except Madge, and about her we are much concerned, as the doctor has come to the conclusion that it is not a sprain, and he is as yet unable to determine what it is." Several weeks later Henry Jr. wrote that he was surprised to learn that she was still limping and commented: "She has certainly had a hard time of it."[2]

Shortly thereafter Madge went to Cincinnati to consult physicians, remaining there for several weeks in a boardinghouse while she received treatment. Sometimes family members visited her, and she explored the city and suburbs. On April 21, following the advice of her doctor, she left off the rubber stocking he had prescribed and took her last dose of cod liver oil, "for which I am extremely thankful," she noted. She hoped her stay would last only another week or two and thought the improvement in her walk was "perceptible now, and the leg has gained almost a quarter of an inch in size."[3]

Aunt Mag rather unhelpfully offered her own advice: "Have you tried walking squarely on your foot without regard to pain? I should not wonder if it would be better than saving it—*if you can stand it.*"[4]

On her return home, Madge continued to keep in touch with her friends and appeared to be healthy except for the pain in her ankle or foot. Friends visited her at Ashland during the summer. Nettie Belle Smith, daughter of Louisville & Nashville (L & N) Railroad president Milton Smith and probably Madge's closest friend, wrote frequently and found her confidante's replies to be "as refreshing as a long horseback ride or a glass of champagne." She added: "I wish I could write a nice long spicy [letter] like you do."[5]

Autumn 1891 found Madge again consulting physicians about her foot, this time in Louisville. Special shoes seemed to improve her walking, "though stiffly of course, on account of the heaviness of the shoes and the iron in the bottom." She was unhappy with the appearance of the shoes, which she thought were "hideous to look at." Happily, she felt her foot had improved because it had not given her any pain since she had been in Louisville. She was able to include an active social life and pleasant shopping excursions in her routine during her stay in the city. Not only did she purchase a new purse, she had two dresses made—a winter one for $50 and a party dress for $52, a very substantial sum at a time when laborers made $15 a month. Back in Louisville before Christmas that year, she enjoyed another wonderful visit with Nettie Belle.[6]

Madge had long desired to go to Europe. Periodically, friends would ask her to accompany them, but she had been unable to do so. On one occasion she informed her father that she could accompany a friend for $650. She cajoled him with the promise that "it will really be more economical for you, for me to go than to stay at home," since she would not be inviting all her friends to visit Ashland and there would thus be far fewer people to feed. She even proposed selling her pony Elspet to raise

The McDowell sisters—Julia, Nettie, and Madeline. Courtesy of Special Collections and Digital Programs, Margaret I. King Library, University of Kentucky, Lexington.

part of the money and thought perhaps she could sell her accounts of the trip to a newspaper. "Of course," she added, "you know that if I can't go, all you have to do is say so; I am not going to be bad-tempered and discontented about it—I can always have a lovely time at home." She further commented that this "is the very nicest opportunity I have had to go," and "I am getting a little superstitious about letting opportunities go by."[7]

Madge did not get her trip to Europe, perhaps because other family needs took priority. As the McDowell children became adults, they entered into the mainstream of Kentucky life—often at the expense of their father. Nettie married Dr. Thomas Bullock in 1892 and moved to Louisville. William "Will" Adair McDowell, after failing financially in Big Stone Gap and relying on his father for several years, eventually became an executive of the L & N Railroad and later president of the Phoenix National Bank & Trust Company in Lexington. Tom followed his father as a horse breeder, ultimately becoming one of the most prominent turfmen in the Bluegrass. A partner in the racing stables of W. K. Vanderbilt, he produced a Kentucky Derby winner in Alan-a-Dale in 1902. Henry Jr. went into law, married his cousin Elsie Clay, and was appointed to a federal judgeship by his father's friend President Theodore Roosevelt. In 1904 Julia, the youngest child, married William Brock, a Lexington banker.[8]

Meanwhile, Henry Clay McDowell faced a growing economic crisis at Big Stone Gap. In February 1891 he sent Will nearly $1,500 to assist him with his personal financial problems, and the son felt he might have to ask his father to endorse notes for him again in the future. In 1893 the Big Stone Gap Improvement Company went into receivership. In addition to his other responsibilities, McDowell continued to assist his brother W. P. McDowell.[9]

Despite economic reverses, the family continued its elaborate entertaining. During 1891 writer Thomas Nelson Page visited Ashland, commenting: "It was like getting back to 'before the war,' a beautiful country, lovely women, fine, cordial men, good books, fine horses. In three weeks I have not heard *money* mentioned. . . . They were . . . delightful . . . entertaining in the old style." Describing the daughters as "lovely girls," he said they had "sweet manners and kind hearts." In addition, *Leslie's Monthly Magazine* recognized the McDowell girls as possessing beauty, wealth, and distinguished family names.[10]

Typical of the McDowells' lush lifestyle was Nettie's wedding on April 19, 1892, where Madge and Julia served as maids of honor. It was a huge, formal affair with an elaborate reception. Although a newspaper article proclaimed that Dr. Bullock had wooed his bride for fourteen years, the match evidently surprised many of Nettie's friends. Because Bullock practiced in Louisville, Henry McDowell sold one of his properties there for $3,000 and purchased "an elegant house in one of the fashionable suburbs" for his eldest daughter at a cost of $10,500. A few weeks after the wedding, one of Madge's friends inquired if Nettie was still embarrassed to call her new husband by his given name, another indication that perhaps the couple had not had a long-standing relationship.[11]

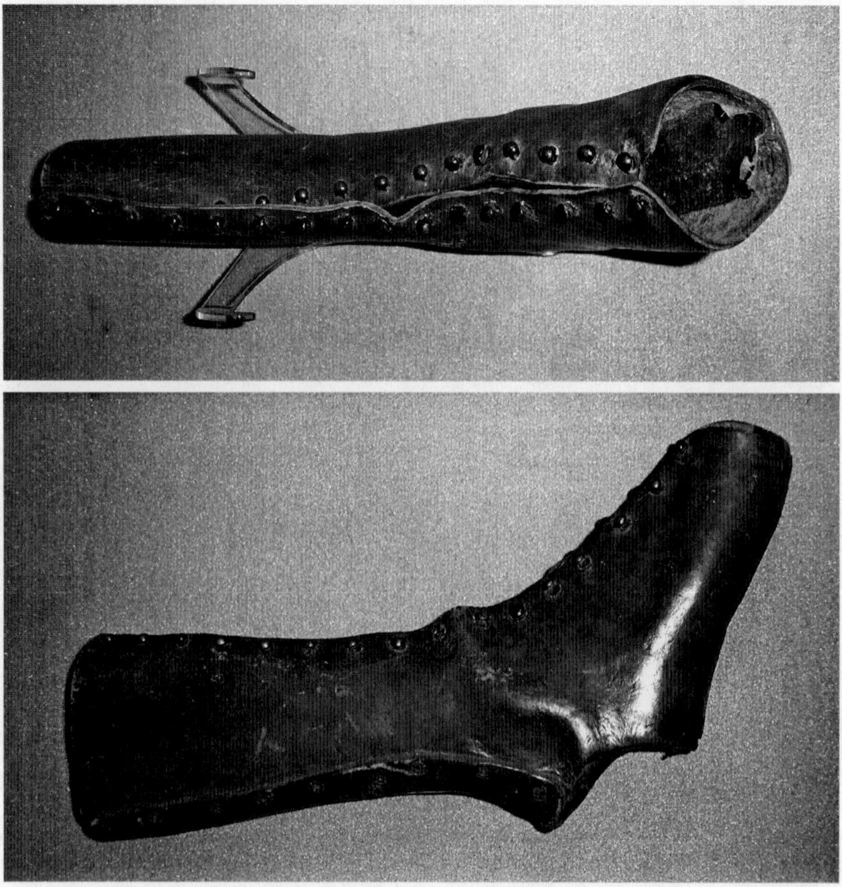

Boot or brace found at Ashland and believed to have belonged to Madeline McDowell. The shape of the boot indicates that it was her right foot that was affected. Courtesy of Ashland, the Henry Clay Estate, Lexington.

After the wedding, Madge's foot still bothered her a great deal. The family discussed sending her to New York City to consult specialists. As Aunt Mag described it, Madge was "hopping around with her leather boot and her new crutches as if it were all fun—She likes the prospect of going to New York—and accepts it all as philosophically as usual." But the trip was postponed. Nettie Belle Smith assumed it was because the foot was better and there was no need to go; however, evidence suggests that the problem continued to plague Madge.[12]

Yet health concerns did not slow down her active social life. Grace Otis and some other girls visited in summer 1892. Describing one planned outing, Madge wrote Nettie Bullock that her own beau for a driving expedition was "yet a little uncertain," but she was "sure" that "he would materialize in time," adding that by the time her girlfriends left, "I will be driven to associating entirely with the young men of Lexington as none of the girls will any longer speak to any of us by that time for jealousy." She missed Nettie's participation in the social "plotting and planning and general evidences of social tact, in which I inevitably fall far short of my illustrious predecessor." She added: "Mamma has a comforting way of saying to me after I have not done something very well—'You haven't the tack [*sic*] that your sister had,' which doesn't succeed in making me jealous in the least."[13]

Not all of the girls' activities were sedate, however. On one occasion, Nettie Belle found Madge's account of a "wolf hunt" so amusing that her family wanted to know if she had made it up. Nettie Belle told them that for Madge, "Escapades like that, and going forty miles for a coon and staying out until four in the morning were ordinary occurrences."[14]

In August 1892, Madge, her parents, Milton and Nettie Belle Smith, and Dr. David W. Yandell traveled to Colorado in Smith's private railroad car for a month's visit. Marion Houston wrote Madge that she envied the western trip because she had always wanted to go to Pike's Peak, adding that she also envied Madge's "pluck and patience in the troublesome time you have had with your ankle." She noted that she was following the election so that "when we have all our 'rights,' and can vote," she would be prepared.[15]

The Colorado trip provided adventure and even a bit of danger. The men spent much of the time hunting and fishing in the Rockies. One day while they were out hunting, the women, left behind in the railroad car on a sidetrack, became bored and hired a man with a two-horse wagon to take them for a drive. When they attempted to ford the Arkansas River in the middle of the stream where the water was about three feet deep, one of the horses reared up and dragged the wagon from the rocky bed of the ford into the quicksand on one side. For long moments it appeared that the horses would be drawn under, and the women thought they would perish. Fortunately, some lumbermen working on the river saw the situation and came to their rescue, using poles and ropes to get the horses and wagon on the ford again.[16]

Thanksgiving found the McDowells celebrating with Nettie and Tom Bullock in Louisville, where they attended plays and parties. One of Madge's friends inquired about Ralph Shaw, the Yale student who had visited her so often at Farmington. "Does he still exist?" Grace Otis asked. Apparently not, at least not for Madge, for his name rarely came up.[17]

The year 1893 proved very eventful for the McDowells. In June and September, Madge made excursions to Chicago to attend the Columbian World's Exposition. Women played a major role in organizing the fair and initiating programs and exhibits that depicted the accomplishments of women and the need for social change to provide them with more opportunities. Whether Madge knew that or whether she attended any of the lectures dealing with social reform or the history of women and their status remains uncertain, but clearly she had a wonderful time on both occasions. On her second return she noted, "My foot feels just about as it did when I left—pretty good for it, but not much for a walking instrument."[18]

In July Henry McDowell Jr. married Elsie Clay, and in November Nettie Bullock gave birth to a son, Henry Clay Bullock. Madge spent two weeks during the summer with Grace Otis, and in August she visited Dr. Howard Vance in Louisville to have her foot checked. He decided she should walk without crutches.[19]

In late December Madge traveled to New York City, Washington, DC, and Annapolis. She stayed at Marion Houston's home in New York part of the time, with Aunt Mag chaperoning at other moments. During this visit she consulted Dr. Virgil P. Gibney, one of the pioneers in orthopedic surgery and head of the New York Society for the Relief of the Ruptured and the Crippled, better known as the Hospital for Ruptured and Crippled, now known as the Hospital for Special Surgery. Gibney prescribed special shoes, and by March she could walk very well, though such activity still caused a good deal of pain and swelling.[20]

Despite the foot problem Madge attended dances at Annapolis, and a young cadet wished she could be there for the June ball. How she managed these events with her painful foot is uncertain, but it evidently did not detract from her popularity.[21]

Soon after her return home she had a house party with Grace Otis from Chicago, Marion Houston from New York, Stites Duvall from Frankfort, and Nettie Belle Smith from Louisville. Later, writing from Scotland, Grace recalled what a good time they had experienced, and Marion subsequently enthused: "I never realized how much I loved you, nor what an altogether superior article you were. I thought you were 'nice,' but did not at all understand the amount of sugar-cane in your makeup. This isn't blarney. I mean it, every word."[22]

Apparently the improvement of Madge's foot was very temporary, because the problem intensified even while she was enjoying herself with her houseguests. Ultimately, she went in June to Louisville, where she had surgery at the Norton Infirmary. Her family feared that she suffered from tuberculosis of the bone, but Dr. Louis Frank wrote her on behalf of Dr. Vance, giving the diagnosis of "an Acute suppercative ostitis non-tubercular in character." He reported that "after careful examination of the pus . . . there are absolutely no Tubercle Bacilli present in those specimens examined (six in number)." He added that some pieces of bone "showed merely necrotic changes" but no tuberculosis. Major McDowell further notified Aunt Mag that there "was not the slightest indication of tuberculosis in Madge's case, as established by what Dr. Bullock thought a most thorough and scientific examination made by an expert of ability—Only one bone was diseased and the whole of that, except the outer shell, was removed—The indications for a thorough cure are considered good."[23]

Soon Madge left the hospital and went to Nettie Bullock's home to recuperate. During this time she received letters and visits from numerous friends. John Fox Jr. wrote that he had heard "how nicely your foot passed through the Surgeon's hands & how good the chance was that you soon wouldn't know one foot from the other."[24]

In the autumn Madge visited Marion Houston in New York, and her foot seemed to have improved. Mrs. McDowell and Aunt Mag supplied clothes for the trip as pre-Christmas gifts, while her mother remarked that Major McDowell had accepted a position as president of Kentucky Utilities at a salary of $1,200 per year. There would not be much work involved, and the money "will help," she noted.[25]

Given the foot problem, the pain it caused, and the hindrance of walking with crutches, it is amazing that Madge took part in so many social activities during these years. Equally notable is the large number of suitors she had, despite the restrictions she endured. She went out with any number of young men during the early to mid-1890s, such as George C. Webb of Lexington, David Prewitt of Pine Grove, Kentucky, and W. H. P. Phyfe of New York City. Sometimes it is impossible to tell if these were just friendships or actual romantic relationships, but it is clear

Madeline McDowell, early 1890s. Courtesy of Special Collections and Digital Programs, Margaret I. King Library, University of Kentucky, Lexington.

that in the early 1890s she had two serious, older suitors in Louisville. Both pursued her tirelessly for several years, although she gave them little encouragement and, in fact, often tried to avoid them. One was William W. Thum, a lawyer and brother of artist Patty Thum, one of Kentucky's first prominent female painters. The other was Harrison Robertson, who worked for the *Louisville Courier-Journal* from 1879 until the 1930s.[26]

In May 1891 Thum invited Madge to attend a music festival. He asked solicitously about her health, remarking: "You make light of your hurt in your letters but I can't help thinking that you are having a hard time." Over the next several years he continued to pursue her in person whenever she was in Louisville and by letter when she was not. He also made occasional stops in Lexington, apparently inviting himself rather than receiving an invitation from her.[27]

By 1894 Thum openly told Madge he loved her. In February he refused to go to a glee club performance because she would not go with him, and in July she cancelled a date they had to go driving. He described that as his "black day," begging: "But you will go another time will you not? If I am too importunate forgive me. I love you so deeply—so wholly that I cannot always keep within measure[.] You are the noblest and sweetest woman in the world." He added: "I feel so strong and passionate a love for you that I create for myself a sort of necessity for some return. . . . I think of you every hour of the day and many hours of the night." Nevertheless, he realized that he should "not misinterpret your sweet kindness and good comradeship for letting me awkwardly try to amuse you."[28]

This proved too much for her. She replied to Thum—ironically drafting her reply on the back of a letter she had received from Harrison Robertson—explaining that she could "not consent to bore you another afternoon as I did yesterday." She stressed: "As soon as the conversation is personal, I become ill at ease & self conscious & can not do either myself or you justice. I have tried to throw this off but have clearly not succeeded." She concluded: "Let me thank you for all your kindness, which I am sorry to have deserved so little."[29]

Thum answered swiftly. He apologized if his letter had been worded so "stupidly" that "it conveyed any criticism." He begged her forgiveness, noting: "I have known that you did not feel toward me as I wished. I longed to have you for my wife. But there are many men who, like me, must arrange their lives to do without love and marriage." Her reply to this missive was obviously a complete rejection and refusal to see him again, for he wrote again begging her to tell him why she seemed actively to dislike him. "I know you do not love me and do not value my poor offer of marriage," he noted, adding: "I have never in my life really loved any one but you and never shall."[30]

What had caused Madge to reject Thum in such an apparently harsh way is unclear, but obviously his devotion made her uncomfortable. Perhaps she had finally concluded that he could be discouraged only by sharp and complete rejection. At least he seems to have been sincere in his pledge that he would never love another woman, for he never married.[31]

The other Louisville suitor, Harrison Robertson, began his courtship in 1892, and his pursuit, which continued even longer than Thum's, received somewhat more favorable consideration. Madge occasionally invited him to attend one of her parties and agreed to correspond with him "when the spirit moves." He felt that inflicting his own letters on her was what she deserved, since "young women who make themselves so attractive . . . to Louisville exiles, and yet who insist on holding themselves aloof from Louisville except for a few days once or twice a year, have no right to expect more merciful punishment." He kept track of Madge's activities through her cousin Susy Ballard, whom he saw at various Louisville social functions. Once he let escape to Susy the information that Madge had agreed to write to him, and then he tried to explain that her letters were too infrequent to be called a "correspondence." He apologized to Madge for letting this slip out since it was generally the prerogative of the lady to reveal such things, but he noted that Susy did not regard "it as a matter of anymore consequence than you do, for she volunteered the comment that she had sometimes corresponded with men whom she did not even like." He often referred to Madge as "Your Royal Highness" or "Your Royal Bluegrass Highness," probably reflecting her aloofness.[32]

Evidently Robertson's awkward apology annoyed Madge, because he hastened to assure her that he had not meant to imply that he was disappointed with her letters, only that they were too infrequent. The correspondence continued despite the brief misunderstanding. Madge professed an interest in seeing some of his poetry, so he sent her some samples but urged her not to feel that she had to say anything about them she did not mean, because he had written them long ago and could contemplate them with "impersonality as I can the school-boy love affairs of which I have told you." Whenever he traveled through Lexington, he always made a point of trying to see her.[33]

In November 1894 Robertson proposed, and Madge rejected him. He wrote her saying that when he left her, he had no intention of reopening the subject, but he felt compelled to do so because he feared she had misunderstood him. He explained that when he first met her, he did not try to see her often because she was so young, but when he encountered her again two years ago, he knew he loved her and found it impossible to believe "that Fate, or Nature, or God, or whatever it is" would not cause her to reciprocate. He continued his impassioned words:

> The love I offered you was not the trivial thing so often bandied about in the name of love. . . . It was the one unquestionable, unreserved, overwhelming love of a man endowed—or cursed—with the power of sounding all the depths of the heart. It seems to me that I lived for you long before I knew you or heard of you, I wanted and worked for you, filling the emptiness of existence without you with anticipation of what life was to be with you. Work was sweet because I thought it was for you; ambition was inspiring because I wanted you to think well of me; . . . I did not desecrate even the word "love" by repeating it to other women, none of whom, however, attractive, I ever mistook for you.[34]

Convinced at last that she would never reciprocate his feelings, he wanted her to remember him as "one who loved you with all the strength and depth, passion and tenderness with which man can love woman." Unlike Thum, Robertson eventually married, but he did not do so for twelve years.[35]

Madge's social life resulted in her acquaintance with many wealthy and prominent young men, but she apparently had high standards. Perhaps none of these young men interested her because her attentions had already been captivated by a charming young Lexington man of her acquaintance, one who would add another "great honored name" to hers. Certainly, if any Kentucky family rivaled the Clays and McDowells in prominence, it was the Breckinridges. They were a family tied closely to the history of Kentucky and the nation. No other surname in Kentucky matches them for length of service or overall achievement. Their sense of the past and the traditions that went with it were transmitted from generation to generation. One member of that family received Madge's special attention—Desha Breckinridge, son of Congressman William Campbell Preston Breckinridge.[36]

Born in 1867, Desha graduated from Princeton University in 1889 and spent two years at Columbia University Law School and one summer at the University of Virginia before joining his father's law practice. Of his experience practicing law, he later said: "Our practice was about equal to our knowledge—mighty little." A snappy dresser, he was attractive to the ladies even though he was not handsome, and in some ways he seemed a perfect match for Madge. Like her, he had grown up surrounded by people important in politics, business, and society. He, too, had a pervasive awareness of being related to important leaders of the past. A woman whose uncle was a law partner of Desha's father and who remembered well that generation of the family probably did not exaggerate when she said: "The Breckinridges always admired each other. They thought there was nothing so great as being a Breckinridge."[37]

Like the McDowells, the Breckinridges originated in Scotland. At the time of the British Restoration they moved to the Highlands from Ayrshire. The harsh life there drove them to Ulster, and from Ireland they came to America in the first half of the eighteenth century. John Breckinridge, the founder of the Kentucky dynasty, introduced and helped author the Kentucky Resolutions opposing the Alien and Sedition acts and served as attorney general in Thomas Jefferson's cabinet. One of his sons, Desha's grandfather Robert Jefferson Breckinridge, lawyer and theologian, was the father of Kentucky's public education system. Robert's nephew John C. Breckinridge served as vice president of the United States and ran for president before becoming a general in the Confederate army. Desha's father, W. C. P. Breckinridge, generally referred to as "Colonel Breckinridge" or simply "the Colonel" because of his service in the Confederacy, or more familiarly as "Willie," married first Lucretia Clay, granddaughter of Henry Clay, and second Issa Desha, Desha's mother, who was the granddaughter of Kentucky governor Joseph Desha. Desha had one brother—Robert—and three sisters—Ella, Sophonisba, and Curry.[38]

Social equals, the McDowells and Breckinridges were friends, though Henry Clay McDowell and Willie Breckinridge had fought on different sides in the Civil War and supported opposing political parties afterward. The friendliness changed abruptly, however, when a sex scandal destroyed Willie Breckinridge's career. Desha's mother had died in 1892, and the following year the Colonel married a cousin, the widowed Louise Wing. Soon thereafter a young woman named Madeline Pollard sued Breckinridge for breach of promise, charging that she had been his mistress for ten years and that he had promised to marry her after Issa's death. The "Silver Tongued Orator of Kentucky," who had served in the U.S. House since 1884, did not deny having had an affair with Pollard, but he asserted in the trial that his accuser had not been innocent and "unspoiled" when he met her, and had lured him as much as he had lured her. He denied that he had ever promised to marry her. The jury was not swayed by this defense and awarded the plaintiff $15,000 in damages. Although Breckinridge would not admit it at the time, the affair ended his political career.[39]

Repercussions of this sordid episode continued for many years. It shocked and divided Lexington society, and many former friends ostracized the Breckinridges. As one Lexington woman described it: "Some of my best friends are on the other side, but I go on, as I did in *war times*, doing my *duty*, regardless of consequence." To complicate matters, the new Mrs. Breckinridge suffered a mental breakdown, exhibiting periods of mania, possibly drug induced, in which she screamed at her husband and stepchildren to the point of causing Willie's children to move out of the house. Desha and his sister Sophonisba, who particularly idolized their father, were crushed by these events. Decades later Sophonisba recalled that awful time and something of the trauma the episode caused. She remembered that toward her mother her father had been "devoted, . . . endlessly kind, and there could not in our minds be any question of his fidelity." But looking back to her mother's long period of invalidism, she noted: "I see how complicated and difficult a burden my Father carried."[40]

Despite the fact that many of her friends ostracized the Breckinridges, Madge continued her friendship with Desha and Sophonisba, even during the height of the scandal. It was an uncomfortable and touchy situation; yet genuine affection existed between Madge and "Nisba," as she was called. Referring to her mother's illness and death in 1893, Sophonisba remarked to her friend: "You were an inspiration and pleasure to me last winter far beyond any thing I could show. I was necessarily so occupied, and my own life from day to day was often so exhausting that I could not freely manifest the inclination I felt."[41]

Madge continued to provide support to Nisba the next year by sending an Easter greeting, which was "very gratefully appreciated, as any sign of friendship and affection is." It came "at a time when such tokens had a peculiar value," Nisba confessed, adding that she and Desha "speak so often of your unfailing kindness that your ears must sometimes grow very hot." Later that year, when Madge gave her friend an embroidered handkerchief for Christmas, Nisba thanked her and noted: "I want your friendship and affection and respect, I want to be worthy of them."[42]

Yet Madge's friendship did not extend to Willie Breckinridge during this time. In December 1893 while traveling to Louisville, she encountered the Colonel and his wife on the train, and Mrs. McDowell subsequently remarked: "I know you were mad when you saw them. I hope you were not annoyed by them." She added that a friend had given her an account of the Pollard affair, and "it was even worse than the published" version. Nevertheless, before leaving for Louisville, Madge had accepted Desha's invitation to go to the Opera House. How difficult it must have been to keep this friendship intact![43]

Social discomfort aside, Madge found encouragement from her trip to Louisville when the doctor reported that "the foot looks better than he has ever seen it," and he thought "the pain is simply caused by the weakness of the muscles." She also enjoyed seeing Nettie's "sweet" baby, Henry Clay Bullock.[44]

Clearly, his father's disgrace seriously affected Desha's life. Yet his loyalty to Willie never wavered, earning him the title "the hero of a hundred fights," because of his readiness to take on the Colonel's detractors, despite the fact that he weighed less than 140 pounds. As Desha expressed his feelings toward his father: "I loved him, I do love him, as I have loved no other man. I approve nothing he has done. I pass judgment upon nothing he has done. He has given me pleasure, for that I thank him; he has given me pain, for that I forgive him."[45]

The tensions increased even more when the Colonel decided to seek reelection to Congress in 1894, despite advice to the contrary. The vicious primary campaign severely divided the Democratic Party. Then, in June, Basil Duke, ex-Confederate general and a nominal Democrat, announced that he supported Henry Clay McDowell, a Republican, as a nonpartisan candidate for the House seat in the Ashland district should Breckinridge win the Democratic nomination. Duke's condemnation of Breckinridge is especially noteworthy since the two had served as comrades in arms under John Hunt Morgan during the Civil War. McDowell strenuously opposed efforts to persuade him to run, but when both Republicans and Democrats urged it, he agreed to consider the proposition. Others began to speak out in his support, and he received many letters from people in both parties urging him to enter the race. His nephew Thomas S. Ballard expressed the typical sentiments of these letters when he implored: "You owe this to your State," because "it would be an insult to Kentucky womanhood, and a disgrace to Kentucky manhood for Breckinridge to be elected." Prominent among McDowell's supporters was Theodore Roosevelt, then head of the Civil Service Commission, who wrote: "I think you could do a very great service to our party by coming into public life." Further, he felt "as an American, I have an interest in seeing Breckenridge [*sic*] retired from public life. I feel it would be an infamy and something to make every American hang his head to have him continued in public service."[46]

Despite the fact that his family seems to have opposed his running, McDowell spoke at a political barbecue in August, saying he believed Breckinridge had met his Waterloo. Without being explicit, he tacitly agreed to run as a nonpartisan candidate should the Democrats nominate Willie. This proved to be unnecessary, because Breckinridge lost the primary in September. Women in the district played a large role in his defeat. Decades later, when she attempted to write an autobiography, Sophonisba maintained that Madeline McDowell had been a leader of those who had opposed the Colonel, but in the process she had fallen in love with Desha. Time and age may have caused Sophonisba to have an inaccurate memory of that episode, however. It would be most unusual for a twenty-two-year-old woman who had never been involved in any type of public endeavor to lead such a movement. While Madge opposed the Colonel in principle, no contemporary evidence has been found to suggest that she led the movement against him. Nevertheless, the whole situation made her friendship with the two Breckinridge children very troublesome. She undoubtedly shared her brother Henry Jr.'s strong relief when Breckinridge lost the primary since it meant that Henry Clay McDowell would not be running.[47]

Even after the primary, public feelings continued to run high, but somehow Madge remained friends with Desha and Nisba. Her attachment to Desha as a special friend must have been evident, for her girlfriends teased her about him. Grace Otis joked that, according to Washington gossip, Congressman Breckinridge was the best-dressed man in the city—"his spring suit cost $15,000." Apparently, Julia McDowell did not approve of her sister's friendship with Desha, because Marion Houston confided to Madge: "Desha is so nice. He is worth an effort but you'd better not tell Julia I said so."[48]

Ironically, at about the same time the Breckinridge scandal emerged, a somewhat similar one threatened the McDowells. In December 1894, a woman calling herself Alice B. Bullock filed suit in the New York Supreme Court alleging that in 1884 she and Nettie's husband, Tom, had entered into a civil contract of marriage as they walked along Fourth Avenue in New York City and that they had cohabited as man and wife. Major McDowell called upon his friend Benjamin Bristow, now a New York attorney, to serve as Dr. Bullock's lawyer. Tom denied the conversation had ever occurred and stated that he could prove he was in Kentucky the day the woman alleged it took place. The case dragged on until February 8, 1898, when the plaintiff, then signing herself Alice B. Snyder, agreed to accept payment of $500 from Henry Clay McDowell and release Thomas Bullock from all claims. The Supreme Court of New York then issued an order dismissing the case. Since this suit was filed in New York State, it is uncertain whether it became common knowledge in Kentucky. Possibly the McDowell family succeeded in suppressing the suit and keeping it from becoming public in Lexington. Nettie informed her father: "You do not know what a comfort to me it is to feel that we will have no further trouble from that source, and how grateful I am to you."[49]

Problems seemed to stalk the family. Shortly before the suit was filed against Tom Bullock, the McDowells and Bullocks grew extremely concerned over the health of Nettie's ten-month-old baby. An illness, possibly meningitis, left the child suffering epileptic seizures and permanent disability. That same year Will McDowell had to close the Appalachian Bank in Big Stone Gap and seek other employment. He would have been better off financially if he had done nothing for the last five or six years, he claimed. He took a position with the Louisville Chair Company for the sum of $1,500 per year but continued to need financial support from his father.[50]

While simultaneously dealing with her foot problem, the Breckinridge scandal, and various family crises, Madge also took classes at the Agricultural and Mechanical College of Kentucky, usually called "State College." Her course work there indicated her interest in social and economic matters. A low mark in political economy in President James K.

Patterson's class distressed her. Yet Patterson later praised his student. "He says you have a very bright mind and are capable of taking a good education. He says you used to ask him some difficult and puzzling questions," Mrs. McDowell reported. "I believe he thinks you ought to be back at the State College now instead of enjoying the pleasures of society."[51]

Like many young women of her era, Madge questioned what to do with her life. The 1890s was a period of expansion in opportunities for women to obtain higher education and participate more openly in public endeavors. Many institutions of higher learning, such as the Agricultural and Mechanical College of Kentucky (now the University of Kentucky), became coeducational. The women's rights movement gained a new lease on life in 1890 when the American Woman Suffrage Association and the National Woman Suffrage Association merged into the National American Woman Suffrage Association. Increasing industrialization and urbanization brought more women into the workforce, especially in nondomestic labor. Out of this emerged the image of a "new woman"—not only freed from the restrictive clothing and social practices of the Victorian era, but also educated, independent, and able to earn her own living. Not surprisingly, many of these women embraced feminism and accepted responsibility for improving the world through social reform.[52]

During this period both Madge and Sophonisba Breckinridge reached adulthood and wrestled with these issues. Madge became enamored with the idea of socialism and began to focus her attention on women's rights. Sophonisba, a graduate of Wellesley, had been admitted to the bar in Kentucky in 1892 but found that a woman could not support herself by practicing law in the state. She considered going to the University of Wisconsin to study economics under Richard Ely or to the University of Michigan Law School, and she wanted Madge to join her. Neither scenario worked out for the two. In autumn 1893 Nisba wrote Madge from Washington about her disappointment at not being able to pursue a law course, especially "if there was any probability of your going in for it with me," but she hoped that if they could not study law together, they could "do some work along the same line in Social study." She admonished her friend: "I do wish you would give your time to Social and Economic questions, and work and write. You have so much ability, such gifts, why not use them in real work." She recommended that Madge send to the "Wisconsin State University at Madison for a catalogue, and follow the Course Prof. Ely gives his students." She believed "there are so few women who can do these things, who have the leisure. You have time and intellect, too, and you do write so well. . . . I believe you could become great but I also think . . . that you can do such work as will help solve the problems that are now occupying earnest men and women." She concluded: "You see I preach, My practice is poor." On reflection, she seems to have feared that Madge would take this advice as criticism, and she subsequently urged her to forgive "the impertinent persistence with which I imply that you either do less than you ought or leave undone more. And, indeed, in spite of such intimation, either implied or expressed, you are *perfectly* satisfactory to me."[53]

In 1895 Sophonisba went to the University of Chicago, where she earned a master's, PhD, and law degree and became a pioneer in the fledgling field of social work. Even before going to Chicago, she began to assume the position of Madge's mentor, a role she would play again and again and one that would have far-reaching consequences for reform in Kentucky. Yet Nisba still seemed unsure of herself and in need of Madge's support.[54]

In correspondence with her friends Madge sometimes discussed her emerging philosophy of life. "Your altruistic, egoistic, socialistic, pessimistic questions put me in a whirl, and my brain didn't work properly for several days after your letter came," Marion Houston noted. She felt better, however, knowing that someone else "undergoes the mental torments that most of the people around don't seem ever to worry about. How they can accept things—traditions, creeds, etc.—as they do 'on faith' without proof or at least reasonably sure evidence, I fail to see." She promised to send a book that introduced the philosophy of Edmund Spencer and agreed that Madge's "idea of a slowly approaching socialism is the right one. No government can be better than the people and they must grow together." She wished they were together to discuss these matters, because "Your mind works so much more clearly than mine, that I feel as if you ought to be able to satisfactorily settle everything that bothers me intellectually."[55]

About this time Madge undertook the project of persuading the Fortnightly Club, the oldest Woman's Club in Lexington, to study German literature and philosophy. At first the group proved reluctant to embark on such a difficult project, and one newspaper even published an article ridiculing the endeavor, but the members finally agreed to her proposal, provided they spread it out over two years. This club eventually merged into the Woman's Club of Central Kentucky, another organization in which Madge would become a leader. As a number of historians have shown, the experience and self-confidence that women gained in voluntary associations during the late nineteenth century helped prepare them for larger roles in public life as a new century swiftly approached. Madge's life serves as a prime example of this, and the Federation of Women's Clubs became one of her primary avenues for promoting reform. It is important to note that although the Woman's Club movement has sometimes received criticism for its conservatism, it, perhaps more than any other voluntary association, educated women about community problems, helped them develop a sense of autonomy, and provided an avenue for escape from the purely domestic sphere.[56]

As Madge continued to seek a meaningful way to use her talents, she experimented with the idea of becoming a writer. In 1895 she delivered, according to her mother, "a beautiful paper" to the Woman's Club at the Chautauqua grounds. Desha wrote Sophonisba that Madge had carried the roses Nisba had sent for the occasion and that she "looked very sweet & unconscious & read well, but as I was on the last row it was pretty hard to hear her." He noted that a large crowd attended all the proceedings, but at least fifty people came only to hear her presentation, which John Fox Jr. described as "very fine." After later reading the paper she had presented, Desha wrote her that "no matter how much you enjoyed writing it I expect I enjoyed reading it more—When I heard you read it or rather saw you & heard parts of it, I thought it good, very good, but not up to what I expected." In fact, he thought he "could have made suggestions which would have improved it—I realize now I was a conceited Jackanapes."[57]

That same year she published an article on Henry Clay in *Century Magazine*, which John Fox Jr. felt was so good she should turn it into a book. "Nobody in Kentucky is quite so well fitted for it in every way as you are. Mr. Clay seems to be in history to stay. I believe you could write the most *interesting* book of him yet written." Describing himself as an "old friend," Ralph Shaw also congratulated her on the article, saying he had always been an "admirer of Kentucky's greatest statesman." Desha, too, encouraged her to write a book on Clay or on the broader subject of Kentucky history, noting various problems with all the state histories published to date. As an opponent of woman suffrage, he advised: "Why not go ahead & show the real equality of woman & man by doing a book equal to man[']s best & let the Susan Anthonys crack their little eddy by their mouthings about the rights of women, you keeping free from that[,] show by your work the title of your sex to equal recognition." The article on Clay, he believed, could do four things: "To make a name for yourself, to help the real advancement of women to aid the present generation to a greater appreciation of their forefathers[,] & rescue from oblivion those of past generations who are worthy of it, [and] to give to Mr. Clay his proper place in American history which has not yet been accorded him." He added: "Knowing neither your plans nor your ambitions I write as one seeing darkly, I only know you have the brain to do all this ably, the love of truth to do it justly." He advised she start it as an experiment and drop it if she grew weary of the task.[58]

At some point during these years she also wrote a short story, titled "An Incident," in which she told the morbid tale of a German boy who, suffering from ill health (implied to be tuberculosis) and unrequited love, killed himself. This unpublished story perhaps served as an outlet for the frustration and depression she surely felt at times because of her foot, even though outwardly she appeared cheerful and optimistic.[59]

Certainly, Madge's social life never flagged. She continued outings with friends and family, including a group trip to Blue Licks in Desha Breckinridge's cart, and she sometimes accompanied Desha to the country club. Friends worried about this relationship. Stites Duvall reported asking Desha about Madge, to which he replied that "he thought Miss Madge was simply flirty." Stites felt "relieved[,] for a wedding present would be right hard on me these times." She added: "I don't want you to marry Desha nor any other Breckinridge, in fact, I'll get it down to any other man, at least not just yet."[60]

The ambivalence Madge had shown with her other suitors apparently spilled over to Desha as well and was probably exacerbated by the fact that neither family looked favorably on the relationship. Although the two corresponded and shared books and articles with each other throughout 1895, Desha constantly chided her for teasing him and not allowing him to reveal his true feelings. Ironically, in view of subsequent events, he wrote her about fidelity:

> One woman wrote of fidelity—"I think it is to keep faithful through good report & evil report, through suffering & if need be through shame: it is to credit no evil of the one loved from other lips & if told that such evil is true by his own to blot it out

> as though it had never been. To keep true to him through all appearances, however against him, through silence, & absence & trial; never to forsake him by one thought & to leave all the world to serve him; that is what seems fidelity to me." I am forbidden to mention that of which I most desire to speak therefore I neither make comment nor ask questions.[61]

Madge frequently sought Desha's opinion of her writing, but she did not find him to be an easy convert on the issue of women's rights. He remembered as a five-year-old telling his grandmother, "men always know better than women." This was an attitude he found hard to shake. Once, when Madge had sent him two of her articles, he informed her:

> I enjoyed both, none the less [*sic*] that I agree with neither. Your especial plea for woman seems to be both more thoughtful & more logical than the article on monometalism. I however believe your premises too narrow & so necessarily your conclusions false. Quite true it is that women were guarded as the most exquisite—the most delicate blossom of chivalry, equally true that women have born only as beasts of the field,—that polyandry has been a recognized state of society in countries from which we have descended in this I do not think there is any principle involved, it is a mere matter of expediency with importance not in the effect on society thro' women's role but in the influence on civilization thro' its effect on woman herself. There are several statements in it I should like to take for texts—I however realize that if I attempted it vitriol would run off my pen more freely than the ink & that you didn't send it to me to be answered.

He noted his "gradual realization of the utter uselessness, the utter hopelessness of what I say making [a] difference to you."[62]

During this time Madge saw other men as well. She reported to her mother, who was out of town, that she had gone to the country club with Jim DeLong, who had kept her waiting for an hour with her gloves on in order to get even with her for the times she had kept him waiting. Delong said he had gone to the country club so often with her that it did not seem natural to get there on time. Likewise, Robert Burns Wilson and John Fox Jr. continued to visit Ashland, and both men sent her flowers.[63]

Meanwhile, Desha appeared uncertain about Madge's affections. After a particularly trying time, he lamented: "I was a fool, a brute last night. I am sorry. I seem to show you the worst side, if there can be a worst when all is bad. I know you forgive me now,—some day you will understand." Another time he wrote: "I have just come back from, where would you guess? Your gate! Forsooth am I not a fool?" He added that "it was beastly hot walking, frightfully long coming back too. This thing of being a coward is infernal." When she asked for his photograph, he assured her that he was "delighted" to send it and "could I have for an instant ever persuaded myself that you really wanted it, I would long since have had a new one taken." He also noted that "I do not want either to annoy you or to evoke even the possibility of friction between you & those you love." When she sent him the book A *Bachelor's Christmas* as a present, he responded: "Honestly do you think it's a proper thing for you to send me such a book as that—don't you think it's enough that I should have the proof of a Bachelor's Xmas every year for the rest of my life on your account without you making me have two the same year? . . . Really are you not ashamed of yourself?" He admitted the gift was "the one bright spot in a rather gloomy day;—after I had received, before I had opened the package, after I knew you had thought of me,—before I knew your thought had been prompted by malice." Nevertheless, he was "awfully glad to learn that the report I heard that you had left for Chicago the first of the week was untrue. I did not believe even you would be so cruel,—even a heart as hard as yours I thought would have pity & not go without giving me a chance to see you again." Yet he had to decline her invitation to attend a banquet but asked to see her before she left for Chicago and perhaps to accompany her as far as Cincinnati.[64]

Shortly after Christmas 1895 she went to Chicago to visit Grace Otis and then on to New York City to consult with Dr. Gibney about her foot, which was again troubling her. While in Chicago, she and Grace toured the University of Chicago with Sophonisba Breckinridge. Evidently Madge was so impressed that she began to make plans to enroll. After she left, Sophonisba sent her a catalog, so she could "plan your work quite definitely. I shall be glad to help you arrange your program in any way in my power." She reported that Madge "quite won every body's heart" while she was there. From Chicago the young woman went on to New York City, where she stayed with the Houstons while she consulted with doctors.[65]

The news the doctors told her ended her aspirations to attend the University of Chicago. She would require another surgery. On hearing this Mrs. McDowell called her "the bravest girl I ever saw" and told her to wait until she could get there to stay with her at the hospital. Her mother and Aunt Mag hurried to New York. Sophonisba promised to "believe with you dear, that this will be as you think—It can't be otherwise, and when you are quite well and strong, and you and I are taking long walks through the park and along the lake front next winter, quarrelling over Social Science and Politics—it will all seem like one of those dreadful dreams."[66]

The surgery appeared successful. Major McDowell wrote his wife that "a great weight has been lifted and I shall move now like another man—Kiss the dear little girl for me and tell her that I had no idea how much I loved her or empathized with her until within the last few days." In fact, he felt "as if I had no other child." With the recovery seeming to go well, Aunt Mag stayed with Madge while Mrs. McDowell returned to Lexington. However, the foot did not heal well, and the doctors kept postponing Madge's return home. As she and the family grew impatient, the doctor told her he thought the "partial operation" would not cure her. Meanwhile, he sent her to another doctor to have her lungs checked. No problem showed up, which did not surprise Madge: "I felt a little like saying I told you so, but really I wouldn't have been much surprised if he had told me that both lungs had entirely disappeared—It wouldn't have seemed much more like a thunder-bolt out of a clear sky than this foot business."[67]

Nettie Bullock informed her mother that "I am distressed about Madge, and wish she was coming home. I wish she was heroic enough to have the foot off and save herself any more pain." However, she acknowledged that "it is easy enough to talk about having it off when it is not your foot, but I am so afraid the ankle might get involved and she might have to lose some of her leg." Nettie did not consider the New York doctors any "better than Tom and Doctor Vance if they do charge so much."[68]

Although liberal in their expenditures for Madge's health, the McDowells still faced financial difficulties, caused largely by the national economic depression of the mid-1890s. They could not sell the property at Big Stone Gap, and Will McDowell even contemplated letting his property go to pay the taxes. Meanwhile, Major McDowell sold two fillies at auction that brought only $15 each, barely covering the auctioneer's fee of $12 each. Three years before, they would have brought $1,000 to $1,200, he claimed. Ultimately, Major McDowell mortgaged some property for $30,000 (equivalent to $774,480 in 2008 dollars) with Northwestern Mutual Life Insurance Company to raise funds.[69]

Madge's friends sympathized with her medical problems and hoped for her swift return. One of her friends informed her that Desha Breckinridge spent most of his evenings at home "and when I see him, there is that far away look in his eyes, which bespeaks the man in love." Finally, in late April 1896, Dr. Gibney allowed her to go home. He thought the foot looked better and the inflammation was "perhaps superficial" and would respond to "country air and good living."[70]

On April 25 she and Aunt Mag reached Lexington, but her joy at being back was tempered by her realization that she might have to return to New York for another operation. Nevertheless, she immediately launched into a busy social schedule, often in the company of Desha. On June 10 the McDowells held a "magnificent reception" at Ashland for Mexican War veterans, who were holding a convention in Lexington. The group named Major and Mrs. McDowell honorary members of the Mexican War Veteran's Association, commemorating Mrs. McDowell's father, Henry Clay Jr., who fell at Buena Vista.[71]

A few days later Madge and Aunt Mag left for New York City and more surgery. Mrs. McDowell did not accompany them, having suffered from ill health since leaving New York in February. By this time the doctors had diagnosed the foot problem as tuberculosis of the bone. Madge stayed with the Houstons until June 21, 1896, when she went into the hospital. The following day Dr. Gibney amputated her foot. On that same day her father's friend Benjamin Bristow died, and McDowell went to New York City for the funeral and to see Madge. The whole family had felt the trauma, and sister Nettie apologized to the recovering patient that "we have taken such a lively interest in your affairs that it may have worried you; but you must remember that you cannot be sweet and lovely without having your family love you dearly and take the deepest interest in your welfare." She also reported that she had recently seen "Mr. Thum, his mother & sister," and that Thum hoped to visit Madge in New York City before he embarked on a trip to Europe. "I held my peace and said neither yea nor nay," Nettie added.[72]

Both Thum and Harrison Robertson used the operation as an excuse to write. Robertson asserted that "it has been long since anything affected me so strongly. I feel for you with all my heart," while Thum reiterated yet again, "I could wish for no greater thing in earth than to . . . comfort you as my dear wife." Perhaps more welcome was the letter from John Fox Jr. that related how he "was so wretched" when he heard she was going to New York "and for what purpose" that "I hadn't the heart to write you a line." He thanked her for sending him her photograph and proclaimed: "You are just about an angel, that's what you are," adding that "it is the best photograph of you that I have seen and I should be glad to have it as a picture even if I didn't know who it was." Her friend Stites Duvall was more upbeat, promising to visit when she returned home and run all her errands. Stites also enigmatically remarked: "As for your 'romance' I must hear more about it."[73]

Madge made a remarkably swift recovery, and by July 6 she visited friends in Englewood, New Jersey. While recuperating, she spent time with Nettie Belle Smith and on August 26 returned to Lexington. Perhaps a friend best summed up the true impact of the nearly six-year ordeal that resulted in an amputation at age twenty-four when she wrote: "You dear Madge, with beautiful consideration for those who love you, have borne suffering and anxiety with such patience and serenity only your mother has altogether realized what you had to endure." Years later, Madge gave a hint of her true feelings about the amputation when she stated that "the loss of the use of one's limbs, of physical power and freedom, is only next to the loss of life."[74]

Although Madge's general health seemed good, tuberculosis of the bone meant that tubercle bacilli had invaded her body and made her susceptible to the disease for the remainder of her life. The actual bacteria causing the tuberculosis had been identified by Robert Koch only in 1882, and there was no effective cure until 1944, when streptomycin was discovered. It has been estimated that in the nineteenth century as much as 90 percent of the population had been exposed to the bacteria, but in a majority of the cases the bacilli were walled off and became active only if the person's immune system became weakened. Yet approximately one billion people succumbed to the ailment in the nineteenth and twentieth centuries alone. In most cases the disease attacked the lungs, but it could also invade the bones, gouging large holes and causing ulceration. Although tuberculosis is a communicable disease, many experts believed there was an inherited predisposition to contract it. In Madge's case both her great-grandfather Henry Clay and her grandfather William Adair

McDowell, as well as several other members of the family, had contracted the disease. It would remain a sword hanging over her head.[75]

What would be the long-term effect of this traumatic amputation? Many young women would have withdrawn from society and lived a cloistered, sheltered life in a sickroom. Others would have become bitter and indulged in self-pity. But for Madge, the coming years would prove that adversity only invigorated her, while physical suffering increased her empathy for the poor, the sick, and the downtrodden. Instead of retreating from the world, Madge began to focus on reforming it. With the amputation of her foot she had experienced one of the greatest traumas that could befall a young woman; yet she had endured without complaint and had hardly slowed her activities. She had seen her ambition to seek higher education outside the state come to naught while she struggled to find a meaningful outlet for her talents. Her belief in women's rights had begun to emerge as she wrote articles on history, economics, and social issues. Through her writing she had started developing an understanding of the power of the press in promoting the ideas in which she believed. She had slowly, perhaps unknowingly, prepared for the challenges that were just ahead.

Chapter 3

"An unholy interest in reforming others" 1897–1900

The knowledge that her days on earth might be cut short seemed only to spur Madge to live life to the fullest and make every minute count as she launched into a wide range of activities. In 1897 she joined John Fox Jr. in an effort to assist Robert Burns Wilson by raising a subscription to publish a collection of his works. Wilson's *The Shadows of the Trees and Other Poems*, which came out in a small printing of 250 copies in 1898, is probably the publication that resulted from this subscription. In February 1897 she went to Cincinnati to have a "slight" operation on her nose, and in April she served as a bridesmaid in a friend's wedding in Louisville. The following month she traveled to Hot Springs, Virginia, with Nettie Belle Smith. In August she and Aunt Mag vacationed at Blue Lick Springs in Nicholas County for a few days, and in the autumn she traveled to New York City for horse shows and to Louisville and Big Stone Gap for visits. She also took lessons and joined the Golfing Club. These many social outings found her more and more in the company of Desha Breckinridge, and he followed her on the trip to Big Stone Gap.[1]

Yet both Madge and Desha worried about her parents' attitude toward him, and their romance continued to be a matter of concern to friends and family. While at Hot Springs she wrote her mother thanking her for being nice to Desha "the other night at the train, for you were so sweet to him . . . he would like to think it wasn't going to change." In fact, he was very grateful for Mrs. McDowell's past kindnesses and "has always been fond of you & always been as anxious for you to be fond of him as he is now for Papa to like him & respect him." The same day she wrote her

On the steps at Ashland, back row: Robert Burns Wilson, John Fox Jr., Anne Clay McDowell; second row: unidentified woman, Madeline McDowell, possibly Julia McDowell, Stites Duvall; front row: Henry Clay McDowell Sr. Courtesy of Special Collections and Digital Programs, Margaret I. King Library, University of Kentucky, Lexington.

father that she had always viewed him as the nicest person in the world and now Desha Breckinridge agreed. She noted: "You were so lovely to Desha that I know he will be better for it all his life, and I do believe that he is worth trying.—You know that I didn't feel a bit certain in the beginning—for that matter I don't suppose I am certain right now for I never am certain of anything in this world—but in every bit of the time that I have taken to try to know him, I have come to respect and admire and believe in him more—I have tried doing without him and it is almost too hard—and he does love me very truly."[2]

Like Madge, Desha had long been seeking direction for his life's work. He had not found it in the practice of law, but in January 1897 he leased the *Lexington Morning Herald* from Henry T. Duncan and Samuel G. Boyle. Colonel Breckinridge proved skeptical at first of the wisdom of this move, but he hoped his son had at last discovered his vocation, and Willie felt that at least the paper gave Desha employment and a certain standing in the world. The *Herald* had had a disastrous year in 1896, but by 1898

Desha, serving as managing editor with his father as the primary editorial writer, had turned it around so well that he was afraid the owners might take it back when the agreement expired. However, they agreed to renew the lease with option to purchase, and in January 1899 Desha exercised that option.[3]

The young newspaperman soon asked Madge to serve as "literary editor" for the paper by writing book reviews. At first reluctant to begin this undertaking, she finally withdrew her objections and ordered: "Send out your magazines!" She then entreated: "We will mention it gently—I hate all thunderclap—and I wouldn't like to see it done up in 'social and personal.'" After a mix-up that resulted in her turning in the first reviews late, she wrote: "Here after, tell me the exact day and time at which you want it, and I will have it there—don't expect it a minute before. I am sorry to have been delinquent so early in the action, but I really didn't understand. . . . I can't judge of the length it will be in print at all, and I do not want it long—Please, read it and cut it properly—Don't try putting it all in as rank flattery to me—I am not susceptible. . . . My things are always so much better before I write them than afterwards. . . . I think you made a mistake in your choice of literary editor."[4]

Evidently her confidence increased, for soon she wrote: "You are very fortunate that I haven't already offered to write your editorial columns for you. I always yearned to be an editor and write some thing every day and express my opinion on every subject in the universe—It is lovely to be able to do it without any personal responsibility, as it were and without being considered to preach."[5]

Madge was already beginning to appreciate the power she could wield by writing for the newspaper. Desha and his father, too, used the *Herald* to advocate their views on many subjects and sometimes to praise one of their own. When the Kentucky Court of Appeals licensed Sophonisba to practice before it in 1897, an article in the *Herald* commented on her many accomplishments, mentioning her continuing study of political economy at the University of Chicago as well as her legal studies. Noting that she came from a well-known, conservative southern family, the paper stated that her admission to the appellate bar gave evidence of the changing relation of women to men and the rising spirit of independence among women. "We know all true men hail her as a comrade in work," the article contended. In the summer Nisba went on to pass the qualifying examinations for the PhD degree.[6]

While the Breckinridges rejoiced over Sophonisba's accomplishments, the McDowells experienced great fear when Major McDowell became ill in July with a "constriction in his chest" that doctors diagnosed as heart disease. He became gravely ill in August following another attack, but by September he had recovered enough to be out and about. Dr. W. O. Bullock Sr., his personal physician, diagnosed the problem as angina and advised the patient to watch his diet, avoid stress and fatigue, and take nitroglycerin. Continued stress from financial problems undoubtedly exacerbated the condition, and Henry Jr. urged his father to sell some of the Louisville real estate in order to lighten the load of debt. Nevertheless, the family continued to pursue its same expensive lifestyle.[7]

Although Madge led a busy social life, according to her mother she studied "a good deal" and devoted much time to ordering and reviewing books for the newspaper. All these activities halted briefly in February 1898 when she and Julia contracted mumps. However, by Easter the girls had recovered sufficiently to accompany their parents on a trip to New Orleans.[8]

By this time whatever uncertainties Madge had about her relationship to Desha had seemingly been resolved. She began to purchase dishes while Desha shopped for rings. The *Herald* announced the engagement on May 28, "without authority," Colonel Breckinridge informed Sophonisba. He also noted that Desha "has never said a word to me about it, and I am somewhat at a loss to know exactly what to do." Apparently concerned about Madge's health problems and her family's predisposition for tuberculosis, Willie explained that he wanted to do what was "right and loving," but "I presume he knows I have no enthusiasm over his marrying into that family and taking the tremendous risks—which with my belief in the prepotency of blood I fear; and yet the girl is intellectual, gracious and very attractive; and any one he chooses will be treated by me with every affection and respect." The following month Loring Andrews of Cincinnati notified Desha that he would make a diamond ring with a three-fourths caret stone for the price of $80.[9]

But the smooth flow of everyday life was again about to be interrupted, this time by events of international consequence. On February 15, the USS *Maine* exploded in the harbor in Havana, Cuba. With the United States supporting the independence of Cuba from Spain and tensions between Spain and the United States escalating, Congress passed a joint resolution for war in April and called for 125,000 military volunteers. The martial spirit, always strong in Kentucky, swept Lexington. Although the *Herald* had not been jingoistic, its managing editor volunteered for the army, joining the staff of his uncle, General Joseph C. Breckinridge. Before leaving Lexington, Desha executed his "Last Will and Testament," leaving "for her who would be my wife, Madeline McDowell," a portion of his estate and his interest in two racehorses. For a time the young soldier was stationed with other Kentucky troops at Chickamauga, where Mrs. McDowell, Madge, and Julia visited him.[10]

Although the war ended too quickly for Desha to see any military action, in August he sent an urgent telegram to his father, asking if Fayette County could provide space for a camp for thirty thousand troops. Henry Clay McDowell stepped forward and offered land on his Ashland estate for the camp, and he also put up $8,000, which was to be reimbursed by the city, to secure Lexington as the location. The camp, located practically at the foot of Ashland's yard, proved to be a significant economic and social boon for Lexington and Fayette County. For weeks the social life of the area centered around the military presence. Stationed at his uncle's new headquarters, Desha returned to Lexington. Major and Mrs. McDowell entertained General Breckinridge and his staff at a dinner and dance, and the following day Madge presided at the raising of the flag and a luncheon at the general's headquarters. Meanwhile, Madge also visited the Eighth Massachusetts Regiment and the Twelfth New York Regiment.[11]

Although it was his philanthropic gesture that had brought the troops to town, Major McDowell found himself somewhat disenchanted with them, noting that "they are the kind of soldiers that not only want feather beds & Pullman Cars, but all the luxuries of life, and can give more trouble than both armies in the Civil War. In fact, they have nothing to do but to complain." Yet McDowell had one streak of good fortune to celebrate when he was able to sell his entire stable of trotting horses in the highest-priced public sale held in the previous three years.[12]

Rumors abounded concerning the McDowell-Breckinridge wedding date. Just as Desha's father had not been told beforehand about the engagement, he also was not informed about the impending marriage until nearly the day for it to take place. He continued to be concerned and mentioned his reservations on several occasions to Sophonisba, noting that Desha seemed worried: "He is not a hilarious expectant groom, but it is a little gloomy and awkward in some of its surroundings and I am not surprised." Desha admitted to Sophonisba that even he had not known the wedding date until recently, for "there were all sorts of discussions etc." The Colonel particularly felt the awkwardness of the situation. Madge wrote inviting him and his wife to attend the wedding, saying: "In spite of various contradictory reports in the newspapers I have set the seventeenth of November on which to take the last advantage of Desha and to leave him no outlook for the future." After receiving this "sweet" letter, Willie related to Nisba that the prospective bride did not seem to realize that the wedding would take place in her father's house and that perhaps McDowell was unwilling to issue a personal invitation. Desha told Sophonisba that he had done everything in his power to ensure that their father would be present at the wedding and to make the occasion as easy as possible for him.[13]

Even the *Herald*'s social editor was either confused or misinformed and announced that the wedding would occur on November 10. As late as the tenth, Willie believed Desha had not yet found a place to live, but four days before the wedding, he reported that the couple had taken rooms in the home of a Mrs. Chenault. The marriage finally took place at noon at Ashland on November 17. It was an informal affair, with only family and Dr. and Mrs. W. O. Bullock Sr. present, and there were no attendants except John Payne, the groom's best man. The Colonel had overcome his obstacles, real or imagined, and attended the ceremony with his wife. Newspaper accounts gushed about the "distinguished family connections on both sides, the brilliant personal endowments of the bride and groom and their universal popularity."[14]

The couple then left by train for New York City, where they stayed at the Fifth Avenue Hotel. Desha wrote his family that the weather was good, and they were having a "pleasant" time. He said he felt like the woman who at age sixty went on her wedding trip and apologized for not writing, saying there were "no pens or ink in this Paradise." They returned via Washington, DC, then went to the home of Desha's sister Ella Chalkley in Lynchburg, Virginia, for the christening of Ella's baby. Willie and Louise urged the newlyweds to stay with them until their apartment was ready. The Colonel told Desha that he wanted Madge to do as she desired but he felt he must extend the invitation "because of the peculiar circumstances surrounding us all," so she would know she was welcome. Perhaps at Madge's urging, but probably by Desha's preference as well, since he did not get along well with his stepmother, the newlyweds stayed

Desha Breckinridge, 1920. From Sophonisba P. Breckinridge, *Madeline McDowell Breckinridge: A Leader in the New South.*

at Ashland between their arrival on December 5 and their move to an apartment on December 13. They did, however, eat Christmas dinner with the Breckinridges.[15]

Madge wrote enthusiastically to Nisba about her wedding gifts and lamented that her friend and sister-in-law had been unable to attend the ceremony. She and Desha had a "fine" time in New York, she related, attending plays and eating all the things they could not get at home. While urging Nisba to visit them so she could do her "hostess act," Madge expressed alarm lest she lose her "new woman principles and want to go to housekeeping." She had long since lost her disapproval of wedding presents, she concluded, and "I believe yet I will some-day rise to being a housewife."[16]

The wedding seemingly ended eight years of turmoil that had begun soon after Madge's return home from Miss Porter's in 1890. She had engaged in a difficult, tension-filled romance that resulted in a marriage that was initially opposed by both families. Yet in many ways the two were well matched. They were both part of the Bluegrass aristocracy; both had emotional scars—she from her illness and he from his father's scandal. Both knew Kentucky needed reform, although they did not agree exactly on what those reforms should be, and both appeared genuinely to love the other. Undoubtedly a complex interplay of factors drew the two together, and despite obstacles, they seemed devoted to each other.

Early in 1899 Major McDowell's health began to fail severely, casting a shadow over Madge's life. In February he was "really in danger" when his cardiovascular problems became exacerbated by an attack of the "grippe." Moreover, he continued to be subjected to stress caused by his financial situation. While contributing $500 to assist two families who were threatened with the loss of their homes, he noted that his income had been reduced by more than half, while his expenses had increased. "I now contribute materially to the support of four families and some individuals, and have been nearly compelled to reduce some of these allowances, in order to make ends meet," he concluded. In addition, a delay occurred in the city's reimbursing him for the $8,000 he had advanced to acquire the military encampment in Lexington the previous year. The city solicitor refused repayment in 1898, saying there was no appropriation in the budget, but when the Lexington Board of Aldermen provided an appropriation in 1899, the solicitor still refused payment on grounds that he could not determine from which fund it should be paid. Claiming that the payment might violate a provision of the new state constitution, he subsequently brought suit to determine if the payment would be constitutional. Editorials in the *Herald* eloquently denounced the solicitor, questioned his motives in bringing the suit, and stated: "There can not be a citizen of Lexington who does not want that money repaid."[17]

By late February McDowell had improved sufficiently for the doctors to urge him to travel south. He and Mrs. McDowell went to Naples, Florida, for more than a month's visit. The warm climate and rest restored him so much that on his return, he proclaimed that he and his wife were "both in perfect health."[18]

Soon after her marriage Madge had embarked on a whirlwind of activities. In January she served on the Executive Committee to plan a carnival at the Opera House for the children's home. She entertained the *Herald* staff, attended various clubs and parties, and maintained cordial relations with Desha's father and stepmother. She and Desha stayed at Ashland while the McDowells were in Florida, and in April they moved into Ashland for an extended stay until they could occupy new rooms on Market Street. When they learned that Desha's sister Curry was returning to Lexington to teach kindergarten, they invited her to live with them. Willie advised her against that plan and wrote to Curry urging her to find a boardinghouse. Nevertheless, she stayed with Madge and Desha for about three weeks before moving to a boardinghouse, although they urged her to remain with them.[19]

Early in the year an event occurred that propelled the young matron into the center of Lexington's growing reform movement. On February 11, 1899, John S. "King" McNamara shot Jacob Keller, a railroad cashier, on Main Street. Each man charged the other with jostling him in the street. Keller, who was known as a peaceful, pleasant man, died two days later. At the time of the shooting police arrested McNamara but then released him on a $1,000 bond. The bond later proved to be invalid because of an irregularity in the signature. McNamara was brought before a magistrate, claimed self-defense, and was again released on a $1,000 bond. He failed to appear at the time set for the examining trial. On the same day that McNamara shot Keller, his brother William J. "Squire" McNamara seriously wounded an officer of the law.[20]

The McNamara gang consisted of the father, known as "Red," and six sons, all of whom seemed to consider themselves above the law, and their acts of violence pointed out the demoralized conditions that existed in local and state government. For a number of years conditions in some areas in the state had resembled civil warfare, and this lawlessness had infiltrated the law enforcement agencies themselves. In fact, throughout the nineteenth century, Kentucky had experienced a growing problem with feuds, murders, and other crimes that had sullied its reputation. Most critics blamed the commonwealth's criminal justice system for this state of affairs, charging that too often the law enforcement agencies and courts permitted the guilty to escape, thereby encouraging others to commit crime. Poorly paid and badly trained prosecutors, packed juries, and governors who abused their pardoning power caused growing criticism of the entire system. Lexington had not escaped this trend; thus, few were surprised when King McNamara absconded and the police made little effort to capture him.[21]

There were those, however, who were incensed at this breach of justice, among them the editor of the *Herald* and his wife. On February 18 Madge and a group of women called a mass meeting at the Merrick Lodge for February 21. They planned to organize and raise money to offer a reward for the capture of McNamara and to hire detectives to find him. The *Herald* noted that since the officers of the law had failed in their job, Lexington would now be protected by the women. This event, it predicted, might be the beginning of the end of an era in which authorities winked at crime, filed away indictments, and allowed witnesses to be spirited off. The next day the *Herald* editorial asked, "Who Is Responsible?" Noting that law enforcement officials had not apprehended King McNamara and had given Squire McNamara only a nominal fine for his acts of violence, the editorial expressed perplexity at the reason for King McNamara's flight, because "for him and his there can be no place so safe as Lexington and in Lexington no refuge so secure as the court of justice." Furthermore, "The root from which this crime grew is deeply embedded in our system, and merely to denounce this young fugitive will not prevent other fruit from ripening upon branches springing from the same roots." Tongue-in-cheek, the editorial suggested that the law making it a crime to carry a concealed weapon should be changed, making it a felony *not* to carry a revolver and making it a crime *to be* killed rather than to kill.[22]

Colonel Breckinridge did not believe the efforts of the women would achieve any lasting results. To Sophonisba he wrote: "I confess that I do not take much stock in this meeting; I see no such feeling in the community as to give any real hope of true reform or proper action." A few days later he again predicted: "Madge is very busy hanging or catching 'King' M'namara;—but the other side is beginning to take courage and the pendulun [*sic*] will soon begin to swing back."[23]

Willie evidently misinterpreted the attitude of the community. As Dr. W. O. Bullock Sr., described it: "A great state of excitement exists over the murder." Men and women crowded into the mass meeting. Madge accepted appointment to a committee to draw up resolutions for the meeting and also served on the Subscription Committee, which raised more than $1,000 as a reward for the capture of McNamara. In addition, Governor William O. Bradley provided a $500 reward from the state. As

Madge explained to her mother, who was in Florida, the duties of catching the fugitive had so absorbed her that she had not had a spare minute to write. Nevertheless, she reported, serving on the McNamara committee had been "a great deal of fun."[24]

Under this public attack officials assembled a special grand jury, which proceeded to indict Squire McNamara on six different counts. When the grand jury called for the bond on which King McNamara had been released, Justice of the Peace Abner Oldham could not produce it. Ultimately, the grand jury indicted both Oldham and Police Judge John J. Riley for malfeasance in office for their handling of the McNamara cases. These indictments were later dismissed, but Squire McNamara received a three-year prison sentence.[25]

The mass meeting did not succeed in capturing King McNamara. He remained a fugitive for more than a decade, and his ultimate capture did not result from the reward raised by the women. From time to time over the years reports came that he had been seen in New York City, Washington State, and various other places around the country. In 1901 police in Sacramento, California, arrested a man they thought to be the fugitive, but he proved not to be McNamara. Finally, on June 14, 1912, the Fayette County sheriff arrested King McNamara at the Seelbach Hotel in Louisville. His brother Squire had been shot and killed in a Lexington saloon soon after his release from prison in 1901. Yet the community protest against lawlessness had not been in vain. Years later Desha would write: "The beginning of the end of that reign of lawlessness came with the murder of Jacob Keller. The meeting, called, organized, and dominated by the women of Lexington, marked the culmination of the subserviency of the men to the reign of lawlessness."[26]

The lack of immediate success in the McNamara case did not deter Madge from promoting other public projects but rather revealed to her the possibilities that could result from concerted action. She conducted a contest for the *Herald* to determine who was the most popular businesswoman in Lexington, continued to write book reviews for the paper, and began to use its pages to open public discussion of reforms that she supported, such as kindergarten education. In March 1899, she initiated a newspaper discussion of the value of kindergarten that foreshadowed the way in which she would use the *Herald* over the next two decades to promote myriad other causes. She printed not only those views supporting her own beliefs, but also those opposed. In fact, in her first article on kindergarten, she quoted a primary teacher disillusioned by children who had been taught by play methods. This type of teaching was impractical, the woman maintained. Madge then asked for responses discussing the methods and purposes of kindergarten. For several days, the *Herald* contained articles advocating and opposing kindergarten education.[27]

From all these discussions, as well as from her reading and association with kindergarten teachers, including her sister-in-law Curry, Madge developed a passionate belief in the value of kindergarten. Her interest in the subject strengthened her concern for all forms of education and pushed her along the road to advocating other educational improvements. The *Herald* continued to be a great asset not only in disseminating information to the public on social problems, but also as a means for Madge to gather her own information in the debates that the paper published.

In spring and summer 1899 Madge turned her attention to yet another project. The McDowell family had joined Christ Church Episcopal soon after arriving in Lexington in 1882. Madge and her sister Nettie became members of a group for young girls called the Gleaners that had been organized to carry out "Christian work." After Nettie's marriage the group became less active, but in 1899 Madge revived it and became its president. The organization opened its membership to women of all denominations, although its work continued to be supervised by the bishop and rector. This seems to have been Madge's only formal connection with organized religion during her adult life, and the endeavor focused more on reforming this world than on preparing for the next.[28]

Madge used the Gleaners to launch a social settlement program in eastern Kentucky, where for two decades the Lexington diocese of the Episcopal Church had maintained a high school in Beattyville, the county seat of Lee County. The diocese had just completed a new school building there, when Madge in summer 1899 joined a horseback tour of the mountains that had been organized by a professor from Berea College. While there, she conceived the idea of using the church's school building in Beattyville and an old mission house across the river in Proctor as a social settlement center for the whole eastern region. After returning home, she organized an excursion of the Gleaners to Beattyville and Proctor. Taking supplies with them, they founded an industrial training school on May 20. Madge's brother Will, by now general manager of the Lexington & Eastern Railroad, helped her with the travel arrangements, while the *Herald* gave "flaming advertisements" to the endeavor.[29]

On the trip the group never reached Proctor because their ferryboat became grounded on a sandbar in the Kentucky River, and they had to be rescued by rowboats. As one woman remembered: "We felt a little like Moses, because we never reached our kingdom-to-come, but . . . gazed longingly at the Mission House on its hill in Proctor." On June 3 friends from Georgetown, Versailles, and Danville joined the Gleaners for a trip to Beattyville and Natural Bridge. Madge took charge of selling tickets to the six coaches full of people who made the trip. In July she embarked on a month-long excursion through the mountains of Kentucky, Virginia, and Tennessee with Katherine Pettit, founder of a social settlement at Hindman, and a group of friends. While she was gone, the Gleaners held a bazaar to raise money for their social work.[30]

During this period Madge's health appeared good as she undertook the rigors of horseback trips in the mountains and even attempted bowling. However, she occasionally admitted that her physical problems limited her activities. Of her attempts to bowl, she noted: "I do it badly and it makes me extremely tired." On one occasion she wrote to Nettie that "I am managing to get along very well now by omitting all walking that isn't obligatory." In late summer or early autumn she and Desha finally left Ashland and moved into their new living quarters. "The house is too sweet for anything," she reported to Nettie, and "Desha is of course perfectly delighted with it all." Nevertheless, her spirits sank as her father's health plummeted. She spent much time at Ashland with him as the family sought additional medical advice, but it brought only the diagnosis that the problem seemed to be "sclerotic change, involving the carotid arteries," and little could be done except for him "to keep very still." In October McDowell noted to Nettie Bullock that "'the Boss [Madge]' switched me over yesterday" to a new doctor. A series of strokes affected McDowell's eyesight, causing the *Herald* to warn that he might not be able to recognize friends. When the major attempted to resign as president of the Lexington & Eastern Railroad, the company refused his resignation and stated that his appointment was for life. That proved to be a short time, indeed, for he died on November 18 at Ashland.[31]

Although McDowell had been an indulgent father to all his children, Madge appears to have been his favorite. He had been a great influence in her life as well, imbuing her with a sense of noblesse oblige as he provided a strong example in both word and deed for philanthropic activities.[32]

McDowell's will left all of his personal estate to his wife and the real

Henry Clay McDowell Sr. Courtesy of Special Collections and Digital Programs, Margaret I. King Library, University of Kentucky, Lexington.

estate to her for her lifetime. At her death the real estate would be held in trust for the six children and managed by Henry Jr. The income would be equally divided among his children, and the daughters' income would be a "separate estate, for their sole and separate use, free from the debts, contracts and control of their husbands." It appears from check stubs in the family papers that the monthly income Madge received usually ranged from $75 to $100 per month, or $1,937 to $2,582 in 2008 dollars.[33]

This money gave Madge a considerable degree of independence, and she did not have to rely on Desha's income from the paper, which turned a profit but still depended on printing contracts from the city government to do so. This situation threatened the *Herald*'s political independence.

The McDowells had always been Republicans while the Breckinridges were Democrats, but neither Madge nor Desha adhered strictly to the party system. Instead, they supported the candidate or party that best represented their own views on public policy, and neither party in Kentucky was reform-oriented enough to please them. In 1900, even though Lexington mayor Henry T. Duncan was known as a reformer, Desha refused to promise that the paper would strictly follow party lines and support all platforms and candidates chosen by the Democrats. As a result, the mayor held up appointment of the *Herald* as the city's printer and threatened to start a new paper. Desha still refused to make a commitment, and the mayor ultimately failed to follow through with the threat of a new paper. The *Herald* soon resumed its role as city printer.[34]

During the winter of 1899–1900, Madge used the *Herald* to highlight the suffering among the poor of the city due to the extremely cold weather. Lexington had no charity committee, though it had usually had one in the past, and by January 1 the city had exhausted its relief fund. Estimating that as many as five hundred people were in dire need, the mayor and police found themselves besieged with requests for aid. The mayor called upon a group of women who had distributed charity in previous years to reorganize the benevolence system. On February 14 that request brought about the founding of the Associated Charities of Lexington, Kentucky, a permanent organization that would implement the modern ideas of relief and social welfare.[35]

Influenced strongly by her sister-in-law Sophonisba, Madge had long been studying the idea of "scientific charity." The University of Chicago emerged as a major center in the development of social work as a profession during the first two decades of the twentieth century, and Nisba became one of the leaders in that movement. In addition, Sophonisba participated in social settlement work with Jane Addams at Hull-House and embarked on scholarly studies of the causes of poverty and juvenile delinquency, while Madge's distant cousin Mary McDowell also pioneered the settlement house movement. Madge had visited these settlements on previous trips to Chicago, and the Gleaners' social settlement experiment in eastern Kentucky reflected their influence. Through Associated Charities Madge implemented many of the techniques and ideas promoted by reform-minded friends and relatives in Chicago.[36]

The concept of charity promoted by the developing social work profession placed strong emphasis on the environmental causes of poverty.

By 1900 these experts agreed that benevolence should be "scientific," that is, it should organize the philanthropic resources of the community efficiently, provide centralized administration, and direct relief in such a way as to avoid destroying the incentive to work. Thus, they stressed the necessity of painstaking investigation and individual treatment of each case, with the goal of eliminating the causes of poverty. The casework system was adopted in an attempt to solve the problems of indiscriminate relief, overlapping private charities, and municipal outdoor relief systems that supposedly encouraged indolence, pauperism, and fraud. Some historians have emphasized the social control aspect of this movement, saying that it represented a response of the troubled middle class to the social dislocations of the post–Civil War industrial city and arguing that organized charity provided the urban community its surest safeguard against revolution. Moreover, many contemporary critics of the casework method called it a cold and calculated way of administering relief. Nevertheless, in the three decades after 1900, paid professionals gradually replaced volunteers in charity organizations and laid the foundations of modern welfare bureaucracy.[37]

Both Madge and Sophonisba passionately defended the casework method, claiming it showed respect for the poor rather than being cold and bureaucratic, and they likely would have refuted any contention that social control was its purpose. In fact, they argued that learning the nature of the problems affecting someone in distress showed respect for that person and was essential for enabling social workers to find a remedy to assist the individual out of poverty. As Nisba expressed it: "It is of course a very easy thing to give a man who asks for a meal some food and send him on, but it is very bad for the man. If we are going to feed him, we ought . . . to find out why he is tramping, and after investigating put him in a way of getting work." She added: "This requires . . . a good deal of specialized knowledge and organized effort." In a variety of ways over the years, in newspaper articles and speeches, Madge reiterated this belief, and she made certain that the Associated Charities of Lexington based its policies on these principles.[38]

The new organization decided to open a downtown headquarters and to employ a full-time executive. In each precinct there would be a committee of two women to investigate applications for aid. The *Herald* gave its complete support to this endeavor, and in March 1900 Madge was elected to the Board of Directors, a position she held most of the time until her death. On March 30 the organization adopted its articles of incorporation and made plans to purchase a lodge and wood yard. The lodge would provide temporary shelter, while the wood yard would apply the labor test by getting rid of those who did not want to work and by preventing the loss of self-respect to those who would prefer a job to direct charity.[39]

Madge continued her efforts to educate the community on the benefits of scientific charity. In April the *Herald* published her article contrasting Lexington's and Louisville's charity organizations. Louisville, she noted, had long practiced organized, cooperative relief rather than indiscriminate charity. Even in the previous two severe winters Louisville had not been inundated with paupers as Lexington had been. She noted that the Associated Charities of Lexington would provide an employment bureau and keep records about the poor, but this would be effective only if people referred private applications for aid to the Associated Charities for investigation. "This would by no means cut off private charity, since the individual, if really interested or charitably inclined, would probably give more after investigation than before, if the case were found worthy. If unworthy, every penny withheld is a positive gain both to the applicant and to the community," she argued, adding that "few people realize how many quarters given on street corners go for whiskey and cocaine and worse."[40]

The social settlement movement found itself closely involved with the issue of poor relief. Although settlements did not plan to dispense charity, the workers there found it difficult to avoid becoming involved in this activity. Jane Addams and the Hull-House group helped organize the Chicago Bureau of Charities, and most settlement workers cooperated by referring needy cases to that organization. Mary McDowell had suggested in 1896 at the National Conference of Charities and Correction that the settlement worker could give inside knowledge to the charity worker, and in most cases this proved to be true. In fact, settlement workers made the first real attacks on urban poverty. Quickly realizing they must deal with the problems of education, labor, housing, parks, playgrounds, and sanitation, they often found themselves lobbying for legislation on these matters and filling positions on public boards.[41]

Madge accepted the ideas and ideals of the social settlement workers. Although she never worked in a settlement house, she continued to visit them whenever possible and reported her findings to the Lexington community. Louisville had the first social settlement house south of the Ohio

River, and after visiting it, Madge wrote that social democracy comprised the basic ideal of the settlement house. The settlement fulfilled its educational role by providing manual training to assist people in learning skills that would help them obtain jobs and its social role by organizing clubs and giving people a recreational outlet. Neighborhood House in Louisville, she asserted, should serve as model for the rest of the South.[42]

During this period Madge built up her fund of information by reading many books on reform. Some of these she reviewed for the *Herald*, sometimes simply to inform the public about projects in other places and sometimes to serve as specific examples for Lexington to follow. She used an article on social settlements in rural New England to advocate additional support for that kind of work in the mountains of eastern Kentucky, writing:

> Being of the class of people who enjoy problem novels and who take an unholy interest in reforming others, I am never able to watch an experiment toward social improvements in any other community without desiring to apply the same experiment to our own. We people of the Blue Grass have been dealt with more generously by nature, our lines have fallen in pleasanter places than have those of our kinsmen in the mountains, and without any spirit of patronizing or of self complacency, it is fair that we should in some way hold out a helping hand to our fellow Kentuckians of the mountains.[43]

On another occasion she reviewed Jacob Riis's *A Ten Years' War* (1900), which dealt with the attack on urban poverty that had taken place in the ten years since he published *How the Other Half Lives*. Riis contended that the decade had brought significant progress, though much more remained to be done. Americans, he asserted, were slow to realize the need for justice to the tenement, feeling that the ideal "all men are created equal" was enough to make it so. Madge found this study to be an inspiration that was "open, convincing and touched with great human sympathy."[44]

Her attitudes toward political reforms were also reflected in her review of John Jay Chapman's *Practical Agitation* (1900). Chapman believed reform movements usually failed because activists tried to do things piecemeal; by compromising, reformers postponed the ultimate victory. Chapman also called upon the individual voter to eschew the political machine. Madge concluded that "it would be hard to point the way to more fascinating reading" than this book. She believed Chapman's ideas could be applied to any location, although he had written primarily of New York City, and she agreed with his argument that too much effort had been expended on reform within the political party system and that a new reform group was coalescing that recognized the fact that machines controlled both political parties. Along the same lines she wrote about the Municipal Voters' League, which she saw as evidence of a "civic renaissance" because it reflected a nonpartisan attempt to secure honest, able leaders who could solve the problems of municipal reform.[45]

Yet Madge did not allow civic reform to interfere with family responsibilities. Soon after drafting the bylaws for the Associated Charities, she accompanied her mother and sister Julia on a trip to Palm Beach, Florida, as they sought warmer weather for their health and a way to distract themselves from the grief they were still experiencing following Major McDowell's death. The women left Lexington on February 15 in a snowstorm and reached Jacksonville, Florida, in unprecedented cold. Madge sent several articles to the *Herald* for publication. In one she complained with disgust that because of "natural southern unprogressiveness," Florida had not prepared for such cold weather. Nevertheless, the beauty and comfort of the Poinciana Hotel, where they first stayed in Palm Beach, enthralled her. She felt Florida provided a "luxury and a gratification of all the senses—a result which makes some of us who are not socialists thank Providence for our American millionaires."[46]

In one witty and amusing article she told of her visit to an ostrich farm near Jacksonville. One characteristic of the ostrich above all others impressed her: "The ostrich is monogamous: he takes one wife and lives with her in his own corrall [*sic*] until death them do part—after which he never takes another. He has another human trait—not that I mean that the second mentioned is human; it would be rather inhuman from a masculine standpoint, I imagine—he is a great kicker."[47]

In this article she also hinted at her political beliefs, including her opposition to the controversial Democratic nominee for governor in 1899, William Goebel. Republican William S. Taylor had apparently defeated Goebel by a narrow margin and was sworn in as governor. Goebel supporters continued to contest the election, and on January 30, 1900, Goebel was shot as he approached the state capitol. The Democratic majority in the state legislature declared Goebel the winner, and he was sworn in on his deathbed the following day. When he died on February 3, Democratic lieutenant governor J. C. W. Beckham succeeded him. Kentucky had two rival governments, and a virtual state of anarchy prevailed until Taylor fled the state in May. This condition of near civil war existed at the time Madge overheard a Kentucky couple speaking at the hotel in Florida. She recorded that the "husband sat a few feet from me and explained to a Floridian in an audible tone the horrible conspiracy worked out in Kentucky against Goebel and his 'law-abiding' followers." She concluded: "It took great self-control to keep me from joining in a conversation to which I was not invited."[48]

The Lexington women returned home on March 9, and by the summer the McDowells faced a new crisis. This time it involved Tom Bullock's health. In June Nettie wrote her mother asking to borrow money from her inheritance and saying that Tom would do three more operations and then quit his medical practice. Apparently he, too, suffered from tuberculosis because letters consistently referred to his cough, one of the major symptoms of the dread disease. By autumn the Bullocks had settled in New Mexico, seeking the sunny, dry climate for a cure. Since Madge and Nettie were very close, this separation distressed both sisters.[49]

Shortly after returning from Florida, Madge launched a major reform effort—founding the Lexington Civic League. This endeavor included much the same group that had organized the previous year's mass meeting to capture King McNamara. The current state of political unrest in the commonwealth resulting from the disputed gubernatorial election had reinvigorated the spirit of reform that had developed during the McNamara case. In a meeting held on April 17, 1900, the women made plans to form a permanent organization to support not only better law enforcement but also other kinds of civic improvements. Madge worked very hard to promote this project. She spoke at a meeting on April 24 about the possibilities of service to the community, and she subsequently became part of the Membership Committee and was elected to the Executive Committee on May 11. Willie Breckinridge, evidently still skeptical of the effort, was propelled by his daughter-in-law's enthusiasm into signing the constitution of the Civic League, which Madge herself had drafted. A few months later he wrote: "It is rather amusing to me to watch Madge active in civic leagues[,] associated charities and other semi-public movements and Desha's tolerance;—recalling his former disapproval of women taking part in such enterprises."[50]

Madge also continued her work in eastern Kentucky with the Gleaners during the summer of 1900. The Proctor Industrial School in Beattyville reopened in April and volunteers from the Gleaners held a month's kindergarten for ninety pupils that summer. They also held cooking, gardening, and carpentry classes. Money for this came from bazaars and other fund-raising efforts they held in Lexington. Already one of the volunteers had discovered that "the church workers knew one unfailing friend . . . and her name was Madge McDowell Breckinridge." In May, while Madge spent some time in Beattyville, Desha stayed with his father. Willie, still not convinced these efforts at social work were worthwhile, was so happy to have Desha staying with him that he felt "her work is not an unmixed evil and bears unexpected and pleasant fruit."[51]

The work in Lee County continued to grow, but Madge gradually ended her involvement with it. She kept the presidency of the Gleaners only a short time. A friend later explained: "As so often happened, she kindled that fire and left others to tend it while she went on to kindle new ones. It seems to be part of her essential heroism. She never stayed for rewards. Other people were warmed by her fires while she was in cold places starting new ones."[52]

The Progressive reform movement was gathering momentum at the turn of the century. Very often the reformers focused on the child as the key to solving existing social problems. While it might be too late to liberate adults from the cycle of poverty, disease, and exploitation, they hoped to prevent the child from following the same path. Thus, many reforms advocated by Progressives focused on children—including attempts to end child labor, to improve health and education standards, and to provide recreational facilities. Of these, education received the most attention. Progressives looked on the public school as the chief instrument of acculturation and of eradicating ethnic and class differences. They sought to expand the school curriculum to satisfy the aptitudes and needs of the children and also to provide the occupational skills necessary in the increasingly industrialized twentieth century. Settlement workers were among the first to become aware of the inadequacy of the educational system for poor children. This led to the movement for compulsory education laws, abolition of child labor, manual and vocational training in the schools, public sanitation, and juvenile courts, as well as for parks and playgrounds to serve the child's recreational needs.[53]

Madge turned her attention to all of these things as she began to construct a career for herself in social reform. Manual training became one of her early interests. She believed manual training would be far more beneficial than traditional education both to society at large and to the vast majority of children who would seek employment in the trades rather than the professions. Kentucky, as well as the rest of the South, needed a trained labor force in order to compete in an industrial nation, she contended: "Broadly speaking it may be said that manual training is a dead letter in the South. In fact the South has only recently awakened to her interests in manufacturing industry; to the fact that cotton alone is no longer king; to the fact that she cannot place her reliance in the production of raw materials, without the capacity to work these materials into finished products of exchange. Kentucky has never awakened to this state of affairs. The manual training school, the industrial, trade, and technical school, seem in fact the logical solution."[54]

She was particularly enthusiastic about the possibilities of manual training in solving the race problem. A paternalist in race relations, she sought to improve conditions for blacks but believed progress could be achieved only gradually. Thus, she accepted the Booker T. Washington model of encouraging manual training as a means of advancement. "The members of the colored race have little capital with which to enter business," she noted, "if they expect to make their livelihood honestly, therefore, they must look to their skill in the industrial arts; they must be taught not to despise labor, but to recognize it as the source of all strength." Lexington's public school system needed many things, she concluded—a nonpartisan school board, better lighted and ventilated buildings, playgrounds for all schools, manual training in both white and colored schools, and a manual training high school that would enable the white boys and girls of Lexington to enter the State College on an equal footing with Louisville youth who had attended a manual training high school. It was even more important, she maintained, for Lexington to introduce manual training in the colored schools. Recent trips to Hampton Institute in Virginia, which had pioneered manual training for African Americans, and the Kentucky Reform School had reinforced her belief in the efficacy of such instruction. "If we can provide this sort of education for the bad boys and girls of our State, why can't we give it to the good boys and girls?" she asked. She noted that she hoped to send one black child in whom she had a special interest to Hampton Institute.[55]

She also related how in one week's time whites in Lexington had killed two blacks. This situation had naturally excited a feeling of unrest among blacks and a belief among them that they were not being granted equal protection of the law. If this state of affairs continued, she warned, there would be an outbreak of violence between the two races for which lawless whites would be responsible. Therefore she argued: "If race antagonism is to be prevented in this community, the two direct steps toward that end are equal justice from the courts and the officers of the law to black and to white, to rich and to poor, and persistent industrial training for the colored races."[56]

There was one source of manual training for blacks in Lexington, and that was in the Colored Orphan Industrial Home. Madge praised this program: "If there are any who are doubting the advantages of manual training in connection with book learning—the advantage of the modern principle of 'learning by doing'—they may be convinced by a glimpse at the children of the Orphan's home with their willing obedience, their industry, their happy faces." The city of Lexington and Fayette County both contributed to this institution, but the bulk of its support came from nonresident philanthropists. Therefore she wrote her article for the *Herald*, "partly as an appeal, partly to bring to the attention of all charitable, all public spirited persons of the community, the purposes, the methods and the excellent record of this institution."[57]

One source of industrial training for whites also existed in Lexington. This was the Saturday Industrial School, founded in 1876. Madge strongly supported this program:

> One cannot see the work that is being done in this Industrial School for the white children of Lexington and in the Colored Orphans' Home for the colored children, without wishing that the significance and the need of this "learning by doing" might be more widely grasped among us. When Lexington has manual training in all her public schools—for white and black; when the State College has a department of domestic science which will provide for its girls' [*sic*] advantages similar to those now provided for the boys—then indeed this former Athens of the West may begin to boast of her institutions for educating and training the young.[58]

Madge was almost as enthusiastic about parks and playgrounds as she was about manual training. In 1900 Lexington did not have a single public park, nor did any of the schools have a playground. Madge pointed to Louisville's experience the previous year. Neighborhood House had sponsored a playground in an ethnically mixed location. As a result of the playground, different ethnic groups learned to work together. In addition, fewer street gang fights took place and fewer drownings occurred from children playing in the river. "There was a general gain in the social virtues, and in the qualities that can become common to all nationalities, which go to make up the right type of independent and self-controlled American citizen," she said. The Lexington School Board was considering the addition of playgrounds to two schools, and Madge urged the board to dedicate these to the use of the children in summer as well as winter.[59]

A short time later the Lexington Railway Company proposed to the Lexington city government a plan to build a park with a convention hall. The hall could be a permanent home for the Chautauqua, an educational and cultural program that sent lecturers and performers on a circuit around the country, while the park would be a first step toward development of a park-playground system. The company asked the city to put up $15,000 and the Railway Company promised to pay the remainder. The *Herald* supported this endeavor and asked readers to send in their opinions for publication.[60]

Madge accomplished very little in either manual training or public parks and playgrounds during the first year of effort. The consciousness of the community to these and other needs grew, however, and she won the support of the Civic League for these causes. During the first two years after her marriage, she could record some important achievements—the beginning of social settlement work by the Gleaners, the formation of Associated Charities and the Lexington Civic League, and the arousal of interest by the community in a variety of other proposed reforms. Moreover, she had developed the methods and techniques that would serve her various causes for the next two decades. She read a great deal on the subjects that interested her, visited sites that could provide firsthand information, and then formulated her opinion. Next, she wrote about the proposed reform extensively in the *Herald* in order to inform and educate the public about the issue. Finally, if at all possible, she secured the support of an organization such as the Civic League or Woman's Club. Later she would also use the tactic of bringing to Lexington speakers who were experts in the field that was the subject of her current reform interest.[61]

By the close of 1900, then, Madge had formulated definite goals and mastered techniques of publicity and organization. Like many other women during the early years of the Progressive reform movement, she had begun to create for herself a career in public reform. As one historian has noted, many young, educated women in the late nineteenth and early twentieth centuries "itched to find socially useful roles for themselves." Jane Addams and many other women accomplished that goal through the settlement house movement; Sophonisba by joining in the development of one of the new academic disciplines developing during the era. By the end of 1900 Madge, using her unique access to a major state newspaper, had begun to create a career for herself in civic reform. She was now ready to launch more ambitious projects on several different fronts.[62]

Chapter 4

"Our hope lies in the children" 1901–1904

From 1901 to 1904 Madge began to build upon many of the ideas that she had already developed and publicized in the *Herald*. In most instances she worked with one of the newly formed organizations—the Civic League, the Associated Charities, or the Woman's Club of Central Kentucky. The latter had formed in 1894 as part of the Kentucky Federation of Women's Clubs, and the Fortnightly Club merged with it in the late 1890s. The reforms Madge promoted through these groups ranged from the founding of parks, playgrounds, and kindergartens to attempts to persuade officials to include manual training in the schools and to secure the passage of compulsory education, a juvenile court, and child labor laws. At this point in her life, no single activity or interest predominated—she addressed one issue after another.[1]

All of these reforms, however, represented aspects of the Progressive reform movement that was developing in the late nineteenth and early twentieth centuries. Madge's close association with Sophonisba Breckinridge put her in direct contact with many of the leading reformers in Chicago, and Sophonisba herself began to emerge as one of the significant social scientists of the day. The Chicago connection proved especially important because "Chicago progressives were often at the heart of national campaigns for legislation or programs intended to address social problems," as one author has noted. Nisba's association with Jane Addams and other social settlement workers at Hull-House—a group whose influence resonated all the way to the nation's capital—her close association with such Progressives as Julia Lathrop, Grace and Edith Abbott, Florence Kelly, Graham Taylor, and many others, plus her research into issues of immigrants, tenements, juvenile delinquency, labor and working

Madeline McDowell Breckinridge, seated at a desk at Ashland. Courtesy of Special Collections and Digital Programs, Margaret I. King Library, University of Kentucky, Lexington.

conditions, and a wide variety of other social problems provided ample fuel for her sister-in-law's reform aspirations.[2]

During the last half century historians have debated the nature of the Progressive reform movement and the people who participated in it. Most agree that the movement resulted from the forces of urbanization, industrialization, and immigration that swept the country in the decades following the Civil War, leaving people with the feeling that they had lost control of their lives to outside forces. Likewise, the supposed increase in corrupt political machines in many cities and the influence of gigantic corporations that wielded unprecedented economic and political power troubled the public. Many historians also agree that Progressives were optimists who believed in human progress and sought to correct problems, often through governmental intervention and regulation. But whether they were looking backward, seeking to restore some idealized version of economic individualism and egalitarianism that had never existed, or were modernizers advocating efficiency, discipline, and centralization—sometimes to the detriment of democracy—whether social control or social justice motivated them, or whether they meant to control business or aid it are issues still being debated. In addition, many studies have emphasized the role Protestant religious and moral values played in the movement. Historians of the 1950s and 1960s often deprecated Progressives as either naive environmental determinists or lackeys of corporate business interests. They also generally described them as urban, middle-class, native-born Americans, usually college-educated professionals. Richard Hofstadter, for example, emphasized a status revolution and depicted the Progressives as members of the old liberal aristocracy who were resentful at being displaced by the nouveau riche business class. Other historians have noted that the conservative counterparts of the Progressives often fit this same demographic description, that some Progressive reforms appealed more to the working class than the middle class, and that much of the legislation they sponsored expanded democracy and benefited lower socioeconomic groups. Virtually all agree that these reformers placed great stress on education as the means of finding the solution to problems.[3]

Certainly, great diversity existed in the Progressive movement, but at all levels women played an important role. Their activities gave greater force to the argument that the participation of women in national affairs would make life more decent. Though Madge Breckinridge emerged as one of the leading reformers—indeed, arguably *the* leading reformer—in Kentucky, in many ways she did not fit the old model of the "typical" Progressive, except that she belonged to the old aristocracy, and even in that she was the daughter of a man involved in many of the business interests of the day. Well educated but without a college degree, she had not experienced an appreciable decline in status. Though the McDowells' financial fortunes had suffered during the 1890s, their social standing and influence had not diminished. Few in the state could rival her family's wealth and none could outclass its prestige. While she did not share completely in the Progressive movement's fears about blacks and immigrants, she did embrace its beliefs in efficiency, the efficacy of law to achieve social ends, and the importance of education. She was not religious in the traditional sense, but her dedication to reform created a sort of civil religion evident in other reformers such as Jane Addams and John Dewey. She, like many women in the early twentieth century, found in reform a means for carving out a career for herself and influencing the world.[4]

In some important ways Madge appears more radical than the typical Progressive. Throughout her life she maintained sympathy for the concept, if not the actual implementation, of socialism. The ravages of big business deeply concerned her, as it did most Progressives, and she once wrote: "Of the daily sucking of the blood of the poor by the great corporations of this country we rarely hear, for the very poor are inarticulate. Their whole energy is consumed in the struggle merely to maintain existence." On one occasion, while surveying the political situation in Nebraska, she pointed out that people in that state were "standing for many of the things that we used to consider socialistic when the Populists or the free silver Democrats advocated them, but which many of us have now come to think are simply progressive." Another time, when recommending a lecturer, she noted that he spoke on "reform movements, such as suffrage and economic reforms, as you may designate Socialism. The average public has already swallowed much of its program, but it is still afraid of the idea of the mouse." If not a true socialist, nevertheless, she grew completely convinced that government must provide a greater variety of services to the people. An example of this was free garbage pickup, for which she argued: "Is not the remedy for it to get over our hysteria about high taxes; to realize that high taxes often mean greater economy; that they mean simply that we are paying jointly for services which otherwise we would have to pay for individually, and at a much higher rate per capita?" She faced an uphill battle in fighting Kentucky's long-standing and enduring tax phobia, but as she accelerated her work in the new century, she experienced some successes—as well as a number of frustrating defeats.[5]

Madge continued to support her earliest reform effort—the Gleaners' social settlement work. Though no longer the group's leader, she served as first vice president in 1901. By this time membership in the group had grown from thirty-five to eighty-three. The Gleaners paid for a cot at Good Samaritan Hospital and conducted work in Lee County. They sponsored remodeling the old mission house in Proctor so it could be used as a social settlement. During the summer volunteers taught kindergarten, cooking, sewing, and woodworking at Beattyville in exchange for their room and board. In September the kindergarten and manual training school moved from Beattyville to the mission house in Proctor. Years later, one of her friends recalled that Madge was the one who looked across the river at the mission house and immediately saw its potential as a social center. The Gleaners funded these activities by personal donations and special events. In December the women held a bazaar, with Madge serving as one of the hostesses, and a few days later they met at the Breckinridge home to wrap Christmas packages to send to students at the Proctor Industrial School.[6]

The major project that Madge undertook during 1901, however, was to provide a park for the children of the West End, or Irishtown, section of the city. The section had developed in the 1840s when a large number of Irish immigrants congregated there to work in factories and on the railroads. Unpaved streets, poor drainage, crowded houses, and inadequate sanitation characterized the area. Sewage contaminated the water supply, while smoke and stench from distilleries polluted the community.[7]

Madge felt the urgent need of improving conditions for Irishtown's children. Believing, along with many settlement workers and kindergarten teachers, in the importance of creative play, and accepting the child-saving rhetoric then popular in educational theory, she began to work for the establishment of a playground in Irishtown. She also believed—as did most social settlement workers—that juvenile delinquency resulted largely from play energies gone wrong, either through restriction or lack of guidance. Thus, the introduction of a playground represented one step toward reforming the neighborhood and teaching the children to be useful citizens. Accordingly, playgrounds had to be supervised by trained personnel in order to achieve the desired goals.[8]

When the Civic League held its first meeting in 1901, Madge presented the offer of a loan for one year of a lot on Manchester Street in Irishtown for use as a playground. The League accepted the offer and appointed Madge to the Playground Committee. The Civic League secured the support of the Woman's Club, many of whose members also belonged to the Civic League, which promised to raise $200 for the project. After much exhausting work in raising money and preparing the lot, the playground opened on June 17 with more than three hundred people in attendance. Benches, flowers, and play equipment covered the transformed lot. Kindergarten and sewing classes met each day. Approximately two hundred excited children, plus a large crowd of adults, attended the park's dedication. Elizabeth Cloud, who was to become one of Madge's closest friends, headed the kindergarten.[9]

Although a few blacks lived in the mainly white Irishtown, only white children could use the playground and kindergarten. In writing about this, Sophonisba, who has been called "a leading white advocate of blacks' rights," remarked that the "policy of the [Civic] League . . . was characterized by reality and not by theory or the doctrinaire. All that could be got for the children was to be claimed and obtained. But the possible was not to be laid on the altar of the chimerical, and the playground in Irishtown and the later school were for white children." She added: "The effort in behalf of the colored children was to get for them what could be got." She also noted that her sister-in-law "was greatly interested in the problems of race relationship, but in her public work she was governed by two principles . . . first, that every human being should live under the conditions making possible reasonably favorable development; second, the possible good of the present should not be sacrificed to the commercial good of the future." In an era fraught with racial conflict, Madge would frequently face this issue in her reform efforts. Sophonisba accurately assessed Madge's approach to the problem, as she veered between sympathetic paternalism and political expediency.[10]

The playground proved to be a great success, with a variety of activities, some of which were open to the entire community. On one occasion nearly 150 Irishtown residents attended an open-air concert. Almost all of them expressed to the sponsors their pleasure at the effect the playground had on their children, and a policeman from the area noted that in the evenings the children gathered to sing the songs they had learned during the day.[11]

The Manchester Street playground remained open for ten weeks. When it closed, Madge summed up her thoughts in an article, "The Passing of the Playground." She viewed the effort as a supplement to the public schools and hoped the playground experiences of kindergarten, drawing, oral history, and manual training would bring a larger percentage of Irishtown children into the public schools. Almost all were of school age, and more planned to enroll in public school at the beginning of the new school year than ever before. Despite this encouraging sign, Madge pointed out that many Irishtown parents hesitated to send their kindergarten- and early-elementary-aged children to public school because they had to walk long distances and cross the dangerous railroad tracks. This situation highlighted the need to establish a kindergarten and elementary school in Irishtown. She summed up the summer's endeavor:

> Sometimes we who have had it in charge have wondered if we had not attempted too much, if the deficiencies in the perfect working of our plan had not come from the fact that we had "bitten off more than we could chew;" if it were not unwise for us to have felt so keenly all the needs of Irishtown and to have tried to answer so many of them at once.
>
> But we have had our reward in that we know we have really answered a number of them. We are not sorry now for anything we have done—we are only sorry for the things we haven't done; we ought to have bitten off just a little more.[12]

The idea that she ought always to do a little more remained forever her attitude toward Irishtown. Of all her causes, this deprived section would remain dearest to her heart, recalled one of her friends decades later. No matter how immersed she subsequently became in causes of national import, she could still find time for Irishtown. Perhaps this interest resulted from the fact that she had such personal contact with the people there, especially the children.[13]

In many ways the summer kindergarten and playground work begun in Irishtown in 1901 foreshadowed the later "Head Start" program, which the federal government initiated in the 1960s. Both sought to help prepare underprivileged children for public school, to broaden their view of the world, and to help them adapt to disciplined activities. As in so many other instances, Madge adopted this idea many years before it became widely accepted.

During most of 1901 Madge's health remained good except for the usual winter cold. However, her mother was unwell for much of the time. Despite this concern and the playground work, the Breckinridges maintained an active social life. They attended family weddings and funerals, frequently entertained guests in their box at the Lexington Opera House, and on occasion traveled to Cincinnati to attend the opera. In August Madge, her mother, and a friend visited Henry Clay McDowell Jr. and his wife in Big Stone Gap, Virginia, where Desha later joined them. Madge and Desha spent a short time in New York City during September but had to return home early because of the illness of Jouett Shouse, who had been left to manage the *Herald.* In the autumn, the McDowell family celebrated President Theodore Roosevelt's appointment of Henry Clay McDowell Jr. as a federal judge for southwestern Virginia. McDowell attributed his appointment to his father's friends as well as Desha Breckinridge's urging of notable persons, another indication of the family's status and extensive social and political contacts.[14]

Along with her other activities Madge still found time to write articles and reviews for the *Herald.* She critiqued a variety of books, wrote an editorial on the public asylum, and had the *Herald* reprint a *San Francisco Chronicle* editorial on public playgrounds. Pursuing another of her interests, she wrote about the Louisville School of Domestic Science. The introduction of domestic science in the public schools and at the State University would have an "inestimable effect on the health and morality of the community in the years to come," she asserted. This idea of domestic science training for girls and vocational—also called manual or industrial—training for boys was gaining support among Progressives who felt that the public school curriculum must become more relevant to the lives of the masses who would not enter the professions. Girls should learn hygiene, housekeeping, sewing, and sanitary food preparation, while boys learned skills that would assist them in finding employment. Although historians have sometimes seen this movement as one designed both for class control and to provide businesses with trained workers, Madge believed it to be a practical approach to education.[15]

For Christmas Madge received a new typewriter. She promptly began taking lessons, and this device soon became an important tool for her writing, including columns on school suffrage, which began to fill the pages of the *Herald.*[16]

Kentucky had been one of the first states to grant some women the right to vote in school elections when the Kentucky General Assembly in 1830 passed a bill to create a statewide public school system. That bill, which included a provision that "widows, femmes sole, and guardians of infants residing and owning property in a school district" could vote in elections for school commissioners, was never implemented, but another act, passed in 1838, created a public school system for the commonwealth and retained the clause allowing some women to vote in school elections. Subsequent acts continued to include that provision, and in 1888 the legislature expanded school suffrage to allow spinsters with wards to vote on school bond issues. Then, in 1894, a bill making Lexington, Covington, and Newport second-class cities (a population-related designation) gave women in those cities the right to vote in school elections as well as the right to serve on school boards. Significantly, black women as well as white could vote, and in the 1895 school election in Lexington more of them did so, a turnout that was repeated in the election of 1901, in which Madge exercised her right to vote and urged other women to do so.[17]

Although Willie and Desha Breckinridge did not support general woman suffrage, the *Herald* encouraged women in Lexington to register and vote in the school election, noting there was a rumor that the legislature at its next session might repeal this provision. This is only one example of how Desha and his father, despite their opposition to woman suffrage, allowed Madge to use the newspaper to bring the issue to the forefront. When a sleet storm interfered with Desha's travel plans, Madge remarked that he felt the bad weather might be a judgment on him "for letting all my woman suffrage articles go into the paper."[18]

In January 1902, the *Herald* urged women to sign a petition asking that the Kentucky General Assembly defeat a bill, sponsored by Lexington political boss and Democratic state representative William F. "Billy" Klair, to rescind school suffrage for women. Race constituted the motive for this move, with supporters of the bill alleging that "1900 colored women and only 700 white women registered and voted" in the 1901 school election. They also claimed the bill would reduce the cost of school elections because the government would no longer have to provide separate voting places for men and women. In truth, Boss Klair's main concern was that black women almost always registered as Republicans, and, indeed, had turned out en masse in 1901 to try to prevent the reappointment of a particularly disliked black Democrat as supervisor of the colored schools and principal of the Fourth Street School. In 1901 the total number of Republicans registered to vote in the school election outnumbered the Democrats 4,393 to 4,073; yet the Democrats won by 572 votes, at least partly because polls did not open until noon, thereby eliminating the opportunity for black domestic servants to vote. As one author has noted, the victory was "far from an honest triumph," and the party machine remained uneasy about its tenuous control of this important source of patronage.[19]

Madge worked hard, not only to defeat the Klair bill but also to extend school suffrage to all women in the state and to allow women to vote in presidential elections. She persuaded Desha to put out two Sunday supplements, one dealing with women and education and one with school suffrage. She also asked Nisba to assist by writing an article on women in higher education and perhaps getting Marion Talbot, dean of women at the University of Chicago, to write a column. Although Sophonisba did not write a piece, Talbot did so.[20]

At one point it appeared that the legislature would reach a compromise on school suffrage, maintaining it with an educational, or literacy, qualification. However, J. Embry Allen, who represented Lexington in the Kentucky senate and who had promised to support such an amendment to the Klair bill, reneged, claiming he had found that "nearly all the men and three fourths of the women of Lexington are opposed to woman suffrage even with the educational qualification." Ultimately, the Klair bill passed by a party vote, with Democrats supporting and Republicans opposing. Madge charged that this made Kentucky the only state to have granted suffrage to women and then taken it away. Likewise, the presidential suffrage bill never made it out of committee, since only Republicans voted to report it favorably. However, one bill that Madge supported passed, making it unlawful to employ a child younger than fourteen "in workshops, mines, mills or factories in this Commonwealth." Although the act contained a loophole allowing a child to work with the written permission of his parents and the county attorney, it was at least a move in the right direction. In 1903 Madge began to promote legislation to allow a woman to be placed on the Board of Trustees of the State College. She persuaded Laura Clay, leader of the women's rights movement in Kentucky, Mary Creegan Roark, an educator, and President James K. Patterson of the State College, who opposed the proposal, to write articles on this subject for the *Herald*.[21]

During the height of Madge's legislative lobbying, her mother fell ill with an apparent attack of appendicitis. Madge and Desha stayed at Ashland during the critical period. Doctors decided not to operate for fear Mrs. McDowell would not survive, and suddenly she began to improve.[22]

In February Madge traveled to Louisville to a Consumers' League meeting to hear Jacob Riis's speech "The Battle with the Slums." Riis, working from the premise that social reform had to begin by altering the environment of the neighborhood, had long been deeply involved in the effort to rid New York City of its tenements, to build public parks, and to improve the general living conditions of the poor. Madge knew his accomplishments, and his talk impressed her. Such lectures formed one of the primary ways she gained information for her own reform work.[23]

A short time later Madge, her mother, and sister Julia left for a two-month visit to California. They went first to Raton, New Mexico, where Nettie Bullock and her family had moved. They all then traveled together to California. Madge wrote Desha every day, telling him of her many experiences.[24]

As always, Madge used this trip to learn more about reforms being carried out in other places. While in San Francisco she studied the playground system, and upon her return to Lexington told the community what she had seen. The city government in San Francisco supported the playgrounds and kept them open all year, she noted. This, she thought, was ideal. The city provided $12,000 per year to be spent under the direction of the Board of Education. Madge's own words clearly reveal the personal satisfaction she derived from the playground movement, as well as from other reforms directed toward children:

> I hadn't seen so many children gathered together in one place, since I was in the thick of Seward Park in New York last fall. I hadn't been so entirely mixed up with such delightful children since our Irishtown playground closed last August. The intimacy was established in five minutes; they crowded around my Kodak . . . until my 2x3 camera could do no more. Children are very nice; they meet one so much more than half way; these children answered questions so enthusiastically, they volunteered so much information they hadn't even been asked, and they pointed out all the best games and the best pieces of apparatus to take pictures of, and as I moved away from this or that ground I could hear them murmur in quite audible tones "Ain't she sweet." Undeserved praise of that kind based on the acquaintance of five minutes is very stimulating; it makes one feel very warm at the heart and in the cheeks, and it makes one want very much to deserve it better of those whom longer acquaintance has made much more cautious in commendation.[25]

Significantly, many of Madge's reform efforts revolved around young people. Probably because of her precarious state of health, she had no children of her own, but she maintained there was "a sex duty upon all women" to see that the next generation would go forward "in the slow struggle toward civilization." That duty fell more heavily on unmarried women or childless married women than on mothers, who were "paying much of their obligations by the nurture and rearing of children." This view formed one of her primary arguments for school suffrage, and she also maintained that mothers must be granted the right to vote on school matters in order to protect their children's interests and health at school.[26]

The philosophy of the Progressive movement, which placed great stress on various issues involving children, also influenced Madge a great deal. One historian has written: "The child was the carrier of tomorrow's hope whose innocence and freedom made him singularly receptive to education in rational, humane behavior. Protect him, nurture him, and in his manhood he would create that bright new world of the Progressives' vision."[27]

In a 1902 *Herald* editorial either Madge or Desha expressed much the same idea: "Fellow citizens, let us remember if we are not satisfied with the present status of affairs, *that our hope lies in the children* of our State, that the remedy lies in improving our system of universal education, of making it such that it will not inculcate book-learning alone, though that should be of the best, but intellectual, moral and physical training of the highest to all our sons and daughters."[28]

Yet Madge seems to have derived more pleasure from her activities involving children than she would have gained from looking at them as the "hope of the future." Children were, in fact, about the only subject on which she became overtly sentimental. Her favorite poems were Rudyard Kipling's "Mother of Mine" and Charlotte Perkins Gilman's "Mother to Child." She especially enjoyed visiting with kindergarteners. It may well have been that she was fulfilling what she believed to be her "sex duty" in sponsoring various reforms for children as a way of compensating for having none of her own. Over the course of her public career, the welfare of children remained her most passionate concern.[29]

After her return from the West Coast, Madge continued to push for a variety of reforms involving children and their education. She held a Civic League meeting at her home to plan the summer's playground program. Two major problems existed—the Manchester Street lot used the year before was no longer available, and the Woman's Club would not pledge financial support as it had the previous year. The Civic League refused to be deterred. Its members decided to combine the concept of a playground and vacation school, to provide this for two months, and to hire a trained supervisor. In an article called "Vacation School versus Playground," Madge explained that both the vacation school and the playground sought to teach social virtues by supervised work and play. Education did not have to be unpleasant to be effective, she maintained. Rather, an excellent educational system would keep a child happy and interested.[30]

Madge served as a member of the Playground Committee that was responsible for finding a location for the playground and vacation school as well as for raising contributions to support the program. The committee finally chose a house on Willard Street for the vacation school and a lot on South Upper Street for the playground. It hired a young woman who had worked in a social settlement in New York City to teach cooking, sewing, and housewifery. Elizabeth Cloud again conducted kindergarten at the vacation school. The committee not only raised money but also received donations of coal, wallpaper, sand, lime, salt, and other supplies for the Willard Street house. When school began, teachers held a "lemonade opening" for both the children and the uptown supporters. Seventy-four children enrolled in the vacation school, fifty of these in the kindergarten. Only eight of the fifty had ever attended the public school kindergarten. As always, in Irishtown water constituted a major problem. Madge persuaded the mayor to put a hydrant and a drinking fountain on Willard Street that would provide water from the city reservoir. This became the first city water available in that section of town.[31]

On July 24 the Upper Street playground opened with outdoor basketball and tennis courts but no outside gymnasium equipment. By August the water hydrant was finally installed on Willard Street, and the water company agreed to cut its rates in half for the playground. Other contributions continued throughout the summer. One woman, for example, provided cantaloupes and watermelons for the children.[32]

As an outgrowth of these activities, Madge scored a significant victory when she attended a meeting of the Board of Education to plead for the establishment of a permanent, public kindergarten in Irishtown. Her speech to that board may have been her first to an official public body. She asked for $350 but received $400, because members of the board agreed that the kindergarten should continue throughout the school year. They chose Elizabeth Cloud and Mary Darby Richardson as teachers for the kindergarten.[33]

As the activities of the playground and kindergarten drew to a close, Madge noted that the Irishtown children appeared less desolate than they had the year before when the playground ended because now they anticipated the new public school kindergarten. They had not even known what a kindergarten was until the previous year, and now they did not want it to end. "The regret the children express, when the next day is Sunday and there isn't to be any lesson, is funny—or pathetic, it is hard to tell which," she wrote.[34]

Madge's desire for a city park system in Lexington also made some progress during the summer of 1902. A *Herald* editorial suggested that the Chautauqua grounds at Woodland Park be opened to the public during the summer months. The paper secured promises from the mayor and fire chief to protect the area, and the park opened. In addition, the Lexington Railway Company, which would profit from fares to and from the park, agreed to provide lights, entertainment, and upkeep for the grounds. In a sermon the Reverend Dean Lee of Christ Church Episcopal urged the city to purchase Woodland Park and open it to the public permanently. The *Herald* adopted this idea immediately, urging the city council to hold a referendum to see if voters would approve such a purchase.[35]

Madge likely instigated the whole plan for Woodland Park to become a public park rather than remain a private one. A friend of Dean Lee, she may well have asked him to make such a suggestion in his sermon. Although she did not sign the *Herald* articles on the subject, she or Desha either wrote them or assigned the topic to one of the reporters. This was typical of the way she operated. A former *Herald* reporter remembered that Madge frequently rushed into the office and virtually ordered a reporter to write an article in support of a cause.[36]

After this initial suggestion, Madge did not allow the park matter to rest. Several months before the next playground season opened, a *Herald* editorial asked: "Does Lexington Need Playgrounds?" She also worked with the Civic League to plan three playgrounds for the summer—Woodland Park, the lot on South Upper Street, and one in Irishtown. The League asked the city for an appropriation of $900 but received only $600. Meanwhile, the city also concluded negotiations for the purchase of Woodland Park. This marked the achievement of a major goal for Madge. It proved to be the first step in the development of a city park system that would in less than twenty years encompass five parks and playgrounds, two vacant play areas, and three playgrounds at children's institutions, with twelve supervisors hired by the city. The people of Lexington were well aware that Madeline McDowell Breckinridge was the person most responsible for this development.[37]

Madge's work, however, could not have succeeded without the generous help of others. One important example of this was the donation from Hector Hillenmeyer's Nurseries of 125 shrubs and trees for the South Upper Street playground and of 5,000 more trees for other city properties.[38]

Another cause Madge had advocated in her speech to the Board of Education did not proceed as rapidly as her request for a permanent kindergarten in Irishtown. In her presentation she had also made a plea for manual or vocational training to be initiated in the schools, but the board responded only by appointing a committee to investigate the matter. Although she achieved no immediate results on this issue, the paper continued to publish articles supporting it. These articles would, she hoped, help educate the public and develop support for the idea.[39]

Madge gained a great opportunity to encourage reforms in education when she took over the editorial writing for the *Herald* during the summer of 1902, a task usually performed by Desha or his father. With them both away, Madge presented a series on Kentucky education. She attacked the commonwealth's lack of progress over the previous fifty years. Kentucky far exceeded the illiteracy rate of 6.4 percent found in some northern states. This disgraceful situation, she charged, could not be blamed on the disruption caused by the Civil War—after all, Chicago recovered from its fire in a decade. Rather, neglect of the public schools resulted from political corruption and public indifference. She termed the Kentucky school system inadequate in every way—a minimum school year of four months, poor equipment, and underpaid and undertrained teachers. Some states had a nine-month school year, playgrounds, vacation schools, kindergartens, and manual training.[40]

The State Teachers' Association proposed a resolution to commend the *Herald* for these editorials. The association then amended the resolution and thanked the entire press in Kentucky for its support of public education. In a subsequent editorial Desha wrote:

> The resolution contained a compliment to which we are not entitled; we are not the author of those articles; and it is due to the writer of them that the credit be not given to one not entitled. We are not permitted to print the name; and the tender relation borne by us to the writer forbids that just encomium which those resolutions implied.
>
> The editorials to which we refer were written by one who has become thoroughly familiar with those former controversies and who is deeply interested in all that is being done for the upbuilding of the State and particularly in every movement for the better training of the children of the State.[41]

By this time, Madge was so deeply enmeshed in her reform activities that she had little time for what she considered the more frivolous things of life. As she informed Nettie Bullock: "I had a fine X-mas. I struck on all the grown-ups . . . didn't send 'em a thing & said I didn't want anything. . . . I didn't have a thing on my plate but $5.00 from Mamma which I pocketed quickly, & a rug from Nisba and Miss Talbot that I had already looked at." She added that she was going to exchange the brass coal bin the Breckinridges had given her for a coal scuttle and give the remainder of their gift away. "Be sure you burn this up," she prudently, but fruitlessly, added.[42]

Inspired by the success of the first five months of kindergarten in Irishtown, Madge turned to the cause of obtaining an elementary school for the West End. A *Herald* editorial pointed out that an industrial department to provide training in cooking and sewing had just begun there in the afternoons. Both the kindergarten and industrial department were full, attended by many who could not be induced to go uptown to school. Further progress would require expansion of the school there, the editorial asserted.[43]

As a new year dawned, Madge turned more of her focus toward the Associated Charities, becoming its president. The group held monthly meetings, usually at the Breckinridge home on North Mill Street. The Board of Directors decided to expand the organization, moving its headquarters to a house on Market Street whose cellar and backyard could be converted to a wood yard. A paid agent would live in the house, and one upstairs room would be furnished as temporary emergency housing for women and children. As always, lack of money remained a problem. The city had appropriated $1,500 to the Associated Charities for 1903, but expenses the year before had totaled $1,700, and with the expanded operations, the cost would rise even higher. The organization needed several workers but could afford to pay only one, so volunteers filled other positions. Donations of money, furniture, and other supplies helped furnish the new headquarters. Many of those gifts came from Madge's family, and the *Herald* gave a desk, bookshelves, and chairs. A bout of severe weather in February 1903 caused the organization to sink deeply into debt. With as many as forty persons per day applying for aid, they had to abandon temporarily the investigation of applicants. Madge then led fund-raising efforts, which by mid-summer put the Associated Charities' finances once more "on pretty firm ground."[44]

Madge remained the person largely responsible for building support for Associated Charities through her publicizing of its goals, methods, and activities. Shortly before she became president, the *Herald* printed an editorial, "Organized Charity," describing the need for organization and investigation in the distribution of charity. Investigation was not heartless, argued the editorial, but beneficial, because it often revealed needs that could not be met by supplying only one load of coal or one sack of groceries. The article called for a minimal city appropriation of $2,000 for the year, pointing out that the community had an obligation to furnish aid for the pauper and dependent class and asserting that this should be paid for by public taxation. In advance of their era, Madge and Desha both recognized that adequate relief could be supplied only by the government, not through private philanthropy alone.[45]

Later, another extensive editorial on the problem of relief appeared, this time called "Scientific Charity." It provided the definition of scientific charity: "This term has been bestowed upon the method of relieving the poor that seeks a basis for its actions in reason and not in sentiment. . . . The new method of 'scientific charity' is much more troublesome, demands much more of time and thought and labor from the giver, and has not the sure return of comfort to the feelings of the giver; for he usually feels dissatisfied with himself rather than solaced, seeing how little he has actually done and how much is needed to be done."[46]

Soon another article in the *Herald*, "Charity Organizations in America," traced the development of benevolence organizations from Germany to Britain to Buffalo, New York, where the first American charity organization was started in 1877. The public must be educated to know that the purpose of charity is "not to keep people comfortable in poverty but to help them out of poverty." By learning the facts of a case, the organization could then use its aid in a way that would raise rather than lower the recipient, the writer claimed. Soon after this appeared in the newspaper, Madge spoke to the Woman's Club in a speech titled "Organized Charity," repeating the same information and opinions that had appeared in the *Herald*.[47]

Likewise, Madge used the pages of the *Herald* to keep education reform before the public. An editorial titled "A Liberal Policy toward Our Schools" noted that an increased appropriation for local schools would include money for the West End (Irishtown) kindergarten and an industrial department there that would include training in cooking and sewing. It added that the School Board hoped next year to build or acquire a structure that would accommodate a primary department as well as a kindergarten. The Civic League also continued having speakers advocating educational improvements, and the Fayette County Equal Rights Association and the Woman's Club both endorsed the League's goals.[48]

Occasionally family events distracted Madge. In early January her mother again became ill with appendicitis, and this time the doctors deemed an operation necessary. The surgery took place at Good Samaritan Hospital on January 6, and Mrs. McDowell returned home in late February. Meanwhile, Nettie and Tom Bullock began the journey back to Kentucky from New Mexico, stopping at Hot Springs, Arkansas, for health reasons. The Bullocks had received a loan from Tom McDowell to finance their trip and their stay in Arkansas. Henry McDowell Jr. urged his sister not to worry about the loan because all the McDowell siblings would stand good for it if their mother did not offer to pay it from her own funds. Likewise, Madge assured her sister all the Bullocks and the McDowells were willing to help. "What is the use of saving up for a rainy day, if you don't know how to shell out when the rainy day comes," she asserted. In fact, she stated, she herself had enough money in the bank to cover the expenses. It seems likely that Tom McDowell had the most to offer, because Madge previously had asked her mother what she thought of Tom as a moneymaker, noting that "he is going to be your millionaire son, and you will have the satisfaction of having some-body in the family who knows how to make money as well as to spend it."[49]

Madge also watched with interest as sister Julia acquired a "devoted beau." Unfortunately, Mrs. McDowell did not approve. She had "no use" for Will Brock's family, plus he was "too delicate" and not as tall as Julia. However, she also noted that people spoke well of him, and Julia said she would not marry for a long time.[50]

Even the most serious family crises did not interfere with Madge's work for long. Continuing her activities with the Civic League, she invited Jane Addams to speak in Lexington; her talk was called "Newer Ideals in Education." She had met the famed Chicago reformer during her stays with Sophonisba and had visited Hull-House many times. Indeed, she borrowed many of her ideas from Addams and other members of the Chicago reform group that centered around the settlement house and the University of Chicago. Madge invited Addams and her traveling companions to stay at the Breckinridge home.[51]

An overflow crowd packed Morrison Chapel at Transylvania University on the evening of Addams's speech. The city council, the Board of Education, and other city officials occupied reserved seats. Her lecture focused on the idea that the child must first be free from labor in order to attend school and must have a chance at recreation and self-expression through playgrounds, kindergartens, and manual training. The Hull-House founder emphasized manual training, pointing out that Germany and England had advanced much further than the United States in providing technical education. "America is singularly slow in this respect," she stated. "We look down upon and despise our skilled labor, but nevertheless it is what counts in the industrial world." She envisioned an ideal school that would have a playground, gymnasium, baths, manual training, cooking classes, and library.[52]

Madge had long ago embraced these "newer ideals." She had studied educational theories and watched them being put into practice in Chicago. Bringing Addams to town simply offered a means of educating and persuading the local population.

There was much to do, because Kentucky did not meet even the first criterion the great social worker had set forth—that a child must be free from labor in order to attend school. The loophole in Kentucky's new child labor law had led to widespread evasion. As a member of the Civic League's Committee on Compulsory School Attendance, Madge grew very concerned about this situation. The compulsory school attendance law, the first enacted in the South, had been in effect since 1896 but was no more effective than the child labor law. It mandated compulsory attendance only twelve weeks a year and lacked any enforcement provisions. Madge and the other members of the committee wanted to see this law amended to require compulsory attendance for the entire term and also compel the hiring of truant officers to enforce the law. This, they believed, would supplement the child labor law and make it more difficult to evade. They hoped it would aid in solving the problems of crime, juvenile delinquency, and illiteracy.[53]

Madge sent a copy of the proposed Compulsory Education Law to Andy B. Ludwig, a factory labor inspector in Kentucky. He approved the plan wholeheartedly, informing her that recent inspections revealed that at least 460 illiterate children worked in Kentucky factories, largely because their uneducated parents saw no need for the children to attend school. Madge gave this information to the Civic League a few days later at a meeting in her home. The group discussed various proposals to solve the problem but could not decide on a plan. However, at year's end a committee of the Civic League met to draft a bill that would extend the compulsory school term and ensure the appointment of truant officers to enforce the law.[54]

Although not yet deeply involved in the women's rights movement, Madge revealed her interest in women's lack of political power in her newspaper articles. In a review of Kate Trimble Woolsey's *Republics versus Woman: Contrasting the Treatment Accorded to Woman in Aristocracies with That Meted Out to Her in Democracies* (London, 1903), Madge criticized the author's literary weaknesses but found much truth in the thesis that women were more oppressed in democracies than under other forms of government. The fact that in monarchial and aristocratic Europe one could find monuments, memorials, streets, cities, and parks named for women, while in the United States one would look in vain for a sign that women had a share in the life or history of the community, proved this point, Madge felt. She also agreed with the author that Chinese women had only one absolute, arbitrary ruler, while American women had forty million. In this community, she said: "When it comes to any political right or privilege whatsoever, even the smallest, men give and take away . . . no protest or prayer of any woman whatsoever making the least difference."[55]

A short time later she participated in the Council of Women that made up part of the Chautauqua. The women involved advocated all sorts of reforms, and speakers included both Madge and Sophonisba. Willie Breckinridge responded to this conclave in his characteristically unpredictable way. He believed the council's actions indicated the women of the state had reached a determination to organize and advocate publicly certain reforms. The Colonel claimed to fear neither change nor the growing power of women, although he disagreed with some of the things they supported: "It has been the habit of those constituting the family of which the writer and the manager [of the *Herald*] are members to do their own thinking and to permit all other members of the family the same privilege," he asserted. He acknowledged that his family had not been united on the leading issues of the day since the American Revolution, "and these differences in sentiment, in judgment and conviction never have caused any estrangements or any diminution in affection." This same attitude had applied to the women of the family as well as the men. "Indeed," he stated, "the women have, as a rule, been the most intellectual and brilliant members of the family; and this has been true for at least one hundred and forty years. . . . The most womanly of women are those who do think for themselves." Clearly, Willie would not seriously oppose either his daughter or daughter-in-law, even if he disagreed with them.[56]

Just as Madge seemed to be making converts and having success, her own health again declined. In early August she left with Desha, her mother, and Julia to seek treatment in Denver, Colorado, at the High Oaks Sanatorium.[57]

The departure for Colorado caused Madge to miss the activities at Woodland Park that marked the closing of the playground season. Nevertheless, the arrangements for the event bore the unmistakable mark of her planning. A wagon transported children from Irishtown to Woodland Park. During the trip they stopped at Ashland, where Madge's Aunt Mag showed them around. One child reportedly said: "This is as near Heaven as I shall ever get." Madge's absence cast a blight over this otherwise happy experience for the children.[58]

Madge and her mother spent most of the winter in Denver. The doctors at High Oaks Sanatorium, Willie reported to Nisba, had discovered Madge had a "slight tendency to weakness in one of her lungs." Desha had insisted she stay in the sanatorium as the doctors suggested because he was anxious about "her hereditary predisposition." Willie added that the doctors did not deem it serious as long as she remained in the Colorado climate until she recuperated. It seems fairly clear from these statements that Madge by this time not only had tuberculosis of the bone, which had necessitated the amputation of a foot, but also pulmonary tuberculosis. From this time on she would appear momentarily to be cured only to suffer a reoccurrence. Thus she lived her life constantly ready to drop what she was doing and undergo treatment.[59]

Madge did not give in to this disease passively, although she was forced to continue her treatment until April 1904. She usually managed to accomplish more while supposedly at rest than most people would under normal circumstances. Such was the case during her stay in Colorado. She used her time to study that state's political system, Judge Ben B. Lindsey's juvenile court system, and Colorado's public health organization's effort against tuberculosis. She then once more wrote articles for the *Herald* based upon her research. The public schools of Denver she called the best west of Boston. The state generally followed an eight-hour workday, and, best of all, women had the right to vote. "The feminine voter," she reported, "is accorded the same dignity as the masculine, is treated with equal respect; the community is apparently unconscious that there is any more question of the advisability of women's voting than of the advisability of men's voting." All this helped "to purify and better politics." In another article she quoted at length from a Denver newspaper article evaluating woman suffrage in Colorado in its tenth year. The *Denver News* asked: "After Ten Years—Futile or Fruitful?" It concluded: "Fruitful—a thousand fold." Madge pointed out that woman suffrage in that state had not changed women's nature or damaged the home, nor had it completely purified politics, but women had as a result been able to exert their influence for positive change. Other progressive measures she found in Colorado included the appointment of women truant officers in Denver and of police matrons in the jails and provision of a special house of detention for juvenile offenders to separate them from hardened criminals.[60]

While Madge was in Colorado her right hand became paralyzed. Years later, one of her friends recalled that after she suffered the paralysis, "by prevailing with her left hand [she] wrote those first articles about little Ben Lindsay's court to rouse Kentucky for Kentucky's children." It seems almost certain she had suffered a "small stroke." The late Dr. Edwin A. Weinstein, professor of neurology at Mt. Sinai School of Medicine, City University of New York, has detailed the usual course of cerebral vascular disease using the case of President Woodrow Wilson. Over twenty years before his massive stroke Wilson had developed weakness and pain in his right hand just as Madge had. This was clinical evidence of structural damage to the nervous system. Weinstein says: "The clinical course of cerebral vascular disease is variable, but tends to be episodic with frequent remissions. The age of onset is between thirty and sixty. The overall duration may be very long with periods of up to twenty-five years reportedly elapsing from initial manifestations to final incapacity. Personality changes are often noticed in this disease." The victim, Weinstein stated, may become more intense and businesslike, finding it difficult to relax or to accept any criticism and opposition. Madge increasingly exhibited these characteristics after 1904.[61]

It is unknown whether Madge realized she had experienced a stroke, but the paralysis surely concerned her, and, coupled with her other health problems, it may have convinced her that she had little time in which to accomplish her goals. She began to push herself harder and harder. As she demanded more of herself, she became increasingly impatient with those who would impede her progress. And as her work increased, her social life seemed gradually to decrease. The picture was not a bright one. At the age of thirty-one, restricted by an artificial limb and suffering from both tuberculosis and cerebral vascular disease, it seemed as if her achievements might all be behind her.

Yet she scarcely paused. Throughout the winter of 1903 and into the spring, Madge continued writing articles on the many reforms being attempted in Colorado. Of all these, the state's juvenile code claimed her primary attention. It was "one of the brightest jewels in Colorado's crown," she said. Judge Ben B. Lindsey had created the unique system in Denver, which was then adopted on a statewide basis. He based his methods on the belief that juvenile delinquents were not criminals but rather misguided and misdirected children who needed aid and encouragement rather than punishment. Devising a system in which cases involving delinquent children were handled separately from criminals, he used probation whenever possible. In more serious cases children were confined in a detention home rather than in jails with adult criminals.[62]

Madge admired this plan for handling juvenile delinquents and immediately began to think about Kentucky's need for such a program. Naturally, she anticipated that the chief objection to it would be its cost.

> The method involves considerable expense, but how infinitesimal as compared to that of allowing these youthful delinquents to become criminals—as is done in most communities by the old

> method! Truly no community is rich enough to afford the old method and none so poor as to reject the new method on grounds of economy. And yet, whenever kindergartens, or manual training in our schools, or playgrounds, or night schools, or juvenile courts, or probation and truancy officers, or any other of the new means of forming children into good citizens is proposed, there arises a great howl of extravagance—though nothing is thought of the outlay for jails and penitentiaries and all the expensive criminal machinery of the law by which we vainly try to reform these children when they have grown into hardened criminals.[63]

Upon her return to Lexington Madge wrote to Lindsey for copies of the Colorado Juvenile Code. She then persuaded the Civic League to invite the judge to come to Lexington to speak. In the meantime, she tried to create interest in a juvenile court system and to prepare the ground for his arrival.[64]

Madge also continued her support for Associated Charities, parks and playgrounds, the Irishtown school, and various other Civic League projects. Even while she was in Colorado, the *Herald* published articles defending Associated Charities from its critics and noting that the organization had dealt with nearly thirteen hundred applications for aid during the last year. Conditions improved considerably for the parks and playgrounds in 1904, and again Madge was responsible. She introduced a resolution asking the Civic League to recommend to the city council that it appropriate $6,000 from a real estate sale for the improvement of the parks. The League and later the city council approved this resolution and proceeded to hire one of the best landscape architect firms in the country, the Olmsted Brothers of Massachusetts, to develop Woodland Park. Madge served on the advisory committee to oversee this project, a position she deserved, for in three short years she had established a rapidly growing, popular playground movement. The Civic League also agreed to pay the salary of a truant officer until January 1905 because the School Board had no funds for the position. In addition, Madge found time to preside at the Women's Council of the Chautauqua and to serve as a delegate from the Fayette County Equal Rights Association to the state meeting of the Kentucky Equal Rights Association (KERA).[65]

The *Herald* ran an article on KERA's accomplishments, noting that after its founding in 1888 by Laura Clay, daughter of the famed emancipa-

The home of Madge and Desha Breckinridge at 337 Linden Walk, Lexington. From Sophonisba P. Breckinridge, *Madeline McDowell Breckinridge: A Leader in the New South.*

tionist Cassius Marcellus Clay, it had successfully lobbied for legislation giving a married woman rather than her husband the right to any wages she earned. It had gotten a provision in the 1891 state constitution allowing the Kentucky General Assembly to regulate school elections (thereby giving women the right to vote in school elections by act of the legislature rather than a constitutional amendment), a married woman's property rights act, the school suffrage provision for women in second-class cities, and various other reforms related to women's education and general welfare. At the KERA state convention, after hearing Dr. Anna Howard Shaw, president of the National American Woman Suffrage Association, Madge began to get more deeply involved in KERA.[66]

Still, Madge did not devote all of her time to reform efforts. She and Desha continued to take part in numerous social events, including receiving guests at Ashland for the 1904 wedding of her sister Julia to William Brock, assistant cashier at the First National Bank. One of the happiest occasions came when the Breckinridges moved into their new house on Linden Walk, where Madge would live for the remainder of her life. Until this time they had resided in a succession of rented accommodations. Near the university, their home was in a new area just being developed by the Aylesford Land Company, of which Desha was vice president. Aunt Mag, an amateur architect, designed their house as well as several others in the subdivision.[67]

Not all of Madge's distractions were as pleasant as her new home. At times she became involved in the Breckinridge family's turmoil and grief. Desha's sister Curry remained very unsettled in life. She wanted to study nursing, but both her father and Desha violently opposed this plan, thinking the life of a nurse would be too strenuous. She and her stepmother did not get along, so Madge and Desha urged her to stay with them rather than in the boardinghouse where she was living. Willie pleaded with her to return to his home, promising that his wife, Louise, would be easier to live with than before. Curry, however, remained undecided about her future.[68]

Then on November 20, 1904, Colonel Breckinridge died after contracting a cold a few weeks earlier. Desha's grief was deep and his tribute to his father eloquent—a blank editorial page. Willie had also left his son with a dilemma—whether to probate his father's will and, if so, how to tell his stepmother that she was not mentioned in the will and how to tell his sister Ella that only Desha, Curry, and Sophonisba were beneficiaries of his father's $5,000 insurance policy. Ultimately, Desha decided to probate the will, and, to his surprise, found his stepmother "calm, controlled, quiet, sweet in manner" in accepting the news. The day before Christmas Desha announced that he had bought the *Lexington Morning Democrat* from W. P. Walton, its owner. Consolidating it with the *Herald* left Lexington with only one morning newspaper and the *Herald* as the major Democratic daily in central Kentucky.[69]

Christmas Day provided Madge with a good opportunity to make an appeal on behalf of children burdened with work. In a *Herald* editorial, she pointed out that Lexington had many children working as delivery boys, newsboys, and at other jobs. Their work usually increased during the Christmas season, resulting in their suffering from cold and exhaustion. Although children often helped support widowed mothers, this economic problem must not stop the attempt to obtain efficient child labor and compulsory education laws, she asserted. In Switzerland, for example, the state provided a school pension for widows with children of school age. This would not be acceptable in the United States at present, so private initiative must fill the breach. The article closed with a plea for contributions to the "Children's Fund" established by the Associated Charities, which would be used to pay mothers the sum their children would earn by working.[70]

The holiday must have been lonely for both Madge and Desha. He still mourned his father and she worried over her mother, who was again in Colorado undergoing treatment at the High Oaks Sanatorium. Nevertheless, Curry, Nisba, and Marion Talbot spent the day with them, and in the afternoon they all went to Ashland to visit with Nettie Bullock and her family.[71]

The passing of Colonel Breckinridge marked the end of an era for Madge and Desha. In the coming years, they would use the pages of the *Herald* even more forcefully for progressive reforms, and Madge would play a greater role in the paper's direction. She would continue with all the projects she had started, while becoming more deeply involved in the woman suffrage movement. Somewhere along the way she made her greatest convert to the cause—her husband—and the *Herald* became the most important paper in the state and one of the most important in the nation supporting that effort. Within a few years Emmeline Pankhurst, the militant British suffragette, would call Desha Breckinridge the strongest male supporter of woman suffrage she had ever met.[72]

Chapter 5

"Whatever a woman can do . . . in the long run she will do" 1905–1907

As a new year, 1905, dawned, Madge's activities reached a frenzy. Had the probable stroke she suffered in Colorado convinced her that she had only a short time in which to achieve her goals? Or perhaps she submerged her fears for the future in work so that she would not have time to think. Whatever her motives, she was not content simply to continue the projects she had already undertaken but in addition launched new endeavors. She initiated a fight against the Salvation Army, began to edit the new "Woman's Page" in the Sunday edition of the *Herald*, and started a crusade against tuberculosis, while continuing her support for the Civic League, Associated Charities, Kentucky Federation of Women's Clubs, the burgeoning parks and playgrounds system, school suffrage, and education improvements.

Yet in spite of these activities, Madge and Desha maintained a very active social life, entertaining friends and relatives and attending teas, plays, and other events, even to the extent that Madge could inform Sophonisba in mid-1905 that "we are getting very social." At the same time she also noted that "most of our projects are going beautifully." She continued her close association with Nisba, urging her to visit, and adding: "I look upon you as an ever present help." On one occasion she informed her sister-in-law that "Cousin Louise," Willie Breckinridge's widow, had recently visited and "was nicer than I ever knew her."[1]

Madge worked through the Civic League to provide shoes for the children in Irishtown and also undertook a new project of establishing a Woman's Club in that area. As in so many instances, she received assistance from a family member. Desha's eldest sister, Ella Chalkley, helped her work out an agenda based on the Hull-House Woman's Club programs. Likewise, Mrs. McDowell, although still undergoing treatment in Colorado, assisted by sending money for Madge to use in whatever cause she deemed most in need. This only made Madge miss her mother more, as she noted: "One has a good many conflicting feelings when one's husband is in one place and one's mother in another."[2]

As second vice president of Associated Charities in 1905, Madge asked in the pages of the *Herald* that the community give the organization greater support. She also raised a disturbing question: Does a community have the right to imprison a man at hard labor and take all the proceeds of his labor when he has a family to support? She related the plight of a family in the West End of Lexington that had been forced to seek aid from the Associated Charities because the father had received a sentence of three months in the workhouse because of drunkenness. Although the mother worked as a cook for $2 per week, such a wage could not support a family. Pointing out that in Switzerland mothers with dependent children received a school pension from the government, she asked: "Isn't direct taxation the most honest means of aiding cases like this?" Another editorial advocated public support for hospitals, children's homes, and other charities. These articles emphasized the belief of both Madge and Desha that private philanthropy could not meet the needs of the poor in an industrialized society. In advocating such a policy they were far ahead of the time, and their thinking ran counter to the attitudes of Kentuckians, and southerners in general, who supported local control and opposed increasing the responsibilities and power of the central government, be it state or national. It would be years before the government would institute a comprehensive welfare program.[3]

Madge also brought to public attention the possibility of a duplication of services between the Associated Charities and the Salvation Army. The Associated Charities invited representatives of the local Salvation Army to attend its first meeting of 1905 so the two organizations could work together. This effort apparently failed. Madge had long harbored doubts about the Salvation Army, and by autumn a *Herald* editorial stated that the paper could no longer be silent on the influence of the Salvation Army, which had announced it would run a coal depot and soup kitchen in Lexington. This action, the paper asserted, would be "a most corrupting element in the city of Lexington" because free soup kitchens had proved to be a "pernicious influence" in the past. For that reason, the mayor several years earlier had asked the women of Lexington to form an organization that would provide charity only when it was really needed. Out of that request had grown the Associated Charities, whose motto was "Charity should do two things: relieve distress, and endeavor to remove the cause of distress." In the *Herald* editor's view, the Salvation Army only addressed the first.[4]

Thus began Madge's lifelong crusade against the Salvation Army. It was to be the most unpopular and perhaps the most questionable of her "causes." She gathered anti–Salvation Army tracts and books, documenting the wealth of that organization and its supposed errors. Criticism centered around the methods the Army used to administer relief, the secrecy of its finances, the wealth of its headquarters, and its poor record keeping, which made it impossible for the public to assess its value in terms of the numbers of people being aided. Madge and most social workers around the country contended that soup kitchens and other forms of indiscriminate aid simply encouraged paupers and professional beggars by making them more comfortable in their poverty. Madge, as well as other social workers, charged that the larger part of donations to the Salvation Army went to the organization's headquarters rather than staying within the community where it was collected, thus diverting funds from local relief agencies such as the Associated Charities. Madge frequently pointed out by contrast that the completely democratic Associated Charities opened its files to public scrutiny while the Salvation Army did not.[5]

Although most professional social workers advocated "scientific charity" and many opposed the Salvation Army, few did so as openly or as zealously as Madge. Indeed, most of the general public viewed the organization in a friendly manner and failed to understand her opposition to it. Even this first editorial attack did not pass unanswered. In a letter to the editor signed "Fair Play," a citizen ridiculed the idea that a little free soup and coal to both the "deserving" and "undeserving" poor would encourage laziness and corrupt the community. With reservations about the ability of bureaucratic charity to solve all the problems of poverty, "Fair Play" continued: "Many hardened wretches would rather freeze or starve than be investigated and run the risk of getting into public print as one of the 'deserving poor,' or, still worse, as one of the husky frauds sometimes unearthed by those who believe charity, like other commodities, should be organized and dispensed by a board of directors." Moreover, "a little independent charity, not cornered by any trust or church, may be the means of sweetening a bitter heart or softening a calloused soul."[6]

Still, the *Herald* did not relent. The previous summer there had been a shortage of farm and domestic labor. Madge believed employers who did not pay a living wage were to blame for this, in part, because they provided little incentive to work. "If we are ever to lift up our laboring class, black or white, in this community, it must be done by making the rewards of industry greater and the rewards of idleness and beggary less," she contended. To her, the Salvation Army's distribution of free coal and soup simply increased the rewards of idleness.[7]

Madge remained sincerely dedicated to improving the lot of the poor, especially children. In February 1905, with the support of a number of organizations, including the Civic League, Associated Charities, the Kentucky Equal Rights Association, and the Women's Christian Temperance Union, she brought to Lexington one of the friends she had made while in Colorado—Judge Ben B. Lindsey. Lindsey had experienced a boyhood so poor and despairing that he had once contemplated suicide. During the 1890s he battled greed and corruption in the Colorado legislature before winning a judgeship in 1900 and developing a juvenile court system. Madge continued her effort to initiate such a system in Kentucky. Lindsey's speech in Lexington, however, dealt only peripherally with the juvenile court. Instead, in "Manual Training as a Preventive of Delinquency in Children" he spoke about how to keep children out of court. One reason children got into trouble, he asserted, was that they could not work with their hands and thus could not find employment. Schools with manual training, he believed, were "moral hospitals" that would train children for a job and thereby help to keep them away from crime.[8]

Madge kept in contact with Lindsey after his return to Colorado and urged him to send her a draft proposal for a Kentucky juvenile court bill so she could begin as much public education as possible before the next legislative session. While on a trip to Chicago, she spent a day in Judge Julian Mack's juvenile court and reported her findings to the *Herald*. She learned from her observations that all too often when a boy was arraigned in court, the father was the true delinquent. From this she concluded that boys should be taught that "primal and ancient obligation that a man owes to support his children." While Madge was publicizing the work of the Chicago juvenile court, two Louisville attorneys prepared a bill to be introduced to the Kentucky legislature. Both Judge Lindsey and Judge Mack promised to read the proposal and make suggestions before the beginning of the legislative session.[9]

While visiting Chicago in April 1905 and going to Judge Mack's court, Madge also found time to attend to some personal matters. She saw her old friend Grace Otis, went to the theater with Jane Addams, and bought her mother an Easter present at Marshall Fields. Most important, however, she had a new limb made of willow wood, which she hoped would be lighter in weight, more comfortable, and better in appearance than her old one. This task necessitated her staying in Chicago for three weeks in order to get the limb made and then test it. The length of time seemed long, even with visits to Hull-House, the juvenile court, and Mary McDowell's settlement house. Nevertheless, a few days later she expressed the belief that "my job here is going to be successful." Yet after her return to Lexington and before a trip to Virginia, she found the limb uncomfortable. She traveled to Louisville, where she had it "gouge[d] out anywhere it occurred to me it might help, and I had good luck, and have been getting along first rate ever since—When I tried going back to the old limb, I was convinced that this one is an improvement."[10]

Madge spent much of summer and autumn 1905 preparing to lobby the Kentucky General Assembly for a juvenile court law. Just before the legislature convened in January 1906, she spoke to the Central Kentucky Woman's Club; her speech was "Legislative Needs." She named as her first priority the establishment of a juvenile court system. Shortly thereafter, a bill that Judges Lindsey and Mack had approved, providing for juvenile courts in first- and second-class cities, with the county judge as the presiding magistrate, was introduced in the house on January 20.[11]

Madge hoped to get Lindsey back to Kentucky in time to speak before the legislature acted, but illness threatened to keep him away. Madge and several other supporters spoke on behalf of the bill to the House Judiciary Committee. In addition, the Civic League sent pamphlets describing the juvenile court system to editors of local papers across the state. At the last minute Lindsey arrived. He stayed with Madge and Desha and on March 2 gave two speeches, one on woman suffrage in Colorado and one on the juvenile court. He warned Kentuckians not to expect too much of either. Woman suffrage, he said, was just and did not make a woman less womanly, but extravagant claims that it purified politics were exaggerations. Likewise, the juvenile court system was not a "cure-all." The school, the church, and the family remained the primary institutions for preventing juvenile crime, he asserted.[12]

On the same day that Lindsey spoke, the house passed the juvenile court bill, and on March 21 the senate followed. Apparently, the bill sparked little opposition. Certainly the educational work of many months—led by Madge—helped explain its widespread support. Lindsey clearly thought so when he wrote to her: "The women of the country are doing the work for the children, and it is such unselfish, devoted and magnificent work as yours . . . who have inspired me to speak the truth in this matter."[13]

In addition to lobbying for the juvenile court bill, Madge in 1906 also actively supported a family desertion bill. Her work with Associated Charities had convinced her of the magnitude of this problem. Statistics of charity organizations proved, she said, that 7–10 percent of all families seeking aid and 25 percent of all children committed to institutions resulted from desertion. In a review of Lillian Brandt's *Family Desertion* (1905), Madge expressed her belief that laziness, intemperance, and a desire to avoid responsibility caused the problem, which she believed required stringent laws.[14]

Another issue that troubled her was that the age of consent for girls in Kentucky was only twelve. The Kentucky Equal Rights Association had agitated since 1893 to raise this to eighteen. Madge, in step with the Progressive movement, argued that it was a relic of barbarism that a girl could not dispose of her property until the age of eighteen, because the courts carefully guarded her against loss or injury, but could "consent to the loss of her character" at any time after age twelve. She and KERA won a partial victory when a 1906 act raised the age of consent to sixteen.[15]

That same year, Madge unsuccessfully supported a bill that would have reorganized the school system by abolishing the old school districts and supplanting them with county boards of education. This bill provided for reducing the number of elected school trustees from nearly 25,000 to 925. Educators hoped that by doing so the quality of the trustees, which in many cases was deplorable, would improve. More planning and lobbying would be required, however, before such a reform could be enacted.[16]

Although she devoted many months to preparing for the legislative session, Madge did not neglect her other goals. She had attempted for a long time to get Lexington schools to start manual training. In autumn 1905 she appeared to be making some progress when the School Board

Sophonisba P. Breckinridge. Courtesy of Special Collections and Digital Programs, Margaret I. King Library, University of Kentucky, Lexington.

indicated it might include such a program in its January budget. Madge feared the all-male board would decide manual training was more important for boys than for girls, so she urged Lexington women to demand that domestic science be included along with carpentry in the curriculum. Just before the board met to draw up its new budget, Madge persuaded the Civic League to sponsor speeches on manual training by Professor Harry G. Brownell of Flexner University School in Louisville and Mrs. W. D. McClintock, Sophonisba Breckinridge, and Marion Talbot, all of the University of Chicago. The League invited the School Board, as well as all city and county officials, to be special guests at the lectures. At the conclusion of the program Superintendent M. A. Cassidy rose to say: "The Board of Education is more than anxious to incorporate manual training in the public school system in Lexington, and I am sure will do so the moment it has the means at its command."[17]

Madge next brought the Woman's Club into the movement. At a meeting in January 1906 the club discussed new ways to promote manual training. That night the School Board met with a committee from the Civic League and the Woman's Club, where Madge and several other women spoke in favor of manual training, especially cooking and carpentry. They also urged the board to ask the city council to levy the full amount of school tax that the law allowed. Nevertheless, the board concluded Lexington could not afford manual training. Madge bitterly pointed out that Lexington could afford to teach Virgil, Caesar, and algebra in its public schools, while 90 percent of the students would eventually earn their living by working with their hands. Still, she did not give up. By the end of 1906 she again attempted to persuade the School Board to include manual training in its next budget. This time the Civic League promised to raise some of the funds necessary to finance the initial expenses of such a program. It also sponsored a speech on manual training by Miss E. E. Langley, a teacher of woodworking at the University of Chicago. While in Lexington, Langley also spoke at an African American church, where Madge introduced her.[18]

At last Madge's diligent work paid off. In its 1907 budget the Lexington School Board appropriated $4,000 for manual training in carpentry and domestic science, beginning in autumn 1907. Many believed Langley's lecture had contributed substantially to this success. Madge, a member of the Civic League's Education Committee, had been able to secure this fine speaker through Sophonisba. Increasing the Chicago connection, the School Board hired two teachers from the University of Chicago to be the manual training teachers. Madge became annoyed when the board would not pay the teachers' expenses to come to Lexington during the summer so they could order the necessary equipment and prepare for the fall semester. This resulted in a two-month delay after the beginning of the school year before manual training could begin. Madge condemned such frugality that caused waste as an attitude characteristic of many public officials.[19]

Having accomplished this much, this relentless reformer conceived a new idea. Why not have a joint city-county manual training high school? Through the *Herald* she sought the opinions of educators in the state. She soon learned that carrying out her proposition would be no simple matter. It would require a change in state law mandating the consolidation of city and county school management and the grading of county schools. Yet many of the educators who informed her of the necessary legal changes also expressed enthusiasm for the proposal. Superintendent Cassidy said: "The educational combination of county and city . . . would be both wise and practical. . . . I hope to live to see this done for the children of Fayette County." The Kentucky superintendent of public instruction also applauded the idea, saying: "Any aid I can give you in your undertaking will be cheerfully given."[20]

Madge quickly put together a comprehensive proposal aimed at creating a joint city-county manual training high school. At the time, county children received only a third-grade education, so extending the county schools to eight grades would be necessary to enable those students to enter high school as equally prepared as the city children. Thus, high school consolidation would require uniting more than fifty one-room, ungraded county schools into a few graded and well-equipped eighth-grade schools. "Now all these ideas we have accepted, we are converted to them, and henceforth there is before us only the simple (!) task of working for them until they are attained—by someone else," Madge asserted. Going a step further, she suggested a possible site for either the proposed high school or one of the consolidated grade schools—the old Bryan Station Fort. She hoped the Daughters of the American Revolution, who had placed a monument there to the brave women who reputedly had carried water to the fort during an Indian siege, might buy the property and donate it to the county to be used both as a park and as a school site. As chair of the Legislative Committee for the Kentucky Federation of Women's Clubs, she began to lay plans to have a school consolidation bill introduced at the 1908 legislative session that would make possible the achievement of these plans.[21]

Madge continued to do much of her reform work through the Woman's Club or a combination of that organization and the Civic League, Associated Charities, and Kentucky Equal Rights Association. Shortly after her return from Chicago in 1905, she reported about a Woman's Club in that city that had undertaken a fight against violations of an antismoke ordinance. "Here is an opportunity for Lexington women, for it is conceded that the demand for clean streets followed by the demand for a clean sky are essentially the province of women," she insisted. At other meetings she spoke on such topics as practical work for Woman's Clubs, current events, and the results of a Louisville meeting of the Consumers' League.[22]

Clubwomen and, in fact, many other citizens across the state were becoming interested in improving the state's public education. At a meeting of the Kentucky Education Association (KEA) in 1905, a group of educators formed the Educational Improvement Commission of Kentucky. While applauding its goals, Madge took issue with the fact that of thirty-three members on its Central Committee, only one was a woman. This represented, she believed, the characteristic attitude of male educators in the state. When she protested to the commission's president, M. O. Winfrey, that women were not fairly represented, he replied that plans were being made to create an independent Women's Committee to aid the Central Committee. To Madge this seemed an insult. She pointed out that eight thousand of Kentucky's nine thousand teachers and most KEA members were women. An independent committee, she argued, would be "a sort of Ladies' Aid Society that will busy itself with the hardest of all work, the raising of money." She believed "the women of Kentucky should . . . protest." She continued: "We should like to see women of Kentucky rally to the cause of the new Educational Commission; but until that commission is reformed on a basis giving reasonable representation to women, and until the Kentucky Education Association shows itself an active ally of the cause of school suffrage for the women of Kentucky, we see no adequate cause why any woman should go out on the disagreeable job of collecting money for the commission to spend." She then sent a letter to members of the Educational Improvement Commission asking whether or not they supported school suffrage. Only two members responded affirmatively. The treasurer of the commission complained that the most "reprehensible" part of her criticism was in urging women not to participate in collecting money for the commission. Madge replied that she admired the spirit in which the treasurer "goes after us" but still disagreed. A school superintendent in Louisville, however, approved Madge's position, saying that more women throughout the state favored educational reform than men and should therefore be a part of the commission.[23]

Eventually Madge won her point. In 1906 the Educational Improvement Commission appointed her to its Executive Committee and also expanded female representation through other appointments. This commission was at least partially responsible for the passage that year of a bill creating two state normal schools to provide for teacher training.[24]

In 1907 the Kentucky Federation of Women's Clubs began a major campaign to reform the state's educational system. As chair of the Legislative Committee, Madge led efforts to lobby for bills the group would support at the 1908 legislative session. She also served as a member of the Education Committee, chaired by Mary Creegan Roark, an educator and wife of the president of the new Eastern Kentucky State Normal School in Richmond. Madge devoted much time to this educational improvement campaign, lecturing students at Lexington High School and speaking at teachers' institutes on the goals of the Woman's Clubs for the public schools. When the local club held a mass meeting at the Fayette County Courthouse to form a School Improvement League, the group made plans to send a representative across the state to organize similar groups. A short time later, Madge and Roark spoke to the State Development Association in Louisville in a speech titled "The Relation of Public Schools to the Commercial Development of Kentucky." Madge pointed out that Kentucky had not only robbed its forests and soil but had also neglected its most important resource—children. Kentucky must stop blaming the Civil War for its educational backwardness, she maintained, and make every effort to upgrade the public schools. Perhaps recalling those ancestors who inspired her commitment to public service, she added: "The fact that Kentucky has led the forward movement of the past should encourage us, not discourage us. What Kentuckians have done Kentuckians may do." She concluded: "To me the inspiration of the past seems to call to the inspiration of the future. I think every Kentuckian may pronounce with the English poet that invocation to the 'Spirits of old that bore me, / and set me meek of mind, / Between great deeds before me / And deeds as great behind!'"[25]

The women had chosen a propitious time in which to pursue education reform. As Richmond lawyer J. A. Sullivan told the new governor, Augustus E. Willson, in 1907: "There is a stronger sentiment for education in Kentucky today than ever before. It amounts to almost a demand that progress be made." The election that year of John Grant Crabbe, city school superintendent in Ashland, Kentucky, to the position of state superintendent of public instruction also provided new hope for school improvements. Crabbe sought to use his office to create a more centralized system of schools with better-trained, better-paid teachers. In the coming years he and the Federation of Women's Clubs would prove useful allies.[26]

In addition to her concern about poor education in Kentucky, Madge believed the state also squandered its most precious resource through child labor. As a member of the Executive Committee of the Kentucky Child Labor Association, she worked for the passage in 1906 of an amendment to the child labor law, making it illegal to employ children under the age of fourteen in shops or factories, limiting the hours children could work, and requiring certain sanitary regulations in businesses employing children. Yet she lamented that the amendment that passed still contained loopholes that allowed for widespread evasion, and she charged that the loopholes had been inserted as a result of manufacturers' lobbying efforts.[27]

Over the years, despite numerous other activities, Madge served in several positions in the Kentucky Child Labor Association (KCLA), including representative to the National Child Labor Committee's meeting in Cincinnati in December 1906 and KCLA's second vice president in 1907 and third vice president in 1910. In addition, in December 1907 she worked on the local Executive, Press, and Reception Committees for the eighteenth annual convention of the Southern Education Association, which met in Lexington.[28]

In 1907 Madge endorsed a mass meeting in Louisville, called by the Woman's Club of that city, to discuss the child labor situation. Both she and Desha supported the unsuccessful child labor bill introduced in Congress by Senator Albert Beveridge of Indiana. Designed to prohibit transporting in interstate commerce goods from factories and mines that employed children, it aroused opposition from states' rights advocates. Madge encountered this argument when she attempted to persuade other newspaper editors to support the bill. For example, Richard W. Knott, editor of the *Louisville Evening Post,* stated that he would do his best to inform the public about the conditions under which children worked, but he was not prepared to support the Beveridge bill since he believed it would be better to deal with the matter by state law rather than federal action. Madge replied to Knott in the pages of the *Herald,* saying the states acting separately could not stop the evil of child labor. If one state passed such a law, manufacturers in that state could not compete with the cheaper labor costs in states without a child labor law, while the states acting separately could not pass a uniform law. Furthermore, the Beveridge bill did not violate states' rights, she asserted, because it used the interstate commerce power that the Constitution clearly gave Congress.[29]

Madge carried her interest in child labor even further when she made a tour of the South during spring 1907. Child labor presented a particular problem in the American South, where 22 percent of the textile labor force consisted of children. Madge worked closely with Edgar Gardner Murphy, the head of the Alabama Child Labor Committee and a founder of the National Child Labor Committee, to attack the problem and to try to ensure that children would have the opportunity for education. She visited the cotton mills in Georgia and South Carolina to see in person the conditions under which children worked. As usual, she shared her experiences with the readers of the *Herald.* She talked to one boy of thirteen who had worked for four years in a mill sixty-seven hours per week. She found that children comprised the majority of workers in the spinning and weaving rooms. In all the mills she experienced "a terrible din of machinery and lint of cotton." At one mill she found herself shocked by a child "with a face unlike any child face I have ever seen before, so wrinkled, so white, so horribly old. It may be unjust to think of this as a cotton mill type, but I shall never forget the strange little figure or cease to associate it with the cotton industry." Such words perhaps revealed the depth of feeling within her regarding the children she never had.[30]

On the trip Madge enjoyed the beautiful scenery and the blossoming spring and devoted an entire article in the *Herald* to a description of the countryside and society around Augusta, Georgia. But she did not allow these things to distract her from the pressing issues in the South. When she reviewed Edgar Gardner Murphy's book *Problems of the Present South* (1907), she found herself especially impressed by the statistics on southern education. Every state in the region had reduced its illiteracy rate between 1880 and 1900; yet huge obstacles remained. Despite the

South's expending a greater percentage of its resources on education than other regions, its education system remained totally inadequate.[31]

Madge's concern for the problems of children led her toward involvement with the National Conference of Charities and Correction, where she served on the Children's Committee. When the Kentucky Conference of Charities and Correction was formed in 1905, Madge served on the Executive Committee, where she used her influence to help determine the reforms it would advocate. At a series of meetings across the state that year the new organization made recommendations that clearly reflected her interests. It proposed the creation of a juvenile court system, a law raising the age of consent from twelve to sixteen, an act making family desertion a felony, and the establishment of a bipartisan state board of charities and correction.[32]

In spring 1906, Madge made plans to attend the annual convention of the National Conference of Charities and Correction, which was to be held in Philadelphia in May. When Governor J. C. W. Beckham appointed a number of Kentucky women as delegates, Madge pointed out what she believed to be his insincerity. He had not named any women to the State Commission for Insane Asylums or to the Prison Commission, she asserted, because he did not approve of women on such boards. This meant that Kentucky women who attended the Philadelphia meeting would have little opportunity to put into practice the things they learned.[33]

Desha, who accompanied Madge to the conference, came away believing that he had developed a greater understanding of the work that needed to be done. From Philadelphia the Breckinridges traveled on to New York for a brief—but much needed—vacation. When they returned home, Madge began to write articles about the things she had learned at the conference. Notably, speakers had attacked the Salvation Army's organization, administration, and financial interests. Madge called upon the Salvation Army to disprove these charges: "For many years it has made in this country an appeal to the sentiments, and it is not unfair that it should be asked to prove to those who are called on to support its work what is the value of that work." She added: "All money and all effort that goes into one kind of charitable work is diverted from other kinds, and it is but common sense that . . . every charity asking public aid should be required to prove its fitness."[34]

Madge not only agreed with criticism of the Salvation Army that she heard at the conference but also heartily endorsed the presidential message in which Dr. Edward T. Devine stated that the cause of a problem must be the focus of attack. Madge expanded this idea: "Are we not hopelessly enmeshed in our halfway efforts to patch rents in the social fabric made by causes of evil that still continually operate? We build hospitals to cure the sick, and we do nothing to prevent the spread of tuberculosis, which brings more sick than any other disease to our hospitals." Likewise, "We take charge of the alcoholic when he is a hopeless wreck, and fail to provide proper legislation in restraint of the liquor trade, or even to enforce such legislation as we have." She added: "We care for the orphaned children of laborers mutilated and murdered by the unnecessary accidents of the railroad traffic and of manufacture, and complacently remain twenty years behind European countries in any legislation to safeguard the life and limb of the workmen." Furthermore, she noted that "we build homes for the victims of prostitution and painfully endeavor to lift again a few of the thousands of fallen girls" but fail "to notice the easily remedied causes of prostitution—the miserable and insufficient wages paid to working girls, the lack of brightness in their lives—or to restrain the illicit traffic by which many adults earn their living at the expense of the youth of the country." "How futile," she concluded, "to bind up the sores, while the cause of the disease is never attacked; to dam the little rivulets of evil, while continually new ones find their way from the great sources of social corruption!"[35]

A short time later Madge attended the annual Kentucky Conference of Charities and Correction, where participants stressed the need for improvement in the state insane asylums. Madge delivered an address, "Asylum Management," advocating the appointment of a woman to the Board of Control. Personal and political considerations rather than merit and experience determined the appointment of workers from the superintendent down, she stated. Thus, she asserted: "We should not be surprised at occasional sensational charges of cruelty to patients; it is a matter for surprise that examples of cruelty do not frequently come to light."[36]

During these years Madge also continued to work for the parks and playgrounds. This did not require as much effort as it had in the past, because now the city provided most of the funds. Nevertheless, she occasionally reminded the public through the *Herald* of the history of the movement, confidently predicting that Lexington would soon have a complete metropolitan park system. It seemed to her that juvenile crime in the city had diminished in the years since the playgrounds opened.[37]

As a member of the Playground Committee of the Civic League, Madge strongly endorsed a law passed in 1906 by the legislature establishing a new Board of Parks Commissioners for second-class cities. The old Parks Board had had advisory power only, but the new one would have full authority to develop the existing parks and create new ones. The Civic League committee soon made a decision to continue the same playgrounds and to attempt to start a new one in the north end of town. An $800 city appropriation, plus private contributions, enabled the League to operate playgrounds at several locations. According to official records, 17,346 children attended these playgrounds in 1906. In addition, progress occurred at Woodland Park, with completion of the auditorium, planting of shrubbery and trees, and construction of walks and tennis courts. In October Madge spoke to the Woman's Club on Lexington playgrounds and wrote additional articles supporting the movement. She urged the School Board to purchase a vacant lot near the school for blacks on Constitution Street and develop it as a playground. She noted that although the Civic League had been ridiculed for its promotion of playgrounds, now President Theodore Roosevelt had spoken on the importance of recreation. "The moral need of recreation is a thing which all social workers will eventually have forced upon them," she insisted.[38]

Even park management could be a complicated issue, however. As Madge reported to a correspondent, the saloon people opposed the men's Sunday afternoon baseball games at the park because it reduced their beer sales. She feared that some of the saloon owners would combine with religious groups to try to end the games. When she and Nisba drove out to the playground in the West End one Sunday afternoon, they watched the men play baseball on one side of the fence while the children played on the other side. Rather sarcastically, she explained: "The fence was introduced as a compromise measure, so that the good, religious ladies who drive and ride bicycles themselves on Sunday, but object to the men of Irishtown who can't afford either drives or bicycles exercising their arms and legs might not have the responsibility of the ball game on their souls." She added: "The game, which used to be very disorderly, was just as nice and respectable and innocent to-day as the children's see-sawing and digging in the sand pile on the other side of the fence."[39]

Elected president of the Civic League in October 1906, Madge was able to score still another victory for civic improvement when she persuaded Professor Charles Zueblin of the University of Chicago to offer a series of lectures, "The New Civic Spirit," in Lexington. Before he arrived she began to educate Lexingtonians by reviewing Zueblin's book A *Decade of Civic Developments* (1905). In subsequent articles she described some of his other activities: In 1891 he founded the Northwestern University Settlement as a laboratory to study Chicago's social problems and as a beachhead in a movement to bring about needed reform in the city. He subsequently became a professor of sociology at the University of Chicago. For Madge, acquiring such a person for a whole series of lectures represented a great triumph. While in Lexington, the professor delivered one free lecture, but the Civic League charged for the series to help defray costs. This successful program provided those attending with many ideas for new reform efforts.[40]

Under Madge's leadership the Civic League embarked in spring 1907 on a city cleanup and beautification plan. Mayor Thomas Combs assisted by proclaiming May 15 "Spring Cleaning Day," with the city picking up garbage free of charge. A *Herald* editorial urged citizens to take advantage of this opportunity. According to Madge, the successful event resulted in the collection of an "incredible" amount of refuse. As a follow-up, in the autumn the League presented a program on beautification.[41]

During this time Madge found another way to use the newspaper to disseminate her ideas. From August 1905 to early 1908 she edited a "Woman's Page" for the Sunday *Herald*. She introduced the page with an explanation about how it would deviate from the norm:

> The Herald proposes to start a "Woman's Page," to be somewhat different from those usually printed in Sunday supplements. It will not bar absolutely the latest fashions in neckware, and suggestions as to how to make Christmas presents out of your old duck shirt, but it does not believe that in the lives of the average woman those things hold so large a place as to justify weekly a full newspaper page. It believes that there are more things in the average woman's philosophy than are now dreamed of by the editor of the Sunday supplement, and the purpose of the new page will be to concern itself somewhat with these other interests. The most active and faithful philanthropists of our country are women; the educational work of our country is largely carried on by women. . . . If an arbitrary sex division of the interests of a newspaper are to be made those things should properly fall to the woman's page,

> as news of the turf and the prize ring and of athletic contests fall to a page intended for men.
>
> It is probable that the page will have a "new woman" flavor, for novelty must always be a controlling feature of newspaper selection.[42]

Within a few months, Madge titled the section "A Woman's Sphere" and added a heading that stated: "Whatever a woman can do, that, by divine ordination she ought to do, by human allowance she should be privileged to do, by force of destiny in the long run she will do."[43]

The success of the Woman's Page was immediate. Within a few weeks Desha remarked in an editorial: "One and only one objection have we to the Woman's Page . . . that it is so much better than the other pages, particularly the editorial page of the paper, that it surpasses them in interest to our readers, whether they be masculine or feminine." He went on to quote an article from the *Kentucky Gazette:*

> The "Woman's Page" generally means a conglomeration of fashion notes, complexion recipes, and heart-to-heart talks on which should precede, the lady or the gentleman, in entering a theater. It is an affront to feminine intelligence and is, as it should be, the butt of the office jokes in newspaperdom.
>
> Six weeks ago the Lexington Herald started a woman's page which is edited on the assumption that women have brains as well as men and that they like to employ those brains on some other subject than dress, etiquette and flirtation.
>
> The new department is ably edited by Mrs. Desha Breckinridge, a woman who has no equal in this section and few superiors anywhere as an authority on civics, children's public needs and rights and some other aspects of sociology. It has already attracted high commendation from Eastern periodicals.[44]

Regularly for the next two years, except when she was on vacation, and then more sporadically until early 1908, Madge edited the Sunday Woman's Page. It gave her an opportunity to present her own views on virtually every subject and to publish articles written by many of the "experts" she consulted. Most important, it allowed her to explain her perception of "a woman's sphere" and expound on her ideas of the "new woman."

Although the term *feminism* did not come into popular usage until a few years later, Madge's columns promoted views that would today be called "feminist." She saw women as a group distinct from and equal to men, and she believed that women could do or be anything they wanted to be if freed from discrimination. Yet she accepted then-current Progressive movement philosophy that as mothers and housekeepers women had an obligation to apply their domestic skills to the public arena and become "municipal housekeepers." Such reasoning manipulated the traditional idea of woman's role as protector of hearth and home, turning it upside down and virtually forcing the new woman into public activity in order to perform her duty as wife and mother. Madge Breckinridge pushed the idea of domestic feminism to the forefront in the Woman's Page, promoting a wide variety of municipal housekeeping projects, including parks, manual training, labor reform, woman suffrage, and antituberculosis and charity organizations. She subsequently reported: "The page has been made to some extent the organ of the Women's Clubs"; however, she could just as accurately have said it reflected the concerns of the Civic League, Associated Charities, Kentucky Equal Rights Association, or education reformers. Sophonisba Breckinridge and others from the University of Chicago often contributed articles, a fact that reveals how much Madge relied on that group for information about the latest developments in social work.[45]

So popular was the Woman's Page in its first few months that Paul Kellogg, editor of *Charities and the Commons*, a magazine touting "scientific charity," asked Madge to write an article detailing specifically the things she had undertaken to do with the Woman's Page. He noted: "We go to a lot of editors and club women throughout the country and those interested in philanthropy, and some of them might take the hint—especially if the article was concrete and told specifically the different things you have undertaken on the page and carried through (or failed to carry through); the attitude of other papers toward it, etc."[46]

Madge replied to Kellogg that "the present page was planned to handle club interests, educational interests, industrial, literary, artistic, religious, civic, whatever came within the scope of the intelligent woman's interest and seemed at the time most pertinent." She added: "Under this definition of Woman's Sphere it will be seen that anything from cabbages to politics can be appropriately treated."[47]

In fact, she used the forum for many different purposes. She reviewed books such as Dorothy Richardson's *The Long Day* (1905), which depicted the life of a workingwoman in the city, and Upton Sinclair's *The Jungle* (1906), which exposed both the filth and the exploitation of laborers in the meatpacking industry. In her review of the former she pointed out the need for manual training for women, as well as legislation regulating hours and conditions of labor, while her review of *The Jungle* focused more on revelations about labor exploitation than the unsanitary handling of meat. She noted that "the methods of the packers in shipping diseased meat handled under the most unsanitary conditions . . . pale before the realization . . . of the utterly inhuman way in which the employee is treated, the way he is considered merely a cog in the vast machinery, a cog out of whom the most work is to be gotten at the slightest expense, who is to be cast aside when injured, or annihilated when a cheaper piece of machinery—be it a woman or a child or a newly arrived immigrant with a lower standard of living—can be put in his place."[48]

She continued this concern in her comment on George Bernard Shaw's play *Mrs. Warren's Profession*. The theme of the play, she explained, was that women were driven to immorality through difficult conditions and poor pay in other occupations. The New York courts had barred the play from being shown, thereby seeming to indicate the belief that such women had chosen prostitution by free will. This assumption, Madge maintained, "is not sustained by the investigation of social workers." She added: "If Bernard Shaw's strangely dull and disagreeable play can waken the ordinary theatre-goer to some serious thought about the conditions of industry, the wages paid to women workers, the punishment now meted out to virtue and the reward to vice, it will not have been written in vain."[49]

During the time when she edited the Woman's Page, Madge often referred jokingly to the almost total absence of fashion news, which usually comprised much of the print in the women's section of most papers. After a trip to New York City, she did offer a fashion tip but admitted: "We fully realize that one fashion note gleaned in a two weeks' trip does not justify the railroad fare." However, "we beg our readers to believe this meager result is not due to the fact that we have spared any grey matter in our effort to master the styles, nor to any failure to realize that occasional fashion notes of the latest and most reliable kind are fitting in a women's page, however advanced." She asserted that "the fact of the matter simply is that we have done our best, and that we ask the congregation not to shout.

Another time we shall turn this important investigation over to someone of acuter perceptions and better qualified."[50]

Although Madge always dressed well—she once mentioned purchasing a suit for $165 and a sealskin coat—she tended to believe that the Bluegrass aristocracy placed too much emphasis on clothing. She noted that "the women of the Blue Grass in proportion to their means do spend a very large amount on dress," and recalled: "A Blue Grass girl some time ago was asked to contribute $5.00 annually to an educational work. . . . She replied that she couldn't afford it; and a little while afterward, when some one commented on the beauty of her dress, remarked that it didn't look like a dress that had cost $90.00, but that was what she had to give for it." This was an attitude she deplored, believing that those with independent income should be taught from childhood that they owed a portion of their wealth to the community.[51]

Madge also strongly urged more women to become involved in business endeavors, a cause she promoted in the Woman's Page. On one occasion she suggested that a woman should start a bakery in Lexington and make it a model of cleanliness and neatness. Another time she urged women to invest in a new company opening in Lexington. The next week, however, she retracted her advice, saying: "It was pointed out to us by a gentleman, often kind enough to show us our faults, that it is hardly good ethics for a newspaper to commend a business enterprise of the management of which it knows nothing." Nevertheless, she continued to recommend that women become involved in business. Most of the readers of the Woman's Page, she thought, belonged to the leisure class, and she asked these women: "Do we women of the so-called better classes furnish . . . a leisure class . . . that is indolent, that puts forth energy only in the effort to entertain itself; that is unthinking, not really aware or awake to the great problems of the age, a class that is conservative and a real drag upon social progress?" She personally felt that "every idle class from tramps up is a menace to any community, from the fact it invariably becomes unthinking and irresponsible; having no duties and no real activities, it is not stimulated to its best endeavor, and from mere inertia it becomes a bulwark of existing conditions however much these may need change and improvement." She admonished women who were proud of their conservatism to "stop and reflect whether it is the conservatism of wisdom or of mere indolence" and to ask "whether they belong to the valuable semi-leisure class in whom is the hope of social advance, or to the hopeless leisure class of the drones, uninterested in the problems of life because removed from its struggle."[52]

Madge particularly wanted to know why no women in central Kentucky had embarked on agricultural careers such as truck farming or dairy and poultry production that women in other parts of the country had found to be profitable. She noted that every year Kentucky imported from other regions large amounts of these products, remarking: "It is humiliating to have to account for this as simply a record of Southern laziness; and for some time we have been seeking in our own minds another explanation of the fact." She found a partial explanation in the fact that relatively few individuals owned large amounts of Bluegrass land. As a result, women on large farms rarely needed to earn money, while those who worked for a living had no capital to invest in land and equipment. Even this was not a sufficient explanation, she concluded, because it was possible to rent land cheaply enough to sell fresh produce profitably in Lexington. She asked: "Is it then, fellow-women, only southern laziness and feminine lack of initiative?"[53]

In government activities, too, Madge believed women had a special role to play. Because of their training and experience in housekeeping, women, she argued, should be on the boards of schools, prisons, jails, and other institutions. "We have a prejudice in favor of women's housekeeping," she said. "The responsibility for the housekeeping of our public schools . . . rests with men, and we do not consider this housekeeping particularly satisfactory." Moreover, she argued that the government should be responsible for inspection of food processing, and women should have a part in that public function through voting. Like many Progressives, she deplored the consequences of the industrial revolution, which had transformed women economically from producers to consumers. Feminist Charlotte Perkins Gilman called it "parasitism," and Madge agreed.[54]

On different occasions Madge expressed her dislike of the condescending and trivial reading materials published for women. She found some hope for improvement in the newer women's magazines, such as *Good Housekeeping* and *Harper's Bazaar*, but referred to the "feeble namby-pamby issues" of *Godey's Lady's Book*, whose stories contained "the same preachment of housewifely devotion and submission and economy." She also criticized books written for girls. In one review, she said the book contained "very pretty little stories for girls," but it was "strictly truthful to say that they are devoid of inspiration." As one who had done most of her serious reading in girlhood, she wondered "if the new generation is growing up of stronger intellectual fibre."[55]

Likewise, she showed contempt for the kinds of columns for women offered by most newspapers. Spoofing such endeavors, in the Woman's Page she proposed:

> The editors of this page have determined to maintain in it, if not regularly, at least from time to time, a column for men, in which matters of interest to the male sex and suited to their intelligence will be discussed. We have often noticed with a spirit of deep gratitude and wonder the very generous space that is given in all Sunday supplements to matters for females, "beauty notes," rules of etiquette, shirt waist patterns, etc. In view of this it seems unfair, when the masculine editor of a paper has taken the radical step of giving up a whole page to the things mis-guided women, devoid of any newspaper instinct, imagine to be interesting to their sex, not to be willing to devote at least one column of this page to matters of interest to males. Hence our decision.
>
> We fear that our invention in the matter will not be equal to that of the masculine editor when he caters to feminine taste: we fear that we shall neither have the fertility nor the cocksureness that he has.

True to her word, Madge presented a column for men, discussing the problems involved in men's shirt fronts![56]

Not only was Madge not afraid to challenge and poke fun at Desha in her columns, but also she could ridicule herself. Always aware that her own servants afforded her the leisure to work for her many causes, she once joked about her own lack of domesticity. She told of her difficulty in coping with kitchen duty when her cook decided to take a vacation during the hottest days of summer. This comprised her "first practical lesson in domestic science, especially in that branch . . . that pertains to the kitchen." In order to cook breakfast, she had to master a new natural gas system that had recently been installed at her home. When she tried unsuccessfully for two hours to get water to boil, "the gas inspector happened to come around and found that the wrong kind of burner had been put in and that the failure of the water to heat couldn't really be counted against our capacity in domestic affairs." After attempting from 7:00 to 9:00 a.m.

to get rice to boil in a double boiler, she finally recognized the impossibility of the task and cooked the rice "in a single boiler and as much of it as wanted to was allowed to stick to the bottom." She lamented the fact that "when we went to State College it offered no domestic science course, and we were consequently obliged to do original research." This episode seemed to prove the validity of her insistence on the inclusion of domestic science for girls in the school curriculum along with carpentry courses for boys and certainly revealed the gender stereotypes maintained even by a "new woman" of the twentieth century.[57]

Yet she did not fear discussing more serious, and possibly inflammatory, topics such as race relations. In fact, she worked that subject into her article on learning to cook. She asked if the cooks who refused to work during the month of August were not acting "within the bounds of reason," adding that "domestic service ought to be such that it could be performed and yet the people who perform it have some time left for a life of their own." Another article called for paying a living wage to the mostly black domestic servants. The so-called "servant question," she stated, was in the minds of many Lexington residents virtually synonymous with the race question. The real problem, she maintained, was not with the blacks but with the whites. Why, she asked, should Lexingtonians "expect our colored race to be moral?" They lived in the poorest housing, with no sewers, water, or gas. Yet white landlords charged exorbitantly high rent, while white employers paid extraordinarily low wages, forcing their servants to seek charity or to steal. Blacks had poor educational facilities and no means of recreation except the saloon and the dance hall. When a race riot occurred in Atlanta, she wrote that the crux of the situation was "the responsibility of the dominant race for outbreaks of lawlessness in either race. . . . Outbreaks of violence are not sporadic; they are simply a manifestation of social disease due to pre-existing conditions."[58]

Perhaps the clearest picture of Madge's attitude toward the "servant problem" was revealed in an article she wrote called "A Personal Experience." She related how she had planned to spend a day with her gardener, "Uncle Henry," planting peonies and lily bulbs. Uncle Henry instead announced that his lodge was meeting to bury a brother. Since he had taken no time off to attend the colored fair, she felt she had to grant his request, but she also knew her bulbs were drying out and "there was bitter disappointment in my heart. In my haste I had about said that all negro labor was unreliable and worthless." Then, instead of planting bulbs she had started to work on the Woman's Page. After she had written awhile, she said that she "made another generalization instead of the one I was first tempted to make: That even negro servants are human beings, with human tastes for funerals and other things, with idiosyncrasies such as we have ourselves." She added: "We can not expect them to show the docility and convenient attributes of the machine that waits ready to be used when we are ready to use it."[59]

Speaking out on servants' wages earned Madge public criticism, her conservative brother Henry noted to his mother. Although "she is exactly right in her position," he asserted, "all reformers must expect opposition and some criticism." However, he believed "the average domestic servant is much more capable of self defense than child laborers and other classes championed by Madge."[60]

On another occasion she criticized the racist attitudes presented in Thomas Dixon's book and play *The Clansman* (1905), which was later made into the movie *Birth of a Nation.* Noting that Dixon apparently disapproved of tolerance and justice for blacks, her article asserted that the result of denying decent treatment to blacks meant the degradation of the white as well as the black race. Dixon's solution to the race problem—deporting blacks—she found ridiculous; what had proven impossible during slavery would be even less attainable now that blacks were free citizens.[61]

While the Progressive Era exhibited many extreme examples of racial repression, including widespread disfranchisement of African Americans across the South, lynching, and other forms of violence, Madge, Desha, and Sophonisba opposed that tide. All three became members of the National Association for the Advancement of Colored People (NAACP) after its formation in 1909, and they frequently spoke out on matters of racial injustice. The black press praised the *Herald* for several of its editorial stands, especially against governmental segregation. This position was undoubtedly fueled in part by the Breckinridge family's heritage of racial liberalism, exhibited in the opposition to slavery of Robert J. Breckinridge, Desha's grandfather, and Willie Breckinridge's support of racial justice in the years after the Civil War, as well as the McDowell family's adherence to the Republican Party, which had enacted emancipation. Although Desha eventually came to favor some forms of disfranchisement of blacks, he continued to oppose many examples of racism and to advocate in the *Herald* measures that would improve conditions for blacks. Both Madge and Sophonisba exhibited an even more assertive stance toward social justice for African Americans. Although by modern standards many of their assumptions would be considered racist, they were considered in their day—and believed themselves to be—liberal on racial issues.[62]

Madge also used the Woman's Page to promote the cause of school suffrage, as well as general woman suffrage. In one column she teased Desha about his position on the subject, saying that the editor of the *Herald* had made a public statement that he supported woman suffrage with an education qualification. "His magnanimity," she wrote, "is only equaled by our own. We desire here publicly to state that we have become convinced of the wisdom of suffrage for men, with an educational qualification. In time, possibly the editor of this page and of the main sheet will be standing on the same suffrage platform." In another article she related how Kentucky suffragist Laura Clay had spent a year in Oregon lobbying for a state woman suffrage amendment, which had been defeated due to a small group of antisuffrage society ladies in Portland and the combined interests of corporations and the liquor industry. One of Madge's main arguments for woman suffrage was that denial of the right to vote equated to taxation without representation. She reported how the names of two women were drawn for jury duty in Lexington and immediately stricken as ineligible because they were females, while shortly thereafter a case appeared on the docket involving the taxes of a woman. "O, the inconsistencies of English-speaking men!" she exclaimed. On another occasion she reviewed Florence Kelley's *Some Ethical Gains through Legislation* (1905), which gave examples of how the ballot in the hands of women could be used to pass legislation to protect women and children and uplift the whole community. In her talks and writings, Madge often noted that states that had granted women school suffrage outranked Kentucky in the quality of education provided to its citizens. "Whether cause or effect," she argued, "educational advance and school suffrage for women go head in hand from Massachusetts to Washington; . . . when Kentucky was blazing the way for the West educationally, she was blazing the way in school suffrage for women," and "as the West has come to the front educationally, leaving Kentucky behind, she has also gone to the front in granting school suffrage to women."[63]

In autumn 1906 Madge sent a letter to several politicians asking their position on a joint resolution to be submitted at the next session of Congress providing for the submission to state legislatures of a constitutional amendment giving women the right to vote. Nearly three weeks later she reported that she had not received a reply either from U.S. senator James B. McCreary or Governor J. C. W. Beckham, who planned to challenge the senator in a nonbinding Democratic primary to be held in 1907 for the U.S. Senate seat that would be awarded by the Kentucky legislature in 1908. W. P. Kimball, candidate for Congress from the district that included Fayette County, had responded, saying that "so far I have not given this matter any serious attention, for the discussion of it with us in Kentucky has gone but little further than the academic stage." Madge replied that "Mr. Kimball's frank confession . . . suggests a similar explanation of the failure to reply both of Governor Beckham and Senator McCreary." Referring to Beckham, she continued: "Surely the great exponent of Southern chivalry, the political candidate who expounds to Southern women the fact that they need no political representation since it is the joy of men to protect them, can not be guilty simply of discourtesy to a polite inquiry from a Kentucky woman." She added that she was convinced that "the affairs and interests of women in general are not given any very serious attention by our masculine representatives in State and National legislative halls. That is exactly the reason for our desire for the suffrage for women." Furthermore, she concluded: "If the discussion of the matter of woman's suffrage in Kentucky, as Mr. Kimball avers, has gotten but little further than the academic stage, it is another instance of the fact recently pointed out by a Kentucky editor that in the stream of progress Kentucky seems moored in an eddy of conservatism."[64]

In addition to publishing articles on suffrage in the Woman's Page, Madge also promoted the cause in other ways. In 1906, for example, after Laura Clay spoke to the Woman's Club on the Oregon suffrage campaign, Madge gave a lecture titled "Necessity for School Suffrage for Women in Kentucky." In this address she supported an educational qualification for voting and argued that women would help improve educational conditions. She also served as a delegate to the annual convention of the Kentucky Equal Rights Association, held in Ashland in November 1906, where she spoke on school suffrage, and the 1907 meeting, held in Richmond.[65]

Despite her concern for these many causes and her work for the newspaper, Madge found time to initiate another new movement. It was a matter that concerned her more personally than any other. It is not surprising in view of her own physical condition that her mind turned more and more to the menace of tuberculosis. In spring 1905, when Louisville initiated plans to build a tuberculosis sanatorium, a *Herald* editorial suggested that Bluegrass counties should attempt to do the same. Such articles frequently appeared in the Lexington newspaper throughout the spring and summer. In one article Madge pointed out, "In the month of July, as in the month of January, tuberculosis leads the death report of the city of Lexington . . . and yet it is the one disease against which our community is not lifting a finger." She added that "every case of tuberculosis among the very poor where several persons are crowded into one small, ill-ventilated sleeping apartment means almost certainly one or more resulting cases; and so the endless chain goes on and we make no effort to break it." She noted that the "Board of Health has no authority to isolate a patient, though every member of that board knows that tuberculosis is a communicable disease. . . . There is no compulsory disinfection of houses . . . [that] would at least do away with so much future waste and misery." Physicians, she reported, had formed a national association for the prevention of tuberculosis, with plans to establish branches in every state. "The Civic League of Lexington," she reported, "will in the autumn take the initiative in this work; its members have been in communication with the Chicago association, and after some public education an effort will be made to establish here an anti-tuberculosis association."[66]

The Civic League planned a meeting for November 20 to organize an antituberculosis society. In announcing this date, Madge noted the urgent need for more information and better statistics about the deadly disease that led the city's mortality lists each month. The day before the meeting, the *Herald* published Madge's article "The White Plague: What Will You Do with It?" She urged all citizens to attend the meeting because in Lexington and Fayette County, as in the whole state, no facility existed in which a tuberculosis patient could receive the fresh air, good food, and rest needed for recovery.[67]

A large group attended the Civic League meeting, which laid plans for both a state and local campaign. Madge addressed the meeting, detailing Louisville's activities in trying to establish a sanatorium. The Board of Health and the Civic League decided to circulate a pamphlet on the prevention of tuberculosis and to register all patients in the county who had been diagnosed with the disease. They also laid groundwork to try to get the legislature at its next session to appropriate money for a state tuberculosis sanatorium. The Civic League soon recognized that a separate organization, devoted only to fighting tuberculosis, should be formed. Madge led in drafting a constitution for the Fayette Tuberculosis Association and was elected to its Executive Committee in December 1905, at the first election of officers. In the coming weeks both the Woman's Club and the state tuberculosis association sponsored talks on the subject by outside experts. One of the speakers pointed out that Lexington had a very high death rate from tuberculosis, and he recommended the treatment first set forth by Madge's grandfather, Dr. William A. McDowell, more than half a century before—pure air, sunlight, nutritious food, and rest.[68]

The new organization acted very quickly in writing a bill to provide for a state tuberculosis sanatorium and getting it introduced during the 1906 legislative session. The measure passed the senate, and Madge believed it had the support of a majority in both houses; however, it was killed in a house committee on the last night of the session, reportedly by the intervention of Governor Beckham. This was a great disappointment, but Madge would not concede defeat. She began immediately to prepare for the next session of the legislature, hoping that both houses would pass the measure.[69]

The state tuberculosis association, like many of Madge's reform efforts, owed much to the ideas of the Progressive reform movement. In the early twentieth century many questions remained about the dreaded and often-fatal disease, but research had answered some of the most pressing uncertainties. Doctors and public health officials, as well as some members of the general public, understood that the disease was contagious and could be spread through sputum, dust, close contact with an infected person, and unsanitary conditions. Victims once thought to have a hereditary disease now were believed merely to have inherited a "predisposition" that could be counteracted by a healthy lifestyle. Thus, Progressives focused on the social and economic conditions that helped spread the disease—malnutrition, crowded and unsanitary housing and working conditions, a lack of clean, fresh air, physical exhaustion, and close proximity to those infected. With the formation of the National Association for the Study and Prevention of Tuberculosis in June 1904, the antituberculosis effort began to expand as local and state societies formed to educate people on ways to prevent the spread of the infection and to help ameliorate social conditions that made certain groups, especially the poor, more susceptible. Reformers created data-gathering programs, promoted laws and regulations such as antispitting ordinances, and began to build a professional bureaucracy of public health officials to attack the disease by imposing hygienic standards on water, food, medicine, and sanitary facilities. As always, Madge was on the leading edge of reform thought.[70]

Both the state tuberculosis association and the Woman's Club had numerous measures Madge expected to work for during the upcoming 1908 legislative session. But her plans to lobby in Frankfort that year were not to be. Others had to take up the causes for which she had prepared the way, for once more she had to seek treatment for tuberculosis. As Sophonisba noted: "She was always prepared for the bell to sound and for plans to be suddenly disarranged."[71]

Since her treatment in Colorado Madge had maintained a schedule that would have been considered impossible by most healthy persons. She served on committees or as an officer of the Civic League, Woman's Club, Associated Charities, Kentucky Equal Rights Association, and the state tuberculosis association, using these organizations to promote a park and playground system for Lexington, education reforms, "scientific" charity, city beautification, woman suffrage, and many other civic improvements. She edited the Woman's Page for the *Herald*, gave talks to and raised money for numerous organizations, and served on the boards of the National and Kentucky Conference of Charities and Correction and the Kentucky Educational Improvement Commission. But failing health once more made it questionable whether she could continue all these efforts. Would she return from her "rest cure" invigorated and determined to continue her reform activities with even fiercer determination, or would the combination of disease and overexertion finally take its toll and force her to retrench?

Chapter 6

"Educational advance and school suffrage for women go hand in hand" 1908–1911

The 1908 meeting of the Kentucky General Assembly proved to be one of the most momentous in the state's history, with school suffrage for women and reform of the commonwealth's public education system among the issues dominating the session. These causes also headed Madge's reform agenda, and she expected to play a major part in lobbying for their passage.

In her roles as a member of the Kentucky Federation of Women's Clubs' Education Committee and chair of its Legislative Committee, Madge began to prepare early for the 1908 session, where one of her primary goals would be school suffrage for women. By the first decade of the twentieth century this cause was far from revolutionary. Women cast ballots in school elections in seventeen states by 1900, while those in Wyoming, Colorado, Utah, and Idaho had full suffrage. In several other states they enjoyed limited forms of suffrage such as voting on bond issues or in municipal elections. This made Madge hopeful she could get the gubernatorial nominees to endorse a school suffrage bill. She wrote letters to Democratic candidate Samuel W. Hager and Republican candidate Augustus E. Willson, asking each to express his position on school suffrage for women. She received a reply from Mary Elizabeth Willson, saying that just as her husband rushed off, he had handed her Mrs. Breckinridge's letter with some notes scribbled on the envelope and asked that she reply. "In trying to decipher his hieroglyphics," Mrs. Willson wrote,

"I find that not one word in ten is readable." But she continued: "I am so heartily in sympathy on the question under discussion I wish I could answer for him." Soon, Madge received the candidate's own reply: "I wish it to be definite and positive for all time that I am earnestly in favor of . . . school suffrage for women." Hager did not respond.[1]

With the election a few days later of Louisville attorney Willson as Kentucky's second Republican governor and of John Grant Crabbe, longtime head of schools in Ashland, Kentucky, as state superintendent of public instruction, the chance for passage of a school suffrage bill seemed excellent. Madge once again wrote Willson, asking him to include an endorsement in his message to the legislature, which "would certainly secure us the votes of such Republican members of the Legislature as were indifferent on the subject and were quite willing to be guided in their action." School suffrage, she asserted, would be "a tremendous advantage in the education revival which is beginning here." Willson agreed, not only advocating the measure in his message to the legislature, but also endorsing the bill in an open letter to the people. Many members of the Democratic Party likewise endorsed the proposal.[2]

In preparation for the legislative struggle, Madge engaged in a frenzy of activities. She organized a mass meeting on January 8 in Lexington, sponsored by the Woman's Club and six other women's groups. F. W. Hinnitt, president of Central University in Danville (now Centre College), asserted in his keynote address that admitting women to the electorate constituted the best way to improve the schools of the state. Madge then read the bill her committee had drafted, and the audience voted unanimously in its favor. Then, at a meeting of the Kentucky Conference of Charities and Correction, she explained that when women in Lexington had been deprived of school suffrage in 1902, they had been assured women could still be elected to the School Board. This, she maintained, was unlikely; although women were still eligible to serve on the School Board, "we also knew that any woman walking the streets of Lexington was liable to be struck by lightning. But. . . . no woman has been struck by lightning on the streets of Lexington; and no woman has been elected to the School Board by masculine votes."[3]

Representative Jere A. Sullivan of Madison County introduced the school suffrage bill in the house on January 21. By that time every significant education body in the state had endorsed it. On five occasions, Madge and a number of other women spoke for the bill before the House

Committee on Education. Passage seemed assured. However, at the critical juncture in late January Madge had to leave the state to seek a "rest cure" in Arizona and California. On February 7, the house committee voted to report the bill favorably. Both the *Lexington Herald* and the *Louisville Courier-Journal* gave their strong editorial endorsement. *Herald* editorials claimed that "no more important bill" would come before the legislature and asserted: "We do not see how any man who has at heart the best interests of the Kentucky schools can bring himself to oppose this measure." But the House Education Committee rescinded its approval and referred the bill to the Committee on Suffrage and Elections, where it died.[4]

Would the outcome have been different if Madge had been able to continue her lobbying efforts? Probably not, though Mary Roark, chair of the Kentucky Federation of Women's Clubs' Education Committee, expressed regret that Breckinridge had been forced to leave "at this critical time." Even though the bill failed, Roark still contended that the Woman's Clubs had done "good work" for the cause of full suffrage for women. The women repeatedly charged that whiskey interests and ward politicians had brought about the defeat. As Madge expressed it: "We had against us conservatism and indifference and prejudice, and lastly the liquor interests which fear even school suffrage for women as the entrance of the first wedge in allowing women a part in public affairs."[5]

Suffragists frequently made this charge because they believed the liquor lobby and the urban political machines financed various antisuffrage associations. This was probably true; because women were closely identified with both the prohibition movement and attempts to defeat political machines, those interests greatly feared woman suffrage. Moreover, legislators, both state and national, who favored prohibition usually—though not always—supported woman suffrage as well. Apparently, many believed woman suffrage would hasten the day for national prohibition. In 1926 suffrage leaders Carrie Chapman Catt and Nettie Rogers Shuler charged in their book *Woman Suffrage and Politics: The Inner Story of the Suffrage Movement*, that the liquor interests had provided a potent "invisible influence" in the opposition to woman suffrage, the full extent of which would never be known. Be that as it may, it is not surprising that in Kentucky, with its many bourbon distilleries, whiskey manufacturers maintained a powerful lobby with the legislature.[6]

Still, Madge and Desha did not stop pressing for school suffrage. A

Herald editorial in August, titled "Men and the School Suffrage," pointed out the light voter turnout in a recent Fayette County school election, where several school districts failed to elect a trustee. The article further noted that a senator from Fayette County had said he supported school suffrage for women with an educational qualification, but added that if white women in the county did not use the privilege, it could be removed in two years. In words surely penned or inspired by Madge, the editorial asked: "Now if this is the right way to test the matter, should we not take it away from the men of Fayette County? Apparently they do not want it."[7]

Despite the failure of the school suffrage measure, the members of the Woman's Clubs could be justly proud of their accomplishments during the 1908 legislative session. They had played an important role in the passage of a number of education reforms, which caused that year's Kentucky General Assembly to become known as the "Education Legislature." The most important among the several acts passed, the School District Law—popularly known as the Sullivan Bill in honor of its sponsor, Jere Sullivan—reorganized the elementary and secondary school system, making the county, not the small trustee units, the key taxing authority. Vestiges of the trustee system remained, however, with each county school retaining one trustee. Together, those subdistrict trustees composed a "school division," which selected teachers. The various chairmen of these made up the county Board of Education. The Sullivan Bill also required that each county establish a high school within two years.[8]

Superintendent Crabbe recognized that many citizens would assume education reform had been completed; yet he and others, including members of the Woman's Clubs, knew much remained to do. As a result, they organized meetings that became known as the "Whirlwind Campaigns," in which thirty speakers gave three hundred public addresses during November and December 1908, with even more speakers involved the following year. Maintaining momentum on education reform proved a daunting task, however, and despite these advances, the state still dropped from fourth in the South in per-pupil spending in 1900 to eleventh in 1920. Obviously, several other southern states—often with clubwomen in the lead—did even more to promote education during those two decades.[9]

Another issue supported by the Kentucky Federation of Women's Clubs came before the 1908 legislative session with seeming success—the creation of a state tuberculosis sanatorium. The bill passed, only to be vetoed by Governor Willson. Well aware of Madge's passionate feelings on the subject, the governor wrote her: "I shall help that cause—dear to me. My father and brother . . . were its victims." He added, however, that "investigation, system, ample information and providing the money must come first. I think this appropriation would be a mere waste. . . . We cannot start this half-thought-out way on an empty treasury." Madge did not take lightly his criticism of the plan. In her report to the Kentucky Federation of Women's Clubs, she answered the governor's objections, concluding that perhaps he believed "the drafters of the measure thought that he would select the six trustees [for the sanatorium] from the Institute for the Feeble-Minded!" Despite this setback the local tuberculosis society made some progress during the year, setting up a dispensary in Lexington and providing free examinations and food. They also sponsored a tuberculosis exhibit in February that informed people about the causes, treatment, and prevention of the disease. Although absent from the state during the time of the exhibit, Madge had served on the local arrangements committee preparing for it.[10]

Most tuberculosis sufferers, of course, could not pursue treatment for the disease in a warm, dry climate as Madge and her mother did. They left Lexington on February 16 for New Orleans, accompanied by Madge's brother Will. The group visited California and spent six weeks in Palm Lodge, Arizona, taking the rest cure, which seemed to produce positive results. Madge spent much time playing bridge, and, according to her mother, obeyed doctor's orders completely. Their treatment included not only rest and relaxation but spinal massage and having coconut butter rubbed into their skin. By April Mrs. McDowell could report that her daughter weighed 110¾ pounds and the doctor pronounced her "sound and well," though she would still have to be careful not to overextend herself. She noted that Madge was "bright," with a "cheerful" disposition, but eager to return home. Mrs. McDowell, unfortunately, retained some tuberculosis bacilli in her sputum as well as some streptococci, and the family remained concerned about her condition. While they were away Madge urged Nettie Bullock to take care of repairs and refurbish several rooms at Ashland but wryly noted "how easy it is for people who are at the rest cure to think up jobs for other people." Unable to take part in legislative lobbying back home, the supposedly resting Madge followed the unfolding events and rejoiced in the successes achieved as the *Herald* continued to give reform efforts front-page coverage.[11]

After their return home in April, Henry Clay McDowell Jr. urged his mother to purchase an automobile "for your own and Madge's benefit." When Mrs. McDowell demurred, he asked her to reconsider. Evidently, before long she made the purchase, because the following year when Madge and a friend ran into a ditch, accounts noted that they were using Mrs. McDowell's car.[12]

Upon her return to Lexington Madge completely ignored the doctor's orders to take things leisurely. Almost immediately, she called a meeting of the Civic League to plan its spring program. The group discussed proposed methods for garbage disposal, voted $30 for flower seeds, requested that the mayor declare another "Spring Cleaning Day," and asked the School Board to contribute to the summer playground.[13]

In May Madge attended the convention of the Kentucky Federation of Women's Clubs in Paducah and in June gave a lecture on education reforms in Kentucky to the biennial national convention of the Federation of Women's Clubs, held in Boston. Shortly after returning home, she attended a meeting of the Education Committee of the Kentucky Federation of Women's Clubs, where the women made plans to send speakers to teachers' institutes and to provide money to assist rural schools. Madge also became the organization's representative on the new Educational Improvement Commission, created by the "Education Legislature" to make recommendations for further reforms to the 1910 General Assembly. Although the legislature did not enact any of the group's recommendations, the creation of the commission provided evidence of the rising demand in the state for improvement of the public school system, which was due in large part to the role of clubwomen and other female reformers, just as in many other southern states. A *Courier-Journal* editorial in 1908 proclaimed that women had taken the initiative and credited them for this new impulse.[14]

Madge continued to promote the cause of education reform, especially school suffrage for women. She collaborated with Mary Roark in writing essays on the subject, some of which appeared in booklet form. These explained her basic arguments for school suffrage. Noting that "educational advance and school suffrage for women go hand in hand," she dismissed completely the objections opponents had made to the reform. "Bad and ignorant" women would vote no more than similar men, and those who said Kentucky had tried woman school suffrage and it had failed were wrong, because the privilege had been too restricted for a fair trial. She acknowledged that a small number of black women would vote, but asked if men were forever going to deprive "intelligent white women" of the vote for that reason. She deplored the inconsistency of men who wanted women to help improve school conditions but opposed granting them suffrage. It was, she asserted, the "height of impudence" to "offer us caresses and cajolements with one hand and a blow and an insult with the other."[15]

Madge observed that Kentucky had a 12 percent illiteracy rate, which was fourth from the bottom when ranked with other states. Men had been so apathetic, they often had not bothered to vote for school trustees, forcing the county superintendents to appoint about two-thirds of them. Thus, she argued, the question was "not whether women are fit for school suffrage but whether men are fit for it." She continued: "If in Kentucky we have to indict one sex or the other for our educational conditions we shall have to indict the male sex. If our public school system has failed to reach our people, it is to the men of Kentucky we must go for explanation, to the sex which writes school laws, establishes schools and, as a rule, superintends them." She provided further evidence by comparing states that permitted women to vote on school matters with those that did not. In every way—illiteracy rate, length of school terms, per capita expenditure on education, and teachers' salaries—states that permitted women to vote in school elections, except one, ranked higher than all of those states that did not, she asserted.[16]

But even as she focused on school suffrage, Madge did not neglect other activities. In August she spoke at a playground meeting, outlining the history of the local park and playground movement and emphasizing that every school should have a playground. In November she presided over the annual meeting of the Civic League, where she was reelected president, and attended the annual meeting of Associated Charities, where she was reelected to the Board of Directors. Yet, almost as if she could not rest, Madge still found time to entertain extensively.[17]

Then, in late January 1909, when a blizzard and record low temperatures descended on Lexington, the charity issue came to the forefront once more. With the weather causing great hardship among the poor, the Salvation Army again proposed to set up a free soup kitchen. On January 31, the *Herald* published Madge's lengthy letter to the editor protesting this plan. She argued that the poor should "not be made a spectacle of" by having to stand in a soup line. If they needed food, it should be sent to their homes. Furthermore, she avowed, free soup offered merely a temporary solution that allowed the well-to-do to feel good about their philanthropy but did nothing to solve the long-term problems of the poor. Lexington had passed the era of soup kitchens and established Associated Charities, which provided a wiser form of charity, she argued. On February 1 the paper published another article by Madge, titled "Evils of Soup Kitchen Are Again Pointed Out." The community would supply most of the funds for the Salvation Army soup kitchen, and citizens must decide whether their resources would be used best by the Salvation Army or Associated Charities, she contended.[18]

Madge took up another charity issue in the pages of the *Herald* when the proprietor of a chattel-loan firm complained in the opposition *Lexington Leader* that his business was under attack by Associated Charities. The proprietor claimed that he ran a legitimate business and was not a "loan shark." In fact, he stated that "we claim to be benefactors to poor people," lending them money when banks would not. Madge published a reply, saying the man went too far in claiming to be a benefactor of the poor. She cited cases in which people had to pay an enormous interest rate. She lamented that Kentucky law did not protect people from these unfair charges. Further evidence of Madge and Desha's growing reputation in the field of charity work came in June when the National Conference of Charities and Correction, held in Buffalo, New York, elected her to the Committee on School and Community and Desha to the Committee on Publicity.[19]

Continuing her activities on behalf of school suffrage as well as general woman suffrage, Madge spoke in May at the Louisville Free Public Library. In announcing this upcoming talk, the *Lexington Leader* called her "one of the most brilliant women in the State." Later, reporting that she spoke for over an hour, the *Leader* stated: "Mrs. Breckinridge's personality and the charming and earnest way in which she advocated the suffragist movement made every argument hit the mark, and nearly every sentence of her speech was greeted with applause."[20]

When the Kentucky Press Association met in June, it asked Madge to speak on woman's work in Kentucky. Her address included a plea for school suffrage in which she declared that it was not right that Kentucky women be classified with criminals and idiots or compared with racehorses and whiskey. "I like to be in neither category," she said. "I do not believe it fair, right or just to let the women do the thinking on school matters and men the voting." Following her talk Jouett Shouse introduced a resolution for the press association officially to endorse woman suffrage in school elections. This caused a "merry good little scrap" until Madge asked that the resolution be withdrawn and changed into a petition that editors might sign individually if they chose.[21]

Madge likewise continued her work with the Civic League and the Woman's Club as the two organizations combined their efforts for city beautification. Moreover, at Owensboro in June Madge gave the report of the Education Committee at the state meeting of the Kentucky Federation of Women's Clubs. The group selected her as a delegate to the national biennial meeting of the Women's Clubs, to be held in Cincinnati in 1910. In addition, she spoke at an education rally attended by a thousand people on July 2 and the following day at a closing program for the Whirlwind Campaign in Fayette County, said at that time to be the greatest educational rally in the history of the state.[22]

Few healthy persons could have maintained such a schedule; yet, despite doctor's orders not to overexert herself, in spring 1909 Madge launched one of the most ambitious projects of her career—a "model" school building for Irishtown. The Lexington school superintendent had noted in his 1908 report that facilities at the West End School, which had grown from kindergarten only to four grades since its beginning in 1902, were as bad as they could be, with 150 pupils crowded into a three-room cottage. Accordingly, the School Board appropriated $10,000 to build a new structure. By this time Madge had formulated a dream of constructing a "model school" that would have a carpentry shop, laundry, gymnasium, shower baths, swimming pool, and assembly hall. In her ideal, teachers would be chosen for merit and efficiency, discipline would be gentle but firm, and manual training would be provided in every grade. In addition, facilities of the school would be open to the public for bathing, swimming, laundry, and meetings. In short, the school would be the social and civic center of the community. Social settlement workers had been the first to visualize the public school as a ready-made neighborhood center where the poor and the well-to-do could come together to work on solving social problems. Madge had gleaned these ideas from Sophonisba, Jane Addams, Mary McDowell, and others involved in Chicago social settlement work. The School Board's appropriation would not provide such a school, so Madge undertook to lead the Civic League in raising an additional $35,000 so it could include all the extras she envisioned. She even persuaded Elizabeth Cloud, principal of the West End School, to go to Chicago for three months to learn how to implement a "model school" program. As Madge informed Jane Addams: "I want her also to learn at Hull House and at Mary McDowell's Settlement how to run a settlement, for I hope some day to have a little settlement house beside our large school house in Irishtown for her to live in."[23]

In spring 1909 Madge began to raise the needed funds. She herself contributed three lots, valued at $350, for the site of the school and $650 in cash. Her mother and Aunt Mag each gave $1,000. She traveled to Chicago in an effort to interest ex-Kentuckians and other friends in the proposed project. She received $1,000 from Robert Todd Lincoln, son of President Abraham Lincoln, and $100 in gold from Lolita Sheldon (Mrs. J. Ogden) Armour, an old friend from Miss Porter's School, who had married into the wealthy meatpacking family. Several other small contributions made this a very profitable trip and showed her fund-raising abilities. She continued her drive by visiting New York City and seeking donations from Andrew Carnegie, James R. Keene, and other philanthropists. Keene, who lived in New York City but owned property in the Bluegrass, rewarded her efforts with $1,000. Robert Woolley, a former Lexingtonian then residing in Washington, DC, sent a contribution and promised to attempt to persuade other out-of-state Kentuckians to do likewise.[24]

Madge made a concerted effort to win local support as well. On May 16, she and Betsy Cloud spoke on the proposed school at a Sunday afternoon concert held in the old West End School. Madge convinced the Commercial Club and the Civic League to join together to discuss the equipment needed for manual training and social work. A banquet at the country club preceded a public meeting at the Opera House, where Madge, Cloud, and Mary McDowell spoke. McDowell discussed the social settlement work in Chicago and endorsed both the model school idea and manual training. Madge's speech, which the *Lexington Leader* published in its entirety and the *Herald* claimed "took the audience almost by storm," centered on the need for the model school in Irishtown. In an impassioned appeal for the children of that neighborhood, she stated: "Those children have a right, just as your children or my children have, just as every child in the world has, to 'rest and food and loving care and all that makes the world so fair.'" She added: "When we make our school building here we must build one thing in the [Irishtown] section that is fair, that is dignified and noble, and that shall serve its end, not only for usefulness but for an inspiration of neatness, order and beauty to the whole community." At the close of her address, after prolonged applause, she stood and said: "I wish you could go down there to the West End and see the way things are, and then maybe you would do something." A Lexington woman recorded in her diary her reaction to the speeches of Mary McDowell and Madeline Breckinridge: "Both spoke well, but Madge was truly eloquent."[25]

In June the Civic League sponsored a lawn fête at Ashland to raise money for the project, with Sayre College students presenting Shakespeare's *As You Like It.* The event, which included a free band concert, folk dances by West End children, acrobatic performances, and pony and automobile rides, proved to be a great success, raising about $500 for the school.[26]

Madge continued to work tirelessly, giving speeches and soliciting money. She also achieved another goal in helping organize a state antituberculosis conference in Lexington in September 1909. Organizers asked every mayor throughout the state to attend and to appoint an additional delegate. Madge made one of the key speeches at the conference, pointing out that while Lexington had excellent hospital accommodations, it had none to treat tuberculosis cases, though that disease caused 17.9 percent of the deaths in the city. "We feel very strongly that the first measure of relief to which we should all bend our energies is to procure a state institution," she asserted. The conference concluded by founding the Kentucky Association for the Prevention and Relief of Tuberculosis. The goals of the new organization included a statewide education campaign, promotion of local antituberculosis societies, and lobbying for a state tuberculosis sanatorium. Chosen as first vice president and member of the new organization's Legislative Committee, Lexington's premier reformer attended a flurry of meetings during November and December.[27]

Madge also attended the Kentucky Equal Rights Association convention in Louisville in November 1909, where she was selected as a delegate to the convention of the National American Woman Suffrage Association for the following year. The KERA convention voted to leave the Kentucky Federation of Women's Clubs entirely in charge of the drive for school suffrage, which meant that Madge and her Legislative Committee would continue to be responsible for the lobbying effort. Since the Kentucky General Assembly met only in even-numbered years, she began preparing a new school suffrage bill, drafted by Sophonisba Breckinridge and John T.

Shelby, Willie Breckinridge's former law partner, which she submitted to Laura Clay for her approval. Madge also secured the endorsement of the Educational Improvement Commission, which asked that the provision limiting female voters to those "able to read and write" be omitted, and Madge agreed. This qualification was reinstated, however, when Senator Claude Thomas of Bourbon County and Representative Eugene Graves of Paducah refused to introduce the bill without the qualification.[28]

Madge's willingness to swing in either direction on the literacy provision, which would exclude most African American women from the polls as well as a large number of white women, reflected her support for immediate, pragmatic success over idealistic principles on the subject of race. Having been told in 1902 that school suffrage was being repealed because "too many illiterate negro women voted," most Kentucky suffragists, including Madge, felt the chance for reinstating and extending it would be greater if an educational or literacy component were included, and they viewed that victory as a step toward full suffrage. As one historian phrased it, "The suffragists had to confront, not a theory on political equality, but an actual condition. . . . Denied the suffrage for all women, they reacted by trying to gain it for their own elite group." In addition, Madge believed "the ignorant vote can be swayed and bent," thereby setting the stage for corruption, but "pure democracy" could be implemented and the educational qualification for voting ended when the masses learned to read and write. Moreover, she did not think that the combination of illiteracy and corruption was confined only to one race, noting that Kentucky had "over 65,000 illiterate white voters" who held the "balance of power." In addition, she charged that although Kentuckians frequently excused their high illiteracy rate by pointing to a "large colored population," in fact "it takes our colored population to bring us up from the rank of forty-second to the glorious one of thirty-seventh in the list." In the final analysis, she did not personally oppose allowing black women to vote, she could see both positives and negatives in an educational or literacy qualification, and she could accept whichever might have the better chance of passage. She also expected that any literacy qualification would be applied equally to black and white women.[29]

Preparing for the General Assembly's consideration of the school suffrage bill, Madge organized a mass meeting at the Lexington Opera House on January 12, 1910, to rally public support for the measure. Although a large crowd attended, members of the legislature conspicuously did not.

Madge followed Superintendent of Public Instruction Crabbe and several others, summing up their arguments and declaring that if all the influence of women were removed from the schools, the system would crash. She urged women to use both aggression and tact in the struggle, which she predicted would not be an easy one. As one of her friends recorded, she also "paid her respects to the liquor interests . . . for their opposition, in a strong and forceful manner." In the next few weeks she spoke at other rallies in central Kentucky, but despite her hard work, she remained pessimistic about the chance for success.[30]

In February Madge, Desha, and several others testified to the Senate Committee on Suffrage and Elections, to which the bill had been referred. The *Lexington Leader* reported that Madge gave a "brilliant argument," which made such a "profound impression" on the committee that it would report the school suffrage bill favorably. A few days later a delegation from the Women's Clubs met with the House Committee on Suffrage and Elections in the Capital Hotel in Frankfort, where Madge presented the reasons why women asked for school suffrage. Desha, Crabbe, Laura Clay, and others followed her. Each gave a forceful and persuasive speech, and nobody publicly stated any opposition to the measure. Nevertheless, speakers felt they had made no impression on Democrat Harry G. Meyers of Covington, chairman of the committee and reputed spokesman of the whiskey interests. When Meyers realized that a majority of the committee members would vote to report the bill without expression, he adjourned the meeting. Later, he managed to secure an unfavorable report. When the bill came before the house, Madge received ten minutes to speak for it, with Meyers answering her. The house defeated the measure, 37-46, with Lexington representative Billy Klair voting against. Some members of the legislature reportedly claimed that if Meyers could make another speech or two in opposition, it would pass overwhelmingly. When the bill came before the senate, it passed by a vote of 17-12, well short of the three-fifths majority necessary for a constitutional amendment, and the house did not take it up again.[31]

Once more Madge declared that whiskey interests had defeated school suffrage. She got in a final word with a stinging article titled "The Women of Kentucky versus the Honorable Harry G. Meyers of Covington, Now of the Legislature." She ridiculed his statement that if the women of the state would come before the legislature with babies in their arms and plead for the vote, the legislature would grant it. Few women would agree that the legislature was the place to take a baby, she asserted. Nor was Meyers correct in his contention that not one of the women who spoke to his committee was a mother. Fourteen of the eighteen women had children. His speech, she charged, had made suffragists out of women who before were "just plain mothers" wanting school suffrage for the benefit of their children. Thus, he had "done much for the cause of full suffrage for women in this State."[32]

One convert Meyers helped make for full suffrage was Desha Breckinridge. Desha had gone to Frankfort favoring only school suffrage, but after comparing Meyers's illogical arguments to those of the women who spoke, he returned home ready to fight "earnestly" for full suffrage and to help educate the rest of the state about the need for it. He also firmly backed his wife in holding the whiskey interests responsible for killing the bill. The liquor lobby, the Breckinridges maintained, constituted the "Third House" of the legislature. Madge reiterated this charge in a speech at the annual convention of the Kentucky Federation of Women's Clubs in May 1910. But, she warned the convention, it would not be enough just to win school suffrage: "I shall be bitterly disappointed if when we obtain school suffrage for women the women of Kentucky are not ready to use it to ten fold better advantage than the men of Kentucky have ever used their school suffrage."[33]

Nevertheless, Madge was not willing to wait for that day before trying to increase the influence of women in Lexington's schools. She continued to make speeches for school suffrage as she planned for the next legislative session and she became a member of KERA's lecture bureau. In May she published a pamphlet, *Some Reasons for Granting School Suffrage to Kentucky Women*, in which she repeated her claim that the strongest argument for school suffrage for women was the dismal state of the public schools after years of "unadulterated male management." "Have men shown by their record their sole fitness to control the school system of Kentucky?" she asked, obviously expecting a resounding no.[34]

In addition, she persuaded the Civic League to endorse two women—Linda Neville and Margaret Brown—for the School Board. The *Herald* gave its unqualified support, proclaiming that women on the School Board would be efficient and effective because they would work for sanitation and for the establishment of kindergarten and manual training. Madge rejoiced when the two women won election by male votes in November.[35]

One of Madge's greatest disappointments during the 1910 session resulted from the legislature's failure to pass an act creating a state tuberculosis sanatorium. In March Madge wrote Governor Willson urging him to include such a measure in the list of subjects to be considered if he called a special session. Again the governor refused: "I have earnest feeling for the battle against tuberculosis. . . . I did not veto the bill of 1908 through lack of sympathy but because the appropriations continually far exceed the revenues." He concluded: "I believe no one in Kentucky has given better study and greater wisdom to Kentucky's problems than you have. No one in the world can more earnestly thank you, for noble, brave, and high-minded usefulness to Kentucky, than I do." Such plaudits did little to soothe Madge's bitterness at that rejection.[36]

Yet, very gradually, she began to see some progress. In 1910 the local tuberculosis society and the Associated Charities joined together and hired Chloe Jackson, a graduate of the Mercy Hospital Training School in Chicago, to work with tubercular patients in Lexington. By February of the following year the local group, now called the Fayette County Tuberculosis Association, opened a free dispensary in the Associated Charities building and hired a second nurse. A number of local physicians also donated time to the dispensary. In May the organizations added a visiting nurse service. At the same time the Tuberculosis Association began developing plans to build a local sanatorium, a goal that would not be achieved for several years. Although she was not always an officer of the organization, Madge remained a member of the Executive Committee. In spring 1911 she began working with the Kentucky Association for the Prevention and Relief of Tuberculosis to plan for the legislative session, and that fall she was reelected to the Board of Directors of the state association and was chosen first vice president.[37]

Meanwhile, Madge continued her efforts to raise money for the Irishtown school, but by May 1910 the Civic League had collected only $9,159.60, with $830 more pledged. Minor fund-raising efforts such as schoolchildren selling garden seeds and the Civic League selling balloons at the July 4 celebration at Woodland Park brought in little revenue. Madge sought and obtained the appointment of three School Board members to work with three Civic League members in making plans for the school, and the Civic League chose her as one of its representatives on this committee. By midsummer they had worked out a contract for the model school and gained the School Board's approval. A later agreement gave the School Board control of the regular school curriculum, including manual training, while a joint committee of the board and Civic League would determine other uses for the facility.[38]

When the Civic League held its annual election in October 1910, Clinton M. Harbison, a young attorney, replaced Madge as president. By this time the League had raised $10,900 for the model school and estimated that it needed another $25,000. The League appointed a campaign committee to secure the remaining funds. Madge led this committee in organizing a nine-day fund-raising blitz, launched on November 14 with the official approval of the School Board. On the preceding Sunday several ministers preached their morning sermon on some aspect of the West End School, and Madge wrote an article on the subject for the Sunday edition of the *Herald* in which she argued that because 90 percent of the children in public school would someday earn their living with their hands, it was folly to teach them Latin and higher mathematics without first instructing them about sanitation, nutrition, and vocational skills. Like many Progressives, she saw vocational training as a means of expanding the options of working-class children, not, as some critics have charged, as a way of limiting them to blue-collar jobs. She explained that the term "model school" simply meant a better one than the community now possessed, and the standards would grow higher every year. In addition, the school would serve social purposes. If young people were provided with a gathering place, they could be better protected from the saloons and other evils that often filled recreation time, she asserted.[39]

Madge had gained a reputation as an outstanding speaker with a strong voice that could be heard in a very large hall. As a result, she often received invitations to lecture, both within Kentucky and without. But when Laura Clay requested her to address the Kentucky Equal Rights Association's annual meeting, to be held in Covington on November 16, 1910, she declined because of the model school campaign, noting that "for this fall at any rate," the Irishtown "school is the paramount issue." While she felt sure Clay thought the school was a small job compared to the cause of woman suffrage, she explained that the Civic League's work for the school had done more for the cause of school suffrage for women than all their other efforts put together. In confidence she told Clay that M. A. Cassidy, superintendent of the Lexington schools, and others had urged her to run for the School Board because of her constant attendance at the board meetings *in spite* of her agitation for women's rights and school suffrage. Furthermore, she believed women's work for the model school could be used to make a stronger plea for school suffrage with the legislature. Despite her absence from the convention, members elected her to KERA's Lecture Bureau.[40]

The drive to raise the final $25,000 opened with a parade of twenty-five hundred schoolchildren, followed by speeches from Madge and Superintendent Cassidy. That night the Civic League sponsored a banquet, where Madge asserted that the model school project represented justice, not charity. On each of the nine days of the campaign, 150 solicitors scoured the city door-to-door asking for pledges. The School Board gave children a two-day holiday to help canvass. On the first day they raised $3,798.50, with about $2,000 of it coming from James Ben Ali Haggin, a prominent Bluegrass horseman, but subscriptions did not flow in quickly or easily. By the fourth day pledges totaled only $8,287. Madge spoke at the YMCA building, the State University, Transylvania University, Hamilton College, and Sayre school during the days of the campaign. On November 15 Desha wrote an editorial urging "every man who reads these lines, who wishes Kentucky to go forward and wishes Lexington to be the leader in that forward movement, to give to this fund both generously and promptly." With obvious reference to his wife, he implored: "The promptness with which a contribution is made will save nervous strain and worry on those who are already carrying more and doing more than their strength justifies."[41]

The entire amount had to be promised in order to hold the pledges. When the Civic League still needed $10,615 on the last day of the drive, the officers decided to ask one hundred women to secure an additional $20 before that night. When they counted the total, they still lacked $3,500. A number of people at the ball that closed the campaign pledged, if necessary, to make up the remainder. These included Madge, Mrs. McDowell, and Nettie Bullock. As both the *Leader* and *Herald* pointed out, the people who guaranteed the money comprised the group that had already given the most in time and money. The *Leader* suggested, and the *Herald* endorsed, a plan to ask those to contribute who had not done so because they felt their contribution was too insignificant to matter. This produced a good response but did not make up the $3,500 guaranteed by Madge and her family.[42]

For months Madge continued to work to collect the pledges, but she failed to complete the task on time. She did take some time off in March to travel with Desha to Cincinnati and on to New York City, but she resumed the fund-raising effort as soon as she returned home. In May 1911 the Joint Committee of the School Board and the Civic League, of which she remained a member, found it necessary to postpone the opening of bids for the school until the middle of June. Madge urged a friend on vacation to use her contacts with the "criminal rich" to try to get additional money. By July the League had only $30,000 in cash, and with the School Board's $10,000, they were still short because they had found it necessary to purchase an additional lot, which would be paid for out of Civic League funds. Madge sent out letters from the Civic League, asking those who had made pledges to pay them promptly. In order to cut the cost of the school, they revised the plans and postponed the swimming pool and a few other luxuries. Nevertheless, the first two sets of bids proved too high. By this time even Madge had become discouraged, and the *Herald* noted that people in Irishtown, as well as Civic League members and citizens in general, had become skeptical about the success of the project. On July 30 the *Herald* published Madge's article "The Model School Is Hanging in Balance," in which she pointed out that $1,800 of the guaranteed funds had yet to be raised. This must be done in time for the School Board to act in August so the building could be roofed before bad weather. Finally, on August 26 the School Board awarded the contract to Congleton Lumber Company for $33,689, exclusive of electrical wiring and heat.[43]

In the month that followed the letting of the contract, Madge raised $2,100 in new pledges. "She is so weary that I believe she has never yet visited the building site," a friend wrote of Madge. "She has worked with tremendous zeal and deserves a rest." She continued to work very hard, however, planning for the cornerstone-laying ceremony and participating in design decisions. The School Board suggested naming the school in her honor, but she asked that it be named for Abraham Lincoln. "I have begged all over the country," she said, "and this would put me in the position of having begged for myself." Moreover, she continued: "There could be nothing finer than that every day these children should have held up to them the example of the Kentucky boy, who arose from poverty and obscurity, who fought his good fight, who triumphed over every handicap, who died the first American, and who though in his life-time he was the target of all the bitterness that engendered the Civil War, is today the beloved of a nation."[44]

Students in a classroom at Lincoln School. Courtesy of Special Collections and Digital Programs, Margaret I. King Library, University of Kentucky, Lexington.

At the cornerstone laying on December 6, 1911, Superintendent Cassidy and State University president Henry S. Barker both praised Madge and gave her credit for the project's success. Cassidy predicted that from the school "will start circles of good influences that will break only on the shore of eternity" and concluded: "All honor to its founder, who has so unselfishly engaged in this work. May her highest hopes be realized and may those of many generations, who get life here, rise up and call her blessed." Barker noted in his address that "this noble edifice is the lifework of one noble woman, who years ago conceived in her mind the idea which has now found fruition. Who shall say she is not a hero?" In a talk that concluded the ceremony, Madge with typical modesty pointed out the hard work by the members of the Civic League. The *Lexington Leader*, the rival of her husband's paper, printed the complete text of her remarks. For her, the event had been "Sunshine in December."[45]

One contact Madge made during her fund-raising efforts paid an unexpected dividend. Anthony Dey, a wealthy Wall Street stockbroker who owned a Bluegrass farm, donated $10,000 in memory of his father-in-law, David C. Humphreys of Woodford County. He asked that the money form a perpetual endowment, the income of which would be used for the children of Lincoln School rather than being invested in "bricks and mortar." The income from the Dey Fund proved to be a valuable asset in carrying out the school's social work program and continues today to provide assistance to needy children and their families.[46]

The year 1911 also found Madge making speeches around the state for school suffrage. In April she traveled to Nashville to address the Fourteenth Annual Conference for Education in the South. She used this forum to emphasize her support for school suffrage, arguing that the entire South would benefit from the participation of women in school elections. The editor of the *New York Evening Post* hailed her speech as the "most brilliant utterance of the entire convention" and maintained that it would be called militant if that word were not associated with lawlessness. At the Kentucky Federation of Women's Clubs annual convention, held in Louisville in May, she predicted school suffrage would come during the 1912 legislative session: "This is the first time I have made this assertion," she said, "and I am confident of the truth of what I assert. It only remains for us to work to arouse great interest among the women of the State so that they will be ready to take up the work of school suffrage when it comes." During summer and fall 1911, Madge organized a campaign for the cause that likely surpassed in intensity the campaigns of those running for state office, including the governorship itself. She sent literature to legislative and gubernatorial candidates, attempting to get them to declare their position. After the election she inundated the winners with material on the subject. In all, the Legislative Committee of the Federation of Women's Clubs sent out one hundred thousand pieces of literature during the year preceding the 1912 meeting of the Kentucky General Assembly. One of the supporters she won over to the cause was Billy Klair, who had sponsored the 1902 bill revoking school suffrage for women in second-class cities. When she and Desha entertained Klair and other leading local politicians in their Linden Walk home in September 1911, the pragmatic Klair had already embarked on a reversal of his position. As one historian has noted, Klair's "support of certain women's reform measures important to Madge Breckinridge was a small price to pay for the favorable press her husband could provide."[47]

The state became even more aroused on the cause of woman suffrage in October 1911 when the National American Woman Suffrage Association (NAWSA) held its annual convention in Louisville. Dissension had grown rampant in NAWSA leadership circles, with New Yorkers and other easterners pitted against southern and western suffragists. Easterners dominated the voting at the convention, defeating Kentucky suffragist

Laura Clay for four different offices. Sophonisba Breckinridge, elected first vice president over Clay, had not even attended the convention, much less sought office. On notice of her election, she wired back: "How did it happen? I cannot take Laura Clay's place. Help me be true & loyal." Clay asserted she would not take the office if Breckinridge declined, so the vote stood. Meanwhile, KERA held its convention simultaneously and reelected Clay president but amended the constitution to provide for rotation in office. KERA delegates also named Madge to its Education Committee.[48]

On the last night of the NAWSA convention Madge shared the podium with notorious militant British suffragist Emmeline Pankhurst. Madge's address, "The Prospect for Suffrage in the South," noted that both the Republican and Democratic parties in Kentucky had now endorsed school suffrage, and she predicted that Kentucky would have full woman suffrage within ten years. In an appeal for southern support for suffrage, she fell back on an argument early suffragists had made: "If the literate women of the South were enfranchised it would insure a preponderance of the Anglo-Saxon over the African, of the literate over the illiterate, and would make legitimate limitation of the male suffrage to the literate easily possible." This theme appealed not only to southern suffragists fighting an uphill battle to win the vote, but also to some northerners concerned with voting by large immigrant populations. But she also used the justice argument, saying that suffrage was a natural right and would solve the problem of taxation without representation.[49]

Despite her defeat for office, Clay proclaimed the NAWSA convention a success because it had created so much interest in suffrage in Kentucky. The convention had, indeed, spawned much newspaper debate, pro and con. One of Madge's friends noted that Desha ran back and forth to the convention so much that he had given the *Herald* readers a rest from politics. But not all newspapermen proved as supportive. Although a *Louisville Courier-Journal* editorial welcomed the convention, editor Henry Watterson opposed woman suffrage. The paper found itself "between the devil and the deep blue sea," he complained, because it favored certain aspects of the women's movement but opposed much as well. A *Lexington Herald* editorial after the convention summed up the NAWSA convention's effect on the state's news media. It charged that the *Courier-Journal* had shown "sensational bad taste" in its attacks on Pankhurst, who was a guest of the city, and reported that the *Louisville Post* gave much space to the convention, though still opposing suffrage, while the *Louisville Herald* converted and embraced the cause.[50]

The NAWSA convention provided a fitting conclusion to a year of great accomplishment for Madge. By the end of 1911 she had succeeded in raising the money necessary for the model school in Irishtown and looked forward to its opening. She had laid the groundwork for passage of school suffrage at the next legislative session and had continued lobbying efforts for a state tuberculosis sanatorium. Would the coming year bring great triumphs on these issues or huge disappointments?

Chapter 7

"Among the most brilliant advocates of votes for women in this country" 1912–1913

The year 1912 opened with a high degree of excitement for Madge and Desha as they traveled to Frankfort in January for the crucial meeting of the legislature. Madge had done her utmost to see that the school suffrage bill would pass and optimistically anticipated success. Nevertheless, she remained in the capital for several days, making speeches and lobbying legislators. When the bill, which included a literacy requirement, came before the house, Harry Meyers offered his usual opposition. Only "bridge whist players and women without children" wanted school suffrage in his hometown of Covington, he asserted. Women really sought full suffrage, he claimed, so that they could vote in wet and dry elections. Despite Meyers's opposition, the bill passed the house on January 25 by a vote of 62-25, with 49 Democrats and 13 Republicans voting in favor, and 18 Democrats and 7 Republicans voting against. A lively floor debate ensued in the upper chamber in March, with Democratic senator E. Bertram of Clinton County arguing that passage of such an act would throw open the home to the "trash of politics." However, Republican senator H. M. Brock of Harlan took the other side, saying that men had failed in their hundred years of controlling the school system, and thus women should be given a chance. After two hours of debate the bill passed the senate, 24-11, with 21 Democrats and 3 Republicans voting in favor and 10 Democrats and 1 Republican voting against. It was a resounding victory that had strong support from both parties.[1]

On March 24, at a public meeting held in Lexington to celebrate the victory of school suffrage, Madge related how women had worked for and finally obtained the right to vote in school elections. She noted that the key had been to engage women's interests in improving educational conditions in the state, and she emphasized the obligation women now had to use this new privilege to improve the school system. She closed by reciting one of her favorite poems, Kipling's "Mother o' Mine." Perhaps the most significant result of the struggle for school suffrage proved to be, as opponents had feared, that many new converts were made for the cause of full suffrage, including an official endorsement by the Kentucky Federation of Women's Clubs.[2]

Reformers also experienced other triumphs during this legislative session. For almost a year Madge had worked through the Civic League to support a change in school laws for second-class cities. Under the League's proposal the School Board would be reduced from twelve members to five, nominations for board members would be by petition of one hundred rather than by a few politicians, and there would be no party designations on the ballot. In June 1911 Madge had become part of a Civic League committee charged with drafting a proposal incorporating these provisions. Its passage by the General Assembly in 1912, according to School Board member Linda Neville, "was procured largely through the efforts of Mrs. Madeline McDowell Breckinridge."[3]

Madge also savored a partial victory when the General Assembly finally passed a tuberculosis bill and the governor signed it. This law established a state tuberculosis commission, appointed by the governor, with a yearly appropriation of $15,000. The new Democratic governor, James B. McCreary, an ex-Confederate who had served with Willie Breckinridge under General John Hunt Morgan, had first won the governorship in 1875 at the age of thirty-seven. Over a long career that included stints in the U.S. House and Senate he earned the nickname "Bothsides" because of his ability to choose the popular side on most issues. This served Madge well, because the popularity of progressive ideas during McCreary's second term caused him to veer toward reform in sharp contrast to his first, mainly conservative, term. He approved the tuberculosis bill, immediately named Madge to the commission, and then reappointed her in 1915 to a four-year term. The law also provided for the creation of tuberculosis districts that were each empowered to establish a sanatorium. A district could be created by the fiscal court or, if the fiscal court failed to act, by an election held in accordance with requirements stipulated in the statute. Since this act did not create a state sanatorium, it was not what Madge wanted; however, she viewed it as a step in the right direction.[4]

While lobbying for various bills before the state legislature, Madge continued to work on the Irishtown school building. By the end of February 1912, the joint committee of the School Board and the Civic League struggled with the need to economize. In April the School Board officially adopted Madge's suggestion to name the school for Abraham Lincoln. The board decided to name the main room, which would serve as an auditorium, gymnasium, and kindergarten, in honor of Major Henry Clay McDowell, whose family had donated its approximate cost of $3,500. In June Madge met with three other members of the joint committee to make plans for using the new building after school hours. When classes began in September, the auditorium still had no lighting, and a waiting list existed for the still-incomplete laundry.[5]

During 1912 Madge traveled widely and made numerous speeches on behalf of suffrage, many of them in campaign states where a woman suffrage amendment would be on the fall ballot. Sophonisba noted that by this time her sister-in-law "was impatient for the opportunity to work directly, and perhaps chiefly, for the vote as an instrument in the accomplishment of the social ends that were ever before her eyes." Historians have often differentiated between early suffragists who demanded suffrage as a natural right and later so-called social feminists who sought the vote as a means to achieve social reforms. In Madge Breckinridge's case, the distinction is artificial. She had long believed in woman suffrage as a natural right, arguing on many occasions that "taxation without representation is tyranny," but devoting more time to the cause became a priority after she concluded from bitter experience that without the vote, women would never have the political power necessary to achieve the other reforms she sought. Thus, from 1912 on she turned aside from many of her old interests to devote her time primarily to suffrage, often using the social feminist argument that women comprised the nation's natural housekeepers and therefore needed the vote in order to protect hearth and home. Indeed, many woman suffrage strategists attached their cause to the Progressive reform agenda in this way in order to win respectability and counter the arguments of the antisuffragists, who frequently charged that women were too delicate and emotional to withstand the turbulent, sometimes dirty, world of politics. Suffragists' use of the argument of municipal housekeeping has been called "a brilliant strategy" because it provided "the common denominator that united women of various persuasions" while at the same time refuting antisuffragists' contentions that allowing women to vote would undermine the home and actually diminish the power of women, who reigned supreme in their own domestic sphere. For Madge, winning the right to vote remained not only a just end in itself but also a necessity for achieving other goals.[6]

Early in 1912 she visited St. Louis, Missouri, where she attended a meeting of the Executive Board of the General Federation of Women's Clubs. In a speech there she attacked the myth of southern chivalry, saying: "On the whole the South has done less for the general protection of women and children than any other part of America." She charged that "the Southern gentleman is back in the Middle Ages when it comes to chivalry. . . . He believes in other men protecting their women as he protects or would fight if it were demanded to protect his women. He overlooks the fact that some women may not have a chivalrous man individual to protect her or to fight for her or for himself." She added: "I have noticed that in the tales of chivalry . . . the lady for whom the Knight fought was always noble, young and beautiful, never plebeian, old or ugly. Who protected the plain, old and ugly woman, I wonder? Who . . . protected the peasant women and the women who did not rank as 'ladies' in those times, climes, and social strata?" She concluded that "on the whole, I have figured that the lady of the Age of Chivalry must have been a desperately oppressed female," and she drew a comparison with "factory girls in the South, children, women who have no Knights to fight for them, but many to oppress them. Therefore, I hold, that these women must, by law, by the vote, protect themselves."[7]

For many years Madge had ridiculed the myth of southern chivalry. In a *Herald* article in 1906 she demonstrated the falseness of chivalry by comparing the age of consent in states where women voted to those where women could not vote. The four states where women had full suffrage set the age of protection at either twenty-one or eighteen, while in the South, where women did not vote, it ranged from ten to sixteen, with only Kentucky in this group having it as high as sixteen. Thus, Madge asked: "Do Southern men protect Southern women at all comparably to the way Western women, granted the right to do it, protect their own sex?"[8]

In St. Louis she predicted that despite these mistaken ideas of chivalry, women would be voting in most southern states within ten years. She also noted that "my husband, who is editor of The Lexington Herald, is in full accord with me on this subject of suffrage." In one of her most revealing statements on the subject, she addressed the issue of race at length. Noting that the liquor interests in Kentucky "draw fearful pictures of the Southern women voting with negroes and lewd, wicked, gun-toting white men," she asked: "So long as women must jostle them on the streets . . . why should they not jostle them in polling places?" Was she in favor of allowing black women to vote? "Yes, I am," she stated. "I wish we could have an educational test for the ballot, but we can't have that, so let the negresses vote, say I." She believed educational qualifications should apply only until general literacy prevailed among the masses; then "I believe in pure democracy," she stated. Acknowledging that race constituted one of the most troublesome issues in the United States, she argued that no state or nation could rightfully, lawfully, or morally deprive any of its inhabitants of equal rights or education. "I feel that negroes cannot be kept in servile positions for all time," she stated, and when they acquire education and property, they will demand "all the rights of the free American citizen." She hoped that by the time this happened white Americans would be "educated enough to handle it." In her pragmatic way, however, she also occasionally used arguments that tried to appease the South's racial views, despite the fact that she considered herself to be liberal on the race issue. There were, she stated, six hundred thousand more white women in the South than black men and women combined, so granting woman suffrage would increase the literate vote without increasing the illiterate vote. "It would be an easy means of obtaining Anglo-Saxon supremacy," she declared. This argument never overcame the white South's fear that woman suffrage ultimately meant racial equality, but this mixed message on the race issue would mark her stance in the coming years. Although personally sympathetic to black voting rights, she nevertheless continued to put expediency first, as she had in the school suffrage fight. Indeed, she noted to an Augusta, Georgia, woman that she had not called on black women "for help and made no effort to bring them in while we were fighting for school suffrage, in fact I discouraged such efforts, because I believed one war was enough at a time." She added that "my idea is to pursue the same policy with regard to the full suffrage." Often her arguments on race, states' rights, and the role of women in society were couched as a response to statements made by antisuffragists or southern suffragists who were virulent racists, which accounts in part for her sometimes inconsistent stance on the race issue. She also frequently pointed out that antisuffragists violated their own tenet that females should not involve themselves in public affairs.[9]

The press in St. Louis reported that this speaker was no northerner, no carpetbagger, no poor white trash, but a true "Southern lady" from one of the most distinguished families in America. Moreover, one newspaper stated: "Her native eloquence, her soft Southern speech toning down the sharpness and keenness of intellect," differentiated her from "the strident suffragette." "She is ranked as among the most brilliant advocates of votes for women in this country," the paper concluded.[10]

At a meeting of the Conference on Education in the South, held in Nashville in April, Madge gave a lecture titled "Public Schools and Southern Development." A newspaper editor noted that although he disagreed completely with her position on equal rights, her speech "for business of analysis and literary expression . . . was better than any thing they had had at the conference." Her success as a speaker, according to Sophonisba, owed much to her use of "incisive though not repelling sarcasm." Wherever she spoke, newspapers commented on that aspect of her speaking technique, as well as "her voice, clear, penetrating, but appealing, her relation to Henry Clay, her simple and dignified bearing, [and] her slender person."[11]

In May she traveled to New York City, where she attended a meeting of the Political Equality League at the home of Alva Belmont, a wealthy patron of the suffrage movement. She visited the Juvenile Court Detention Home as well as the night court and took the opportunity to purchase a coat and shoes, lamenting to her mother: "I always feel as if I were feebleminded when I try to shop—I wish it never had to be done." She also went to Kinderhook, New York, where she visited an old friend, Marion Houston Smith. Shortly after her return from New York, she spoke to a group of society women in Cincinnati, whose position on suffrage she described as "zealous enough to provide enthusiasm for all other women."[12]

In June Madge embarked on a trip to San Francisco to attend the annual convention of the Federation of Women's Clubs. She used the journey to campaign for woman suffrage, making stops in Denver, Colorado Springs, Salt Lake City, and Sacramento. Receptions, sightseeing expeditions, parades, and suffrage speeches filled her days. The *San Francisco Chronicle*, she reported to Nettie Bullock, would be publishing her five-minute speech to the Commercial Club of that city. While she enjoyed the excursion very much, she became somewhat homesick and wrote Desha that it felt as if she had "been away from Lexington & you a very long time."[13]

Madge toured Ohio in the last few days of August before voters went to the polls on September 3 to vote on woman suffrage. Ohioans rejected the suffrage amendment, but Madge had already gone on to other campaign states. In September she spoke in Michigan, Oregon, Wisconsin, Nevada, and Kansas, all of which had upcoming votes on suffrage. While in Oregon she debated the Reverend Clarence True Wilson, secretary of the Committee of Temperance and Morals of the Methodist Church. A report of this encounter stated: "Three thousand people saw him [Wilson], completely routed, retire from the platform, while, Mrs. Breckinridge and 'the cause' got a tremendous ovation."[14]

As soon as she returned to Lexington, the seemingly tireless Madge became deeply involved in the School Board election. When the Civic League endorsed five candidates, she helped secure the necessary number of names on the petitions for their nomination. Very concerned that women would not use their school suffrage, she worked hard to ensure that women would register and take advantage of the opportunity to vote. She agreed to serve as chairman of the Civic League committee responsible for organizing support both for the nominees and for two bond issues to complete the sewer and park systems. At a Civic League meeting in October, she spoke on the proposed School Board. But soon that election became embroiled in controversy. A "Patrons' School Board Ticket" entered the field against the Civic League ticket. The "patrons" remained nameless, but, according to rumor, one of them was a Democratic Party boss. These anonymous persons claimed an interest in all schools, not just one, and asserted that the schools should be divorced from "politics and fads"—an obvious attack on the model school and the women involved in reforms such as domestic science, manual training, and physical education. Even worse, rumors—apparently started by those favoring the patrons' ticket—began to circulate, accusing Madge and Linda Neville, one of the Civic League's nominees for the School Board, of being interested in the Irishtown school because they owned property there and the school would increase the property's value. Desha ardently defended the two women in an editorial, "Who Is Above Slander?" The Nevilles, he said, had held property in Irishtown for two generations, but at the time the Civic League embarked on the model school campaign, Linda Neville had been totally occupied in caring for her father. Furthermore, he added, Madge owned no property in Irishtown and never had, except for the two lots she bought and donated to the School Board. He concluded: "In addition she gave to the West End School money which she saved through self-denial and sacrifice of pleasures." The controversy ended abruptly when the voters made their decision, electing Neville and the entire Civic League ticket by a large majority and at the same time endorsing both bond issues that the League advocated.[15]

If Madge's work on behalf of various reforms earned her some enemies, it was, perhaps, to be expected. There are often those who, whether from sincere conviction, jealousy, or some other reason, will oppose those who take the lead in public affairs. But Madge seldom allowed criticism to deter her. In fact, at the twenty-third annual convention of the Kentucky Equal Rights Association she accepted even more responsibility. Laura Clay, who had founded KERA in 1888 and had served as its president ever since, decided to step down, and she chose Madge as her successor. With plans already under way for KERA to begin a drive for a state constitutional amendment giving Kentucky women full suffrage, Clay believed that because the question in Kentucky had become political, Madge could "carry on the work better than I can."[16]

One of the most exciting events of Madge's life occurred on November 30 with the dedication of Lincoln School. Madge herself had prepared the invitations. At the Civic League's request, Sophonisba Breckinridge spoke at the event, after which Madge related how two days earlier in Louisville she had seen depicted in photographs "splendid" scenes of Lincoln School. Thus, she noted, it already served as a "model" to Louisville and to the remainder of the state.[17]

The year 1912 had indeed been a momentous, successful one for Madge. The passage of school suffrage, the creation of a state tuberculosis commission, the dedication of the Irishtown school, and her election as president of the Kentucky Equal Rights Association comprised her greatest achievements. One of her goals for Lincoln School came to fruition with the opening of the Outdoor School on the roof, to provide fresh air, rest, and nourishing food to children from families that had tuberculosis. The School Board supplied money for moveable desks and for the teacher's salary, while the Tuberculosis Society, the Elks Lodge, and private donors contributed money for additional equipment. Many of the thirty children selected for the Outdoor School were anemic, but none had an active case of tuberculosis. The school required them to take a daily shower and

WHAT

—THE—

KENTUCKY EQUAL RIGHTS ASSOCIATION

HAS DONE

—AND—

THE WORK FOR THE FUTURE.

In 1888 the Kentucky Equal Rights Association was organized, for the purpose of obtaining for women equality with men in educationul, industrial, legal and political rights.

We found on the statute books a law that permitted a husband to collect his wife's wages.

We found Kentucky the only State that did not permit a married woman to make a will.

We found that marriage gave to the husband all the wife's personal property, which could be reduced to possession, and the use of all her real estate, owned at the time or acquired by her after marriage, with power to rent the same for not more than three years at a time and receive the rent.

We found that the common law of curtesy and dower prevailed; whereby, on the death of the wife the husband inherited absolutely all personalty not hitherto reduced to possession, and when there were children, a life interest in all her real estate; while the wife, when there were children, inherited one-third of her husband's personalty and a life interest in one-third of his real estate possessed during marriage.

In 1890 we secured a law which made the wife's wages payable only to herself.

From the long Legislature of 1892–93, we secured a law giving a married woman the right to make a will and control her real estate.

Finally, from the General Assembly of 1894 we secured the enactment of the present righteous Husband and Wife law.

Excerpt from a pamphlet of the Kentucky Equal Rights Association. Courtesy of Special Collections and Digital Programs, Margaret I. King Library, University of Kentucky, Lexington.

also provided extra food. Madge hoped this plan, based in large part on her grandfather McDowell's prescribed treatment of tuberculosis, would give these high-risk children a better chance to avoid the dreaded disease. When health officials from Kentucky and several other states, as well as from the Rockefeller Sanitary Commission, located in Washington, DC, toured Lincoln School in the fall, they praised its ventilation and sanitary conditions, saying it should be heralded throughout the South as a model for both city and rural schools.[18]

Fortunately, by June 1913 the swimming pool opened. Both children and adults put the new pool and showers to good use during the hot summer months. Irishtown women flocked to the laundry, paying 10¢ per load. Madge, pointing out that most houses in the area still had no running water, recalled that when the Civic League first opened a playground on Manchester Street, it had been responsible for getting a water hydrant in the area, providing the first uncontaminated water for that neighborhood. The next year the League had secured two fire hydrants and a public drinking fountain. Most families still carried water from these for drinking and for household uses. Thus, the laundry, showers, and swimming pool of Lincoln School proved to be valuable assets to the entire community.[19]

The school continued to be a rousing success. Robert Todd Lincoln donated a portrait of his father, and by autumn 1913 the School Board found it necessary to appoint an extra first-grade teacher. The Civic League furnished a medical assistant to the school, and the state tuberculosis association gave additional equipment for the Outdoor School. As the news of this model institution spread, the *Ladies Home Journal* asked Madge to write a description and provide pictures of the project. By this time Madge was so deeply involved in the suffrage struggle that she could not find time to write the article herself. She did send pictures and information to Mary I. Wood of the *Journal* staff, who then wrote an article about Lincoln School. In spring 1914 newspapers as far away as San Jose, California, carried stories of the school.[20]

Although Lincoln School remained dear to Madge's heart, her election to the presidency of KERA required her to spend most of her time and energy on suffrage. Under her guidance KERA lost much of its evangelical tone and became more organized and bureaucratic but also more exciting as she embraced a variety of new tactics. One historian has called her "a good public speaker, an inspiring and innovative leader, and a

Outdoor School on the roof of Lincoln School. Courtesy of Special Collections and Digital Programs, Margaret I. King Library, University of Kentucky, Lexington.

skilled administrator." She initiated hikes for suffrage, with women following the lines of the Cincinnati Southern Railroad in relays, making speeches along the way. The hikes were supplemented with automobile trips through the Bluegrass, especially on county court days when rural people came to town. "Since we have come along in the pink tea of the suffrage fight there is no reason that we should make a funeral of it," Madge proclaimed. She adopted the publicity technique of setting up suffrage tents at fairs and other places of interest. At the Blue Grass Fair the Fayette County Equal Rights Association attracted much attention with its suffrage tent; the *Herald* urged people to "drop in at the tent" and promised "a couch where you may take a nap if the suffragists will stop talking to you long enough." Suffragists gave speeches at almost every teachers' institute, which usually resulted in the formation of a county suffrage league. To further stimulate interest, KERA offered prizes to schools, colleges, and other institutions of higher learning for the best papers written on the subject of woman suffrage. Not everyone favored these tactics, however, and Laura Clay warned her successor that such activities as parades and hikes might not be popular with the main body of people.[21]

Suffragists became indignant in April 1913 when the Kentucky Education Association (KEA) denied them a place on its program, even though Madge had specifically asked to be heard. The *Lexington Leader* expressed the opinion that KEA had refused because equal rights would mean equal pay for female instructors. Officials of KEA denied that allegation, but they undoubtedly were chagrined when KERA set up a tent next to the KEA meeting place, passed out suffrage literature, and made speeches at various times throughout the day.[22]

Perhaps Madge's greatest contribution to the cause consisted of making suffrage interesting and arousing people from their apathy. Her techniques of organization and administration seemed to work, despite Laura Clay's reservations. In the first year of her presidency, KERA membership rose from 1,779 to 4,655 and by the end of 1914 it stood at 10,577. This growth resulted in part from the method Madge devised of distributing non-dues-paying membership cards at meetings after someone at the meeting called for forming a suffrage organization. This gave KERA an expanded list of contacts with whom to correspond, though many of these groups represented mere paper organizations. In early February 1913 KERA established its first official state headquarters in the McClelland Building in Lexington. About the same time they hired Urey Estes, a Kentucky graduate of the University of Chicago, to organize new suffrage leagues in the state. Madge confided: "I frankly confess that the idea of ordering about and 'bossing' such a man in the execution of our work is extremely attractive to me. Why, in some small town, he ought to attract almost as much attention as a fire engine." In addition to Estes, KERA hired Ora Adams, Mercer County school superintendent, as a full-time suffrage speaker for part of the summer.[23]

Madge did not confine her suffrage interest to the United States. She followed the movement in other countries as well, especially Great Britain. During these years the militant British suffragettes, led by Emmeline Pankhurst, made headlines throughout the United States for their assaults on Parliament. Most of the press criticized their tactics, but the *Lexington Herald* proved to be an exception. Both Madge and Desha had formed favorable opinions of Pankhurst when she spoke to the NAWSA convention in Louisville in 1911, and they continued to admire the British suffragette, although Madge did not fully endorse the use of violence, believing the tactics used by the British militants would not be necessary to win the vote in the United States.[24]

Madge enjoyed bringing to the state unusual speakers who would arouse interest in suffrage and generate extensive publicity for the cause. One such person she brought to Kentucky in 1913 was Ethel Snowden, the wife of Philip Snowden, a member of the British Parliament and future chancellor of the exchequer. A militant who had been arrested in England, called a "wicked suffragette," and disowned by her family for supporting her husband's Labour Party, Snowden gave a speech in Lexington in 1913 that, according to the *Herald*, "electrified" the audience. After the lecture Madge announced that KERA planned to get a bill introduced at the next legislative session that would grant Kentucky women full suffrage.[25]

Madge also brought the controversial Max Eastman to Lexington. A writer and a socialist, Eastman in 1909 had organized the Men's League for Woman Suffrage because, he said, "to me it seemed the big fight for freedom in my time." Speaking in Louisville and Lexington in November 1913, he opposed the "romantic" idea that woman suffrage would lead to moral elevation and purification of politics in the United States but urged it as a simple act of justice.[26]

Madge herself also made speeches across the commonwealth and beyond its borders during the year. From Paducah in the west to Middlesboro in the east, she traveled, forming a new suffrage association here, revitalizing an old one there. She spoke to the state convention of the Federation of Women's Clubs, to a gathering of Kentucky newspaper editors, and to college groups. At Georgetown she urged the audience, which included many college students, to let Congressman James Campbell Cantrill, a Georgetown native, know of their support for a federal woman suffrage amendment. At the State University in Lexington she spoke "with great force and logical argument" to a somewhat hostile group, ridiculing the idea that women should not vote because they could not fight in the defense of their country. If necessary, she said, women could fight and they could pull hair. The editor of the school's newspaper, the *Idea*, responded in a somewhat facetious way to her speech: "We who have the misfortune to belong to the unlawful and heartless sterner sex felt that the great lives of our able statesmen had been lived in vain, and prayed that the mountains might fall on us to hide us from the wrath to come." But in a more serious tone, he concluded: "Mrs. Breckinridge is an old State student and we are proud that she is courageous enough to have the spirit to stand by her convictions even against great odds."[27]

Not all editors proved as generous in evaluating the suffrage leader as the young editor of the *Idea.* Indeed, in 1913 acrimony expressed against the suffrage movement by Kentucky's preeminent newspaperman reached unparalleled levels. Henry Watterson's attacks in the *Louisville Courier-Journal* provoked sharp replies from both Madge and Desha. Watterson had long opposed woman suffrage, at least in part, the Breckinridges charged, because of his alliance with whiskey interests. In April 1913 Watterson responded to the Snowden visit with vitriolic editorials saying, in Madge's words, "impolite things about all women who are suffragists." His attack proved, she said, that the old southern "belief in an aristocratic form of government, in the divine right of certain persons or classes of persons to rule, has always continually interfered with Mr. Watterson's attempt to be a Democrat. The people, to him, are the mob." In response to the editor's contention that the *Courier-Journal* had always supported the emancipation of women from the thralldom of the Middle Ages, she replied: "If the Courier could only wake up and find that we are no longer fighting about the Middle Ages, but are somewhat concerned with matters of the twentieth century, the superior quality of its male leadership might be more readily acknowledged by Kentucky women."[28]

Instead, Watterson continued his attack on the movement, predicting that if women were granted an unrestricted right to vote, it would cause as much "havoc" as did the Fifteenth Amendment, which enfranchised "a race unfit by antecedents and education to exercise the rights conferred upon it." Women, rather, should be protected from the "passion and dirt of party politics," lest they become the "insane, self-exploiting and self-seeking women of the Pankhurst type" who were about to begin a "sex war" that would end in "rebellion to God." A *Herald* editorial charged Watterson with "suffragephobia," and stated: "It comes with but ill grace from the venerable editor of The Louisville Courier-Journal to prate as a moralist or to attempt to classify & describe with invidious and vicious innuendo, those the laces of whose shoes he is unfit to tie."[29]

These stinging broadsides finally led to a confrontation between the two editors. In an exchange of letters Watterson called Desha Breckinridge "an unmanly man and a dishonest journalist" and implied that he would physically fight the Lexington editor if he were not too old and infirm. Desha responded: "You claim exemption from attack or insult because of your age and condition. You do not let sex, age, or conditions bar your brutal attacks, on those who lead the movement for votes for women." He added: "My wife, the daughter of a man who was your friend and whose friend you professed to be, is the official head of that movement in Kentucky. I have in the past let my regard for your age and condition keep me from characterizing as they deserved utterances and actions of yours." He continued: "Your characterization, denunciation and slander of those the hem of whose garment you are not fit to touch demands that someone tell the truth to and about you." To Madge, who was out of town when the controversy erupted, Desha wrote that if Watterson "keeps on I'll make his name a by-word in Kentucky so that there will be none to do him honor except those who use him for their own purposes." (The conflict between the two editors over distribution of federal patronage in Kentucky by Woodrow Wilson's administration, especially Desha's desire for the position of collector of internal revenue, probably exacerbated their differences over suffrage.)[30]

Events had carried both parties a great distance from that day in May 1898 when Watterson had written Desha: "I was very much disappointed in failing to see you when in Lexington. . . . Allow me to congratulate you [upon his coming marriage] with all my heart. You are going to get one of the sweetest girls in the world and to enter one of the sweetest families." Even in 1911, a mere two years before the heated exchange, Desha had written Watterson that "my regard for your judgment is so great that . . . [your] advice . . . is conclusive with me."[31]

Although Watterson might have been the most vehement antisuffrage editor in the state, his paper was by no means the only one to oppose giving women the vote. In January 1913, the *Louisville Evening Post* refuted the claims made by suffragists that the lack of political power constituted an important factor in the wage differential between men and women. In a lengthy letter to the editor Madge answered this argument, asserting that the industrial changes that had thrust women into the marketplace had made the ballot more necessary to them than ever. Citing a study made by the Russell Sage Foundation, which had concluded that the vast majority of working girls received less than a living wage, she averred: "The principle that the laborer is worthy of his hire should not be violated in the case of the young girl worker." Yet she admitted: "No woman suffragist who isn't a fool believes that wages will rise automatically with the granting of the suffrage."[32]

In the midst of all these controversies on the home front, Madge still found time for several trips outside the state. In February, according to the *Herald*, she "captured the hearts of Tennessee solons" with her "intelligent analysis" of the suffrage question in a speech to the legislature of that state. In April she went to St. Louis to attend the Mississippi Valley Suffrage Conference. Despite experiencing difficulties with the trains and arriving in St. Louis almost a day late, she found the meeting to be a valuable experience because women from eighteen states compared their methods and experiences. Although many others seemed to like her speech, "What Women May Do for Women through the Ballot," she considered it "pretty bad."[33]

A short time later, at the height of Desha's confrontation with Watterson, Madge embarked on a suffrage tour in Virginia with her mother, who accompanied her as far as Henry Clay McDowell Jr.'s home in Lynchburg. Though rather conservative, Henry expressed pride in his sister's work, noting to Mrs. McDowell, "I have bragged a great deal about Madge here and I want these people to hear her." Nevertheless, he could not be persuaded to introduce her when she spoke in Lynchburg, as Madge laughingly informed her audience. She lectured in several cities, citing the liquor interests and organized vice as the chief opponents of woman suffrage. One man who heard her speak in Richmond, Virginia, wrote Desha Breckinridge that "she was master of her subject, and, with it, convincing," adding, "this is no empty flattery." At another stop, in Staunton, Madge discovered that "one old man had ridden in 50 miles from Bath county to hear a woman speak. . . . He expressed himself as not at all convinced—he thought I wasn't following St. Paul's injunction to keep silent—but he had evidently enjoyed his evening." Virginia suffragist Lila Meade Valentine accompanied Madge on a visit to the governor's wife, and based on that experience as well as speaking with people in her audiences, Madge concluded that Virginia had much further to go than Kentucky before woman suffrage could succeed. From Virginia, Madge went on to New York, while her mother returned home. During this trip she also attended a meeting of the National Association for the Study and Prevention of Tuberculosis in Washington, DC, and, thus inspired, renewed her efforts to get Fayette County to build a sanatorium.[34]

Keeping up such an intense schedule would have taxed the most robust person, and, in fact, Madge reported to Laura Clay that she was working herself to death. Yet despite the fact that her health remained fragile, she seemed to do well during most of the year. Her physician, Josephine Hunt, one of Lexington's first female doctors, wanted to see her weight increase to 135 pounds and prescribed a diet that included eating all the foods she liked best, drinking cream with two eggs between meals, and taking a spoonful of olive oil after each meal. Hunt also recommended two hours of rest each day after lunch, though it seems unlikely that Madge followed that recommendation. She did, however, relax in September, when she and Desha went to French Lick Springs Hotel in Indiana to take the baths and drink the mineral water. Even then, she stopped in Louisville for a suffrage meeting on the way. Though she drank the water, she protested: "I can't say I enjoy the job." Nevertheless, she added: "I am enjoying Desha: or does that go without saying?"[35]

While in New York City in October 1913, Madge met with Alva Belmont and invited her to attend the upcoming KERA convention. Belmont had other commitments but donated $200 to the cause. Most important, Madge went to Madison Square Garden to hear Emmeline Pankhurst. When immigration officials had attempted to prevent Pankhurst from coming ashore when she arrived in the United States for her speaking tour, the *Herald* had defended her, proclaiming her detainment "unjust." Madge found the British suffragette's appearance to be "very charming," but a closer look revealed her to be pale, much thinner, and older-looking than she had been two years before. After listening to her, Madge found herself "ready to admit that the advance of the suffrage both in England and in this country is principally due to the militant agitation," and said she had begun to think perhaps the militants were right in their approach. Madge later reported her favorable impression of Pankhurst to the Fayette ERA.[36]

On her return home Madge prepared for the annual KERA convention to be held in November. She insisted her mother attend, because "I want you first for the pleasure of having you & then I want you to add prestige to the cause for Mr. Watterson's benefit." Evidence of the success of her first year as president showed at the convention, where more than five times as many delegates attended as the year before. Although she did not believe there was any chance the next legislature would pass it, Madge worked diligently at the convention to lay plans for the introduction of a bill to provide a state constitutional amendment giving women the vote.[37]

Shortly after beginning her second year as KERA president, Madge left for Washington, DC, to attend the national convention. At the

NAWSA convention she made a rousing speech calling for the enactment of a federal constitutional amendment for woman suffrage. At this time NAWSA used its resources to campaign for state woman suffrage amendments as well as a federal amendment. Many southerners opposed a federal amendment on states' rights grounds, concerned that such an amendment would bring about federal intervention in southern elections and overturn the various devices they had contrived to eliminate the votes of black men. Others believed that an extension of the franchise was an issue belonging to the states, as it had until the passage of the Fifteenth Amendment.[38]

In 1913 Louisiana suffragist Kate M. Gordon, who had resigned from the NAWSA board in 1909 because of its support for a federal amendment, formed the Southern States Woman Suffrage Conference (SSWSC) to work for suffrage by state amendments only. When Gordon sought to recruit Madge to her cause, Laura Clay accurately warned her that Breckinridge "was not a States' Rights Woman." Madge, who wanted suffrage however it might be obtained, signed the call by Gordon to hold an organizational meeting for a southern suffrage society, but ultimately she declined to join SSWSC. Nevertheless, she exploited southerners' fear of a federal amendment by pointing out in her speech at the NAWSA convention that if southern men opposed a federal amendment, they should immediately grant women the vote by state action.[39]

Dissatisfaction with Anna Howard Shaw's weak leadership, her lack of organizational skills, and her inability to control dissent within NAWSA continued to grow. The National found itself challenged by the SSWSC to work only for state amendments and by still another group to work only for a federal amendment. The Congressional Union (CU), led by Alice Paul and Lucy Burns, had begun as the Congressional Committee of NAWSA but soon broke away when the National rejected a policy of focusing all its efforts on a federal amendment. The CU adopted some of the civil disobedience tactics of the militant British suffragettes. Later renamed the Woman's Party, this group's members soon became distinguished from the old-line suffragists, and the name "suffragette" came to be applied to them. Although Madge felt that adopting such tactics as hunger strikes and civil disobedience would not be necessary in the United States, Sophonisba believed there was "no reason to think that she would not have done so had she thought the denial of the women's claim sufficiently persistent" to leave no other choice.[40]

In 1913 the chance that Congress would pass a federal amendment, while not good, appeared better than it had been for years. The former Senate Woman Suffrage Committee had been reactivated in spring 1913 and had reported the amendment favorably. Although proponents could not muster enough support in the Senate to pass it at this time, at least they had taken the initial step. As the NAWSA convention met in Washington, Woodrow Wilson made his first State of the Union address. His failure to mention woman suffrage infuriated the women, and they quickly organized a march on the White House. Madge, along with Anna Howard Shaw and Mrs. Medill McCormick, daughter of the late Republican leader Mark Hanna, led a group representing each state to the White House. The president pled illness, so the women had to wait a few days before seeing him, only to learn that he would not try to influence Congress. Nearly a thousand women later converged at the capitol to urge the House to create a standing committee on woman suffrage. As one of the speakers who addressed the House Rules Committee, Madge urged lawmakers to hurry with the federal amendment lest Kentucky beat them to it by state amendment. These events marked the beginning of more assertive tactics on the part of suffragists in trying to pressure the president and Congress. This especially exciting convention culminated with the election of new officers, including Madge as second vice president and member of its Congressional Committee, and Jane Addams as first vice president. Dr. Shaw remained president. Madge's election, said the *Louisville Herald*, was an honor to Kentucky and was due to "her spirit, intellect and enthusiasm."[41]

As a fitting tribute to her 1912–13 term as president of KERA, the *Lexington Leader* provided its readers with a full account of Madeline McDowell Breckinridge's achievements. While she had accomplished much in the previous two years, much remained to be done as she developed her strategy for lobbying the upcoming meeting of the Kentucky General Assembly for a woman suffrage amendment and planned once again to extend her suffrage speeches across the country.[42]

Chapter 8

"An able speaker, a brilliant woman" 1914–1915

In 1914 Madge determined to work with even greater zeal for suffrage on both the state and national level. As Sophonisba noted, Madge "was not sure that only through the federal amendment would all the women of the United States become politically free, but she was perfectly willing to obtain the vote by that method." Yet she never forgot that both congressmen and state legislators answered to their constituents and that federal amendments had to be ratified by three-fourths of the states. Thus, she realized that additional states needed to adopt woman suffrage in order to increase the pressure in Washington for a federal amendment and to ensure that when Congress passed such an amendment, the requisite number of states would ratify.[1]

Madge also knew that many in Congress opposed woman suffrage, including her own congressman, J. Campbell Cantrill. After her return from Washington in December 1913, she continued the effort to get Cantrill and other members of the House Rules Committee to create a special woman suffrage committee. She even persuaded the local suffrage association in Cantrill's hometown of Georgetown to pass a resolution asking him to support creation of such a committee. A number of his friends also promised to talk to him. While Madge believed that he was "an utterly hopeless party, as he belongs to the liquor people," she also felt "a little 'pestering' can't do any harm and, at least, it will be good for him to know that his friends and neighbors are interested in Woman Suffrage." In a telegram to the congressman she urged him "in the name of thousands of women of Kentucky who earnestly desire and are anxious to secure the right of the ballot" to vote for creating a committee; however, in keeping with her assessment, he voted against the proposal. In a letter to the editor of the *Herald*, a writer, probably Madge, signing herself "A Woman of the Ashland District," called upon the congressman to explain his position, asking whether he also opposed a state amendment, and, if so, why?[2]

Cantrill's actions led a group of women, including Madge, to begin an attempt to defeat him in the next election. They sponsored the candidacy of Claude Thomas of Paris in the Democratic primary, but he was "woefully beaten." "Cantrill is a perfectly outrageous person," Madge asserted, "but he had the money and the organization of the whiskey interests behind him." Cantrill, however, did not stand alone as the only Kentucky politician who exasperated Madge. In spring 1914, when a majority in the U.S. Senate (but not the necessary two-thirds majority) voted for a woman suffrage amendment, Kentucky senator Ollie James spoke against it, claiming that the women of his state did not want the vote. In a *Herald* editorial Madge angrily asked by what authority James spoke for Kentucky women. She further warned that if the Democratic Party "wishes to be a party of the living and not the dead," it had to give tangible evidence of its commitment to democracy.[3]

Because many senators and representatives held views similar to those of Cantrill and James, little chance existed in 1914 for the passage of a federal amendment for woman suffrage. In Kentucky as well, Madge saw little hope for an amendment; yet when the General Assembly convened in January, she led KERA in a massive campaign to get the legislature to pass and submit to voters a suffrage amendment that had been drafted by her cousin, Louisville attorney Robert A. McDowell. She had thoroughly prepared for the session by making sure legislators received literature and letters from their local Equal Rights Associations, and KERA supplied members of the General Assembly and forty-three newspaper editors with four-month subscriptions to the *Woman's Journal*, a publication of NAWSA. In addition, Madge raised money from Kentuckians and others to finance the lobbying effort.[4]

KERA established a headquarters in Frankfort for the duration of the legislative session, and Madge opened the campaign by addressing members of the General Assembly in the lobby of the Capital Hotel on January 7. Most of them appeared friendly, and, even though not necessarily interested in suffrage, seemed to have concluded that they should learn more about the subject. This led to passage of a resolution asking both Madge and Laura Clay to address a joint session of the legislature. When the two women spoke to a "standing room only" crowd in the House Chamber on

Laura Clay, founder of the Kentucky Equal Rights Association. Courtesy of Special Collections and Digital Programs, Margaret I. King Library, University of Kentucky, Lexington.

January 15, it marked the first time a woman had addressed a joint session. Women came from all over central Kentucky to witness the event. Madge asserted to the group that "the woman question is the most important political question we are confronted with today." She continued by pointing out the vital role women had played in the state in improving laws and fighting "political corruption, vice, and filth."[5]

Desha could not restrain his desire to editorialize on this event. He realized people might think his views prejudiced by his "relation to one of the gentlewomen who spoke," but he insisted he could be frank and just. "By the instinctive turn of our mind and by habit of thought," he admitted he was as likely as anyone to oppose woman suffrage. Although a late convert to the cause, he could now think of no valid argument against woman suffrage. He found the arguments of both his wife and Laura Clay "unanswerable." "We confess, confidentially," he said, "that we were rather predisposed in Mrs. Breckinridge's favor; but we know that because of that predisposition we are a more severe critic than is any other." All his life, he noted, he had heard great speakers, and these two women ranked among the best, making it impossible to argue that the women of Kentucky were not equal to men "in intellect, in courage and in sense of duty."[6]

Madge spoke again on January 21, along with Nevada suffragist Anne H. Martin, to a group of about four hundred in the Capital Hotel. Martin later delivered a suffrage speech at the Fayette County Courthouse. Other meetings followed, and the bill providing for submission to the voters of a state woman suffrage amendment received a favorable report from committees in both houses. A constitutional provision allowing only two amendments to be offered in one election stymied the effort, however. Two amendments had been passed at the previous session and had been voted on, but the secretary of state had not advertised them properly, so the Court of Appeals ruled they must be resubmitted to voters. This provided reluctant legislators with the excuse they needed for voting against the suffrage amendment, and the house defeated the measure 51-29. Madge felt some of the speeches made against it were "rather distressing to a Kentuckian with any State pride." However, she believed the effort had not been in vain. The cause had made new converts among legislators and women across the commonwealth.[7]

Madge seized the opportunity to extend the KERA organization as she tirelessly spoke for the cause, across state and nation. In March she attended a NAWSA meeting in New York and in April proclaimed at a suffrage rally in Boston that when women won the vote, they would not allow children to "work under inhumane conditions, for the mothers will protect them with the ballots in their hands." The next day she reportedly became the second woman to be allowed to speak at Harvard University. In Louisville that same month she addressed the annual Conference on Education in the South with "Why Suffrage Should Be Granted Women." Later in the spring she organized a mass meeting at the Opera House in Lexington, where she, Grace Abbott of the University of Chicago, and Frances Ingram, a social settlement worker in Louisville, spoke on various aspects of the women's movement. On May 1 KERA held an automobile parade to celebrate Universal Suffrage Day. Later in the month, despite misgivings about leaving her ill mother, Madge traveled to Memphis for a meeting of the National Conference of Charities and Correction, where she talked about Lincoln School and social hygiene. While in Memphis she enjoyed the company of Grace and Edith Abbott as well as Sophonisba, whom she described to Desha as "the sweetest thing in the world." After her return to Kentucky, she conducted a whirlwind tour across the state, speaking in seven cities. She then returned to Lexington for still another speech before leaving for a NAWSA board meeting in Chicago, where she gave a talk at the banquet, spent some time with Nisba, and emerged rested and "fat." (Madge usually weighed in the vicinity of 110 pounds.) She attempted to get Desha to accompany her to Chicago, but he declined in favor of attending his twenty-fifth reunion at Princeton.[8]

In addition to many speeches in Kentucky, Madge made a total of thirty-two talks outside the state during 1914. In June she visited Cincinnati, Chicago, and Washington, DC. While in the nation's capital, she, Dr. Anna Howard Shaw, and Jane Addams delivered a petition to the vice president and the Speaker of the House with the signatures of 462,000 suffragists calling for a federal amendment. She then traveled to Columbus, Ohio, in August, and on to Missouri and Nebraska in September, spending a week in each state. October found her again in Cincinnati.[9]

During summer 1914, KERA hired a woman to help organize the suffrage work. By August the Fayette ERA had acquired more than a thousand members and hoped to use the *Herald*'s tent at the Blue Grass Fair to double that number. In addition, teachers' institutes around the state hosted suffrage speakers. Madge had some difficulties in arranging for the annual KERA convention because of her numerous engagements. Finally, the board set the place and date for November 5–7 at Owensboro.

Louisiana suffragist Kate Gordon became the keynote speaker, despite the fact that Madge disagreed with Gordon's opposition to a federal amendment and had declined membership in the SSWSC. Nevertheless, the convention proved a great success, and Madge could point to a tenfold increase in membership since she had assumed leadership only two years before.[10]

As she concluded the KERA convention, Madge prepared to leave for the NAWSA convention to be held November 12–17 in Nashville. The National continued to experience dissension over how much emphasis to place on the federal, or Susan B. Anthony, amendment, as well as what to do about the weak leadership of its president, Dr. Anna Howard Shaw. Because the Anthony amendment used the same language as the Fifteenth Amendment (except that it substituted the word "sex" for "race"), many southerners opposed it on states' rights grounds. Kate Gordon and her SSWSC led this group. Living in Louisiana where blacks comprised nearly one-half of the population, Gordon served as a prime example of the suffragist who was an extreme racist and hard-line defender of states' rights. She opposed the federal amendment adamantly and once wrote Madge: "We are working the negro prejudice to our advantage."[11]

A portion of the states' rights advocates and a few others in NAWSA supported the Shaforth-Palmer federal amendment, which had been proposed by NAWSA's Congressional Committee, headed by Ruth Hanna McCormick, in the hope of placating the states' rights suffragists. This amendment provided that in any state where 8 percent of the voters petitioned for a woman suffrage amendment to the state constitution, that state would be required to hold a referendum. This would have enfranchised women only if the amendment submitted in the referendum were approved. A halfway measure that did not appease many of those in the states' rights group, the proposal also failed to satisfy most other suffragists. As one historian has noted, the Shaforth-Palmer amendment "pleased no one and nearly split the organization." McCormick defended it by explaining to the state suffrage presidents that "the doctrine of states rights does not alone stand against suffrage, back of that is the race question." Thus, suffragists needed to ascertain whether politicians opposed a federal amendment "because it was repugnant to the state's rights doctrine, or whether they were hiding behind that doctrine because of prejudice against the cause" of woman suffrage itself.[12]

Madge, as a member of the Congressional Committee in charge of congressional work for the southern states, made her position clear from the very beginning: she would take suffrage any way she could get it. She refused to let the race issue or constitutional doctrines interfere with her true goal—the ballot. According to Sophonisba, she was "inclined to go with Mrs. McCormick's Congressional Committee . . . though she was never convinced either of its intrinsic value nor of the wisdom of appearing to lobby actively for" it. After the convention, Madge noted to McCormick: "You know that I am personally very doubtful about the value of the Shaforth, yet in spite of myself, in Nashville I was warmly arguing for it." She added that work on the national level was a "knotty problem" and that she felt unequal to deciding what would be the wisest course.[13]

Other problems arose for NAWSA when the CU adopted the English suffragettes' technique of holding the party in power responsible and trying to defeat its candidates. Madge, although not as critical of Alice Paul and the CU as some of the other NAWSA leaders, nevertheless noted that while the CU wanted NAWSA to cooperate with it, its leaders seemed unwilling to reciprocate. "I rather think that sort of unity out of the question," she concluded. The tactic of holding the party in power responsible was one she opposed more than she did many of the other so-called militant tactics of the CU. She sent a letter to former *Herald* employee Jouett Shouse, now a Kansas state senator who was running for a seat in the U.S. House of Representatives, assuring him that NAWSA would not try to defeat Democrats in Kansas and stating that if any group planned to do so, it was the CU. She noted that Paul once led NAWSA's Congressional Committee, of which Madge herself was now a member, but explained that the National had severed its connection with the CU eight months earlier. She told her friend that Kansas "could not have a better representative in Congress than you."[14]

The NAWSA convention maintained its nonpartisan stance and achieved a truce of sorts when it adopted a resolution pledging not to campaign against any member of Congress without the consent of the suffrage association of that state and not to hold any political party responsible for the acts of any individual member. The Congressional Committee also announced its intention to work for the Shaforth amendment because its members doubted the Anthony amendment could be passed until more states enacted woman suffrage. Thus, differences over the Anthony and Shaforth amendments as well as states' rights continued to plague NAWSA. Madge took a moderate course in these controversies.

She favored trying to defeat antisuffrage candidates and continued to support both state and federal amendments.[15]

In these controversies she played a peripheral role. However, she occupied a central position in the most divisive issue of the 1914 convention. Dissatisfaction had been growing with the leadership of the president, Dr. Anna Howard Shaw, for quite some time. A fine public speaker, Shaw had proven to be a disorganized and weak administrator. By 1914 a strong sentiment existed among suffragists outside the Northeast to replace her with a more effective leader. Madge was one of those who saw the need for change, noting on one occasion that "perhaps we haven't the wisest person in charge." When Sophonisba reported that New York suffragists seemed completely out of touch with the feeling of suffragists elsewhere on the issue of Shaw's leadership, Madge replied: "The Dr. Shaw matter does begin to seem hopeless. I suppose we will just drift along as before." As the time drew near for the convention, however, a group of women within the organization decided to attempt to persuade Shaw to accept a position as president emerita and become a full-time lecturer, leaving the way open for the election of a new president with more administrative ability.[16]

The person favored for the presidency was Madeline McDowell Breckinridge. In early November, Gertrude L. Leonard asked Madge whether she would accept the position if Shaw agreed to step down or, if Shaw refused, would be willing to fight for the office. Madge agonized over the problem. She believed "if Miss Shaw will never consent peaceably to get out[,] somebody ought to make the fight." As she wavered on this decision, Madge sought Sophonisba's advice. After talking it over with Jane Addams, Sophonisba replied that she and Addams both thought Madge "the very best presidential material in the country," but they agreed that even if Madge should fight Shaw and win, the "difficulties growing out of Miss Shaw's antagonisms would make the position so difficult as to render the sacrifice of time and strength really futile." In a caucus before the opening of the convention Dr. Shaw flatly refused to accept the office of president emerita and allow Breckinridge to become president without a contest. Upon hearing this, Madge declined to challenge the incumbent and was subsequently reelected second vice president.[17]

Madge's role in the 1914 NAWSA convention earned plaudits from a number of people. Her cousin wrote Aunt Mag that he had enjoyed visiting with Madge in Nashville "and seeing how she was looked up to by everybody else." Jane Addams likewise wrote her friend how much she admired her actions in Nashville and appreciated all her efforts. In addition, Sophonisba applauded her sister-in-law: "It is sweet to see how in all the accounts there is a total lack of suggestion of self-seeking or anything but devotion on your part." She added: "I care so much for the things that you can do and that practically you alone can do that I hate to have your strength taken with futile and exhausting bickering."[18]

Still, Madge's refusal to challenge Shaw for the presidency did not bring peace to the organization. Madge soon became embroiled in a controversy within the Executive Board, one exacerbated by Shaw's resentment of the Kentuckian's earlier proposed candidacy. The controversy concerned the selection of Jane Addams as vice president. Apparently, Addams had written Shaw a letter stating she would accept the position of "honorary" vice president on the condition that her name not be used to endorse official actions of the Executive Board. Then she had written a second letter refusing the office and had sent a copy to Madge. At the board meeting Shaw read only the first letter until Madge reminded her there was a second one and stated she had a copy. Shaw then presented only a portion of the second letter, making it seem as if Addams would accept the position so long as the board did not use her name to endorse its actions. Madge continued to argue that Addams had refused the office, but the board followed Shaw's recommendation and elected her anyway. Subsequently, Addams declined the position and thanked her Kentucky friend for her efforts. Shaw evidently then blamed Madge for Addams's withdrawal. As a result, Madge decided that it would be best to resign from the board because she could no longer work in harmony with Shaw. Both Addams and Sophonisba persuaded her not to resign immediately, because to do so would expose schisms within the organization.[19]

On February 5 Madge wrote Dr. Shaw, officially resigning from the position of second vice president of NAWSA. The resignation was to take effect no later than April 1, although Shaw did not announce it and seek a replacement until the June meeting of the Executive Board. In explaining the resignation to a New York suffragist, Madge said she did not resign in order to have her feelings soothed but because she felt her time could be better spent on some other aspect of suffrage work. She added: "I wish that I had several different lives, and that one of them might be given to suffrage. As it is, I want to give all I can spare out of this one for suffrage." To continued suggestions that she make a fight against Shaw for the presidency of the NAWSA, she gave a firm: "No." As she noted to Kate Gordon: "I have so many other responsibilities besides suffrage that I have to fight for time and must regret any useless waste of it."[20]

Swiftly on the heels of the NAWSA convention, Madge embarked on a speaking trip across the South—going to New Orleans, Houston, Galveston, Austin, Dallas, Tuscaloosa, Birmingham, Montgomery, Columbus, Atlanta, Savannah, and Augusta. The suffrage campaign totaled three weeks, and she spent seven nights sleeping on a train and making at least one speech every day except Sunday. Over and over, she argued that the South had the greatest need for woman suffrage, "and it is in the South that we encounter the most difficulty" in getting it. Furthermore, she explained why women required the vote:

> It is the sphere of government that has changed; not the sphere of women. The government has grown away from the foundation principles. The women are only demanding the vote to keep the rights which they had when the government was founded. The original purpose of our government was to control measures for offense and defense. Now it has branched out into a thousand directions. It has taken charge of the schools; women have always been the educators. It has interested itself in charities and hospitals; from the beginning, nursing the sick and aiding neighbors were duties imposed on the women. In order to maintain their positions as teachers and neighbors women have had to go out and seek the vote. I do not say that had the government not been slowly developing into a paternal government[,] women would not have sought the ballot. I am a democrat and as such I believe in the right of women to vote.[21]

Newspapers across the South gave Madge's speeches extensive, and usually favorable, coverage. The *Houston Post* reported that "as the great-granddaughter of Henry Clay, she is said to have inherited his power of oratory combined with a degree of personal magnetism that has made her one of the foremost public speakers of her sex in the South." An Atlanta paper called her "an able speaker, a brilliant woman, a leader in the various movements which have kept the progressive women of the country busy for many years." When sending newspaper clippings about the speeches to her mother, Madge noted with wry humor: "I am sure you are tired of reading newspaper notices of me and the same old speech—so don't read the enclosed if you don't want to."[22]

Along the way in her travels she ran into former Lexington residents and an old friend from Miss Porter's School. All in all, she had a "good time" on the trip and experienced only one major disappointment. Desha had to make a trip to New York City, while Madge planned to attend a meeting there, so they hoped to get together and have a few days of vacation. "I am quite excited over the idea of seeing you in New York, and am very glad we are going—Even if it is only a little bit of a holiday, we'll have the trip back together," she wrote Desha. However, it was not to be; Madge's meeting was postponed, so she extended her speaking engagements in the South. "It seemed to me I couldn't get reconciled—I was looking forward to the little holiday with you so much . . . and it seemed too good to be true to do my duty and yet get the fun of being with you," she lamented. "I think you have a right to feel positively bitter about it," she concluded, "but I must stop crying over skimmed milk & the trouble I gave you now. And maybe time will finally pass till we see each other again—And then I'm not going away any more until you do." She added that she had received only two newspapers and two letters from Desha during the trip, "so if it hadn't been for the telegrams, I'd feel very like an orphan." As it happened, they both arrived back in Lexington on December 20, Madge a half hour before Desha, which allowed her to greet him "looking as if I had been here always." As for Desha, he found Madge appearing better than he expected after such a grueling expedition.[23]

While devoting most of the year to suffrage work, Madge felt she had "woefully neglected" Lincoln School. She continued to try to raise money for cots for the Outdoor School and solicited funds from Robert Todd Lincoln to finish the playground. She related how the effort to raise money to build the school had "nearly killed me," and noted that "toward the end, I took to trying to earn it, instead of begging it, by making speeches! Then I felt meaner than a sheep-killing dog when I took money for the speeches." She added: "I was pushed into the state suffrage work before this other job was complete and I must yet, when I can catch my breath, go back on it. My first experience reduced me to skin and bone and the upshot of all this is that I dread money raising as a burnt child dreads the fire." Yet she was able to close out the year with a Christmas celebration at Lincoln School. Somehow, during 1914 she also found time to help establish the Baby Health Service in Lexington, a privately funded organization to provide free baby formula and supplemental food to impoverished families.[24]

The Breckinridges celebrated New Year's Eve at a party held by their close friends Mary and Clarence LeBus at Hinata, their home on Russell Cave Pike outside Lexington. Both Madge and Desha needed relaxation and seemed vulnerable at this time. Often finding himself alone as Madge traveled for suffrage, Desha commented to his sister Curry: "I know you are lonely; I know whenever I have the blues I am lonely, no matter with whom I am . . . and . . . it doesn't make a damn bit of difference what I do or what anybody else does, and I just gather that you are in somewhat that condition that I have been in on numerous occasions, and that Madge gets in quite often." Madge seemed to deal with depression by immersing herself in work. As she confessed to a friend: "I know that often when one is in deep grief it is a relief to have something outside with which to busy one's thoughts and occupy one's time." This tactic she used again and again in the coming years, even when health concerns should have dictated rest and relaxation. In fact, in late January 1915 she embarked on a suffrage trip to Pennsylvania, then went on to New York.[25]

By this time the strain of so much traveling and speaking began to exert its toll on Madge. It was probably because of exhaustion that she at last consented to go on a three-week vacation with Desha in March. They went first to New York and then sailed for Bermuda. It was Desha's intention, she said, to take her to a place where she couldn't talk or even think about suffrage. Unfortunately, the weather in Bermuda proved to be cold, but they did get some much-needed rest.[26]

The vacation provided only a brief respite from suffrage work. Madge returned apparently reinvigorated and ready to extend her suffrage campaign in the South. In April she journeyed to North and South Carolina, where she described her travel as "one night stands . . . & much traveling to & fro." People often commented on the fact that she was Henry Clay's great-granddaughter and compared her oratorical powers to Clay's. Madge took advantage of this connection, noting that in North Carolina "the Raleigh newspaper came out with an article announcing that they would meet me at the train with a brass band and parade through the streets. It was an April Fool joke, but it made the suffragists tear their hair. They are trying to get suffrage there in the most lady-like manner, without having anybody find out they want it." Again she found her family connections helpful, commenting: "As I spoke under the portrait of my great-grandfather, and as he had dedicated the capitol in the forties, that lent a little respectability to me and suffrage. I think it also comforted them when the Bishop of North Carolina called, because he is one of my mother's Hart relatives."[27]

Madge encountered a hesitancy about suffrage in all of the southern states she visited, and she worked ardently to change that attitude. In June she toured Arkansas and then went on to spend a week in West Virginia. She planned a three-week effort in the campaign states of New York, New Jersey, and Massachusetts beginning in September, but by that time her health forced her to cancel those trips. The grueling work she subjected herself to is evident in the words of a West Virginia woman, written just after Madge's tour in that state: "I know you must have been worn to a frazzle with two street meetings the same day. I don't wonder that your family and friends are loath to have you leave their watchful eyes, for I don't believe you know how to take proper care of yourself."[28]

Despite all of the activity outside the state, Madge did not neglect her duties as president of KERA. She spoke in many places around the state and made sure suffrage speakers attended all teachers' institutes where the school superintendent had invited them. KERA barraged legislators, preachers, and newspaper editors with suffrage material. This work began to bear fruit as a number of organizations, including the Kentucky Federation of Women's Clubs, the Kentucky Methodist-Episcopal Conference, the Grange, the Christian Churches of Kentucky, the Women's Christian Temperance Union, the state American Federation of Labor, and the Progressive and Republican parties all endorsed woman suffrage in 1915. Membership in KERA rose to 15,557. Yet on different occasions Madge expressed feelings of frustration at the slow progress being made. Even the Fayette ERA, which had more than one thousand members, virtually ceased to exist except when there was a special speaker or entertainment, she lamented, and in 1920, on the verge of victory, she believed "there is not a corporal's guard of active suffragists in Kentucky." Near the end of 1915 she complained: "I feel desperate about the slight advance I find in real suffrage interest in Kentucky. We can get plenty of people to sign cards, but we cannot get anybody who cares enough to do anything."[29]

But politicians discouraged Madge the most. In January 1915, when the U.S. House of Representatives voted on the federal amendment, only one Kentucky congressman, John W. Langley, the lone Republican in the state delegation, supported the amendment. Madge warned Democrats

Banner of the Kentucky Equal Rights Association. Courtesy of the Kentucky Historical Society, Frankfort.

that the Republican Party was gaining the favor of suffragists. Later she won the promise of A. O. Stanley, Democratic gubernatorial candidate, not to veto a woman suffrage amendment if the legislature should agree to submit one to the voters. When Governor James B. McCreary called upon the women of Kentucky to participate in the preparedness campaign on the eve of America's entry into World War I, Madge replied with asperity, asking him how he expected women to feel any burden for preparedness when they were denied a voice in government. "Kentucky women," she warned, "are not idiots—even though they are closely related to Kentucky men. You can't ignore them and treat them as though they were kindergarten children, and then when work is needed expect them to do a man's share." Yet she also declined the invitation of the Woman's Peace Party to serve as "Peace Chairman for Kentucky," saying that "I believe in a certain amount of preparedness" and "I am keen that the United States should get in [World War I] on the side of the allies and help to bring about permanent peace by whipping Germany to a finish." Furthermore, she declared: "I consider that entirely peaceful, just as I would consider that forceful resistance to a burglar . . . was in the interest of law and order and permanent peace."[30]

Surely Madge's moments of discouragement were only temporary, because in 1915 she organized several spectacularly successful suffrage events. In April British suffragist Emmeline Pethick-Lawrence came to Lexington. A member of the Pankhurst group, she had gone to jail and participated in hunger strikes before being expelled from that organization in 1912 because she opposed the violent destruction of private property. Pethick-Lawrence gave a rousing speech at the Ben Ali Theatre, while Madge presided over the meeting and added many new members to the KERA roster.[31]

On May 1 KERA celebrated National Suffrage Day with a parade in Lexington culminating in speeches, folk dancing, and other activities at Duncan Park. A few days later the Fayette ERA presented a play, *How the Vote Was Won,* in the ballroom of the Phoenix Hotel. A suffrage film at the Ben Ali and a banquet at the Phoenix soon followed as suffragists geared up for a spring and summer full of activity. Madge's speech at the annual Federation of Women's Clubs' convention, "The Long Way Round or Otherwise," related the very slow process by which women had obtained the creation of various commissions and had secured passage of several laws such as school suffrage. Referring to the alleged reason the legislature had deprived women in second-class cities of school suffrage in 1902, she suggested satirically that women were once again in danger of losing school suffrage "since two women in Pike County sold their votes." The Federation convention closed with passage of a resolution calling for submission of a state amendment for woman suffrage at the next legislative session. Although fairly late in endorsing full suffrage, the Woman's Clubs, both in Kentucky and nationally, had long encouraged activities that stretched females from their traditional domestic sphere into the sphere of public activity. Thus, as one historian has noted, "the clubs were not estranged from feminism," but "made a significant contribution to women's struggle for autonomy." That had certainly proved to be the case for Madge, who gained much of her early public experience working as legislative chair for the Kentucky Federation of Women's Clubs.[32]

Undoubtedly Madge would have accomplished more in her third year as state suffrage leader if she had not again become ill with tuberculosis. As it was, by September she not only had to cancel speaking engagements in campaign states, she also found herself barely able to plan the annual KERA convention to be held in November 1915. In addition, her mother became virtually bedridden. Nevertheless, Madge persisted, and, disobeying doctor's orders for complete bed rest, produced a successful convention that proved a fitting conclusion to her three years as president. She asked all merchants in Lexington to decorate their store windows in yellow and to display a suffrage pennant, and she enlisted Mary LeBus to organize the banquet concluding the convention. Ethel Snowden again came to Lexington to speak. Madge held a reception at her mother's home for Snowden and all the convention delegates. In her closing address as president Madge stated her belief in rotation in office. Mrs. Thomas Jefferson (Elise) Smith, granddaughter of Cassius Marcellus Clay and niece of Laura Clay, became the new president. The convention voted to carry the fight to the state legislature again in 1916 and elected Madge as campaign chair to lead the struggle. Laura Clay urged her to reserve her strength, saying: "Remember there are a few things which no one can do so well as you; and limit yourself to them and leave other things to others who can do them, even if not quite so well as you." Another friend, commenting on a speech Madge had made, noted: "You *never* did better than that last night at Lexington. It was *superb.* If only I could have forgotten how worn out you were."[33]

Even in the midst of so much suffrage activity, Madge still somehow found time to promote the activities of the Civic League, Lincoln School, the Tuberculosis Society—which had evolved into the Public Health Nursing Association—and the Associated Charities. These organizations continued to be very much intertwined, with many of the same people serving on their boards and focusing on the same goals. For example, the Civic League helped raise money for Lincoln School, whose Outdoor School comprised an attempt to protect at-risk children from contracting tuberculosis.

In early 1915 Lincoln School's most critical problem concerned its milk supply. A local dairy had been donating fifteen gallons of skimmed milk and two quarts of cream daily. Outdoor School children consumed the cream and part of the skimmed milk, while the kindergarten and first grade used the remainder. When the owner of the dairy died, his executors discontinued the donations. The Civic League then began to purchase whole milk for the kindergarten and first grade. Madge began to seek contributions, either in money or in milk. She wrote Susanna (Mrs. Johnson) Camden of Versailles asking if the Camden dairy would supply the needs of the Outdoor School. She entreated: "I am sure you would feel like helping these little children if only you could see them," but added, "I do hope you will feel when I ask you anything that you must do just what you would do if a person you did not know, but in whose integrity you had confidence ask[ed] you. I do despise holding up friends." Mrs. Camden replied to this appeal with a check, saying it was easier to pay for the milk than to arrange for delivery from their dairy.[34]

In another attempt to raise money for the Outdoor School Madge helped sponsor a ball at the Phoenix Hotel. Funds went to purchase needed equipment, including cots, "Eskimo" suits, blankets, and sleeping bags. Madge also served on the board of the Public Health Nursing Association, which provided a medical helper at Lincoln School and also supplied about $75 per month for food for these children. Meanwhile, Lincoln School continued to be a beehive of community activity. Students were encouraged to grow small garden plots, and school officials passed out rakes and hoes very much as they did library books. A Mother's Club, Men's Saturday Night Gymnasium, Junior Citizen's League, and various social clubs used the school's facilities.[35]

The playground remained unfinished. Concerned that if she continued to beg money for many projects, people would stop giving to anything, Madge nevertheless undertook to build a "model" playground, an idea first implemented at Hull-House in 1893. During the previous year, the Civic League had purchased additional space on High Street to provide more room for the playground. The League deeded this lot to the School Board, and Madge set out to persuade the board to put in sidewalks, guttering, and drainage. When she thought she had obtained these, she then began to contact people for donations of $1,000 to $1,500. She wrote Jouett Shouse, now a congressman from Kansas: "I am out begging again for Irishtown School—woe is me—and am seeking ex-Kentuckians of philanthropic bent and loyal effections [*sic*]." "You can understand," she continued, "as I can't make an outsider, why, though the school has been an unqualified success, it is difficult to get more money for it here in Lexington. This community gets tired of a philanthropy very soon and wants a bran-new [*sic*] one." She added: "As an upshot of the work that was done for Lincoln School a sentiment seems to be that nothing more ought to be done for it, that it has had more than its share and that, sometimes even a little evidence of resentment for what has been done." As a maker of playground equipment explained to Madge: "Now Miss Betsy [Cloud] may be the mortar that holds the structure together but everyone knows you were the architect and hustled for the bricks." That continued to be the case.[36]

Although she received a check for $50 from Jouett Shouse, as well as several other contributions, the playground plans grew so rapidly the funds could not keep pace. The Civic League decided to attempt to buy property on Valley Avenue, which would even out the line and provide enough space for a baseball diamond. By now they also realized that part of the cost of the curbing, guttering, and sidewalks would have to come from League funds rather than from the School Board and estimated the cost at $5,000. Although very ill with tuberculosis in spring 1916, Madge continued to make contacts for donations. Throughout the previous winter she herself had provided much of the money necessary for Lincoln School's social work, and there was "not much prospect of ever getting it back." She appealed to the John F. Slater Fund to double its contribution from $300 to $600 per year. When that was refused, she replied in a fit of despair: "Whenever we have one of these meetings of the Public Health Nursing Association, the Associated Charities or the Civic League and I face the despairing budget of another society, I am strongly tempted to quit and throw up the sponge." She lamented: "I stayed awake until 2: o'clock last night trying to work out where we were to get the money for

Civic League jobs, and then got up in despair. Your letter received in the morning mail is the first blow today. Truly things are never so dark that they can't get a little darker."[37]

Yet she did not give up. She continued to appeal to ex-Kentuckians and philanthropists throughout the country, attempting to persuade Mrs. Joseph B. Russell of Cambridge, Massachusetts, to purchase the additional land needed and promising to name the baseball diamond the Otis S. Tenney Field after Mrs. Russell's father, a Lexingtonian who had recently died. Often in her letters Madge included pictures of the children and activities of Lincoln School. In one she wrote: "The 'model' in the case of the school has absolutely worked." She continued: "The school work, the social work, the health work in the school—we have added a fresh air school—has won the highest commendation from authorities. The school is constantly visited by teachers from the Eastern Normal School, and persons from other parts of the State." Yet, she added: "Though our Civic League has gotten some little interior parks in Lexington it has not yet gotten one park or model playground around a public school. This we believe would be just as valuable a model as the school has been and it is to this end that I want to earnestly ask that you help us." Yet work on the playground progressed at a very slow pace.[38]

Madge remained the driving force behind the Civic League, often presiding at meetings even when someone else, usually someone she had recruited, served as president. (One friend recorded in her diary that she had been "terrified because she [Madge] wanted me elected president" of the Civic League.) Madge also remained on the city's Playground Committee and served on the boards of virtually all the major civic organizations in Lexington. She also continued to solicit funds from Clarence and Mary LeBus and other well-to-do friends and family for many of these endeavors. The fund-raising must have seemed unending; as she wrote to Mary LeBus on one occasion: "With many thanks for you help and hoping that you have now contracted the habit of working for us and will continue to do so, until death us do part."[39]

Madge's commitment to the antituberculosis movement also remained strong as the organization grew and changed. The Tuberculosis Society, founded in 1905, had expanded into the Public Health Nursing Association in 1911, providing a visiting nurse service and free clinics for the poor. Madge followed a local approach to the tuberculosis problem over the years, although her ultimate goal continued to be the creation of county and state tuberculosis sanatoria. This goal still proved elusive, as the Fayette Fiscal Court took no immediate action for creating a tuberculosis district under the 1912 tuberculosis act, which provided that if the fiscal court failed to act, an election could be held to establish a tuberculosis district with the power to create a sanatorium. In autumn 1913 Madge helped gear up a vigorous campaign in support of establishing such a district. As usual, she used the pages of the *Herald* to promote the cause. She also made speeches and helped the association promulgate its message through a massive literature campaign. The effort succeeded at the November election, when the Fayette County electorate approved the creation of a tuberculosis district by a margin of about 4.5 votes to 1. Then, when the Board of Trustees for the district was established on March 24, 1914, Madge became one of its members. This, coupled with her position on the state Tuberculosis Commission, gave her the opportunity to work on both the statewide and local levels.[40]

Almost as soon as it was created, the Board of Trustees for the tuberculosis district began to plan for a sanatorium in Lexington. Much to Madge's dismay, this goal did not materialize swiftly, because the fiscal court would not appropriate money for the purpose. Finally, in 1915 the court provided $2,536.35 out of its general fund for the first payment on a tract of land that had been chosen as the site for the facility.[41]

During much of the time when she played an active role in fighting tuberculosis in Fayette County, Madge also waged the battle on the state level. As vice president of the state Tuberculosis Commission she became embroiled in its money problems and political squabbles. Although the legislature in 1912 appropriated $15,000 annually for the work of the commission, all except $1,578.14 was held up until the last month of the fiscal year 1912–13. The commission by then had a secretary and a stenographer and had prepared a large amount of literature, although it had not had the money to distribute it. After a Court of Appeals decision freed the appropriation, the commission felt compelled to make up two years' work in one. It began an intensive publicity program that included sending speakers to teachers' institutes and passing out more than 110,000 pieces of literature. When in 1916 the state inspector and examiner made a report criticizing the large amount the commission had spent in its second year, Madge felt compelled to reply. To Dr. H. S. Keller, another member of the commission, she wrote: "I think the old members of the Commission who are still on must of necessity defend" its actions "by replying to this report." "How I can do the work that it will require in addition to the other things I have to do, I can't see, but when you are killing yourself anyway, you might as well kill yourself a little deader, I suppose," she complained. And reply to the report she did. In four typewritten pages she answered every one of the inspector's criticisms and explained: "The plans for the expenditure of this second year were deliberately made, the members believed then, and believe now, that they were wise, and were doing their duty only, in spending for the eradication of tuberculosis in the first two Fiscal Years, the $30,000 appropriated by the legislature for that purpose rather than to allow that money to revert to the State Treasury to be used for other purposes, as it would have done on the first of July 1914, if not spent by the commission."[42]

The commission faced another major problem in securing a qualified, forceful person as the executive secretary who would be in charge of coordinating tuberculosis work throughout the state. In 1915 when Roy French, the first secretary, resigned, Madge believed she had the perfect candidate for the position—Jessie O. Yancey, Mason County school superintendent and a registered nurse. Madge secured recommendations for Yancey from such eminent people as Dr. Henry Hardin Cherry, president of Western Kentucky State Normal School. But Madge could not overcome the prejudice against having a woman in charge, and, ever the pragmatist, she lamented to her protégée: "Whatever we may think theoretically about the capacity of women, you know we are living in a time [when] women are not holding equal positions with men nor having the opportunity for them with equal pay," a process that must be accomplished "by steps and not try to leap the whole wall at once." Madge felt compelled to give in to the other members, perhaps believing that her identification with woman suffrage, rather than Yancey's superior qualifications, would be viewed as her real motive if she persisted. The commission then voted to hire Dr. L. M. Maus of the U.S. Army Medical Corps at a salary of $1,500 per year, although he had no experience at all in tuberculosis work. Before the year was over, Madge felt her position had been vindicated, because Maus proved to be totally unsuited to the job. In 1916 Madge would again resume her support for Yancey to become executive secretary as soon as Maus's term expired. "And this year," she stated, "I think it is due the Tuberculosis cause that I act on my own best judgment and do all I can to procure the election of the person whom I am entirely convinced is the most advantageous person for us to elect."[43]

It must have appeared to Madge that success never came easily for any of her causes. Each battle had to be fought again and again, and sufficient funding always required a struggle. During the years 1914–15 Madge had kept an almost unbelievable schedule: leading KERA, campaigning for suffrage around the country, and working on Lincoln School, tuberculosis, and other civic projects. With her health in a precarious condition, the question as 1915 ended was how much effort she would be able to give these causes in the future and whether or not she would be able to garner the resources needed to keep these endeavors alive.

Chapter 9

"I cannot keep her from doing more than she ought to do" 1916–1918

Although exhausted from her three years as president of the Kentucky Equal Rights Association and ill with tuberculosis, Madge Breckinridge seemingly approached the 1916 legislative session with the same zeal and determination as always. Upon relinquishing the presidency of KERA, she accepted the position of legislative campaign chair, which gave her the responsibility for organizing the drive to get the General Assembly to pass a state constitutional amendment for woman suffrage. On January 4 she formally opened KERA headquarters in Frankfort. Madge stayed in the capital to work for the cause as often as her health would allow, but she found it necessary to delegate much of the responsibility. Nevertheless, she continued an active role in the struggle through her letter writing.[1]

Because suffragists considered the whiskey interests among their chief opponents, Madge compiled a list of prohibitionist members of the legislature. She felt these men might be persuaded to support suffrage because it would enable them to add many new votes for prohibition. She also invited the British suffragist, actress, and author Beatrice Forbes-Robertson Hale to speak to the legislature and to be a guest in the Breckinridge home. At the same time, Madge persuaded Senator Thomas A. Combs and Representative W. C. G. Hobbs, both Lexington Democrats, to introduce the suffrage bill in their respective chambers. KERA sponsored an elaborate luncheon for a number of house and senate members at the Capital Hotel on January 13, and five days later Madge attended a joint session of the legislature to hear Hale's address. A week afterward, Madge, KERA president Elise Smith, and several others spoke to the Senate Committee on Suffrage and Elections. After listening to the women, the committee voted to report the bill favorably, and on March 8 it passed the Senate by a 26-8 vote.[2]

Although encouraged by the senate's action, Madge realized the chance for success in the house was not nearly so good since the new, "wet" Democratic governor, Augustus Owsley Stanley, would use the powers of his administration to defeat the bill in that body. A native of Henderson in western Kentucky, Stanley had been elected to Congress in 1902 and then had won the race for governor in 1915 by a mere 471 votes. He had made a name for himself as a flamboyant campaigner, eloquent public speaker, and opponent of monopolies and trusts. Although his administration would develop a record for progressive reform, he proved reluctant to embrace woman suffrage. Both Stanley and U.S. senator Ollie James sought to make the issue a partisan one, claiming that it was a movement of Republican women and would help only that party, while some antiprohibitionists came out in favor of submitting both a woman suffrage amendment and a statewide liquor prohibition amendment to the voters, presumably hoping both would fail. Speaking to the House Committee on Constitutional Amendments, Madge refuted the claim that suffrage comprised a partisan issue, pointing out that although Kentucky Republicans had officially endorsed woman suffrage while Democrats had not, many Democrats in Kentucky supported the cause, and the party's national leader, President Woodrow Wilson, favored woman suffrage by state amendment. Despite the pleas of Madge and several others, the house committee voted 5-4 to report the bill unfavorably. The full house, however, voted 51-40 to put the bill on its calendar, and it also voted 37-35 to refuse to call from committee a bill that would have abolished woman suffrage in school elections. Madge and the other suffragists in the gallery cheered loudly at the announcement of these votes, although the 51-40 tally did not constitute a sufficient majority necessary to bring the suffrage bill to a vote of the full body.[3]

By the end of February Madge had concluded that the bill might pass the General Assembly, despite Stanley's opposition. Allegedly, before the legislature even met, the House Rules Committee had been organized in Louisville with the purpose of defeating woman suffrage, but now the governor promised Mary LeBus that he would do nothing further to defeat the measure. In a continuing effort to woo the prohibitionists, the Lexington Women's Christian Temperance Union gave a banquet for members of the legislature known to support statewide prohibition. Although not an active prohibitionist herself, Madge gave the address, noting that scientists and criminologists now agreed on the negative effects of alcohol. On March 2 when a surprise attempt to bring the bill to a vote in the house occurred, almost all the "drys" voted for it, but the motion again failed to receive the necessary majority. The *Lexington Herald* charged: "Dodge, twist and delay has been the program of the very men in the House who have been backing the Governor's liquor legislation program and in the suffrage bill today they resorted to the same tactics."[4]

Still, Madge maintained a faint hope that the measure might yet pass. In early March KERA brought Helen Ring Robinson of Colorado, the only female in the U.S. Senate, to Kentucky to speak. Nevertheless, the house voted 45-46 not to call the suffrage bill from committee. The *Herald* proclaimed: "Governor Stanley and the whiskey and beer interests which are in absolute control of the Governor and of the present Democratic organization won a victory over the women of Kentucky today." The article further charged that Harry G. Meyers of Covington, "the brains of the wets in the House," left his sick room to vote against the bill. This was the third and final attempt to bring the measure before the full house. In an article Madge summed up the session, pointing out that opposition had come not from conservative rural districts but primarily from the urban areas of Louisville, Covington, and Newport, where brewers and distillers wielded political power. This type of article led one member of the legislature to inform Madge that "your cause has been hurt during the last Legislature on account of the ultra-radical position of the Lexington Herald." The legislator said he had never publicly declared for woman suffrage but "was well near the point of so doing at one time." Across the top of his letter Madge wrote with wry humor: "Easily Deterred."[5]

Just before the house took its last vote, an event occurred that incensed both Madge and Desha. Governor Stanley released a telegram he had received from Senator Ollie James and Congressman J. Campbell Cantrill, advising that at a meeting held in James's office and attended by all but one of the Kentucky Democratic house members, "the opinion was expressed that it was not within the province of the members of Congress to offer advice to the Legislature, but each man present expressed himself as strongly opposed to the Woman Suffrage Amendment and hoped that it would be defeated in accordance with the action of the last Democratic State Convention." The one absent member of the house delegation could not be located in time for the conference, the telegram stated. Immediately, Desha telegraphed each of the Democratic congressmen, as well as Senators James and J. C. W. Beckham, asking for "explanation, simplification, or denial" of the statements made in the telegram. Madge followed Desha's telegrams with letters. Both Breckinridges asked who formulated the idea for the conference, who attended, and which persons authorized the telegram. Desha further pointed out that "as far as I am aware this is the first time a delegation in Congress has presumed to attempt to influence the legislature of Kentucky through a telegram addressed to the Governor." Furthermore, he charged, the telegram was inaccurate and misleading, since it implied that the Democratic State Convention had opposed submission of a suffrage amendment to the voters. "Do not both of you know that no action was taken by that Convention?" he inquired of James and Cantrill. In fact, the Democrats had not voted to *oppose* submission, they had rejected a resolution to *favor* it, a completely different action, in Desha's thinking.[6]

When the Breckinridges received replies to their inquiries, it soon became evident that the telegram *had* been misleading. They learned that Democratic congressmen William J. Fields and Robert Young Thomas Jr.—both of whom supported submission of a state amendment—had not been invited to the conference. Four of the five who attended stated they had not authorized the telegram, while the fifth did not clarify whether he had given authorization. All five, however, did oppose submission of a suffrage amendment. Congressman Alben Barkley explained that he wanted the 1916 election to be a referendum on President Wilson and did not want it complicated by the suffrage issue. Such an event might result in "a failure to record the real wishes of the people upon either question." In his memoirs, perhaps remembering his later efforts on behalf of the Anthony amendment rather than this episode, Barkley stated: "I also recall our efforts to give women the right to vote. I never had any trouble with the ladies, for I was on their side all the time." In 1916, however, he made excuses for opposing submission of the amendment, because he surely knew it would not have been voted upon until 1917 and thus would not have interfered at all with the presidential election the previous year. Senator Beckham, although an opponent of woman suffrage, was undoubtedly relieved to be able to tell Madge and Desha that he had not taken part in the meeting; he piously stated that he did not believe it proper for a senator to advise the General Assembly. On the other hand,

Ollie James continued to come under fire from the Breckinridges when he voted against submission to the states of a federal amendment because "I believe that this is a matter that can be best dealt with by the states, each state acting for itself." This statement prompted Desha to remind James that he had also opposed the submission of a state amendment to the voters of Kentucky and to predict that it would soon be difficult for James to defend opposition to both a federal and a state amendment.[7]

Throughout the spring and part of the summer after the close of the 1916 legislative session, Madge remained fairly active in suffrage work. When those outside the state sought her opinion on the Congressional Union's activities, she replied that, although she favored the Anthony amendment, if it passed Congress tomorrow, there was not yet a sufficient number of state legislatures that would ratify it. Thus, work needed to make progress on the state as well as the national level in order to build support. The CU, she felt, had done some good publicity work but had made many enemies for suffrage as well, and its policy of holding the party in power responsible would not work in the South, with its one-party system. In March Madge spoke in Louisville to a group from NAWSA, which included Carrie Chapman Catt, the organization's new president. Catt impressed Madge so much that she wrote: "I wish that we could have her for National President always." The next month Madge traveled to Cincinnati to interview Walter J. Millard for a position as lecturer for the Fayette ERA. She proceeded to hire him for one month's work and upon his arrival in Lexington gave a luncheon to introduce him to the members of the local suffrage organization. A few days later she accompanied him and Mary LeBus to a suffrage meeting in Paris, Kentucky. On May 6 she participated in the largest suffrage parade ever held in the state, where nearly one thousand women rode or walked from Gratz Park in Lexington to Cheapside near the Fayette County Courthouse for an open-air meeting. She spoke on May 18 at a state meeting of the Kentucky Federation of Women's Clubs in Maysville and made plans to march in a suffrage parade in Chicago, "though I shall only be able to march a short way and then fall out," she warned. She also led a group of women who called on the City Board of Commissioners to ask for the appointment of a police court matron to supervise all female prisoners and court witnesses. Then in June she gave two lectures in Bloomington, Indiana. These would be her last public appearances for some time.[8]

During the first half of 1916 Madge had labored diligently not only for suffrage but also on tuberculosis work, both on the local and state levels. Her only concession to doctor's orders for rest up to this point had been in January, when she declined election to the Board of Directors of the Associated Charities, saying she could not attend afternoon meetings, presumably because she had been ordered to rest at that time. Henry McDowell Jr. believed she was taking the "rest cure" after the close of the legislative session; yet the volume of her suffrage and tuberculosis activities clearly shows that she did not consistently follow doctor's orders, and she herself admitted: "I just couldn't rest from the legislative cold as the doctor wanted me to." In addition, she continued to entertain friends and family with dinner and cards.[9]

Madge also found herself advising KERA treasurer Rebecca Judah on ways to raise money. She maintained that more Louisville women should help because "the money in Kentucky is in Louisville," and she found it sad that so few cared even $100 worth about suffrage and that they were mostly "the ones who cared that much about forty years ago."[10]

At the same time that Madge was directing KERA's campaign for a state suffrage amendment, she also found herself more deeply involved in the plan to build a local tuberculosis sanatorium. In January 1916 the Fayette County Fiscal Court authorized a levy of 3¢ on every $100 of taxable property to help build such a facility. This produced $17,450, enough to get started but not enough to complete the project, estimated to cost a total of $61,000. Aunt Mag's contribution of $10,000 to construct the children's building in memory of her father, while generous, complicated the planning process since it gave her the feeling that she should have a major role in determining the design. As an amateur architect, she had definite ideas of how the children's building should look, and, unfortunately, Madge had to play the role of mediator between Aunt Mag and the architects. Agreeing that the original design for the children's building looked "rather prison-like," Madge noted: "It doesn't seem fair to persuade her to put her money into a building with which she is not satisfied." Nevertheless, the work proceeded and by June 1916 the Board of Trustees of the Tuberculosis Sanatorium, on which Madge served, had purchased the land and finalized the plans for three buildings.[11]

Simultaneously, Madge continued to hold her seat on the state Tuberculosis Commission. In February she spoke at the first annual tuberculosis conference, which was held in Frankfort. When the Tuberculosis Commission sought a new executive secretary, Madge again promoted

Jessie O. Yancey. Unfortunately, she came no closer to success in 1916 than she had previously. This time Governor Stanley entered the picture, as both he and his new appointee on the commission, Dr. Archibald Dixon, opposed having a woman as secretary, allegedly because the secretary would have to visit state institutions, and that was not "woman's work." Madge stated clearly and unequivocally her belief that the governor simply wanted to use all appointive offices for political purposes. This situation drove Madge and her cousin Tevis Camden, also one of the original members of the commission and daughter of former U.S. senator Johnson N. Camden, to resign. Madge wrote Governor Stanley: "I can not under existing circumstances render any service for the tuberculosis cause commensurate with the effort entailed. My conception of carrying out the purposes of the law is, I believe, very divergent from yours." Ironically, the governor appointed Jessie O. Yancey to serve the remainder of Madge's term.[12]

Even though most of her time in recent years had been devoted to suffrage and tuberculosis work, Madge continued to try to keep the other reform organizations afloat. These groups relied on her organizational and fund-raising skills. The Lexington Civic League, for example, had become virtually moribund as a consequence of her preoccupation with other matters. In midsummer she attempted to revive it by publishing a lengthy article in the *Herald*, pointing out the League's many accomplishments and stating the need for funds to support social work at Lincoln School, park and playground activities, and other projects normally funded by the organization. As some of the Civic League members recalled many years later, the group came to life mainly when Madge had a cause, and she did not hesitate to draft members to do the work she wanted them to do. In all these endeavors she relied on the *Herald* as a major marketing tool. She received one bit of good news in June 1916, when the Slater Fund informed her it was donating $300 for the Lexington Colored Public Schools.[13]

By this time Madge's health had declined significantly. Her personal battle with tuberculosis mirrored her fierce struggle against the disease in the public health sector. For years she had violated the major recommendation for tubercular patients—to get plenty of rest—and her penchant for overworking finally took its toll. Her attempts to cut back on activities and follow the rest cure at home had failed, and Desha began to seek a tuberculosis facility where she could receive the most up-to-date treatment. From August 1916 until the middle of 1918, she underwent frequent medical treatment.[14]

Luxury sanatoria existed in Colorado Springs and Asheville, North Carolina, but the pioneering facility—founded by Dr. Edward L. Trudeau, one of the country's leading experts on tuberculosis—was at Saranac Lake, New York. Suffering from the disease himself in the 1870s, Trudeau had improved while resting and eating nutritious food in the Adirondacks. This led him to establish the Adirondack Cottage Sanitarium in the 1880s for the treatment of tuberculosis. After his death in 1915, the facility continued, becoming the Trudeau Sanatorium two years later. Madge and Desha decided to go there. As they were preparing to leave for Saranac Lake in late July 1916, Desha wrote his sister Curry that Madge "is still working like a dog and is very much worn out and I doubt whether she will stand the trip, but in case she gets the least bit tired we will leave the motor [car]."[15]

It appears that Madge did not become a patient in the sanitarium itself but instead stayed in the Santanoni Apartments in Saranac Lake, where rates for lodging, meals, lights, linens, and blankets totaled $38 to $50 ($750 to $987 in 2008 dollars) per week for two people. Although apparently no patient records with names attached have survived, documents show that the treatment given patients at the sanitarium consisted mainly of rest, a diet emphasizing eggs, milk, and cod liver oil, regular weighing and taking of temperature, and fresh air. The regimen permitted exercise only if a patient had no fever. Madge's letters indicate that those staying in the apartments experienced fewer restrictions than patients in the sanitarium itself; however, she followed the same basic program. Desha stayed with her most of the time, and Madge reported to Nettie Bullock that the apartment was much nicer than they had expected. During their first days there, they entertained Mary LeBus and some other friends. The rest cure really began on August 5, when these guests departed for Saratoga for the afternoon races. "You may be sure it was hard for Desha to let them go," Madge wrote her mother: "If Cherry Blossom [Desha's horse] should happen to run this afternoon I don't know how he could stand it." In a bantering tone she also mentioned that they had celebrated Desha's birthday, and "Mrs. LeBus got a birth-day cake at the bakery, which wasn't much to look at, but was better to look at than it was to eat, & had 7 candles on it—He insisted that was her age, but the rest of us thought it was about the right age for each one of them."[16]

Not surprisingly, Madge remained involved in decisions about her various Lexington projects. Just before leaving home, she had written a letter concerning playground equipment for Lincoln School, and after reaching Saranac Lake, she learned the School Board had hired the person she wanted for play director at the school. Yet for the most part she attempted to follow the rest regimen and appeared optimistic and content in letters to her mother, stating that "it is really questionable whether there is anything the matter with me. . . . And I am really enjoying being free from all the jobs and not having it my duty to telephone anybody, or to go to any meetings or to decide any questions, or to persuade any body to do things." Nevertheless, she let Nettie know that the X-rays showed evidence there had been tuberculosis and "some evidence of existing T.B., though I believe that wouldn't be considered very definite except for the existence of symptoms." She added that "it seems reasonable to suppose that if I have had it when I didn't know it, that when a slight cough persists for a yr. and a half that there is some now." The doctor ordered her "not to stretch, not to walk down town, not to breathe unnecessarily for 6 weeks." She kept urging Nettie to come to Saranac Lake for treatment also, and she reported that Desha, too, had gained five pounds but lost two of them, saying "he insists . . . that's what comes of giving up smoking, doing nothing & taking too much advice from your wife." When her mother sent $200, Madge informed Nettie she would not cash the check because "I have plenty of money in the bank & Desha's taking care of me."[17]

While undergoing the rest cure, Madge agreed to write an article for the November issue of the *Journal of Outdoor Life* about Aunt Mag's donation to the tuberculosis sanatorium and Dr. William Adair McDowell's work in fighting tuberculosis. As time passed, Madge seemed to grow more restless. Though the doctors advised her to remain for more treatment, possibly for up to a year, or to go to Colorado, Asheville, or Arizona, she decided to return home in October. Desha attributed her decision to her concern for her mother and Aunt Mag, saying that she feared each winter would be their last. Madge agreed to make a studied attempt to continue the rest cure at home. She begged Nettie's help in overcoming "the little family temptations—X-mas & Thanksgiving & every day." After her return, Desha and friends described her condition as improved but still weak.[18]

To be sure, the various organizations in Lexington sorely missed her guidance. An item under "Suffragist Notes" in the *Herald* in September noted that "we miss our campaign chairman, Mrs. Desha Breckinridge, more than we can tell. . . . Requests for speeches from her . . . are received at headquarters, and no name suggested by the President seems quite to fill the bills." In addition, the Kentucky Federation of Women's Clubs Board of Directors nominated her as first honorary vice president "because of the inspiration and great good and splendid work" she had done for Kentucky women. She accepted this because it was "just an honor—without work." Yet being at home made it nearly impossible for her to maintain her regimen of rest. Although Desha at times reported that "she is doing fairly well . . . really much better than could be expected," about keeping quiet, by the end of the year he lamented that she was "not doing so well as I should like" because "I cannot keep her from doing more than she ought to do."[19]

The biggest project Madge undertook after her return from Saranac Lake consisted of organizing the cornerstone-laying ceremony on November 15, 1916, for the service and children's buildings for the tuberculosis sanatorium. Dr. B. L. Wyatt, whom Madge had met at Saranac Lake and who was her choice to head the sanatorium in Lexington, served as featured speaker. Proceedings included a memorial service for Dr. William Adair McDowell, which noted how he had been ridiculed during his lifetime for treating tuberculosis by rest, nutrition, and fresh air. At the ceremony officials announced that the children's building, largely funded by his daughter, would be a memorial to him. The institution would bear the name Blue Grass Sanatorium and would admit patients from outside Fayette County if space permitted. Another speaker pointed to Madge and called her "the only soldier who has been in the trenches from the beginning to the success of the movement." A friend thought that Madge looked better at the event than she had in some time, and Desha noted that while she had experienced three very strenuous days, she promised to resume her regimen of rest right away. He also reported that Dr. Wyatt would probably become the sanatorium superintendent, and, if so, it could be attributed "in large measure" to Madge's influence, because Wyatt had been offered much more money elsewhere. She ultimately succeeded in getting Dr. Wyatt as head of the sanatorium for the first year, and her power would continue to be felt in the coming years as she consistently secured the appointment of her personal choice as superintendent of the institution.[20]

Pledged to rest immediately after the cornerstone ceremony, Madge found herself unable to attend the annual KERA convention, held in Louisville November 15–16. Her health also compelled her to resign as chair of KERA's Legislative Campaign Committee. She did, however, pledge to contribute $100 for the coming year to KERA and $1,000 to a $1 million fund being raised by NAWSA. The members of the convention sent a telegram to let Madge know they were thinking of her. Delegates to the convention then proceeded to adopt a new constitution and elect Christine Bradley South, daughter of Kentucky's first Republican governor, William O. Bradley, as the new president. Madge sent South a letter of congratulations and apologized that she could not be of more help. To another friend she commented that, while some of the Louisville suffragists opposed South because of her father's prominence in the Republican Party, that fact "doesn't bother me in the least," because it would require the votes of Republicans to win suffrage, and it would be a long time before "we get the Democrats as a whole."[21]

Although Madge continued trying to live quietly, she accompanied Desha to Hinata, the LeBus home, after Christmas dinner to visit Mary, who had undergone surgery at Mayo Clinic in Minnesota a few weeks earlier. Madge became increasingly concerned about her mother and Aunt Mag, both of whom apparently suffered from tuberculosis. Mrs. McDowell's health had declined in 1912, and although she had improved from the critical condition she was in at that time, she remained in a precarious state. This made Madge hesitant to leave Kentucky for long periods for her own treatment. Her deepest fear was realized on February 3, 1917, in the midst of bitterly cold weather, when Anne Clay McDowell died in her sleep, just two weeks short of her eightieth birthday. Her death dealt a terrific blow to Madge. "She reproaches herself for not having done more for her," Desha said, "though she did all it was possible." The *Herald*'s editorial the following day read "To Know Her Was to Love Her," and it extolled Mrs. McDowell's thoughtfulness of others. Out of respect for her generosity, Lincoln School dismissed classes for the day of the funeral. The fact that Henry McDowell Jr. was too ill with the grippe to attend their mother's funeral further increased Madge's anxiety. From the symptoms described it seems likely that he, too, had tuberculosis, and for some time Madge had been urging him to go to a clinic in Rochester, New York, for a physical examination. Her pleas and those of other members in the family were to no avail. "He has got less sense than I have, and that is about the worst I can say," Madge complained.[22]

Anne "Nannie" Clay McDowell at Ashland. Courtesy of Special Collections and Digital Programs, Margaret I. King Library, University of Kentucky, Lexington.

In an action that perhaps constituted one of her attempts to distract herself from personal problems, Madge entered into a major confrontation with her old adversary, the Salvation Army, shortly before her mother's death. It began in January 1917 when the Salvation Army requested an appropriation from the city of Lexington to help establish an emergency home and hospital dispensary. Madge soon launched what Sophonisba described as "one of the most heroic encounters ever engaged in. One knows not where to turn for analogy unless it be to the driving of the money-changers from the Temple." In a number of articles in the *Herald* Madge opposed the Salvation Army appropriation on several grounds, pointing out that Lexington had two well-equipped hospitals plus the Public Health Nursing Association, which offered a free clinic and dispensary for the poor. Likewise, Associated Charities had long provided emergency housing for wayfarers. Public funds partially, though inadequately, funded all of these organizations. Why, Madge asked, divert limited public resources to an organization that would simply duplicate the functions of agencies already established? In addition, Madge argued that the Army was more a religious than a charity organization and that to allocate tax money to it posed a violation of the constitutional principle of separation of church and state. She reiterated her complaint that the Salvation Army sent a portion of local donations to its headquarters and made no public accounting for its use of funds. The only portion of the organization's relief work that Madge thought more effective than the Associated Charities' was its fund-raising. "Their soliciting work," she stated, "should be the envy and despair of every local philanthropic organization." She also charged that one of the organization's methods of solicitation was illegal: the Army sent its female workers into saloons to ask for donations, violating a city ordinance barring women from such establishments.[23]

Madge stated on January 29: "There has never been a time when I less wanted to put in time on a controversy with the Salvation Army," but the following day she announced, "I shall if the appropriation is made, bring an injunction suit to prevent payment." She hoped this threat would discourage city officials from making the appropriation, but it did not, so on April 11 she filed suit in Fayette Circuit Court, seeking an injunction to stop the transfer of $720 to the Salvation Army. Judge Charles Kerr granted the injunction. Thus began the most controversial episode in Madge's career. Apparently in a fit of pique at being challenged, the mayor decided the injunction applied to all charitable appropriations, including

St. Joseph's and Good Samaritan Hospitals, as well as Associated Charities, forcing these institutions to borrow in order to continue their operations. A *Lexington Leader* article charged that the injunction had tied up the funds for other welfare purposes. The *Herald* hotly denied that the injunction held up any payment except to the Salvation Army, because the suit challenged no other item in the appropriation ordinance. Rather, Desha insisted, the mayor, without justification, stopped all charity grants in order to discredit Madge and make her position unpopular.[24]

The *Leader* stood behind its story, saying it had not alleged that Mrs. Breckinridge "intended" to hold up all appropriations, but merely that "as a result" of the suit they were held up. The *Leader* further denied the charge that it meant to harm the plaintiff, saying such allegations were "mere drivel." In fact, *Leader* editor Harry Giovannoli, a member of the Associated Charities Board of Directors and chairman of its Finance Committee, believed the matter should be settled by the courts. Later, the *Leader* denied taking sides in the controversy but stated that many cities gave aid to the Army and "whether there is a place for it in Lexington may easily be a debatable question."[25]

Meanwhile, despite her own illness and her mother's death, Madge marshaled information against the Salvation Army and continued to publicize it. Although she was virtually alone in the anti–Salvation Army crusade in Lexington, she collected vast amounts of material written by professional social workers and proponents of scientific charity throughout the United States and Great Britain who agreed with her views. The National Conference of Charities and Correction condemned the Army's form of charity work, and a Pittsburgh charity official wrote her: "Let me tell you how glad I am that at least someone has emerged with the enterprise and courage to oppose the institutional aggrandizement of the Salvation Army."[26]

When Captain John Hundley, head of the Lexington Salvation Army, testified in court, he did little to help his cause. He admitted that records from his predecessor were meager and indecipherable, and while he claimed the Army had aided 440 families between October 1916 and May 1917, he could not say whether this meant 440 separate families or an unknown number of families 440 times. Madge, therefore, charged that "not even the Recording Angel himself, used as he must be to tangled and devious records, could tell with the Salvation Army books before him exactly what the Salvation Army has done in the way of relief." She also pointed out that Hundley counted rent on his headquarters as direct relief, yet the public viewed the rent of the Associated Charities building as "one of the reprehensible overhead expenses that prove that 'organized' charity is 'cold.'"[27]

Finally, on October 15 Judge Charles Kerr ruled the Salvation Army appropriation invalid but approved all other charitable appropriations. Kerr's decision, however, implied that a city appropriation to the Army would be permissible if the city specified that it would be used for relief rather than religious purposes. Five days after the decision the city commissioners again voted $720 to the Salvation Army to be used to provide food and shelter to the needy. Madge again sought and obtained an injunction. This time neither the Army nor the city fought the injunction. Thus, through stubborn determination, she had taken on the City Commission, the mayor, the Salvation Army, and, to a large extent, the *Lexington Leader* and public opinion—and she had won. Yet how much had she really gained? It is doubtful if she achieved much additional support for Associated Charities or turned many people against the Salvation Army. Of all her endeavors this was perhaps the most futile, the most misunderstood, and the most unpopular. Even Sophonisba admitted it was "a fight few thought worth making, not because the issues were not of sufficient importance, but because the fruits of victory would be so elusive and difficult to share."[28]

Desha constantly complained that Madge attempted to do too much. Both the tuberculosis sanatorium and the Lincoln School playground projects drained much of her energy. When public money provided for construction of the Blue Grass Sanatorium proved insufficient, Madge decided to raise money from private sources to supplement the public appropriation just as she had done with Lincoln School. To those who questioned this approach, she replied in a *Herald* article that the project needed an additional $55,000 to complete and open the institution, and "there is no hope for any more money from the County for the Sanatorium until next year." At a mass meeting in the courthouse, citizens decided to undertake a two-week campaign to raise the funds. Madge put into this effort all the things she had learned in previous money-raising endeavors and, assisted this time by professional fund-raisers, surpassed the goal by raising almost $57,000 in pledges in two weeks. This enabled the Blue Grass Sanatorium to open its doors in August 1917. Soon patients occupied all fifty-two beds. Most were indigents but a few, at least initially, paid part of the cost of treatment. As Madge explained, having some paying patients kept it from assuming "too much the aspect of a 'poor-house.'"[29]

Likewise, Madge continued fund-raising efforts to provide a model playground for Lincoln School. She became impatient with the man responsible for buying additional property, complaining that "he just dilly-dallies about it" with the owner, who did not want to sell. She raised only small sums of money until November, when Mrs. Joseph B. Russell of Cambridge, Massachusetts, contributed $2,000 in memory of her father, Otis S. Tenney. This completed the funds needed for purchasing property and equipment. Madge also found herself defending Lincoln School from criticism over the use of its facilities for entertaining the influx of soldiers that had developed due to World War I. Girls, accompanied by their mothers or an older chaperone, helped provide programs for the soldiers who flocked to the school in the evening, when schoolrooms and auditorium were used as reading and clubrooms, and the Civic League held dances. An anonymous critic urged the editor of the *Lexington Leader* to investigate these dances—for the protection of the soldiers who might come in contact with "bad" girls. This critic believed those supervising the dancers could not possibly know all the girls attending. Madge immediately replied in the *Herald* with an open letter to the *Leader*'s editor. She pointed out that Lincoln School had held dances for all of the five winters since it had opened. Elizabeth Cloud, principal of the school, chaperoned all the dances, and, because she had taught in the Irishtown area for more than ten years, she knew the young people and asked any unknown girls to leave. Furthermore, Madge asserted: "We elders have gotten away from the attitude of some churches in the past that tried to wipe dancing off the face of the earth by the threat of eternal punishment, and still did not succeed."[30]

All of these matters distracted Madge and kept her from resting. Desha kept trying to get her to go away for further treatment, and finally in August 1917 she and Nettie Bullock departed for Asheville, North Carolina. Nettie soon returned home after her husband became ill, but Curry Breckinridge, now a trained nurse, came to stay with Madge at St. Joseph's Sanatorium. Madge proclaimed she was "reveling in the rest-cure," noting that "Desha comes & visits me & goes shopping for all my possible wants." She came home in the autumn to attend the twentieth-eighth annual KERA convention, where she introduced Nellie McClung

Family gathering at Ashland, May 19, 1917, to celebrate the birthdays of Madeline McDowell Breckinridge (seated fourth from left in second row from back) and Magdalen Harvey McDowell (seated to the left of Madeline). Courtesy of Special Collections and Digital Programs, Margaret I. King Library, University of Kentucky, Lexington.

of Canada, one of the featured speakers. Later, she returned to Asheville to spend the winter, although she complained that Asheville had more rain and mist than Lexington and speculated that if she lived in Asheville, doctors would probably send her to Lexington.[31]

During this period Madge did little suffrage work, although she corresponded with a number of suffragists. She continued to advise KERA treasurer Rebecca Judah on fund-raising, which unfortunately only stirred up controversy. Through the years in her many attempts to raise money, Madge had developed a technique whereby she would contribute a certain amount, such as $100, provided nine others could be found to donate the same amount. Usually, she had gone out and found the other nine pledges herself. In 1917, when she promised a conditional $100 to KERA, she was not physically able to raise the matching contributions, so she suggested ways in which the treasurer might do this. Judah replied that it was not fair for Madge to give money on those conditions and called many of her suggestions "impossible." Madge responded that she believed her plan of conditional giving was "not only reasonable, but the best way for raising the most money for the KERA." Furthermore, she did not think her other suggestions were impossible; in fact, if Mrs. Judah could not get other newspapers to contribute, "then I certainly shall not urge Desha to contribute for the Herald another year . . . $100.00 is a small sum, and unless it has some value in bringing in other money, there is no use at all in the Herald putting it in." This episode led Madge to vow she would make no further suggestions, because she had "the feeling that they are not desired."[32]

All in all, 1917 was a difficult year for Madge. Her own illness, her mother's death, continuing fund-raising responsibilities for Lincoln School and the tuberculosis sanatorium, and dissension within state and national suffrage organizations all proved to be depressing problems. But Madge bore an even greater burden, one that perhaps hurt her more than any other—her husband was unfaithful. Although the couple appeared devoted to each other, with Desha signing his letters, "With great love your husband," and Madge addressing him as "Dear heart," at some point during the teens Desha developed a romantic relationship with another woman—Mary LeBus, one of Madge's suffrage associates. The Breckinridges and the LeBuses had become close friends after the LeBuses moved from Cynthiana, Kentucky, to Lexington in 1909; Madge and Desha became frequent guests at Hinata. Clarence LeBus served as president of the Burley Tobacco Growers Association, and ill health and overwork plagued him, much as it did Madge. Both Desha and Mary enjoyed parties and socializing, while their spouses were often away from home or busy with more serious endeavors. Mary LeBus was a very attractive woman, described by friends as "very handsome and . . . wonderfully gowned" and by Madge as the "tall and showy type." Within a few years it seemed every gossipy tongue in Lexington commented on the affair between Mary LeBus and Desha Breckinridge. Even students on the campus of the University of Kentucky repeated stories of how the *Herald* editor had exited in his pajamas down the fire escape of the Phoenix Hotel just as Clarence LeBus stepped into his wife's room. Exactly when the affair started and how long it took Madge to discover it is uncertain, but friends eventually learned that she knew about the situation. Though she continued to socialize with the LeBuses and encouraged Mary to participate in suffrage activities, she mentioned on one occasion to one of Mary's cousins that she tried to involve her rival in reform activities to keep her busy and away from Desha. Occasionally Madge revealed a hint of disapproval of Mary, once commenting to Sophonisba: "It is really hard to get even a few dollars from her. . . . She only spends foolishly on what she considers fun. . . . It always seems much harder to get at your own personal friends, and especially at your husband's personal friends."[33]

Though Madge always retained Desha's affection and strong public support, the situation must have been extremely humiliating and painful for the Lexington aristocrat. That she managed to ignore the affair is a demonstration of the degree of determination she had exercised in concealing her emotions ever since the foot amputation. One source indicated to a historian of the Breckinridge family that Desha had carried on a relationship with another woman living near them on Linden Walk even before he began his affair with Mary LeBus, so perhaps Madge had steeled herself to accept his unfaithfulness, especially in light of her own physical limitations. Desha's actions seem particularly ironic in light of the letter he had written her many years before on the subject of fidelity.[34]

Unfortunately, as 1918 dawned, some of Madge's problems seemed to grow worse. Division within KERA grew deeper, in large part because of events beyond the state. By this time political support for a federal woman suffrage amendment had increased in Congress. The tide began to turn in 1916, when President Wilson, perhaps inspired by the need to win many of the northern and western votes that had gone to the Progressive Party four years earlier, more forcefully endorsed woman suffrage, preferring state action if possible, but implying that he would accept a federal amendment if necessary. Thus, the Democratic platform in 1916 reflected Wilson's new conviction that the federal government must play a more active role in bringing about reform. By 1918 the great contributions women had made to the war effort after U.S. entry into World War I helped propel Wilson into announcing on January 9 his unconditional support for the Anthony amendment. The following day the House of Representatives gave it the necessary two-thirds approval, so for the first time in its long history, the amendment appeared to be on the verge of success. Wilson appealed to the U.S. Senate with the argument that "its adoption is clearly necessary to the successful prosecution of the war and the successful realization of the objects for which the war is being fought." Despite this plea, the Senate rejected the amendment; but, thanks in large part to the pressure exerted by the president, a significant change began to take place in the position of many Kentucky Democrats on the suffrage issue, with most of the state's congressional delegation who had previously opposed suffrage now endorsing it. Congressman J. Campbell Cantrill, for instance, formerly a suffrage opponent, now warned southern Democrats that failure to support the amendment could cost them their committee chairmanships.[35]

Significant changes had also taken place in NAWSA after Carrie Chapman Catt succeeded Anna Howard Shaw as president in 1916. Catt revitalized the organization and devised a "Winning Plan," which required the National to concentrate primarily on supporting the federal amendment and to assist only those states that had a good chance of obtaining woman suffrage by state action. She based this plan on the belief that the larger the number of congressmen from woman suffrage states, the greater the chance for the federal amendment to pass Congress. As one historian has noted, under Catt's leadership NAWSA became one of the most effective single-issue pressure groups in U.S. history. Suffragists won important state victories in Rhode Island and New York in 1917, and the KERA convention initiated plans for a major state campaign to take place during the 1918 meeting of the Kentucky General Assembly. Catt, however, asked the Kentuckians to abandon the plan and join with NAWSA in concentrating all resources upon a few states with the greatest likelihood of success. Madge believed that 1918 presented the first real chance in her lifetime to secure a state amendment; yet she and a majority of Kentucky suffragists agreed to support the National's policy, although Madge said they "will never know what they asked us to give up."[36]

The increasing emphasis on the federal amendment had a disturbing effect on KERA. Laura Clay, founder of the organization and an avid supporter of states' rights, had advocated the Anthony amendment for purposes of agitation when there was no possibility it would pass Congress. When Wilson endorsed it, she had gone along for a time, but she opposed acceding to NAWSA's request to forego a state campaign in 1918 and became very bitter about losing that opportunity. Soon she turned from her apparent acceptance of the federal amendment and declared her intent to speak out publicly against it. Desha Breckinridge urged her not to submit letters to the paper opposing the amendment because it would help the antisuffragists. For a short time she agreed to hold off her opposition, but in October 1918 she submitted her resignation as a member of the board of KERA because that body had voted to censure U.S. Senate candidate A. O. Stanley if he did not support the federal amendment. Such action, she contended, would be partisan. She was persuaded to withdraw her resignation and remain on the board when Stanley's support of the amendment made the censure unnecessary. However, this only postponed the dissension that threatened to split KERA and left Madge "greatly distressed" about Clay's attitude.[37]

Another, more personal blow fell in 1918 when Desha's youngest sister, Curry, died. She had served as a nurse in war-torn France beginning in 1915. After the United States entered the war, she came home to help organize a medical unit to go to France to aid wounded soldiers. While at home she contracted an illness diagnosed as "an attack of what they call grippe," which affected her heart. In April 1918 Sophonisba admitted her to Presbyterian Hospital in Chicago, where she lingered in great pain until her death on June 23 at the age of forty-two. Her life had been brief and tragic, beset by early family problems, frequent melancholy, and poor health, as well as the difficulty of finding her niche in life. Both Madge and Desha grieved at her passing, feeling they had somehow failed her and wishing futilely that they might have done more.[38]

Madge again spent much of the summer at Saranac Lake undergoing treatment for tuberculosis. Both in Asheville during the previous winter and later in Lexington and Saranac Lake, she worked with the Civic League to provide extra food for children at Lincoln School and stayed actively involved in the tuberculosis sanatorium, helping to bring Dr. Edward J. Murray of Denver, Colorado, as the hospital's new superintendent. In June she accepted the presidency of the Civic League once more. During this time KERA honored her by raising funds to send a nurse, "known as the 'Madeline McDowell Breckinridge Nurse,'" to France with the medical unit Curry had helped organize. Madge returned home in the autumn, finally declared "cured," only to experience another trauma with the death of Aunt Mag on December 26 at the age of eighty-nine. Magdalen McDowell was more than a beloved aunt; she had provided a role model for her niece. In a day when it was thought improper for a woman to engage in such activities, she worked as both an artist and an architect. Undoubtedly her independent spirit and her utter disregard for the social restrictions that would have confined her to "woman's work" helped liberate Madge from those same conventions.[39]

Following her usual pattern, Madge submerged her grief by plunging

Magdalen Harvey McDowell at Ashland. Courtesy of Special Collections and Digital Programs, Margaret I. King Library, University of Kentucky, Lexington.

into the work necessary to carry out her aunt's wish that she serve as executor of her estate. Meanwhile, Henry Clay McDowell Jr. continued the process of settling the estate of Henry Clay McDowell Sr. and his wife, consisting of $390,828 (equivalent to $5,592,913 in 2008 dollars) subject to inheritance tax that had been left in trust to their children. With Aunt Mag's death the old way of life had ended, and the McDowell children pondered whether or not to sell Ashland.[40]

Madge had endured much sorrow in the previous two years, and many decisions about her family's property remained to be decided. However, she rarely allowed personal problems to divert her from her reform goals, and, in fact, seemed to derive solace from her many public projects. Now that her health had improved, suffragists would once more look to her for leadership. With suffrage success seemingly a bright spot on the horizon, the question now appeared to be whether Madge could meet the challenge and lead the cause to victory.

Chapter 10

Kentucky's "most distinguished woman citizen" 1919–1920

After being pronounced cured of tuberculosis in autumn 1918, Madge Breckinridge felt reinvigorated and eager to move forward for the cause of woman suffrage. The international influenza epidemic had caused the annual KERA convention to be postponed until the following spring, and when it met in March 1919, Madge again became president. Prospects for the federal amendment had never looked brighter, even though the U.S. Senate had failed by one vote on February 10 to give it the necessary two-thirds majority. NAWSA now constituted a mass movement whose strength had grown exponentially since Catt devised her "Winning Plan." At the same time, demonstrations by the National Woman's Party and the government's attack on its right of assembly through arrest, imprisonment, and force-feeding led many in Washington to question the government's actions. Together, the two suffrage groups, though not consciously cooperating, caused a backlash that coerced the Wilson administration to endorse the federal amendment. As a result, Kentucky's entire congressional delegation with the exception of Senator J. C. W. Beckham now supported the amendment. Strong resistance continued, however, in the Deep South, where the Anthony amendment remained inextricably linked with the issue of black voting rights and the perception that it would threaten white supremacy. Some antisuffragists even went so far as to imply that the tactics used to prevent black men from voting could not be applied to black women. (Apparently, they feared the much-vaunted concept of "southern chivalry" applied to black women enough to prevent widespread violence or threats thereof from being used to pre-

Portrait of Madeline McDowell Breckinridge by Dixie Selden, 1920. The portrait hangs at Ashland. Courtesy of Special Collections and Digital Programs, Margaret I. King Library, University of Kentucky, Lexington.

vent their voting.) Mainstream southern suffragists tried to ignore the race issue whenever possible, and when forced to address it, argued that the federal amendment would add more white women to the electorate than the total of black men and black women combined, if all were allowed to vote. Yet few could deny that equal suffrage meant political, and possibly social, equality.[1]

Despite the fact that Kentucky, with a black population of only 9.5 percent in 1920, had implemented a number of segregationist policies, it had never taken the final step of disfranchising blacks. Nevertheless, culturally it identified in many ways with the Deep South—with some historians even arguing that Kentucky joined the Confederacy *after* the Civil War—and many in the commonwealth clung to the states' rights philosophy. This climate created a challenge for support of the Anthony amendment. Thus, the final episode of the suffrage movement in Kentucky revolved around the issue of states' rights versus federal amendment and the contrasting attitudes of the state's two leading suffragists—Madeline McDowell Breckinridge and Laura Clay.[2]

In February 1919 the *Herald* published arguments for and against the federal amendment by Laura Clay, Lexington attorney John T. Shelby, Desha Breckinridge, and Madeline McDowell Breckinridge. Laura Clay launched the debate with a letter to the editor stating that her chief objection to the Anthony amendment centered on section 2, which stated: "Congress shall have power to enforce this article by legislation," the exact wording of section 2 of the Fifteenth Amendment. It was this "federal supervision of state elections" to which Clay objected, believing that if the amendment were passed, any partisan majority in Congress might thereby force its will on some state. She believed the Republican Party had used section 2 of the Fifteenth Amendment during Reconstruction primarily to maintain itself in power rather than to protect the ex-slaves, and the effect of the Anthony amendment might be even greater because the amendment would enfranchise one-half of the population and might lead to federal intervention in every election in every state. Moreover, she maintained, in virtual defiance of her life's work, that while woman suffrage was an important issue, it was not more important than state control of state elections.[3]

John T. Shelby, former law partner of W. C. P. Breckinridge and one of his defending attorneys in the Madeline Pollard lawsuit, stated his belief that the federal amendment would violate "the spirit of the Constitution." Desha replied by asking Shelby if the constitutionality of a federal amendment on voting rights had not already been settled by the Fifteenth Amendment. Shelby responded that he did not mean that the Anthony amendment would be unconstitutional in a legal sense, only that it would interfere with the rights of the "sovereign states." He feared that one group of states using the amending power to impose its will on others would ultimately break up the Union. To Desha it seemed as reasonable to contend that the "spirit of the Constitution" permitted a state to secede, despite the decision of the Civil War, as it was to say that the Anthony amendment violated the "spirit of the Constitution" despite the precedent of the Fifteenth Amendment. Shelby replied that it was "a matter of surprise, indeed of paternal sorrow, that The Herald" would advocate passage of the suffrage amendment based on the precedent of the "wrongful" passage of the Fifteenth Amendment.[4]

On February 22 Madge wrote the *Herald* editor that she wanted to explain her own views on the amendment "since I disagree somewhat with you, with Mr. Shelby, and with Miss Laura Clay." She agreed with the editor's conclusions, she stated, but she arrived at them by a more direct route. The Constitution gave the states the right to determine the electorate, but it also provided a way to amend the Constitution. The "so-called 'crime of the Fifteenth Amendment'" consisted of the federal government's forcing it on unwilling states. This would not be the case in the present situation, because the states would ratify joyfully. In fact, "as Senator [William P.] Pollock of South Carolina—(once the State of Nullification!)—pointed out during the suffrage debate in the Senate last week, when a considerable body of citizens desire an amendment submitted, it is a denial of states' rights not to allow the states to pass upon it." As for Clay's fear of a Force Bill reminiscent of those of 1870 and 1871, Madge thought it was "a bogey, ingeniously conjured up, but which will very speedily vanish into air." She continued: "Miss Clay knows well the answers for Southern standpatters to the colored woman bogey. She has, I am sure, quoted them when urging suffrage by the states' rights route in Southern States: there are more white women in the South than colored men and women combined—(why is the Democratic party so timorous?)—; such honest and proper qualifications as may limit male suffrage may also limit suffrage for women." She added: "Colored women who meet these qualifications deserve the same protection in their political rights as do white women meeting them."[5]

Madge further stated that ever since she had reached voting age, she had "ardently desired to have and to exercise political rights." She had, therefore, spent most of her life working for the franchise when she would have preferred working for other reforms that Kentucky needed.

Laura Clay, she pointed out, was an even more striking example of one who could have accomplished much for Kentucky if she had not had to spend her life working for the political means necessary to serve her state. Madge explained that she had never feared the federal government, because it was not an alien government imposed from without but was "our own representative government" just as was the government in Frankfort. Her father had often said that his family followed George Washington and Alexander Hamilton rather than Thomas Jefferson; Henry Clay rather than Andrew Jackson; Lincoln rather than Jefferson Davis. Despite this heritage, she said: "I think still sometimes that I'm a better Jeffersonian Democrat than, say the editor of The Herald. While I'm not afraid of the central government, neither am I afraid of the people."[6]

In reply Laura Clay lamented that she had been misunderstood by "even so careful a reader as Mrs. Breckinridge." She had never, she protested, supposed that the evils of federal supervision would be limited to states that tried to deny woman suffrage. Rather, the supreme party in Congress would use the power to further its own selfish purpose to the detriment of all states. If a state amendment had been presented to the Kentucky General Assembly in 1918, it would have passed, she argued. Kentucky would have another chance in 1920, and she urged Madge to use her "great abilities and wide influence" to further the suffrage cause by state action.[7]

Clay's biographer has argued that it is erroneous to conclude that Clay's "sole fear was that the federal government would force the southern states to let Negro women vote." Rather, he asserts, her opposition to the federal amendment centered "on the principle of federal-state relations." If so, this fear seems irrational in view of the federal government's failure to intervene during the next forty years in southern elections to enforce the Fifteenth Amendment. Moreover, Clay's correspondence indicates that while she did not fear the black vote in Kentucky, neither she nor her emancipationist parents believed in racial equality, and she had great sympathy for those areas of the South with large black populations. Though her racism lacked the virulence of Kate Gordon, the two women maintained a deep friendship and an extensive correspondence, working together for a "whites only" suffrage policy for the Deep South, a stance they failed to persuade NAWSA to follow. In the final analysis, it seems likely, as one historian of the southern suffrage movement concluded, that "Clay's statements on race and suffrage, including the statement that in predominantly black areas of the South, unrestricted suffrage would mean 'an abandonment of civilization as white Americans have lived it, and a decline to a state of society suited to the mental and moral development of negroes,' suggested that racism had a great deal to do with her defense of state sovereignty."[8]

Whatever Clay's motivations, by this time Madge had committed herself fully to the federal amendment. After her election as president of KERA in March 1919, the organization adopted a platform asking Congress to submit the federal amendment to the states and imploring the Kentucky legislature to ratify it. Since the General Assembly could grant presidential suffrage without a state constitutional amendment, the platform also asked for a presidential woman suffrage bill so that women could vote for president in 1920 even if the Anthony amendment had not yet been passed and been ratified by the requisite number of states. Whether a state amendment would be proposed in 1920 was left to the discretion of the board in consultation with NAWSA. Laura Clay opposed the platform and refused to stand for election to any office, although she received several nominations. After a spirited debate the convention voted down her motion to begin immediately a campaign for a state amendment. Although Clay was later able to secure endorsement of the Fayette ERA for a state amendment, she did not succeed in persuading the KERA board, which voted against a state campaign when it met on March 31. Clay's influence in the organization she founded had clearly vanished.[9]

A frightening event occurred on the way back to Lexington from the KERA convention in Louisville when a tire blew on Mary LeBus's limousine, causing the car to crash into a telephone pole. Madge, Mary, and two other women were transferred to a Shelbyville hospital, where they remained for a few days. LeBus was the most severely injured, but all four women recovered. A few days later Madge left to attend the NAWSA convention in St. Louis, saying: "I went when I wasn't very well able to navigate, having left the house only twice after the automobile accident." Although at the NAWSA convention Laura Clay continued to oppose the Anthony amendment and attempted to get approval for a Kentucky state campaign, supporters of the federal amendment believed they were on the verge of success, needing only one vote in the U.S. Senate, so they overwhelmingly defeated Clay's proposals.[10]

It became obvious by May that KERA board members could not be persuaded to mount a state campaign. This position was sealed on June

4 when the U.S. Senate finally passed the Anthony amendment. In the final vote only two members of the Kentucky congressional delegation voted against it—Democratic congressman Arthur B. Rouse, a native of Burlington, Kentucky, and Senator J. C. W. Beckham, who remained consistent to the end, telling the Senate that he "did not wish to give women the ballot because they are entirely too good for it." Congressmen J. Campbell Cantrill and Alben Barkley and Senator A. O. Stanley, all of whom had previously opposed woman suffrage, reversed their positions and now advocated the federal amendment. In fact, so strong was Cantrill's stance that Maud Wood Park, chair of the Congressional Committee of NAWSA, compared it to St. Paul's conversion on the road to Damascus. With Barkley and Cantrill's support, Kentucky Democrats endorsed ratification in their 1919 party platform, and both Edwin P. Morrow, the Republican nominee for governor, and Governor James D. Black, the Democratic candidate, likewise favored ratification.[11]

The day after the U.S. Senate approved the Anthony amendment, Laura Clay withdrew from KERA, again predicting that historical results similar to those following the passage of the Fifteenth Amendment would occur if the federal amendment were ratified. Since KERA had voted to support the National and work only for the federal amendment, "there is no longer any consistency for a firm believer in State rights, as I am, for remaining," she wrote Madge, who accepted this resignation with "deepest regret," noting that Clay had been president of KERA for the first twenty-five years of its existence. The KERA board, Madge stated, had now decided to ask the legislature in 1920 to pass a presidential suffrage bill and to ratify the Anthony amendment. Madge predicted that both of these proposals had an "excellent" chance for passage.[12]

Laura Clay managed to take a small group of KERA members with her when she withdrew. The dissidents soon established the Citizens' Committee for a State Suffrage Amendment and set up headquarters on North Upper Street in Lexington. Christine South reported to Madge that a rumor was circulating charging that KERA intended to try to defeat Beckham in the next primary. South, who believed Clay hoped to get Beckham's organization to oppose ratification, was not sure Clay was behind this rumor, "though I strongly suspect that she is."[13]

The Clay group spoke to the state Democratic Platform Committee in an attempt to prevent it from endorsing the federal amendment, but the effort failed. Although frustrated by the states' rights group, Madge refused to be intimidated by it. Over the years she and Laura Clay had often differed on tactics, but Madge still held Clay in esteem because of her many contributions to the suffrage cause. At the same time she recognized Clay's shortcomings, once saying of the tall, imposing suffragist: "She isn't a bit tactful, but she is not small in any way, mentally or spiritually more than physically." As the 1919 KERA convention approached, Madge conceded that "Miss Laura could do a little handling from the sidelines if she wanted to" even though she would not be attending. Madge did not expect her to attempt this; however, "it would not bother me if it happened, and personally, I have not the slightest idea of resigning the City of Lexington to Miss Laura." She added that "we are all on good terms," and the split seemed more serious to those at a distance than to those in Lexington.[14]

Ignoring the KERA split as much as possible, Madge on July 4 launched the campaign in Kentucky to secure ratification of the Anthony amendment. That day she and Mary Scrugham, an organizer sent to Kentucky by NAWSA, spoke at Pikeville and in the next few weeks held meetings throughout eastern Kentucky. Setting out by 6:00 a.m., Madge spoke in two or three places each day. The National undertook a drive about this time to try to get enough states to call a special legislative session to consider the amendment, so that it could be ratified and go into effect in 1919. Since Kentucky's General Assembly would not meet until January 1920, Madge and the KERA board decided they would not ask for a special session unless it became clear that the amendment could be ratified before the end of the year. Nevertheless, Madge set out to determine the position of the legislators on ratification and to discover whether they favored a special session and would waive payment of their expenses to attend. She received a variety of replies. Senator Charles M. Harriss, a Democrat from Versailles, enclosed a clipping that quoted him as saying: "'Our Ladies' have long since ceased to be the vine that secures its life from the tree to which it clings. . . . May the day hasten in which each of 'Our Ladies' will have . . . a ballot in her hand." He added: "I am willing to waive mileage, per diem, Magna Charta and the Habeas Corpus" to attend a special session. Dr. H. T. Morris, Republican senator from Greenup, stated that "the American woman is the most adorable creation of God; her intelligence is a demonstrated fact"; but, he continued, "I do not believe in the principle of woman suffrage . . . because I do not believe that equal suffrage would be a recognition of the accomplishments of American woman, but would in time destroy that which she has attained." He then provided the encouraging news that 90 percent of his constituents would favor a referendum on the subject. Republican senator J. L. Early of Stanley in western Kentucky informed her: "If Governor Black will call an extra session at once and there is complaint of the cost, just charge it to the Republican party and exonerate him of all blame. We will be glad to be charged with so worthy a cause." Still another Republican said: "Yes I believe in woman suffrage. My mother taught me that 50 years ago. . . . I believe in women doing anything they want to do. It is none of my business and besides any of them have got as much or more sense than I have."[15]

Despite her preoccupation with the suffrage movement, Madge did not neglect tuberculosis work. In April she attended a meeting of the board of the state tuberculosis association. The group had not been active for a while due to an alliance between the Kentucky Tuberculosis Commission and the State Board of Health, but an appropriation made by the Red Cross necessitated reviving the board in order to handle the funds. The *Herald* reminded its readers of the ravages of the disease in the community, and in the autumn Madge became vice president of the state tuberculosis association. She also gave a speech in Cleveland in support of the League of Nations and presided at a dinner in Washington, DC, calling for international peace and American entry into the League. Somehow she also found time to take instruction on driving an automobile.[16]

In addition to her civic pursuits, Madge became recipient of the remaining portion of Aunt Mag's estate that had not been consumed by the tuberculosis sanatorium pledge. The McDowell heirs also sold off a portion of the Ashland estate bordering Hanover, High, and Main streets, to be developed as a subdivision designed by the Olmsted Brothers, who had planned New York's Central Park and Lexington's Woodland Park. Madge at least rested during much of August and September as she and Desha visited Mary LeBus's Nantucket estate. They enjoyed clambakes and sightseeing and made a brief trip to New York City for Desha to attend a meeting of the Publishers' Association Board, while Madge met with Carrie Chapman Catt to discuss suffrage strategy.[17]

Strangely, Madge's reports of the Nantucket visit to Nettie Bullock seem fairly content, with her leaving the date of their return to Desha and noting that she wanted him to get as much rest as possible. She did, however, complain that things "seem a little slow and lonesome" as "Desha and Mrs. LeBus go bathing in the morning, and I have been doing a little suffrage and Tb. work with the stenographer." Perhaps she did not know of the affair as early as some of her friends assumed; perhaps she did know at one level, but did not want to believe. The most likely explanation for her behavior is that she saw the affair as an outgrowth of her illness and looked away with a knowing eye. Perhaps she and Desha had an agreement, either spoken or tacit, that Desha—a man whom friends recalled had "always liked the ladies"—could have relationships with other women. Yet, in the end, Madge's emotional state remains a mystery, even now. Clearly she loved Desha and did not want to lose him, and, in his own way, Desha appears to have cared a great deal for her. Certainly, neither of them would have wanted the notoriety of a divorce, and it is a subject to which Madge would not have referred in writing. Her mentioning of it to friends seems to have come at rare times of particular stress, when she lost control and blurted her true feelings.[18]

Back in Lexington in October Madge reported to the Fayette ERA that all candidates for office in the Fayette district favored ratification of the Anthony amendment. By this time it had become apparent that the necessary thirty-six states would not ratify before the end of the year, so KERA leaders dropped plans to try to get Governor James D. Black to call a special session. Black, who was completing the term of A. O. Stanley, now in the U.S. Senate, had long supported suffrage, and when he received a telegram from the governor of Louisiana asking all southern governors to oppose the federal amendment in favor of state action, he gave Madge an interview for publication strongly supporting ratification of the Anthony amendment. "It is too late now," Madge insisted, for southern governors and legislators "to begin to show such a passionate desire to grant suffrage by the states' rights method."[19]

State senator Thomas A. Combs of Lexington reported to Desha Breckinridge that the Democrats' platform would endorse the Anthony amendment and stated that Congressman Cantrill was now "quite active" on behalf of suffrage. With both Democratic and Republican platforms in favor, Madge began to devise plans to secure ratification of the amendment on the first day of the legislative session. This would be an unprecedented accomplishment, because the legislature had never before passed a substantive measure on its opening day. She and Christine South conferred with the newly elected governor, Edwin P. Morrow, who was South's first cousin, about strategy. Morrow—a Somerset attorney and nephew of William O. Bradley, the state's first Republican governor—had handily defeated incumbent Black in the 1919 gubernatorial election. The Morrows and Breckinridges were old friends, dating from the years when Morrow had lived in Lexington and taught at a night school with Curry Breckinridge. With Christine's help, Madge easily won Morrow's support for first-day ratification. Madge then made plans to hold the KERA convention simultaneously with the convening of the 1920 legislature and began negotiations to secure Emmeline Pankhurst as a speaker for the convention. When NAWSA president Carrie Chapman Catt questioned this choice, Madge replied: "We are having Mrs. Pankhurst because we think her the very best Barnum circus drawing-card we can possibly get. . . . The bad odor of militancy is forgotten in her war work and in the triumph of the Suffrage cause in England." Plans to begin the KERA convention at the same time the legislature convened and to have both Pankhurst and Catt as speakers ran into snags as Madge experienced "a devil of a time" trying to reconcile Pankhurst's and Catt's managers "and the Lexington Opera House and the positive advice of our legislative friends." Ultimately, KERA officials decided to hold the convention in Lexington and travel by train to Frankfort for the opening session of the legislature.[20]

Madge felt so optimistic that KERA and the Woman's Club in Lexington sponsored a series of lectures on politics and citizenship, given by Mary Scrugham, a doctoral student in history at Columbia University. The *Herald* published these lectures, which were designed to help educate women in the new responsibilities they would assume as voters. Despite this apparent confidence in success, Madge still had many problems to solve, including KERA's lack of money. In December 1919 she stated: "I have simply had to go straight ahead with the state work . . . as if there were money in the treasury, paying bills myself and trying to get something put in." Other annoyances concerned the division within the suffrage movement. When the National Woman's Party sent representatives to Louisville to work for the federal amendment, Madge refused the request of some NAWSA officials to oppose them publicly. "I have previously declined to aid the Congressional Union in Kentucky or to ask their aid and will again do so," she said, "but I will not publicly fight them, for I believe the less said, the better."[21]

A more critical issue concerned Laura Clay's Citizens' Committee for a State Suffrage Amendment. This division in the Kentucky movement puzzled Catt, who wrote of Clay: "I cannot think that she is quite in her right mind to take the attitude she has. I can see she might feel too much opposed to the method to work with it and for it, but it seems to me a normal minded suffragist would have vision to see that the suffrage is coming this way and that, therefore, she had better drop out and let it come." This situation caused the NAWSA president to seek Madge's counsel on what to do about presenting Clay with one of the certificates of honor that the National was preparing for every current and former state president and major leaders. She explained: "We workers of the long ago were bound together by a bond of comradeship and faith which I believe to be a little stronger than any that binds the later comers into the movement and I therefore have no feeling of enmity, hatred or any other related feeling for Laura Clay." "Now, whatever are we going to do about Laura Clay?" she asked. Noting that "no one deserves a certificate of honor more than she as a token for her many years of hard work and certain sacrifice," she wondered how "can we honor a woman who, when the last turn of the road was reached, ceased to march forward with us, but instead turned about and did everything she could to impede our progress? It is an amazing condition. What do you think we ought to do about it?"[22]

"It beats me!" Madge replied. "I could not bear for you not to honor Miss Laura, and I think you will have to do it with a foot-note that in the latter days she dissented from the policy of the National." Madge hoped that soon suffrage would be achieved, and "we can forget and forgive everybody." Yet for the present she found "it a little hard to forget and forgive myself, as I keep hearing from stupid legislatures [*sic*] that Miss Laura has gotten to first, last or both times."[23]

Knowing the Clay group was hard at work, Madge did not take success for granted. By the time for the legislature to convene in January 1920, she could confidently predict victory. Still, she continued to press the issue, pointing out in a January 2 article in the *Frankfort State Journal* that it was a bit late to argue that Kentucky should have another chance to give women the right to vote through a state amendment; Kentucky men had had 127 years to enfranchise women but had not done so. Moreover, she predicted that the enforcement clause of the Anthony amendment would be innocuous, because it gave Congress no more power than it already possessed under Article I of the U.S. Constitution. In another article she argued that ratification by three-fourths of the state legislatures was a "distinct acknowledgement" of the principle of states' rights.[24]

As the crucial morning of January 6 dawned, Madge met with the delegates to the KERA convention at the Phoenix Hotel in Lexington. The women then traveled to Frankfort to witness the opening of the legislature at noon. In his message to the General Assembly Governor Morrow called earnestly for approval of the federal amendment. Hopes for instant ratification soon dwindled, however, as states' rights opponents demonstrated their intent to fight to the bitter end. Madge moved from the house to the senate to the governor's office, directing the fight. The house completed its action first, ratifying the amendment 72-25. The senate became the site of an acrimonious states' rights debate. As the *Herald* reported the next day: "Caesar and the dead empire of Rome were called up from the seventh century to typify the inevitable result of indulging in a federal government." Finally, the senate ratified the amendment 30-8. Madge's first comment after her return to Lexington: "Hurrah!"[25]

On the evening of January 6 Governor Morrow and Katrina Ely Tiffany of New York, an avid suffragist married to the grandson of the founder of Tiffany and Company, spoke in Lexington at the KERA convention. The next afternoon Madge gave a reception at Ashland and a dinner at her home for Emmeline Pankhurst, followed by the closing session of the thirtieth, and last, KERA convention. The meeting, highlighted by Pankhurst's address, drew a packed house. Madge announced that the governor had invited KERA members to Frankfort the next day to watch him sign the joint resolution of the two houses passing the amendment. She also announced that when the Anthony amendment received ratification by the thirty-sixth state and went into effect, KERA would become the League of Women Voters. Noting that Laura Clay had toiled incessantly and virtually single-handedly to keep KERA going and had spent much of her wealth for the cause, she expressed the organization's gratitude to its founder. Madge and a group of suffragists watched the next day as Morrow signed the resolutions making Kentucky the twenty-fourth state to approve the amendment. (Only three other states in the South—Tennessee, Arkansas, and Texas—ratified.) As Desha later recalled these events, they "were the culmination of three months['] intense labor during which she [Madge] wrote hundreds of letters, innumerable newspaper articles, made numerous trips for the purpose of inducing members of the Legislation [*sic*] to vote for the ratification of the Amendment." So intense was her work during the final three days, she "seemed more like a spirit than a being fettered by human limitations."[26]

Later in the month a representative and a senator from Fayette Coun-

Surrounded by suffragists, Governor Edwin P. Morrow signs Kentucky's ratification of the Nineteenth Amendment. Madeline McDowell Breckinridge stands behind him, second from the right. Courtesy of the Kentucky Historical Society, Frankfort.

ty each introduced a bill to submit a state woman suffrage amendment to Kentucky voters. Madge commented: "I think that the gentlemen are just about 127 years too late." Still, she hoped to see the legislature pass a presidential suffrage bill so that Kentucky women could be assured of voting in the autumn presidential election even if the required twelve additional states had not ratified the Anthony amendment by that time. Sarah Clay Bennett, sister of Laura Clay and also a states' rights advocate, put up the money for lobbying to push the presidential suffrage bill through. The move for a state amendment, which KERA now opposed but Laura Clay continued to support, was killed with Morrow's help, and in March the senate followed the house in approving the presidential suffrage bill.[27]

In a mood of celebration, Madge spoke at the "Jubilee" suffrage convention on Valentine's Day in Chicago, where she joyfully recited a parody of "My Old Kentucky Home":

> The sun shines bright in my old Kentucky home,
> 'Tis winter, the ladies are gay,
> The corn tops gone, prohibitions in the swing,
> The colonel's in eclipse and the women in the ring.
> We'll get all our rights with the help of Uncle Sam,
> For the way that they come, we don't give a — —;
> Weep no more, my lady, Oh, weep no more today,
> For we'll vote one vote for the old Kentucky home.
> The old Kentucky home, far away.[28]

During the spring Madge also began her last major task for the suffrage movement—writing the "Kentucky" chapter for the final volume of *The History of Woman Suffrage* being edited by Ida H. Harper. Madge collected from Laura Clay the early reports and other records, and, when she completed her first draft, submitted it to Clay for her criticism. Although Clay did not agree with Madge's statement that the suffrage movement in Kentucky had come to a "successful close" with the ratification of the federal amendment, Madge let the statement stand.[29]

After achieving ratification of the Anthony amendment, Madge immediately turned her attention to other projects. Desha wrote Sophonisba that his wife was busier than ever: "I really see no hope for her ever showing any signs of intelligent self-restraint." Even though she had a cold and lost her voice for a day or two, she continued working into the night. During this time she also sat for E. Sophonisba Hergersheimer to paint her portrait, undoubtedly one of those activities that irritated her because of the time it consumed, but one she must have felt obligated to do, because, according to Sophonisba, children at Lincoln School had raised the funds to have the portrait painted to hang in their institution.[30]

One of the causes she still worked for diligently was the antituberculosis movement. As vice president of the state association and chair of its Legislative Committee, she sought passage of a bill giving state aid to the tuberculosis districts. In the 1920 General Assembly this measure ran up against a bill to convert Hazelwood Sanatorium near Louisville into a state institution. Madge did not believe this would be very helpful to the commonwealth as a whole and feared Hazelwood would turn into a large,

Madeline McDowell Breckinridge by E. Sophonisba Hergersheimer, 1920. The portrait hung in Lincoln School until it was moved to the Madeline McDowell Breckinridge Elementary School, which opened in 1963. Courtesy of Special Collections and Digital Programs, Margaret I. King Library, University of Kentucky, Lexington.

politically controlled, and poorly administered institution. However, she promised not to oppose the measure, adding: "I have been in the T.B. game in Kentucky long enough now to be willing to take anything we can get."[31]

Madge employed a lawyer to draft a bill for state aid to the district sanatoria, which she believed would benefit the entire state rather than one region. She took the bill to Frankfort and persuaded legislators to introduce it in both chambers. She then wrote newspaper editorials and letters to the legislators, to the governor and lieutenant governor, and to members of the Kentucky Society for the Prevention and Relief of Tuberculosis, urging all of them to support the bill. Occasionally her weariness, her frustration, and her feeling that time was too short to accomplish her goals became evident in her letters. To Governor Morrow, who had urged economy and patience, she wrote: "The Tb. fight in Kentucky from start to finish has been work, persuade, fight, until when you get anything you are so weary you can hardly rejoice in it." To Lieutenant Governor Thruston Ballard, her cousin, she wrote: "You cannot do a thing for Tb. with sympathy. It takes money. . . . It is wicked the way public authorities are letting people die in Kentucky from Tb. and never conceding it to be any part of their business to help save them." When she thought the House Rules Committee was about to kill the bill, she entreated Morrow to try to save it, explaining, perhaps with prescience: "I don't know whether I will ever be here to get things in as good a state another two years hence." When both the bill making Hazelwood a state sanatorium and the one giving state aid to the tuberculosis districts passed, Madge could feel that Kentucky had at last assumed some responsibility for fighting its major killer.[32]

In March 1920 Madge participated in the NAWSA convention in St. Louis. She then decided to attend a meeting of the International Women's Suffrage Alliance, which would convene in Geneva, Switzerland, in June. Madge had wanted to go to Europe at least since the time she offered to sell her pony to finance such an excursion. She had vacillated about the trip, but Desha urged her to go, believing she would be forced to rest at least on the voyage. Finally, he agreed to accompany her for part of the trip. After the conference, Madge planned to join an eighty-day tour of Europe, led by her friend Sara McGarvey.[33]

Before she left, Madge and Desha wrote new wills. At Madge's suggestion, since they had no children, Desha changed his to give more of his estate to his siblings and less to his wife because "she has a separate estate of her own that insures her against want." In April the Breckinridges traveled to New York City, Desha to attend a meeting of the Associated Press and Madge to have a new limb made, a task she had "been trying indefinitely to get the time to do." While they were in New York, Madge joined Carrie Chapman Catt on a suffrage campaign in Connecticut to try to get that state to ratify the Anthony amendment. Although suffering from a bad cold, Madge spoke gamely at events in Bridgeport, Stamford, New Haven, and Norwalk, and "said about two words" at the governor's hearing in Hartford. Nevertheless, the governor refused to call a special session to ratify the amendment.[34]

Madge had counted on her husband's accompanying her on the trip to Europe, even though he would shortly have to return home. "I don't quite know how I would have started without Desha," she wrote Nettie Bullock. However, on May 19 she sailed alone. It is unclear why Desha did not go, but during the voyage, which was warm, calm, and "one of the most delightful experiences in the world," Madge wrote Nettie that "I was so paralyzed with grief the first day or two after I didn't let Desha go—& I still am for that matter—that I couldn't get the most out of it." Later on the trip she wrote Desha: "I should think you would hate me for all the bad times there were on that New York trip—and if I had just let you go with me we would both have been so happy!" Had her frustration over his affair at last boiled over into a fight while they were in New York? Whatever the reason for the "bad times," Madge obviously blamed herself rather than Desha. Friends observed her depression throughout the trip and attributed it to her concern about Desha's amorous affair and her disappointment in his not accompanying her.[35]

In Paris before going to the conference in Geneva, Madge visited her old friend Nettie Belle Smith Feltner, who lived there with her husband, Thomas Feltner. "Nobody ought ever to die without seeing Notre Dame," Madge proclaimed. At the suffrage conference she met Lady Astor and listened to many women speak who were from "strange countries where women are voting & sitting in Parliament." She found herself "disappointed to find how my languages of twenty years ago have left me," complaining that she missed much of the French speeches—though she had no trouble reading them in the newspapers the next day—and caught only "occasional bits & words of the German ones." Nevertheless, she spoke French better than anyone in her party and thus became the translator.[36]

After the conference, they stayed in Nettie Belle's apartment in Paris while waiting for the Sara McGarvey trip to begin. The tour proved to be arduous, and Madge sometimes rested in the hotel while her companions engaged in activities she could not manage, such as climbing the glacier at Mt. Blanc. At one point she lamented that "I can't keep comfortable & have been awfully lame much of the time," but several weeks into the trip, she reported to Desha that "I am not having the miserable time that I was having for over a month after I got here—The trip is very strenuous and not under the best conditions, but they all look out for me . . . I always have a seat, no matter who has to stand." All in all she was getting along "very well in spite of the heat—I am no more lame than is to be expected with the heat and the walking." Despite "all the hardships, I'd much rather have the trip than never to have" gone to Europe. Proclaiming herself a "natural-born sight-seer," she reported: "I go to bed so tired & so lame at night, & I get up & go back at it the next day with renewed eagerness." But she added: "I do envy people, though, who are good & strong physically—Except for the lameness & consequent weariness, though, I have been perfectly well—I haven't had a sign of a cough since I got here."[37]

Madge's impressions of Europe varied. She found the Folies Bergère in Paris "more shocking even than desired," while "the reality" of the Gothic cathedrals "uplifts me quite beyond words to describe." "Scoff no more at my religious ardor," she wrote Desha after attending services in four cathedrals in one day. Switzerland she found to be "so cool and so clean and so bracing." While Italy was hot and dirty, Sorrento was extremely beautiful. She did not mind in the least when two barefoot Italian men carried her up the steps in a chair at one of the hotels. She described Rheims as a "city of ruins," but noted the crops growing between what had once been the German and French lines and commented that she was unsure which was more impressive—the destruction caused by the war or "the amazing industry that is rebuilding." The poverty fanned her reformer instincts as she developed "a passionate desire to start model schools or at least baths enough to get" the children clean, and "each time I see another blind beggar I decide that Linda Neville must come over & found a society for the prevention of blindness."[38]

Madge longed for Desha's presence throughout the trip and wrote him affectionate letters detailing her homesickness and expressing the desire that someday they should tour Europe together. Frequently referring to him as "my darling" and sending "love and kisses," she lamented on a boat trip on Lake Geneva: "I do wish so much for you! . . . I wish

I could have these first impressions of beauty with you." While she was gone, Desha traveled to Canada and later to Denver, Los Angeles, and San Francisco. After receiving a postcard written on the road between Kansas City and Denver, Madge teased her husband, whose handwriting was notoriously hard to read, that hearing from him was so good, "I take back anything disagreeable or disrespectful I may ever have said about your writing—It seems the most beautiful in the world to me!" She fretted over what gifts to bring home to Desha and told him she had his birthday present but had been unable to ship it: "I wrote a tender card to tell you how I hoped there would be many more birthdays & that I would be with you for all the rest." When Desha developed problems with his eyes and teeth, she worried and expressed the hope that his planned visit to Nantucket would provide helpful rest, and she thanked him for sending her money, saying: "You are a sweet thing." She suggested that when she returned home, they both should go to Mayo Clinic and "see about that blood pressure of yours & why I don't get fat." Yet by late August she felt so well she could write: "I've concluded I'm about the strongest person in the party—and I'm not lame now."[39]

On September 11 the party finally sailed for New York City from Southampton, England. Desha went to New York to meet the ship, which was delayed by bad weather. Madge made plans to consult about her new limb while in New York and hoped they could have a short vacation together before going home. However, that did not occur, and they reached Lexington on September 24.[40]

Immediately upon her return to the United States, Madge undertook her last crusade—a fight for American entry into the League of Nations. Speaking to the Woman's Citizenship class of the YWCA in her first public address following the trip to Europe, she found a large crowd gathered, when she had expected only two dozen women. "Why did all these people come?" she asked with her customary modesty. Her host replied: "Mrs. Breckinridge they came because Lexington loves you and wants to hear you." As she stood and spoke, she recalled how on the battlefield of Verdun she had first learned of Tennessee's ratification of the Anthony amendment, completing the thirty-six states necessary for adding the Nineteenth Amendment to the Constitution. Asserting that "the League substitutes right for might," she urged women to consider seriously the issue of the League of Nations when they cast their ballots in the November election. This was her recurring theme while campaigning for the

Democratic presidential ticket. Even before her trip to Europe Madge had spoken for the League, but as the election neared she became more emphatic. "The women of America must fight world war with the League of Nations, and the only way to do this is to vote the straight Democratic ticket for Governor [James M.] Cox and the League of Nations in November," she argued as she traveled in Kentucky, Missouri, and Nebraska, often on a freight train. During these speaking tours she left at 5:00 a.m. and spoke in a different place every afternoon and evening.[41]

Madge had earlier said of woman suffrage: "I do not expect a miracle; I shall be satisfied if the women do not disgrace themselves." Voting for the Democratic ticket of Cox and Franklin D. Roosevelt, she did not agree with the apparent decision women made by helping elect Warren G. Harding as president and thereby defeating U.S. entry into the League of Nations. However, she remained hopeful about the future effect of their voting and was encouraged by the larger-than-expected turnout of women in Kentucky and the fact that her home state went for the Democratic ticket. The *Herald* announced on November 3 that all arguments about woman suffrage had been answered the previous day when women voted all over the country for the first time, proving conclusively that women valued their new right enough to participate. Madge showed her optimism by working on plans for a convention of the League of Women Voters, a nonpartisan organization that would advocate constructive legislation and teach women to be enlightened citizens. The old KERA board set the date of November 27 to meet in Lexington with the Committee on Organization of the Kentucky League of Women Voters. Meanwhile, Madge, again serving as president of the Civic League, called a meeting at the *Herald* building on November 11 to hear reports of summer activities and plan the winter program. She also accepted a position on a committee of the newly organized Community Service League of Lexington.[42]

During the time after her return from Europe, Madge and Desha entertained family and friends, both in their home and at a theater party at the Opera House. They regretfully declined to move into Ashland because of the expense to renovate and maintain it and because they felt their health was not up to the task. On November 23 Madge telephoned Desha about final plans for Thanksgiving dinner and then began to gather items to give to the needy. Desha told her he would be home for lunch early but instead stopped at the barbershop. When he arrived at the house, he discovered that a servant had found Madge lying on the floor, felled by a stroke. Physicians from Cincinnati and Lexington declared she had a blood clot in an artery in the brain. The next day Desha wrote Sophonisba that Madge could move her right hand and leg, and he hoped that "with her wonderful vitality" she would have a steady improvement, though doctors warned they could not truly judge her condition for twenty-four to forty-eight hours. He noted that she had seemed very well when she came home from her western trip until she got a cold and then slipped on the floor, spraining her knee. Since then, she had been confined to the house and had become nervous and restless. He further explained that she had no pain and was quiet, though not comatose, and the doctors thought the condition might be due to the same cause that had left her right hand paralyzed nearly two decades earlier. He had not been in Denver with her when that incident occurred, he recalled, and had not realized the seriousness until she returned home. Even then, she learned to write with her left hand and made light of the situation. This stroke, however, she could not overcome. On Thanksgiving Day, November 25, she died at her home on Linden Walk at the age of forty-eight. Her funeral took place two days later at her family's beloved Ashland with the Reverend Robert K. Massie, dean of Christ Church Cathedral, officiating. She was laid to rest near her father and mother in the Lexington Cemetery.[43]

Tributes poured in from many individuals, from every organization in Lexington, and from others throughout the state. Newspapers called her Kentucky's "most distinguished woman citizen" and one of the "greatest women orators in the U.S." Perhaps the most eloquent tribute was Desha's editorial, "She Is Dead," which he published in the *Herald* the day after her funeral. He recalled how she had once been "the best tennis player, the most tireless dancer, the most daring rider." After becoming lame "there was no more tennis, and no more dancing, and she drove instead of rode," but "there was never complaint, never a suggestion of loss." He continued: "And then, grown to womanhood, she left the stately home where love surrounded and luxury attended her and went to one room to make a home for him she crowned with the glory of her love." Recalling how she had gone up and down the streets begging for money for playgrounds and schools, he noted: "Timid, shrinking, reserved, she forgot herself, forgot bodily ills, physical handicap, when her heart and her brain told her there was an opportunity to give joy and render service to others. . . . She knew sorrow, she knew weariness, she knew pain. She never knew fear, nor envy, nor malice. . . . Her body is at rest."[44]

Epilogue

"She belonged to Kentucky"

News of Madge's death shocked her friends and allies—and, indeed, all who knew her. That spirit, that determination, that force for good, was no more. Uncertainty gripped Lexingtonians. What would happen to the organizations she had led for so long? Who would assume leadership? Would her legacy endure?

Her dominant role in civic affairs became clear when on December 5, 1920, the *Herald* published several pages of tributes to her from many organizations and groups in Lexington and Fayette County. The Civic League, the African American community, the Lexington Board of Education, the city commissioners, the bar association, union groups, the Kentucky Federation of Women's Clubs, the children of Lincoln School, and many more passed resolutions expressing their grief. Cora Wilson Stewart, founder of Moonlight Schools for illiterate adults in eastern Kentucky, received a letter that summed up the feelings of many. "I wish for Mrs. B.," the writer stated, "that she can know now what her friends thought of her. . . . Yes God was good to Mrs. Breckinridge. He let her live long enough to see the good results of her life's work—in woman suffrage, tuberculosis etc.—then took her away from all suffering." The woman added: "I was told she said, she was never for a moment free from pain. What a beautiful way to go!" Close friend Marion Houston Smith wrote Nettie Bullock: "We all need her so much. . . . I verily believe no one ever before joined so brilliant an intellect to so tender & affectionate nature." Linda Neville told Nettie: "My thoughts are of you and Madge, and my work does not hold my interest as before," while Jane Addams recorded for the *Survey* that "social workers will bear a sense of personal sorrow and a loss of gallant comradeship" as a result of Madeline Breckinridge's death. "Few women have a larger list of achievements to be placed to their credit," she concluded, adding that "all these developed from her surpassing love for the children." A whimsical handmade card in the family papers shows the outline of a tombstone with the words:

Breckinridge
Rest in Peace, oh!
Madge McDowell
She hung herself, with a
Turkish towel
with a Crown upon her forehead
You can bet
She's making every Angel
a
suffragette.

The *Register of the Kentucky Historical Society* also paid tribute, stating: "Perhaps no other woman in America contributed more toward the final triumph of equal suffrage."[1]

One friend recalled how Madge sat in Rock Creek Cemetery in Washington, DC, in 1919 and contemplated Augustus Saint-Gaudens's statue *Grief*, noting that since early womanhood Madge had stared death in the face, unafraid. Another friend, obviously believing that her final speaking tour had caused her death, concluded: "The League of Nations is the only cause I have ever known great enough for Madge to die for." And most telling of all, two years after her death, Desha wrote in an editorial celebrating his twenty-fifth anniversary at the *Herald*: "From January, 1897, to 1920 Madeline McDowell Breckinridge was the inspiring and dominant factor in all The Herald did for good. To her it was also solely an instrument that might be used to make more effective effort for the community to which she gave herself."[2]

Perhaps Cora Wilson Stewart's correspondent had best captured the almost serendipitous timing of Madge's death. In many ways, she died at the high point of her career—achievement of woman suffrage, progress toward development of state tuberculosis sanatoria, completion of the Lincoln School's model playground, and attaining her lifelong ambition to tour Europe. Yet, pain and depression marked her last year as well—pain caused by her artificial limb, by Desha's infidelity, and by the difficult decisions relating to her family's beloved Ashland. Her poignant

Desha Breckinridge. Courtesy of Special Collections and Digital Programs, Margaret I. King Library, University of Kentucky, Lexington.

letters from Europe to her husband expressing her longing to be with him were contradicted by her actions when, soon after arriving home, she departed on a tour for the League of Nations. It appeared she could not be content *with* Desha anymore than she could be satisfied *without* him. The confusion she had felt that long-ago day when she had written her father, "I have tried doing without him and it is almost too hard" apparently still resonated in her life as, unable to face losing him, she attempted to ignore his affair. And it is clear that, despite everything, Desha not only had great pride in her achievements but also held great affection for her, possibly more than even he was aware during her life. His doctor recalled that during the time immediately following her death, Desha "was very nervous and lost a great deal of weight." In the coming years he devoted much of his time to perpetuating her memory.[3]

A little over a year after Madge's death the Kentucky League of Women Voters presented a portrait of Madge to the Kentucky Historical Society. In accepting it, Governor Edwin Morrow said: "Never a braver spirit, a more serene or greater soul wrought for Kentucky than that of Madeline McDowell Breckinridge. Childless, she loved all childhood; feeble of body, her heart went out to all the helpless and afflicted. Loving the good, she was beloved by all the good. She thought pure thoughts, spoke brave words, did generous deeds."[4]

The community began almost immediately to experience the void Madge's death left in the corporate fabric. The League of Women Voters became one of the first organizations to face a crisis of leadership. Before her death, Madge had called a meeting of its Organization Committee for November 27, and at Desha's insistence, the meeting went forward. Instead of planning the transformation of KERA into the League of Women Voters, however, the group passed a resolution on Madge's death and then attended her funeral. On December 15 the new league was officially launched, with University of Chicago graduate Mary Bronaugh, a Hopkinsville native and Madge's personal choice for the position, as chair. At the meeting the former KERA treasurer reported that in the two weeks before her death, Madge had raised $500 for the Kentucky League—even though it did not officially exist—to contribute to the National League of Women Voters. During the month of December, the *Herald* ran a number of editorials supporting this new organization, but Desha remained distressed because of its lack of experienced leadership. A number of years later Sophonisba lamented that the League of Women Voters in Lexington had not become all it could be, and would have been, if Madge had survived. Indeed, as historians have noted, the suffrage campaign brought women of different classes, sections, and ethnicity together in a unity of purpose so far never achieved by the League of Women Voters or any other organization. Women tended to vote the same way as their husbands, and politics continued to be primarily a male domain.[5]

This was not the only organization that sorely missed her leadership. The director of the Public Health Nursing Association wrote another Lexington woman, saying: "I know you, like myself, are heartbroken over Mrs. Breckinridge's death. I wonder if there will ever be anyone to take her place. It would be difficult to fill, that I know." The Woman's Club made its entire December meeting a memorial service, with Madge's recently painted portrait for Lincoln School hanging on the wall, flanked by palms, white chrysanthemums, and candles. Many of the women gave brief talks about her work. The group then adopted a resolution of appreciation and devotion and closed with the song "Farewell." On December 3 another of Madge's goals reached fruition when the Community House at Duncan Park officially opened. The city commissioner of public property paid tribute to Madeline McDowell Breckinridge, who was, he said, "almost directly responsible for the organization of Duncan Park, and who had always been the leading spirit in community . . . work in Lexington." The Civic League undertook an extensive program at the Community House that included the formation of the "Madeline Club," a girls' service group named in Madge's honor.[6]

Lincoln School also continued to remember Madge. Years before her death the children there had started a fund to pay for having her portrait painted. Although she had begged that the money raised by the children be used for something else, she had finally consented in the last busy months of her life to sit for the portrait. Plans for its presentation shortly before Christmas had already been made before her unexpected death. The program continued without her presence. Robert K. Massie of Christ Church Episcopal Cathedral told the children: "Though you do not understand what a great woman she was, you will when you grow older. You will realize what a great love she had for you." Another speaker noted: "She was Kentucky's most gifted daughter and the Lincoln School's best friend. When the cornerstone of the building was laid, she was afraid that, over her earnest protestations, the school would be named for her" and instead insisted that it be named for Abraham Lincoln. A few days later members of the Civic League distributed Christmas gifts to the children of Lincoln School, an activity that had been under Madge's direct supervision ever since the school's founding.[7]

Desha was determined that Lincoln School would not forget its founder. In May 1921 he and Nettie Bullock planned a party for the Lincoln School children at Ashland in honor of Madge's birthday. This became a tradition, and in 1928 Desha wrote his cousin Breckinridge Long, longtime State Department official and later U.S. ambassador to Italy: "I am having a picnic on Friday which I give every year to the children of Lincoln School, in memory of Madge whose birthday is the 20th. . . . I am anxious to be at it . . . it is going to be at Lincoln School, as Nettie Bullock is too ill to have it at Ashland."[8]

It had long been Madge and Nettie's dream that Ashland be preserved as a shrine to Henry Clay. Although Desha tried to use a part of Madge's estate for that purpose, it was not until Nettie Bullock died in 1948, leaving half her estate to the Henry Clay Memorial Foundation, that the idea came to fruition. Ashland, with twenty surrounding acres, opened to the public in 1950 and is a National Historical Landmark.[9]

The Lexington Civic League, too, had to adjust to existence without its leader. Madge had always been the guiding spirit of the League; thus, it had never developed a close organization, although it had maintained a number of standing committees. It functioned primarily when Madge had a new idea, and occasionally she was able to rally the whole community behind a project. Especially in the last few years it had seldom met except when she decided to call a meeting. Reportedly, she orchestrated these gatherings in an adept and somewhat dictatorial manner. One did not dare to make a motion unless it was something Madge approved, recalled her successor as Civic League president, Florence Shelby Cantrill, who would subsequently serve in the state legislature and become the first woman to win a seat on Lexington's city commission. Cantrill recalled that sometimes Madge railroaded her plans through the Civic League and volunteered people for jobs whether they wanted them or not. At the time Madge died the Civic League planned to merge with the Community Service League of Fayette County. This it did on January 1, 1921, but the consolidated group retained the name "Civic League," partially in order to perpetuate Madge's memory. Her death had been, according to Cantrill, "a stunning blow and serious loss" to the organization. There was a tendency thereafter for older workers to seek to retire, while younger people proved hesitant about taking the vanguard. Although the Civic League continued its existence for many years, the organization seems never to have recovered the vitality it had under Madge's leadership.[10]

Soon after Madge's death Desha and Sophonisba conceived the idea for Nisba to write Madge's biography. They corresponded with numerous people who had worked with her on various projects, and concluded a contract with the University of Chicago Press. This constituted a fitting end for Madge's long association with the University of Chicago, which had exerted an immense influence on her reform ideas. She had brought innumerable speakers from that institution to Lexington, and had hired its graduates to do suffrage and playground work and to teach manual training and kindergarten. She had borrowed ideas from the Chicago School of Civics and Philanthropy, which studied social problems and proposed solutions, and from Chicago settlement house workers such as Jane Addams. Still, Nisba fretted that she could not do the subject justice. "It is such a wonderful story that it should have the pen of an artist," she lamented, and when she finished it, she felt "it ought to be so much better than it is." Nevertheless, Desha, who had compiled a narrative of his wife's work for the Anthony amendment, believed his sister's introduction to the book was "perfect." Madge's sister-in-law Elsie McDowell noted the difficulty of the job, saying: "It seems to me not an easy matter for one who loved Madge so deeply to write of her for the public." When she finished the project, Sophonisba boxed up Madge's papers, along with many others from the Breckinridge family, and donated them to the Library of Congress.[11]

Gradually, the family adjusted to Madge's absence, but a sense of melancholy pervaded their references to her. Desha still advocated many of her causes, continued the *Herald*'s progressive record, and tried to perpetuate his wife's memory in the community. In 1925 he pondered whether to purchase a memorial chair in Madge's honor at the National Daughters of the American Revolution building in Washington, DC, but after consulting Nettie and Sophonisba, he concluded Madge would have preferred the money be given to "Lincoln School or the Sanatorium than spent for a memorial" to herself. Others, too, did not quickly forget Madge, and they created memorials to her memory. In 1923 a group donated money to develop a health camp for tubercular children on Versailles Road in Lexington, a mile or so beyond the gates of Keeneland racetrack. Called the Madeline McDowell Breckinridge Fresh Air Camp, the Public Health Nursing Association originally ran it. Since 1961 the Greater Lexington YMCA has leased the property, and it is still used as a summer day camp for underprivileged children. After Lincoln School closed in 1966, the Fayette County school system moved the Lincoln School portrait to the Madeline McDowell Breckinridge Elementary School, which had opened in another part of town in 1963. Another of her legacies, the Baby Health Service, which she helped found in 1914, continues in the twenty-first century to provide free health care, medicine, and immunizations to more than five thousand needy children annually.[12]

In the latter years of his life Desha often displayed a sentimental attachment to his wife's memory. As late as 1933 he dispersed some of her jewelry to one of his nieces and gave a string of gold beads and a "little pearl pin" that was one of his first gifts to Madge, "and of which she was very fond," to Nisba. In 1928, almost eight years after Madge's death, he telegraphed Nettie Bullock that he and Mary LeBus "were married at noon know you will wish both Good Luck and Happiness." According to one friend, this marriage took place at the urging of friends, who told Desha that he owed it to Mary, now a widow, because their names had been linked for so long. A family member claimed Gertrude Bayne Breckinridge, daughter-in-law of Desha's uncle Joseph Breckinridge, had encouraged him to marry Mary, and, shortly thereafter, he did so.[13]

When Desha's health began to deteriorate in 1929, his doctor noted that he had played hard, worked hard, smoked, and drank "a good deal." His only serious illness had come during Madge's trip to Europe when he lost the vision in his left eye, apparently from a detached retina. Now, he began to experience stomach problems and fatigue and exhibited a degree of arteriosclerosis "somewhat in advance of his years." By 1933 he had become very ill with stomach cancer, which required two operations. Probably because Desha had suffered financial losses from the Great Depression and kept his finances separate from those of his second wife, Nisba paid part of his medical expenses, recalling how he had always helped the family financially and how forty years before he had given her the money to go to Chicago. He slowly improved, only to suffer a stroke in September 1934. He died at Hinata on February 18, 1935, at age sixty-seven. As the *New York Times* reported in his obituary, he had been "for nearly forty years one of the most powerful and colorful figures in Kentucky journalism and politics."[14]

Together, Madge and Desha Breckinridge had contributed much to the spirit of progressive reform in Kentucky. Using the pages of the *Herald* to promote their causes, they each had sought to live up to the legacy they received as a result of being born to "one great honored name." Imbued with a sense of noblesse oblige from childhood, Madge always remained aware of the many ways in which her ancestors had served Kentucky—Henry Clay, Judge Samuel McDowell, and other members of that family, including her father in his philanthropic activities. Once, when sending a photograph of herself to be used in suffrage publicity, she commented that it had been taken "in the library at Ashland—'The Home of Henry

Clay'—my mother's home, which, since we are using Henry Clay strictly for advertising purposes, is of some value." After her marriage she also focused on the contributions of Desha's family to the state, on one occasion writing a whole series of editorials for the *Herald* on the development of public education, detailing the role of her husband's grandfather, Robert J. Breckinridge. Her family connections lent prestige and respectability to her causes. As one person who had ridden thirty miles on horseback to Pikeville to hear her speak in 1919 recalled: "It seemed as if the mantle of 'Harry of the West' had fallen on her shoulders, and as she closed, our eyes were filled with tears." One author, writing about one of Madge's first cousins, has said: "The Clays bore the legacy of Henry Clay like an albatross about their necks." For some this undoubtedly proved true, but not for Madge; she turned the legacy into an instrument to use for her own purposes, trading on her and Desha's families' heritage to win a hearing for her causes. As she once wrote to her mother: "You will see that here in Missouri they are working your grand-father over-time in the suffrage cause—Everybody whose father or grand-father had voted for him in Missouri had to come hear me speak." Few would ridicule or even openly criticize one of her elite status. In addition, Madge was fortunate to have the family connection to Sophonisba Breckinridge, one of the pioneers in the social work field. Through her she had access to the latest in social science research at the University of Chicago and to many of the major leaders of the Progressive movement. Sophonisba Breckinridge's importance in the field of social work was noted in a University of Chicago press release stating that the school she established at the University of Chicago was "the first social service school in the world—[it] raised social work to a science and a profession."[15]

But Madge's motivation came not only from family influence but personal experience. Lame from the age of eighteen, with her foot amputated six years later, illness transformed her adult life. From a carefree girl who enjoyed clothes and parties, she gradually changed to a serious woman concerned for the poor, the ill, and the downtrodden. The link between her personal bout with tuberculosis and her passion for fighting the dread disease is evident; the connection between her other reforms and her physical condition is less clear, but there, too, her health likely had a major impact. Childless in an era when women's lives were expected to center around their children, she focused her reform interests on improving opportunities for all children. Even her work for suffrage resulted primarily from her desire to achieve the power necessary to effect reforms in other areas.[16]

Gradually, the girl who had loved parties and clothes evolved into a serious woman who actively resented the time she had to spend on everyday chores. To some she appeared dogmatic, even autocratic, and many of her letters in the Library of Congress collection bear this out. On one occasion, when a man refused a Civic League office, she replied: "If no one wants a Civic League, I do not see why I should kill myself keeping it alive." In another letter, she castigated a Lexington merchant for not fulfilling her request, saying: "I begrudge the time it takes to shop in the first place, and there aren't many things I want enough to do many times over." Many of her closest associates in the Civic League, Associated Charities, and other organizations seemed awestruck by her; however, occasionally someone ventured to voice a direct criticism. As one man wrote: "Your constructive energy is so great and your desire to make every minute count is so strong and you actually do so much more than any other individual to accomplish results while day light lasts, that I fear you become impatient with those who because of less ability—lack of time and independent means cannot go at the pace you set." He also warned that "I am of the opinion that your personality IS the mainspring of the Charity Organization as now constituted," and "if in the course of human events something should happen to the mainspring—what then?" Sometimes Madge's prodding must have been irritating to even her closest friends and associates. One of them, Margaret Preston Johnston, received a letter congratulating her on her new baby, which the writer said would save Margaret from having to serve as secretary for all of "Madge's pet organizations." "Now," the woman continued sarcastically, "will be the chance of your life to tell Madge what she ought to do to make your child's life happier. How 'the little one craves play' and surroundings of beauty, etc."[17]

Yet her personal correspondence, found primarily in the Henry Clay Memorial Foundation Papers, reveals a different side to her personality. The warmth and charm that so many commented about after her death comes through clearly in her correspondence with family and close friends. As Margaret Preston Johnston wrote Desha: "She was so kind and affectionate, always," and since her death "I have longed for her to know how much she was beloved in this State. I loved and admired her for many years, and yet I feel as if none of us expressed that love and admiration completely while she was here with us."[18]

Evidence also indicates that Madge used her reform work to escape personal problems such as her mother's and Aunt Mag's last illnesses and her husband's infidelity. Indeed, some of her closest friends believed she went to Europe in 1920 to escape Lexington gossip. The frenzy of speeches and traveling during her years as KERA president, the lawsuit against the city appropriation to the Salvation Army during her mother's final illness and death, the trip to Europe followed by an extensive tour on behalf of the League of Nations—all of which taxed her limited physical resources and sometimes threatened her life—occurred at particularly stressful times in her personal life and indicated her almost obsessive dedication to the causes that she supported. Perhaps a sense of urgency fueled by the awareness that her time on earth might be cut short, combined with an attempt to submerge her personal problems in work, pushed her to such extremes.[19]

Madge could count many achievements in reform—a juvenile court system, compulsory education and improved child labor laws, manual training in public schools, state-supported tuberculosis sanatoria, the Irishtown school and social settlement, and Lexington's park and playground system. She had served as an officer of the National Conference of Social Work and the National Child Labor Committee. But it was in the area of woman suffrage that she most clearly left her mark. As Thomas A. Combs wrote her in April 1920: "Except for you and Desha I doubt if Kentucky would yet be ready to ratify the Anthony Amendment." She also contributed substantially to the national movement by traveling and speaking around the country. However, by declining to challenge Anna Howard Shaw for the NAWSA presidency, she gave up the chance to be a preeminent figure on the national scene.[20]

Her legacy included virtually every reform achieved in Kentucky during the first two decades of the twentieth century, many of which had become public policy by the time of her death and continued to expand in the years to come. They were reforms that fit the Progressive movement's goals of modernization and efficiency based on social science research and tempered by a deep sense of social responsibility for the underprivileged, especially children. Like a number of other southern suffragists she was able to accomplish so much in that area, in part, because her family's prestige and legacy of public service ensured her a public hearing. As Sophonisba described her sister-in-law: "She belonged to Kentucky by right of five generations of service and devotion. What interested Kentucky was her interest; what interested her must be of concern to the community with whose life her life was one."[21]

It could be argued that Madeline McDowell Breckinridge remains the most important woman in Kentucky history; certainly, she provides the best example of the Progressive movement in the state. Also a significant leader in the national woman suffrage movement, she stands as a model for other reformers in the range of her interests, in the depth of her commitment, in the personal courage of her whole life. Facing serious adversity, confronting seemingly insurmountable barriers, coping with challenge after challenge, she seldom hesitated in her relentless pursuit of what she perceived to be the right path toward justice and equality. The children she never had, the sick, the poor, the women of the nation—all demanded her devotion. The outpouring of grief at her death evidenced that to the end, despite her sometimes forceful leadership style and impatience with those less dedicated than she, Madge retained a portion of the warmth and charm that had endeared her to so many friends and suitors during her girlhood. Her life's work left a legacy to her city, her state, and to women across the United States that still endures. She died young but she lived well.

Appendix

Selections from Articles and Speeches of Madeline McDowell Breckinridge

A Day in Judge Mack's Juvenile Court in Chicago

A day in Judge Mack's Juvenile Court in Chicago is apt to be a day full of the sound of weeping and wailing and gnashing of teeth. Children accused of some petty crime when they are told to give their version, when the judge bids them "look up at him and speak out," usually dissolve in tears; this doesn't indicate either guilt or innocence; sometimes the judge's kindly bantering, "what you scared of" restores confidence, if not composure; sometimes it seems as if no human power could stop the flow. But the most vociferous wailing comes from the small boys upon whom sentences are passed that are not to their mind. John Worthy is a juvenal [*sic*] penal institution, a prison school within the city; St. Charles is a State Industrial school in the country, which means protracted banishment from the joys of the streets. There were no more copious tears shed, no more bitter wailings voiced, one morning that I sat by and listened, than by three small boys to whom these fates were allotted. They had wasted no tears before the sentence; they had defended themselves with a pretty good show of confidence, but when the judge, after listening and questioning good naturedly, spoke their doom with the same calm kindness, the boys knew that the time had passed for defense and had come for appeal. They had all been before the court a number of times before; they were confirmed street urchins with the waywardness and the impudence of the species; but the casual observer would have been taken in, would have had hard work to resist the impulse to pity, when the big gray eyes of the youngest overflowed, the muscles around the mouth worked pathetically and he clutched the bar of justice and held on even after the bailiffs of the court were hustling him away, wailing, "Please, jedge, yer honor, give me one more chance. Oh, please, jedge, yer honor." Nor did the wail of these three cease as long as there was a chance that "jedge, yer honor" might be moved; they could be heard resounding all down the court house corridor to the elevator shaft.

Three other boys who had run away from a Catholic institution and who gave as their proper reasons for so doing that they had been given sour milk to drink and that the brother beat them with a horsewhip, were almost as vociferous in their distress because they weren't sent to St. Charles; they had come to the conclusion that as a choice of evils St. Charles was preferable to the discipline of the brothers. They told the judge that they would get more beatings now for running away; he encouraged them to face the music, and he sent a private injunction to the brother to try milder methods of receiving the prodigal sons this time, but he destroyed the fallacy in those youthful minds that by running away they could escape the long arm of justice.

But not all the cases are even mildly comic. There is the mother, whose one redeeming trait is her love for her child, told that she has been given her last chance and that the court will this time have to take her child away from her; she doesn't weep, this mother, but she takes her child to a corner of the court room and sits holding it in her lap and coddling it till the officers of the institution to which it has been confided come to take it, and the sight is touching. There is the mother with a child of six, whose father had deserted it and left it to her support, and for whom the struggle and the sorrow have been too much; she is convinced now that "things" are following her, and she consents to let the child be taken because it will then be safe from the "following things." The probation officer is told to take the mother to the Hull House physician for examination, and one chokes down a feeling in the throat, hoping that the fact of the juvenile court having taken cognizance in this case may finally mean for the mother restoration to mental health and to her child. There is another mother with seven children, from four to eleven, whose husband has abandoned her; another, with five children, the oldest fourteen, whose husband is insane; another mother, whose husband is in the hospital with tuberculosis, brought into court with her four children—one other is in a feeble-minded institute—on the charge of neglect and intemperance. Two children are taken away from her to be cared for temporarily; the oldest, who is over the child labor law limit, is left to help in the support of the family and she is allowed to keep her baby, under the watch of a probation officer, if she will sign the pledge. "A woman who can't drink moderately," says the Judge, "must give it up entirely if she wants to keep her children; it is the only way," and the woman says she will try. Another mother, whose husband had gone South to work and who has been ill in Memphis for several weeks, asks that the court take two of her children temporarily and put them where they will be supported; she thinks she can earn enough to support the other two and to pay the back rent that is owed, and that she won't have to give up her home and have the added expense of moving. The court undertakes to help her carry her load.

One cannot spend a day in the Juvenile Court without wishing that our next President might be imbued with a sense of the duty of fatherhood and might "preach a crusade," as our present President is doing, on the duty of motherhood. On dependent children's day in the court one believes that a new course of instruction should be introduced into all our boys' schools on the primal and ancient obligation that a man owes to support his children; and not to desert and leave the job to the mother whenever the family becomes too big for ease and comfort. On delinquents' day in court one wants added to that course another, to the effect that a father's responsibility does not stop with providing bread and meat for his children; that the bringing up of those children in proper habits and morals is a little his job as well as the mother's. Often, and often, when a small boy is being arraigned, the true delinquent is the father. Illinois' experience in her Juvenile Court has made so clear this fact of ultimate responsibility, of the share that the neglectful parent and the adult law-breaker bear in the downfall of children, that she is trying now to have added to her law the "adult contributory negligence" clause that makes Colorado's juvenile code so effective.

When delinquents' cases are taken up in the court many of them have amusing features. There are angry mothers and fathers, one side accusing the other—and throwing in a little gratuitous accusation of the other fellow's children who are not on trial; there are usually two sides in these neighborhood depredations and street quarrels, and the judge hears them both, as a rule both at once, for it is more than human nature that one set of parents should preserve respectful silence while the other talks. Sometimes a foreign mother, whose child long suspected and finally caught in the act of stealing rubber balls from a street peddler or trifling articles from the school room has been brought into court by the school principal, is sure that the principal is simply down on her boy and expostulates and denies loudly in two languages and regularly drowns the voice of the calm little school teacher until the judge restrains her. The judge is no great stickler for the order or dignity of the court; his anxiety is to get at the facts and he knows that one way of doing it is to hear all sides—at once if necessary—so that the human qualities of anger or sorrow or mental unsoundness that enter into the testimony may be weighed with it. And after he has spoken if one witness or another comes back with an added bit of testimony he is quite ready to modify a decision. Once he is convinced of the right and wrong in the matter, though; once he has decided, he loses no time; the court bailiffs hurry off weeping and expostulating parents and children and neighbors, and the next case is entered into before the sounds of dissension from the first are stilled; then one begins to understand how Judge Mack can get through in the time allowed him the Herculean task that now falls to the Juvenile Court of Chicago. . . .

There are eighteen probation officers attached to the Juvenile Court at Chicago—all but four of them women—and, in addition, members of the police force are detailed when needed to assist. For Chicago is a big city, with many little children in it needing "correction, aid and encouragement," children both of the foreign-born and of American parents. The probation officers are appointed by the judge, though usually suggested by the Volunteer Juvenile Court committee—a committee that raises from individuals and organizations the salaries of the probation officers, and that also has charge of and partially supports the Detention Home. Bills to provide both for the salaries of probation officers and the support of the Detention Home from county funds are now before the legislature. Illinois' system—if it may be so called—has grown with the need and has not kept pace with it; it did not spring full-fledged and it is made as wonderfully effective as it is by the devoted and unpaid labors of many men and women.

Source: Lexington Herald, *April 24, 1905.*

Cotton Mills of the South

We had a great desire to see it go in cotton and come out olive oil! But we were just too late. Last year's crop was short in this section and the cotton oil mill at Camden had closed down about two weeks earlier than usual. The season for this industry is short; it lasts only from September to April at the latest; the heat in the room where the oil is pressed out is always great; later in the season the heat is so great that the oil made under such circumstances would become rancid. But while the season lasts and the crop holds out the mill runs night and day, employing from seventy-five to a hundred Negro men. And the Camden mill is but one of twenty-three in the State of South Carolina, and eight odd over the South, belonging to the same company.

This mill in addition to the cotton seed which it buys already ginned absorbs a good deal of the local cotton crop. We climbed up a step-ladder to see the silent gin—the miracle-working machine which is said to be the idea of a woman! The planter's wagon drives under a shed at one side, the baskets of cotton are grasped and lifted up by machinery; the cotton passes through the gin, the seed going down a chute in the middle, and presently the blade cotton is lowered out of a window on the opposite side on to the waiting wagon. Thence it goes to be made into mattresses. To look at only one boll of cotton and think of the weary process of picking away by hand the cotton from the seed—from which nature surely meant that it should never be separated—makes one wonder that even the great of the earth could have clothed themselves in cotton goods in the days before the gin. . . .

We were not too late for the cotton mills and we came out from them with a much greater respect for unbleached cotton than we had ever felt before. They were doing their twelve hours a day amid a terrible din of machinery and lint of cotton. A boy of thirteen, who had been in the mills four years, told us that he went to work in the "new mill," as they call it, the one with the most up-to-date machinery, at six in the morning and worked until twelve; after three-quarters of an hour for dinner he went back to work at a quarter of one and worked till seven; there is a half holiday on Saturday. As the child gave them to us—though he was not in the least complaining and seemed quite content with his job—the hours seemed much longer than as the manager briefly stated them: sixty-seven hours a week. One can readily understand the temptation to employ child labor when one sees how little the perfection of the machinery leaves to the human hand to do. The human motions in several of the processes are so simple, so slight, so mechanical that it seems a perfectly natural thing to turn them over to a child; yet when one sees them being made with a lightning-like rapidity the thought of the long, monotonous hours makes one's head swim and one's body tired. In the spinning and weaving rooms the majority of the workers seemed to be children. In other rooms where in the preceding processes the soft, white stuff is being handled more in bulk, the greater numbers of the workers are men.

In the older mill, the machinery of which is not so improved a type, many hand processes are being done by women. To see a woman stooping over her frame catching and placing a thread with a tiny steel crochet needle with the utmost rapidity, with eye and hand never diverted from their job, and to learn that she received 20 cents an hour for this setting up for weaving, makes 20 cents seem a very valuable piece of money, one not to be idly and wantonly fooled away. She doesn't complain either of the hours, only that she is laid off so often, that the mill shuts down so frequently and the chance to work is gone. Another evidence that the machinery in this mill is a little antiquated—and also that supervision is not very strict—is seen in the fact that the children are not working at such speed and that there are some loafing times between, when they frolic at the end of the great room, and make faces through the windows and giggle at a chance visitor outside.—And yet among these children is one with a face unlike any child face I have ever seen before, so wrinkled, so white, so horribly old—the skin drawn tightly over the bones, little eyes deep-set and crossed, the tow-head covered with whiter cotton line, increasing the look of age, and the whole set on an emaciated body like that of an old man rather than of a child. It may be unjust to think of this as a cotton mill type, but I shall never forget the strange little figure nor cease to associate it with the cotton industry. Whether this child is the result of the cotton mills or not, I thought, he is in the cotton mills, and if the children are to be in the mills rather than in the schools, then there should be a medical inspector in the mills who would remove such a child to a hospital, where surely he must belong. The children in the mill seemed younger than in the other mill; one little girl was ten, another was "going on" eleven, another, with her feet tied up in rags because they were sore, was twelve, and had as helper her little sister of eight. She did not know what wages she made, her mother drew her wages and she thought that none of the children under twelve got wages—presumably they were all "helpers"—she had three brothers and a father also in the mill. The oldest brother had gone over to the "new mill" because wages were better there. Conversations in the mill had to be brief, for it was almost impossible to make one's self heard in the roar. The children seemed quite used to it, as to the other incidents of the machinery. Two children seemed to be playing a sort of game of tag near some exposed hands with never a notion of danger. It seemed quite dreadful to me in view of the information a girl who was returning from her dinner had given me outside the mill; that a child of nine had gotten his finger mashed off the Saturday before. She would be glad, she added knowingly, if they would pass a law to take the children out of the mills. She was sending her baby brother, who "had the toothache" all night, down to a dentist—presumably to have his tooth pulled. "How early their troubles begin!" I said to myself. But perhaps I was looking at life through the colored cotton mill glasses, for the child himself seemed quite proud that he was going to the dentist, and tried to tell me about it in English that was not yet comprehensible.

Source: Lexington Herald, *March 17, 1907.*

A Model Public School

[By special request Mrs. Desha Breckinridge has consented to try to reproduce here what she said at the opera house Tuesday night.]

The Civic League has asked you here tonight to consider with us the plan for a model public school in the city of Lexington and the means by which we are to get it.

Perhaps it is necessary for us to realize that we have need of educational improvement. We have been saying to ourselves for sometime, in the manner of Kentuckians, that we have one of the best public school systems in the country, and unless someone insists that Kentuckians look the facts in the face they are very apt to believe just what they say of themselves to others. As a State we stand disgracefully low in the tables of illiteracy. To the dismay of our own local community, it has recently been shown that in ten Blue Grass counties, of which Fayette is one, there are but 92 fewer native white illiterates than in the whole State of Massachusetts, a State with almost double the population of Kentucky and a large foreign element.

Fayette County's Poor Showing

In 1907 the county of Fayette, which was spending over $185,000 of county revenues, devoted but little over $2,000 of this to her public schools. Since that time we have gotten from the Legislature a new county school board law, one of the special objects of which was to bring about local county taxation for the benefit of schools, and this year Fayette county will spend $4,000 for her schools while she spends $65,000 for her roads. Now the roads over which the children go to school are important, but the schools to which they go are likewise important, and the present proportion of expenses simply indicates that our county officials, the men who are deciding the business methods of our county, have not at present a proper appreciation of the importance of our schools.

If you should ask—you who are contentedly saying that we have a perfect system of schools in Lexington—those who are intimately acquainted with the schools about them, they would not tell you that any single school in Lexington is a model. The superintendent would not; the members of the board would not. And if you should talk for five minutes to a principal or teacher, showing any intelligent interest or knowledge of the subject, he or she would begin to pour out to you a list of the things needed for the schools.

Women Are Needed

Personally I do not believe that we shall ever have model schools, as good schools even as the money that is spent for them should provide, while we divide our community into two classes, the women who are doing the thinking about educational matters and the men who are doing the voting. Having started out 70 years ago by granting the first school suffrage to women of any English-speaking people, Kentucky, by a final stroke at her last Legislature, contentedly reduced herself to an oriental position by declaring that men only were fit for school suffrage. It is rather singular that this reactionary attitude on the part of Kentucky men has gone on side by side with the most remarkable and important development of public interest in educational affairs that Kentucky has seen in the seventy years past.

Movement Backed by Women

And this movement has been conceived and executed and financed to a large extent by Kentucky women. Of all the ridiculous political disabilities that men have ever put upon women the most ridiculous is to debar them from a share in the control of the public schools—to say to them on the one hand, "Women, your glorious mission is to bear and to rear children," and on the other hand, to say to them, "When those children are six years old—or four years old, now that we have kindergartens—they must go into the public schools, and there you may not go with them. How the public schools are conducted is a matter for men, not for women, Mothers have nothing to do with the education of their children."

As a matter of fact, even debarred as they are from any authority, the mothers of this community know more and care more about what is going on in the public schools than do the fathers. A mother came to me the other day, wanting me to look into a matter in the public schools which she thought very wrong and to get it remedied. It was a thing about which I had never thought, but I have thought of it since and I have asked people in this and other communities whose experience is much wider than mine, and I am convinced that that mother was right.

Devoid of Power to Act

I told her that I was not on the School Board, that I was as devoid of any power in the matter as was she, and when she left I decided that this hard job was perhaps not my job, and I wrote to her and suggested that she have her husband, the father of the boy, talk with the members of the School Board about it.

Now that was a month or so ago and I do not believe that anything has been done. I mention it simply to show you that there is a difference in women's standard and men's standard of what the public school should be, and I believe if we want to bring up our children in the best way we should be getting the judgment and advice of the mother sex instead of ignoring it. We should have women on our School Boards and women as principals and women as inspectors "nosing" about in our schools and finding out the little apparently insignificant things that are perhaps the things of vital importance that should be changed and bettered.

Male and Female Standard

We had an example the other day of the difference in the male and female standard. A stranger came into our midst, a woman, and she went into the cellars and basements of our public schools, and she did not like them, and a few days later the gentlemen of our School Board went around and looked at them and they said they were all right. Now even male janitors could have made a change in those cellars and basements in the two or three days intervening between visits, but if the men of our School Board had gone with Mrs. Crane I think their views and hers about the conditions of those cellars and basements would have been different.

Our men have minds above cellars. It takes a woman who has had herself to see to the cleaning and whitewashing to know how a cellar or basement ought to be. If you do not believe it I suggest that some of you women go and look at the cellars of some of the most prominent business houses in our city, even those within the fire limits and see if you think they are right. We cannot expect men who have looked down upon housekeeping for many centuries and considered it a menial task fit only for women to know very much about it.

What Do We Mean By a Model School

Now if we are going to have a model school in Lexington what do we mean by it? In the first place we mean a school in which teachers are chosen for merit and efficiency; a school in which there are provided for our children the very best teachers that can be obtained for the money to be laid out, no matter where we go to get those teachers; a school in which a teacher who is doing her best knows that she will hold her place while she deserved it and does not have the Damocles sword of an annual election, for which all sorts of wire pulling are necessary, hanging over her head; a school in which the curriculum is the result of the careful thought of big minds; in which discipline is gentle but absolutely firm, in which book teaching is of the highest type; and in which that indescribable process of character building is going on constantly from the influence of a high type of men and women in charge of the children.

Ideals of Perfect School

. . . Our model school must have in it thorough equipment for hand training in every grade. It must have in it certain physical equipment and space for neighborhood uses, some time back considered out of the province of the public school, and it is these things I want to talk about. . . .

Commercial Value of Education

There can be no longer any question about the practical and commercial value of education. . . . everywhere there is a direct relation between the amount spent for education and the average earning capacity of the people. For every dollar earned per inhabitant in Kentucky Indiana earns $1.57. When we go further to the application of the latest educational discovery, the discovery that it is wasteful to try to train the mind alone, but that you must train the hands and body with it, the illustration is even more striking. . . .

Private Initiative

I want you to realize a little how other communities have waked up to the commercial and moral value of hand training in the public schools, and want to refer to the way in which most of the great advances in educational matters have come from the initiative and generosity of private individuals. It is impossible to ask that any community shall act as a whole through its public representatives until long after there have been many individuals who are ready to act privately to attain a desired end. . . .

The Habit of Public Giving

Our own community has not as yet contracted the habit of public giving. Sometimes in Louisville when I have looked at the magnificent Manual Training High School, the gift of one citizen, and at the building in which the charity organization society has its headquarters, the gift of another; and at the beautiful drinking fountains and gateways and bridges on the streets and in the parks, I have wished that that contagion of public spirit might reach this Blue Grass region. At the present the attitude of many of us toward the State or the city seems to be to "do" it, to give as little as we can and to get as much. It seems sometimes as if we had forgotten that this government was our own government and that what we gave to the public we were, after all, but giving to ourselves. . . .

Community Use of School Buildings

Another thing that we want our model school to give besides hand-training is the opportunity for community use. It is slowly dawning upon us that the public schools belong to the public, and that they have the right to use them both in school hours and out. Of all the wicked extravagances the most wicked, it seems to me, is to tax people—and poor people, for every landlord, no matter how disgraceful the hovel which he rents, makes his tenants pay the taxes on the rental which he fixes—to tax poor people for the purpose of erecting costly school buildings and then to allow these school buildings to stand idle 165 days out of the year and 19 hours out of every 24 of the days they are in use. While the people have need of them for every sort of use our school buildings are closed and idle for half of the afternoons, for all of the evenings, on Saturdays and on Sundays and through three months of the summer while our janitors are taking the rest cure. And there is no place for our people, whose homes are too small for more than domestic uses, to meet with their fellowmen as every rightly constructed human being wants to do.

How Money Is Wasted

The men must go to the saloons for their political meetings. The young people, if they want to dance or to enjoy themselves in other ways, must go to the skating rinks and the cheap dance halls and the five-cent theaters; and they go unchaperoned, and there are often deplorable consequences. Then we go to work in our juvenile courts and our reform schools we spend the money that we should have spent to keep these young people from going wrong. And the pity of it is, that a broken thing mended is never what a whole thing might have been, even if we succeed in mending and not in further scarring and disfiguring the young character which is handled so roughly in police courts and jails and State Institutions. . . .

Our Next School

Now the model school we want for Lexington is to be built in the West End simply because that is the next school we are to build. Bye and bye we want such a model school for every school in Lexington. Surely it will not be many years before our people demand that every school building in Lexington for white or for colored be equipped for manual training work, so that this may be given to all our boys and girls and not just to an occasional few who are picked out and sent from their school to the manual training center. And after we get these schools all up to the standard we are now setting, you may rest assured that somebody will come along with a standard of a school building way in advance of any we have now; and then we will begin aiming for that. One's wagon should always be hitched to a star.

The West End School

I believe I can tell you best what we need in all of these model schools we are to have, by telling you a little of the history of the school in the West End, and why we want the things in it that we do want. Seven years ago the Woman's Club and the Civic League started a little playground in what is commonly known as Irishtown on a lot loaned to us by Mr. Richard Stoll. The second year this property had been sold and we could not get it for a playground, so we started a little vacation school with cooking, and sewing, and out-door kindergarten in a slip of a yard, and sand piles, and swings, and see-saws and basketball, and croquet. Then we went to the School Board and showed them that in a list of 80 children of kindergarten and primary age but four were even registered up town and they were not attending school. We showed them that there were children of 14 and 15 who could neither read nor write and that the public school system was passing over the heads of these children, who really needed it most. The School Board started a kindergarten with our little playground instructor, Miss Betsy Cloud in charge—who is about the best thing that has ever happened to that end of town—and to that kindergarten the School Board has added one thing after another.

One Grade Crowded Out

There is a school now of 150 pupils and one grade was lost this fall simply because the children could not be accommodated in the funny little school-rooms that have been made out of the two converted dwelling houses that are the school. And we are not pushing the School Board any longer about this West End School. They are pushing us, and right now they are eager to build and we are begging for time that we may try to raise a little more money.

For seven years we have had a beautiful vision of what the new school building in that section was going to be and how it would have in it a kitchen, a carpenter shop and a laundry with stationary wash tubs where the girls might learn the fine art of laundry work and where the mothers might bring their washing out of school hours, as they do to the municipal laundries in the European cities; of how it would have a gymnasium and shower baths for the use of young and old alike and a swimming pool; perhaps a little room that might be used for a library and a club-room; and either an assembly hall or a kindergarten room so large that by putting funeral chairs into it we could on short notice convert it in time into an assembly hall. And if we can not afford a separate assembly hall we want a stage at the end of the kindergarten room where the piano and the cupboards for the kindergarten work may go, which you see is really an economy of space, and a teacher's room to one side of it where a sick child may be taken or a business matter gone over with the principal in school hours, and in which in the evening may be converted into that fascinating place where wigs are put on and eyebrows are blackened and ready-made expressions created by the fine hand of the artist—a green room. For the children who read and learn and play Shakespeare and Schiller in their youth are going to have tastes above Anna Held and "The Merry Widow" and the five-cent theater when they grow up. . . .

An Experiment Station

We like to claim that the manual training in our public schools grew out of the humble little work started in the West End School; and that the playground and park movement grew out of that. And we believe now that, if we can open there a model school which the board will allow the superintendent to use as a sort of experiment station where the curriculum may be loosened and adapted to the model set by the School of Education in Chicago, the influence of this school in the West End will go not only through all the schools of Lexington eventually, but through all the school of Central Kentucky. And even further, for no Kentucky movement has ever yet hid its light under a bushel; and we will see that there is plenty of free space in the newspapers to proclaim our shining example throughout the length and breadth of the State.

Observations of Seven Years

In the seven years that we have been in the West End we have seen boys go to the penitentiary and girls go wrong in one way or another for the lack, we believe, of being taught in the school to use their hands to make an honest living, and of being given some outlet for social intercourse under proper conditions. And the things we have seen there, you could have seen in many other parts of town if you had only watched for them closely.

The school we are planning to build will be fed from the section known as Irishtown and from Davis Bottom, and the territory extending over to the tobacco factories and the Southern depot and from Spiegel Heights and from the new and growing section beyond the Cincinnati Southern tracks that cross the Versailles road. The lot picked out is in the very center of this district. The building must be so constructed that it may be added on to from year to year.

Good Work of the Teachers

Sometimes we have gotten discouraged with our work in the West End. It seemed as if there were but little result. But when we remember that for seven years through the school and the playground, winter and summer, there have been with these children every day women of refinement and high character who are teaching them not only what is in the books but all the little unconscious things that go to make up a good man or a good woman, we must know that the work has not been in vain. And, however hard it is, however exacting, we know too that those children are worthy of it. I have seen them sitting with their little bare feet under the kindergarten tables and their heads bowed over them, saying the grace that the teachers have taught them:

"Father we thank thee for the night
And for the blessed morning light;
For rest and food and loving care
And all that makes the world so fair."

And I have said to myself: "Those children have a right, just as your children or my children have, just as every child in the world has, to 'rest and food and loving care and all that makes the world so fair.'" And I have said to myself: "When we make our school building here we must build one thing in the section that is fair, that is dignified and noble, and that shall serve its ends not only for usefulness but for an inspiration of neatness order and beauty to the whole community."

Isn't it a vision worth waiting for and working for, and giving to, and even worth begging for? Will you help us to get it?

Source: Lexington Herald, *May 30, 1909.*

Woman's Suffrage Is Sure to Come

Excerpt from two-hour speech given by Madeline McDowell Breckinridge on December 15 in Savannah. Newspaper commentary is in brackets.

I think I am perfectly safe in saying that the granting of the ballot to women generally in this country will come within the next quarter or half-century. We now have eleven states in which whole or partial suffrage has been given. The very biggest statesmen in the country have said that they believe women's suffrage is coming and I believe that anyone who is not totally blind can see now that it is coming just as surely as the sun rises and sets.

Speaker [Camp] Clark in an interview with a delegation of women advocates of equal suffrage said that he believes woman's suffrage was inevitable. I think this is one of our greatest weaknesses. We all think it is inevitable and we are apt to underestimate the difficulties and the opposition that undoubtedly confronts us in our fight for the ballot.

Woman's cause is not won until it is won throughout the entire nation, and one of the greatest forces with which we must reckon is the force of inertia. This exists among a large percentage of women all over the country. The women are complacent to sit idly by and say that it can't be done or that their time is so taken up with their duties at home that they are unable to get out and work for the cause, even though they feel down deep in their hearts that in asking for a voice in the affairs of their states and their nation they are but asking for that which is justly due them.

Other forces opposed to granting suffrage to the women are the liquor and vice interests and the interests who know that child labor will be speedily abolished after equal suffrage goes into effect.

[Mrs. Breckinridge told of the experiences of those who had fought for suffrage in Kentucky and gained a partial victory. She said that as a result of the limited power given the women of her state some very good and successful laws had been enacted in Kentucky; that commissions on schools and illiteracy have been established and that the laws provided that on all the commissions appointed for educational purposes women must be appointed as well as men. The result, she said, had been that a far greater percentage of the state funds have been spent for educational purposes, the conditions in the schools have shown marked improvement and the percentage of adult illiteracy in the state has been cut down to almost nothing. The part women has [*sic*] played in the wars of the world was one of Mrs. Breckinridge's most forceful arguments in favor of giving the ballot to women.]

If there were no better argument in favor of giving the ballot to women, war would be an entirely sufficient one. When we think of patriotism we think of war and when we think of war we think of men who march off to war 'mid the playing of patriotic airs, the beating of drums, and the waving of flags. We forget the hundreds of thousands of women who have been and are being made widows, whose sons are taken away from them in the cruel, bloody game of war—a war which was precipitated by an act of their nation in which they had no voice.

But the mere fact that war is all wrong, that it is barbarous and criminal and awful and terrible to think of in this stage of civilization is not the only argument in favor of woman's suffrage that war gives us. Has [*sic*] not women, since the very earliest days when nations took up arms against each other, made sacrifices that make this plea of hers for the right to help conduct the affairs of her nation, but a request for, but a portion of, that which has been her right?

[Mrs. Breckinridge dwelt strongly upon the great need of new laws and the enforcement of existing laws in the South and explained that the giving of the right to vote to women would help greatly to accomplish those things which the South needs most.]

It is only because I love my Southland that I regret and recognize the fact that the South is so lawless; that educational, health and other conditions in the South are far in the rear of the pace that has been set in the North and West.

When I think of how little Georgia spends for the education of her children I try to remember Sherman's march through the state to the sea—how women were made widows and children made orphans and homes wrecked and pillaged and the path taken by the Union soldiers so devastated that not even a crow could find sustenance in the fields. But even when I am thinking of this, I realize that this is no excuse for the conditions that exist to-day in Georgia; that the heroic sacrifices made by the people of the South in their war for "states' rights" is no excuse for the fact that the South is not now leading all other sections of the country in the passage of good laws, in the enforcement of laws and in the health and educational conditions.

A great argument in favor of woman's suffrage is contained in the educational statistics of Georgia as compared with some of the Western states where equal suffrage is now in effect. Do you know that in Georgia the average salary paid to your schoolteachers is but $250 and that in the state of Washington it is $600 and in the state of California it is $900? This shows that the sacrifice is being borne by your teachers.

[Mrs. Breckinridge dealt a blow at the cotton goods manufacturers of the South who employ cheap child labor in their mills.]

It is the child labor that fills our juvenile courts. The young boy and girl criminals that we are turning out in large numbers each year do not come from the children who are reared in the homes and are given the playgrounds and the schools to play and become educated in.

There are cotton mills in the South that have been moved here from Northern states where the employment of child labor has been prohibited. Shall we allow these men to come down here and commercialize our children, stunt their bodies and their minds in the dirty, unsanitary and poor paying mills?

And right here I may add that the man who employs child labor will be a factor in the fight against woman's suffrage. This man knows that he will not be allowed to employ this sort of labor once woman is given the right to enact and enforce laws forbidding it.

[Mrs. Breckinridge condemned the statement made by opponents of woman's suffrage that women, if given the right to vote, will go out of their sphere.]

We have never gone out of our sphere in anything that we have undertaken. The very earliest movement of woman to help the world, the movement toward nursing, which was at one time considered the proper thing for woman only in her own home or in the home of her very dear friends, has been so broadened now that nursing is a profession in which woman is entirely within her sphere. The government of this and other countries has taken up this movement and the Red Cross societies of which the woman nurse is the prime factor, are among the greatest and most efficient organizations in the world.

The sphere of the woman is as broad as she chooses to make it. She is the mother of men and any undertaking she may endeavor to engage in which aids and makes more pleasant, more profitable and more enlightened the life of men is within her sphere. . . .

I want to make an urgent appeal to the women of this community for support in efforts to obtain the right of the mother to the guardianship of her child; the right of the young girl to protection up to a greater age than now embraced by the age of consent, and the right of the working woman to protection in the length of her working hours. These are things which are all badly needed, particularly in your own state.

Source: Savannah Morning News, *December 16, 1914.*

Are We the Gates of Hell, and a Field for Foreign Missions? If So, What Shall We Do about It?

The Salvation Army is a religious organization and a relief society. This fact makes it difficult for many people to weigh the relief work on its own merits. I believe that in determining whether they wish to maintain the headquarters of the association and to finance its work, the people of Lexington should separately weigh the merits of each function of the organization. To speak briefly of the religious function first.

It does not seem to me that Lexington is or should be a missionary field. I noticed in last Saturday's papers invitations to church from twenty churches. These did not include the two Catholic churches. These church organizations are all supported by our home people; some of them by great sacrifices and self-denial on the part of some. Is it necessary that these same people should also support the missionaries of an out-side religious organization? Lexington is not a very large place; I feel sure that the clergy and members of twenty-two churches can carry and are carrying the teachings of their churches to the poor of the city.

If we are the "Gates of Hell"—and sometimes I am inclined to think so when I learn that we have 104 or 105 licensed saloons in a town of 40,000, and that there were in 1915 eighty-eight deaths from violence in Fayette County as compared to six in Bloody Breathitt and fifty-seven in Campbell, whose people we were helping to reform last winter by act of Legislature—if we are the "Gates of Hell," I think it is time we found it out ourselves and set about to remedy conditions. I do not believe they will ever be remedied by foreign missionaries. And it is a pity for us to get the notion that by dropping small change into a tambourine we can get our own job done by someone else.

I do not consider the relief work of the Salvation Army sound, and I believe no citizen ought to support it until he has assured himself that it is. My opinion is based not only on careful reports of the methods of the army throughout the country made by experienced and conscientious social workers, but on investigation of such facts concerning the local work of the Salvation Army as have been brought to light by their own newspaper articles and appeals.

But I especially deplore the fact that when local people have for a good many years now been making through certain central organizations a brave effort to bring order out of chaos in what is known as "outdoor relief"—relief to the poor in their homes, that these efforts should be broken down as they are in many cases, by the efforts of another relief society coming in from the outside. I know how difficult it is for the organizations under home rule to get the money necessary for really helping the poor and the sick. For real help often does not mean "small change," it means study, thought, effort, time, and considerable sums of money. Our people are a liberal people when it comes to food, clothes, automobiles, theatre or movie tickets, but they are a fairly careful people when it comes to doubtful expenditures like charities. When $2,500 of local money goes to the Salvation Army, as their published report of expenditures for the year September 1914–15 (I have seen no financial report from the Salvation Army since) showed it did go, we can feel pretty sure that $2,500 was withdrawn from the support of our local relief workers. Which group is it better worth our while to support and to try to improve and reform if they need improving and reforming?

Source: Lexington Herald, *January 18, 1917.*

Notes

Abbreviations

ACM	Anne Clay "Nannie" McDowell
BFP	Breckinridge Family Papers, Manuscript Division, Library of Congress, Washington, DC
DB	Desha Breckinridge
FCHQ	*Filson Club History Quarterly*
HCM Jr.	Henry Clay McDowell Jr.
HCM Sr.	Henry Clay McDowell Sr.
HCMFP	Henry Clay Memorial Foundation Papers, Special Collections and Digital Programs, Margaret I. King Library, University of Kentucky, Lexington
LC	Library of Congress, Washington, DC
MM	Madeline McDowell
MMB	Madeline McDowell Breckinridge
Register	*Register of the Kentucky Historical Society*
SPB	Sophonisba Preston Breckinridge
UC	University of Chicago
UK	University of Kentucky, Lexington
WCPB	William Campbell Preston Breckinridge

Chapter 1: One Great Honored Name

1. SPB, *Madeline McDowell Breckinridge: A Leader in the New South* (Chicago, 1921), 10; McDowell genealogy, HCMFP.

2. SPB, *Breckinridge*, 1, 8–9, 11; SPB, "Madeline McDowell Breckinridge," in *Southern Pioneers in Social Interpretation*, ed. Howard W. Odum (Chapel Hill, NC, 1925), 186; James Lane Allen, *The Blue-Grass Region of Kentucky* (New York, 1892), 36.

3. SPB, *Breckinridge*, 1.

4. Ibid.

5. Lowell H. Harrison and James C. Klotter, A *New History of Kentucky* (Lexington, 1997), 19, 53, 67, 58–64; John E. Kleber, ed., *The Kentucky Encyclopedia* (Lexington, 1992), s.v. "District of Kentucky." For more on the McDowell

genealogy, see Thomas Marshall Green, *Historic Families of Kentucky* (1889; repr., Baltimore, 1966), 1, 3, 30, 39, 75–78, passim; Charles Kerr, "A Life Connecting the Past with the Present," Bessie Taul Conkwright Clippings, Filson Historical Society, Louisville; typescript on genealogy, Preston Johnston Papers, Special Collections and Digital Programs, Margaret I. King Library, UK; John M. Brown, *Memoranda of the Preston Family* (1842; repr., Frankfort, 1870); Anna Mary Moon, *Sketches of the Shelby, McDowell, Deaderick, and Anderson Families* (Chattanooga, 1933).

6. SPB, *Breckinridge*, 4; Green, *Historic Families*, 75, 76; "High Tribute to Dr. M'Dowell Is Paid by Dr. S. P. Sprague," Conkwright Clippings; Frederick Eberson, *Portraits: Kentucky Pioneers in Community Health and Medicine* (Lexington, 1968), 1, 12. On Ephraim McDowell, see Laman A. Gray, "Ephraim McDowell, Father of Abdominal Surgery, Biographical Data," *FCHQ* 43 (1969): 216–29; Willard Rouse Jillson, "Flamma Clara Maturae Medicinae Kentuckiensis," *FCHQ* 21 (1947): 103–29; Ephraim McDowell 1771–1830 Folder, clipping files, Martin D. Schmidt Library, Thomas D. Clark Center for Kentucky History, Frankfort.

7. SPB, *Breckinridge*, 10, 17–18; Green, *Historic Families*, 78. Kathleen McCarthy has defined *noblesse oblige* not only as "the duties of the rich to the society which has enriched them," but also "the notion that successful citizens owe a dual obligation of time and money to the communities in which they have prospered." Kathleen D. McCarthy, *Noblesse Oblige: Charity and Cultural Philanthropy in Chicago, 1849–1929* (Chicago, 1982), ix. Both definitions describe the attitudes of the McDowell family.

8. Diary of Anne Clay, February 11, 16, 17, 1856, HCMFP. One of the wedding presents was a silver coffee and tea service from her grandfather Henry Clay's good friend Dr. William N. Mercer of New Orleans. See Anne "Nannie" Clay to Grandma [Susannah] Price, November 3, 1857, HCMFP. Mrs. Price was actually Nannie Clay's great-aunt and the sister of Lucretia Hart Clay, as well as the mother of Nannie's guardian, Nannette Price Smith.

9. For Anne Clay's birth and her mother and father's deaths, see James F. Hopkins, Mary W. M. Hargreaves, Robert Seager II, and Melba Porter Hay, eds., *The Papers of Henry Clay*, 11 vols. (Lexington, 1959–92), 9:31, 391–92, 10:312. Anne Clay to Henry Clay [III], June 8, 1847; Aunt Ep to Henry Clay [III], May 1 [1847], both in HCMFP.

10. Document commissioning Henry Clay McDowell into the Union army, November 19, 1861; HCM Sr. to ACM, March 27, April 21, 1862; Thomas J. Clay to ACM, March 3, 1863; J. Stoddard Johnston to HCM Sr., October 13, 1863; document commissioning HCM Sr. as a federal marshal, October 17, 1862, all in HCMFP.

11. HCM Sr. to ACM, November 4, 1880, HCMFP; *Lexington Herald*, November 28, 1920.

12. Last Will and Testament of Maria Harvey McDowell, May 21, 1875,

probated December 16, 1876; HCM Jr. to ACM, December 12, 1875, November 4, 1880; HCM Sr. to Magdalen Harvey McDowell, June 15, 1866, August 13 [1867?], October 30, 1880, April 29, June [14?], 1885; A. K. Kennedy to Magdalen McDowell, May 27, 1874; application for patent on fireplace, by Magdalen McDowell, May 1889, all in HCMFP. For the story of Josephine Simpson Erwin Clay, see Henry Clay Simpson, *Josephine Clay: Pioneer Horsewoman of the Bluegrass* (Louisville, 2005).

13. William L. and Frances Breckinridge to HCM Sr., April 15, 1868, deed conveying lots in Chicago; note for $75,000 between HCM Sr. and W. N. Haldeman, April 4, 1874, both in HCMFP.

14. *Frankfort Triweekly Yeoman,* November 5, 8, 1881.

15. Mattie F. Denby to Magdalen McDowell, November 10, 1881; Mattie P. Robinson to ACM, November 9, 1881; HCM Jr. to ACM, November 28, 1881, April 29, October 8, 15, 1882, n.d. [October/November], November 12, 1882; William A. McDowell to Nettie McDowell, October 23, 1882; Stites Duvall to ACM, March 2, 18, 1882, May 14, 1883, all in HCMFP. The papers also contain a plat showing the Woodlake property consisting of 430 acres on the Frankfort and Georgetown Turnpike. Accompanying the plat is a document, dated October 21, 1883, that certifies that these 430 acres have been purchased by John C. Noel at $70.25 per acre. According to the *Frankfort Triweekly Yeoman,* October 19, 1882, this was a "very low" price. The paper also noted that another tract of 153.5 acres sold for $45.80 per acre.

16. Richard Troutman, "Henry Clay and His 'Ashland' Estate," *FCHQ* 30 (1956): 160; undated Chicago newspaper clipping enclosed in Mrs. W. S. Browrard to HCM Sr., n.d.; HCM Jr. to MM, February 25, 1883; Robert Burns Wilson to MM, n.d.; Ashland Guest Book containing handwritten copy of "Evening at Ashland," by Robert Burns Wilson, June 19, 1889, all in HCMFP; Harriet R. Holman, ed., "The Kentucky Journal of Thomas Nelson Page," *Register* 68 (1970): 11, 14. For more on Robert Burns Wilson, see J. Winston Coleman Jr., *Robert Burns Wilson: Kentucky Painter, Novelist and Poet* (Lexington, 1956). Also see Eric Brooks, *Ashland: The Henry Clay Estate* (Charleston, SC, 2007), for a pictorial view of Ashland over the years.

17. SPB, *Breckinridge,* 11.

18. Ibid., 14–15.

19. "Mrs. Higgins's Private School" report card, April 1, 1887; "Miss Butler's Day School" report card, June 1, 1888, January 18, June 1, 1889; Nettie McDowell to Magdalen McDowell, June 17, 1885; MM to Magdalen McDowell, July 24, 1886, all in HCMFP.

20. Nettie McDowell to Magdalen McDowell, August 14, 1885; MM to ACM, September 2, 1886; Nettie Belle Smith to MM, February 18, [18??]; MM to Nettie McDowell Bullock, June 9, 18, [189?], all in HCMFP; MM journal, October 29, 1892, BFP. The Breckinridge Family Papers in the Library of Congress comprise a massive collection that was unprocessed when the author first

researched them in 1976. A portion of the letters have been pasted into large books and numbered by volume. The notes reflect the volume number where applicable. The papers not included in the volumes have since been organized by name and date.

21. *Louisville Courier-Journal*, February 17, 1889; MM to ACM, August 20, 1883, February 17, 1889, HCMFP.

22. HCM Jr. to ACM, September 19, 1880, November 2, 1884, February 1, March 22, 1885; William A. McDowell to ACM, May 27, 1883; Thomas McDowell to ACM, October 17, 18, 1884, December 8, 1885, all in HCMFP.

23. William A. McDowell to HCM Sr., March 15, 1884; HCM Sr. to Magdalen McDowell, June 15, 1866, October 30, 1880, June 14, 1884; W. P. McDowell to HCM Sr., March 12, 23, July 14, 1889, October 5, 1890, February 16, March 3, August 8, November 3, December 19, 1893; promissory note, HCM Sr. to Kentucky University, June 9, 1882, January 15, 1885; Chicago newspaper in Browrard to H. C. McDowell, all in HCMFP. Will McDowell's allowance of $1,500 in 1884 would be equivalent to $35,856 in 2008 dollars. For this calculation, see www.minneapolisfed.org/community_education/teacher/calc/hist1800.cfm.

24. For a discussion of the land boom, see Hambleton Tapp, "Rogers Clark Ballard Thruston, Good Kentuckian, November 6, 1858–December 30, 1946," *FCHQ* 21 (1947): 103–29. Thruston claimed that John Fox Jr.'s character, Jack Hale, in *The Trail of the Lonesome Pine* (1908) was a composite of himself, Henry Clay McDowell Jr., and James M. Hodge. See also Hambleton Tapp, "Rogers Clark Ballard Thruston (1858–1946), Good Kentuckian," *Register* 45 (1947): 118. The articles in the *Filson Club History Quarterly* and the *Register of the Kentucky Historical Society* are virtually the same. The former, however, contains a picture of Thruston as a child that was painted by Magdalen Harvey McDowell. See also "The Great Future of Big Stone Gap," pamphlet, HCMFP.

25. *Ashland Catalogue of Trotting Stock for 1883, Belonging to H. C. McDowell* (Frankfort, 1883); Thomas McDowell to HCM Sr., January 30, 1885, HCMFP.

26. Notice of Incorporation of Goff Land Company, May 9, 1887; Articles of Incorporation for Dictator Cannel Coal Company, July 14, 1887; HCM Sr. to John Fox Jr., March 26, 1890 (copy); "The Great Future of Big Stone Gap"; HCM Sr. to ACM, October 22, 1885, June 25, 1887; HCM Jr. to HCM Sr., March 5, 1886; HCM Jr. to ACM, June 25, 1887; MM to ACM, May 17, 1890; Magdalen McDowell to MM, June 19, 1890, all in HCMFP; Tapp, "Rogers Clark Ballard Thruston," *Register*, 114–15; Ronald D Eller, "The Coal Barons of the Appalachian South, 1880–1930," *Appalachian Journal* 4 (1977): 195–207; Stuart Seely Sprague, "The Great Appalachian Iron and Coal Town Boom of 1889–1893," *Appalachian Journal* 4 (1977): 216–23.

27. Barbara Welter, "The Cult of True Womanhood, 1820–1860," *American Quarterly* 18 (1966): 151–74; Barbara Welter, *Dimity Convictions: The American Woman in the Nineteenth Century* (Athens, OH, 1976), 3–41; Marjorie Spruill

Wheeler, *New Women of the New South: The Leaders of the Woman Suffrage Movement in the Southern States* (New York, 1993), 6–8.

28. Marie Hagen Carpentier to MM, April 23, 1889, HCMFP; SPB, *Breckinridge*, 15; Barbara Miller Solomon, *In the Company of Educated Women: A History of Women and Higher Education in America* (New Haven, CT, 1985), 43–77; Roberta Frankfort, *Collegiate Women: Domesticity and Career in Turn-of-the-Century America* (New York, 1977), xiii, xv–xviii.

29. *Lexington Leader*, July 17, 26, 1889.

30. HCM Sr. to MM, September 13, 1889; MM to ACM, October 5, 8, 1889; wedding invitation to marriage of Marion Houston and Datus Clifford Smith, August 10, 1904; HCM Sr. to ACM, September 15, 1889, all in HCMFP.

31. MM to ACM, October 8, 11, 23, 1889; MM to HCM Sr., October 13, 1889, all in HCMFP.

32. MM to ACM, October 20, November 6, December 13, 15, 1889, all in HCMFP.

33. MM to ACM, March 2, 1890; MM to Nettie McDowell, March 5, 1890; ACM to MM, March 18, [1890], all in HCMFP.

34. MM to Nettie McDowell, March 5, 1890, HCMFP.

35. MM to ACM, April 2, 1890; MM to HCM Sr., April 23, 1890; Nettie McDowell to MM, April 27, 1890, all in HCMFP.

36. MM to ACM, May 2, 11, 1890, HCMFP.

37. MM to ACM, May 17, 18, June 17, 1890; MM to Julia McDowell, May 25, 1890, all in HCMFP.

38. SPB, *Breckinridge*, 15; Magdalen McDowell to MM, June 19, 1890; Grace Otis to MM, July 3, 1890, both in HCMFP.

39. T. W. Spindle to HCM Sr., October 29, November 12, 1890; St. John Boyle to HCM Sr., November 28, 1890; R. A. Ayers to HCM Sr., December 18, 28, 1890, all in HCMFP.

40. *Annual Register of the State College of Kentucky, 1890–91* (Lexington, 1891); *Annual Register of the State College of Kentucky, 1891–92* (Lexington, 1892); *Annual Register of the State College of Kentucky, 1892–93* (Lexington, 1893); *Catalogue of the State College of Kentucky, 1893–94* (Lexington, 1894).

Chapter 2: A Thunder-Bolt Out of a Clear Sky

1. HCM Jr. to ACM, August 24, 1890; Grace Otis to MM, September 27, 1890, both in HCMFP.

2. Grace Otis to MM, January 6, 1891; W. W. Thum to MM, January 29, 1891; HCM Sr. to W. A. McDowell, January 31, 1891; HCM Sr. to ACM, March 18, 1891, all in HCMFP.

3. MM to ACM, April 14, 22, n.d., 1891, HCMFP.

4. Magdalen McDowell to MM, April 19, 1891, HCMFP.

5. Nettie Belle Smith to MM, August 14, n.d., 1891, HCMFP. For Milton

H. Smith's role in the Louisville & Nashville Railroad, see Maury Klein, *History of the Louisville & Nashville Railroad* (Lexington, 2003), 186, 276, 383, 418, passim; and Milton Hannibal Smith Family Collection, 1797–1958, Special Collections, Kentucky Historical Society, Frankfort.

6. MM to ACM, September 27, 1891; Milton Smith to HCM Sr., December 18, 1891, both in HCMFP.

7. MM to HCM Sr., April 26, 1897, HCMFP.

8. Invitation to wedding of Nannette (Nettie) McDowell to Dr. Thomas S. Bullock, April 19, 1892; HCM Jr. to HCM Sr., June 24, 1892; invitation to wedding of Elsie Clay to HCM Jr., July 5, 1893, all in HCMFP; *Lexington Herald*, November 13, 1904. For Henry Clay McDowell Jr.'s service on the federal judiciary, see http://www.fjc.gov/servlet/tGetInfo?jid=1545. William Adair McDowell graduated from Yale and married twice, first in 1887 to Alice Dudley and second to Mrs. Katherine Ramsey in 1914. When Will died at almost sixty-two years of age in 1925, he left an estate of $136,384.13, according to his son, William C. McDowell, executor. For his obituary, see newspaper clippings [ca. August 14, 1925], HCMFP.

9. R. A. Ayers to HCM Sr., November 28, December 18, 23, 1890, January 10, 1891; St. John Boyle to HCM Sr., November 28, 1890; Will McDowell to HCM Sr., February 8, 1891; Agreement, November 17, 1891; Order Appointing Receivers for the Big Stone Gap Improvement Company, May 26, 1893; R. C. Ballard Thruston to HCM Sr., May 29, 1893; W. P. McDowell to HCM Sr., February 16, March 3, August 8, November 3, December 19, 1893, all in HCMFP. The land boom in Big Stone Gap, Virginia, was similar to that in Middlesboro, Kentucky, and in numerous places throughout the Appalachian region in the period 1889 to 1893. It rested on the assumption that iron and coal resources in the area could attract industry and jobs and bring a great population expansion. For a discussion of this phenomenon and its decline following the panic of 1893, see Sprague, "The Great Appalachian Iron and Coal Town Boom," 216–23.

10. Holman, "Kentucky Journal," 11, 14; Evelyn Kennedy, "Some Kentucky Women," *Leslie's Monthly Magazine*, October 1897, 394–95. See also SPB, *Breckinridge*, 12–14, which includes the full text of the sonnet "Evening at Ashland."

11. Invitation to the wedding of Nannette McDowell to Dr. Thomas S. Bullock, April 19, 1892; unidentified, undated newspaper clipping; Marion Houston to MM, May 8, 1892, all in HCMFP; Nellie Kinkead to SPB, April 2, 1892, reel 2, SPB Papers, LC. Reel number indicates citations for the Sophonisba P. Breckinridge Papers at the Library of Congress on microfilm; if no reel number is given, the author refers to the original.

12. Magdalen McDowell to Nettie Bullock, May 17, 1892; Nettie Belle Smith to MM, June 4, 1892, both in HCMFP.

13. MM to Nettie Bullock, June 9, [1892], HCMFP.

14. Nettie Belle Smith to MM, February 18??, HCMFP; diary of MM, October 29, 1892, BFP.

15. Milton H. Smith to HCM Sr., July 27, 1892; Nettie Belle Smith to MM, August 7, 1892; Marion Houston to MM, October 28, 1892, all in HCMFP.

16. *Lexington Press,* September 14, 1892.

17. ACM diary, November 24, December 16, 21, 1892; Grace Otis to MM, April 1, 1892, all in HCMFP.

18. Anne Firor Scott, *Natural Allies: Women's Associations in American History* (Chicago, 1991), 129–32; MM to Nettie Bullock, September 17, 1893; Grace Otis to MM, n.d.; ACM to MM, September 10, 1893, all in HCMFP.

19. Wedding invitation of Elsie Clay to HCM Jr., July 5, 1893; ACM diary, July 5, August 14, 15, November 27, 1893; Nettie Bullock to MM, September 24, 1893, all in HCMFP.

20. MM to DB, November 28, 1893, BFP; ACM to MM, December 10, 1893; George C. Webb to MM, December 28, 1893; MM to ACM, n.d., March 30, [1894]; MM to HCM Sr., January 8, 1894, all in HCMFP; Berry Craig, "Charting the Evolution of the Hospital for Special Surgery," *O&P Business News,* September 15, 2002, 53, 54, 56.

21. Julia McDowell to Nettie Bullock, January 4, 1894; MM to HCM Sr., January 8, 1894; ACM to MM, January 20, 1894; Grace Otis to MM, February 26, April 20, 1894; Edward Watson to MM, March 10, 1894; MM to ACM, May 30, [1894], all in HCMFP.

22. Grace Otis to MM, May 6, July 22, 1894; Marion Houston to MM, May 18, June 27, 1894, all in HCMFP.

23. Nettie Bullock to HCM Sr., May 22, 1894; Dr. Louis Frank to MM, June 30, 1894; HCM Sr. to Magdalen McDowell, July 5, 1894, all in HCMFP.

24. MM to ACM, July 7, 1894; John Fox Jr. to MM, July 18, 1894; Marion Houston to MM, July 1, 23, 1894, all in HCMFP.

25. ACM to Nettie Bullock, October 17, 1894; Marion Houston to MM, November 11, 1894; Nettie Bullock to ACM, November 27, 1894, all in HCMFP.

26. George C. Webb to MM, December 28, 1893; David Prewitt to MM, August 28, 1895; W. H. P. Phyfe to MM, December 14, 1895, January 22, February 24, May 5, June 25, 1896, all in HCMFP. For Thum and Robertson, see W. T. Owens, ed., *Who's Who in Louisville . . . 1926* (Louisville, 1926).

27. W. W. Thum to MM, December 5, 1890, January 21, May 2, 20, July 5, 1891, December 20, 1892, January 26, April 28, June 5, August 10, 1894, all in HCMFP.

28. W. W. Thum to MM, February 19, July 20, 1894, both in HCMFP.

29. MM to W. W. Thum, n.d., 1894, HCMFP.

30. W. W. Thum to MM, July 21, 24, 1894, HCMFP.

31. Owens, *Who's Who in Louisville . . . 1926.*

32. Harrison Robertson to MM, n.d., n.d., Thursday n.d., December 2, 12, 21, 31, 1892, January 1, 1893, all in HCMFP.

33. Harrison Robertson to MM, May 6, 9, 17, 23, 31, 1893, July 22, 30, September 3, 1894, all in HCMFP.

34. Harrison Robertson to MM, November 12, 1894, HCMFP.

35. Ibid.; Owens, *Who's Who in Louisville . . . 1926.*

36. James C. Klotter, *The Breckinridges of Kentucky, 1760–1981* (Lexington, 1986), ix, passim.

37. Ibid., 210; Florence Shelby Cantrill, interviews with author, March 25, October 25, 1976.

38. Klotter, *Breckinridges*, 31–32, 58–60, 111–12, 121, 140–85. For John Breckinridge, see Lowell H. Harrison, *John Breckinridge: Jeffersonian Republican* (Louisville, 1969), esp. 1, 138; Harrison, "Attorney General John Breckinridge," *FCHQ* 36 (1962): 319–28; Harrison, "John Breckinridge: Kentucky Planter, Speculator and Businessman," *FCHQ* 34 (1960): 205–27; Harrison, "John Breckinridge's Bluegrass Plantation Agreement to Operate, 1806," *FCHQ* 31 (1957): 104–14. For John C. Breckinridge, see William C. Davis, *Breckinridge: Statesman, Soldier, Symbol* (Baton Rouge, 1974), esp. 6–8. On the Breckinridge genealogy, see also Alexander Brown, *The Cabells and Their Kin* (New York, 1895).

39. *Louisville Courier-Journal*, November 6, 1891. For a detailed account of the scandal, see Klotter, *Breckinridges*, 153–70; and Klotter, "Sex, Scandal, and Suffrage in the Gilded Age," *Historian* 42 (1980): 225–43.

40. Mrs. Waller O. Bullock Sr. to Samuel Bullock, October 24, 1894, Bullock Family Papers, Special Collections and Digital Programs, Margaret I. King Library, UK; WCPB to SPB, November 12, 1895, vol. 484, BFP; Klotter, *Breckinridges*, 182–83, 199–200, 208–12; SPB typescript autobiography, SPB Papers, Special Collections Research Center, Joseph Regenstein Library, UC, 2–11.

41. SPB to MM, September 20, 1893, HCMFP.

42. SPB to MM, April 23, December 30, 1894, both in HCMFP.

43. ACM to MM, December 10, 1893, HCMFP; MM to DB, November 28, 1893, BFP.

44. MM to ACM, n.d. [December 1893], HCMFP.

45. Quoted in Klotter, *Breckinridges*, 210–11.

46. Basil Duke to HCM Sr., June 14, 16, 1894; H. Clay Howard to HCM Sr., August 19, 23, 25, 30, 1894; unidentified newspaper clipping [1894]; Thomas S. Ballard to HCM Sr., May 28, 1894; Theodore Roosevelt to HCM Sr., May 7, 1894, all in HCMFP. At one time during the Civil War, Duke and Willie Breckinridge served together as colonels commanding brigades under General John Hunt Morgan. See James A. Ramage, *Rebel Raider: The Life of General John Hunt Morgan* (Lexington, 1986), 139. For Duke's public statement against Breckinridge and in favor of McDowell, see *New York Times*, June 14, 1894.

47. Klotter, *Breckinridges*, 161–69; *New York Times*, August 23, 1894; SPB autobiography, 11, passim; unidentified newspaper clipping; HCM Jr. to Elsie J. Kelly, September 16, 1894; HCM Jr. to ACM, May 20, July 15, 1894, all in HCMFP. For other accounts of the Breckinridge campaign, see Paul E. Fuller,

"Congressman Breckinridge and the Ladies; or, Sex, Politics and Morality in the Gilded Age," *Adena* 2 (1977): 1–13; and Fuller, "An Early Venture of Kentucky Women in Politics: The Breckinridge Congressional Campaign of 1894," *FCHQ* 63 (1989): 224–42.

48. Grace Otis to MM, April 20, 1894; Marion Houston to MM, June 28, 1894, both in HCMFP.

49. T. S. Bullock to HCM Sr., June 29, 1895; *Alice B. Bullock v. Thomas S. Bullock*, December Term 1894, New York Supreme Court; Benjamin H. Bristow to HCM Sr., January 25, March 18, October 11, 1895; Bristow, Peet & Opdyke to Thomas Bullock, June 25, 1895; Agreement and Court Order, February 8, 1898; William B. Bristow to HCM Sr., February 16, 1898; Nettie Bullock to HCM Sr., March 1, 1898, all in HCMFP.

50. Mrs. [Waller O.] Bullock Sr. to Nettie Bullock, November 4, 1894; ACM to Nettie Bullock, December 12, 1894; Dr. W. O. Bullock Jr. to Army Exemption Board, August 9, 1914; W. A. McDowell to HCM Sr., April 29, May 29, June 17, 30, October 6, 1895, all in HCMFP.

51. MM to HCM Sr., July 5, 1894; ACM to MM, December 4, 1894, both in HCMFP.

52. In the last several decades there has been an outpouring of scholarly work in women's history, much of it documenting, among other things, the transformation that took place as a "new woman" developed during the late nineteenth and early twentieth centuries, one who had a different perception of the roles females should play in public life. Among these are Lois W. Banner, *Women in Modern America: A Brief History* (New York, 1974), 1–44; Nancy F. Cott, *The Grounding of Modern Feminism* (New Haven, CT, 1997); Cott, *Root of Bitterness: Documents of the Social History of American Women* (New York, 1972); Cott and Elizabeth H. Pleck, *A History of Her Own: Toward a New Social History of American Women* (New York, 1979); Nancy Schrom Dye, "The Louisville Woolen Mills Strike of 1887: A Case Study of Working Women, the Knights of Labor, and Union Organization in the New South," *Register* 82 (1984): 136–50; Sara M. Evans, *Born for Liberty: A History of Women in America* (New York, 1991); Jean E. Friedman and William G. Shade, eds., *Our American Sisters*, 2nd ed. (Boston, 1976); Paul E. Fuller, *Laura Clay and the Woman's Rights Movement* (Lexington, 1975); Linda Gordon, ed., *Women, the State, and Welfare* (Madison, WI, 1990); Linda K. Kerber, *No Constitutional Right to Be Ladies: Women and the Obligations of Citizenship* (New York, 1998); Kerber, *Toward an Intellectual History of Women: Essays* (Chapel Hill, NC, 1997); Kerber, Alice Kessler-Harris, and Kathryn Kish Sklar, eds., *U.S. History as Women's History: New Feminist Essays* (Chapel Hill, NC, 1995); Gerda Lerner, *The Majority Finds Its Past: Placing Women in History* (New York, 1979); Mary P. Ryan, *Womanhood in America, from Colonial Times to the Present* (New York, 1975); Dorothy Schneider and Carl J. Schneider, *American Women in the Progressive Era, 1900–1920* (New York, 1993); Anne Firor Scott, ed., *The American Woman: Who Was She?* (Englewood Cliffs, NJ, 1971);

Scott, *Making the Invisible Women Visible* (Urbana, IL, 1984); Scott, "The 'New Woman' in the New South," *South Atlantic Quarterly* 6 (1962): 473–83; Scott, *The Southern Lady: From Pedestal to Politics, 1830–1930* (Chicago, 1970); Mary Martha Thomas, *The New Woman in Alabama: Social Reforms and Suffrage, 1890–1920* (Tuscaloosa, AL, 1993); Welter, "The Cult of True Womanhood, 1820–1860," 151–74; Wheeler, *New Women of the New South*.

53. Marion Houston to MM, October 23, 1894; DB to MM, ? 18, 1895; SPB to MM, September 20, 1893, October 3, 1894, n.d., all in HCMFP; Nancy Ellen Barr, "A Profession for Women: Education, Social Service Administration, and Feminism in the Life of Sophonisba P. Breckinridge" (PhD diss., Emory University, 1993), 116. On January 23, 1897, the *Lexington Herald* reported that on the preceding day Sophonisba had become the first woman admitted to the practice of law before the Kentucky Court of Appeals. She also received an honorary doctorate from the University of Kentucky in 1925. See also *Lexington Herald*, June 2, 1925; *The World Today*, SPB Papers, UC; Anthony R. Travis, "Sophonisba Breckinridge, Militant Feminist," *Mid-America* 58 (1976): 111–18.

54. SPB to MM, n.d., April 23, September 20, 1893, October 3, December 27, 30, 1894, September 3, 1895, all in HCMFP; Barr, "A Profession for Women," 120; *Lexington Herald*, June 22, 1897. For information on Sophonisba Breckinridge, also see James C. Klotter, "Family Influences on a Progressive: The Early Years of Sophonisba P. Breckinridge," in *Kentucky Profiles: Biographical Essays in Honor of Holman Hamilton*, ed. Klotter and Peter J. Sehlinger (Frankfort, 1982), 121–54; Klotter, *Breckinridges*, 189–207; Ellen Fitzpatrick, *Endless Crusade: Women Social Scientists and Progressive Reform* (New York, 1990), 3–14, passim; Lela B. Costin, *Two Sisters for Social Justice: A Biography of Grace and Edith Abbott* (Urbana, IL, 1983), 59–67, 227–28, passim; Cathy Coghlan, "An Examination of the Contributions of Sophonisba Preston Breckinridge (1866–1948) to the Discipline of Sociology" (PhD diss., Texas Woman's University, 2002). Unfortunately, there is not a full-length biography of this important Progressive Era social scientist.

55. Marion Houston to MM, October 23, 1894, HCMFP.

56. SPB to MM, October 3, 1894, HCMFP; "Program of Fortnightly Club, 1894–96," by a Mrs. Harrison to DB, December 2, 1920, BFP. For works discussing the importance of club work in preparing women for reform endeavors during the Progressive Era, as well as participation in the woman suffrage movement, see Karen J. Blair, *The Clubwoman as Feminist: True Womanhood Redefined, 1868–1914* (New York, 1980); Anne Ruggles Gere, *Intimate Practices: Literacy and Cultural Work in U.S. Women's Clubs, 1880–1920* (Urbana, IL, 1997); Gordon, *Women, the State, and Welfare*; Kathleen D. McCarthy, ed., *Lady Bountiful Revisited: Women, Philanthropy, and Power* (New Brunswick, NJ, 1990), 93, 117–19; McCarthy, *Noblesse Oblige*, 47; Scott, *Natural Allies*; Anne Firor Scott, "Women's Voluntary Associations: From Charity to Reform," in McCarthy, *Lady Bountiful*, 35–54, esp. 46.

57. ACM diary, July 10, 1895; HCM Sr. to ACM, July 16, 1895; DB to

MM, June 24, 1895, all in HCMFP; DB to SPB, July 13, 1895, reel 2, SPB Papers, LC. The Chautauqua Association, chartered in Lexington in 1887, was based on a movement that had begun in Lake Chautauqua, New York. The organization sponsored a variety of cultural, educational, and recreational programs. See John D. Wright Jr., *Lexington: Heart of the Bluegrass* (Lexington, 1982), 100.

58. John Fox Jr. to MM, n.d.; Ralph Shaw to MM, September 2, 1895; DB to MM, ? 24, 1895, all in HCMFP; MM, "Recollections of Henry Clay," *Century Magazine*, May 1895, 765–70.

59. MM, "An Incident," unpublished story, BFP.

60. WCPB to SPB, October 13, 1895, vol. 483, BFP; DB to MM, October 7, 1895; Stites Duvall to MM, n.d., both in HCMFP.

61. DB to MM, August 7, ? 24, 1895, both in HCMFP.

62. Klotter, *Breckinridges*, 215; DB to MM, April 6, 1895, HCMFP.

63. MM to ACM, August 4, 1895; John Fox Jr. to MM, n.d.; Robert Burns Wilson to MM, Ju [June or July?] 7, 1895, n.d., all in HCMFP.

64. DB to MM, August 7, November 10, December 27, 1895, all in HCMFP.

65. Will McDowell to ACM, December 23, 1895; Nettie Bullock to MM, December 13, 1895; SPB to MM, January 3, 4, 26, 1896; ACM to MM, January 18, 1896, all in HCMFP.

66. ACM to MM, January 23, 1896; ACM diary, January 27, 1896; SPB to MM, January 26, 1896, all in HCMFP.

67. HCM Sr. to ACM, February 2, 9, March 16, 1896; ACM diary, February 19, 1896; ACM to MM, April 11, 1896; MM to ACM, April 20, 1896, all in HCMFP; *Lexington Herald*, February 26, March 27, 31, 1896.

68. Nettie Bullock to ACM, April 23, 1896, HCMFP.

69. Will McDowell to HCM Sr., June 17, November 3, 6, 1896; George W. Davy to Messrs. Buchanan & Son, February 14, 1896; Bond, June 3, 1896, all in HCMFP; Waller O. Bullock Sr. to Waller O. Bullock Jr., April 9, 1896, Bullock Family Papers. For calculating the consumer price index, see www.minneapolisfed.org/community_education/teacher/calc/hist1800.cfm.

70. HCM Sr. to MM, February 12, 1896; Alice Shirley Mulligan to MM, February 22, 1896; Garland Barr to MM, February 23, 1896; MM to ACM, April 2?, 1896, all in HCMFP.

71. ACM diary, April 25, 1896, HCMFP; *Lexington Herald*, May 14, 16, 17, 19, 20, 22, 29, 31, June 9, 10, 11, 1896.

72. *Lexington Herald*, June 12, 17, 1896; ACM diary, June 16, 22, 26, 1896; Nettie Bullock to MM, June 28, 1896, all in HCMFP.

73. Harrison Robertson to MM, July 20, 1896; W. W. Thum to MM, June 24, 1896; John Fox Jr. to MM, July 1, 1896; Stites Duvall to MM, n.d., all in HCMFP.

74. ACM diary, July 6, 24, 25, August 26, 1896; Lula Simpson to MM, August n.d., 1896, all in HCMFP; *Lexington Herald*, December 8, 1907.

75. *The Merck Manual of Diagnosis and Therapy* (Rahway, NJ, 1950), 1250–51; David L. Ellison, *Healing Tuberculosis in the Woods: Medicine and Science at the End of the Nineteenth Century* (Westport, CT, 1994), 30; Michael E. Teller, *The Tuberculosis Movement: A Public Health Campaign in the Progressive Era* (Westport, CT, 1988), 1–2, 95–97; Dr. Joe T. Petty to author, December 18, 1976. Worldwide, tuberculosis continues to be a major threat, with an estimated 29,700 cases of XDR (extremely drug-resistant) tuberculosis in 2004. Annelies Van Rie and Donald Enarson, "XDR Tuberculosis: An Indicator of Public Health Negligence," *Lancet*, November 4–10, 2006, 1554–55.

Chapter 3: An Unholy Interest in Reforming Others

1. John Fox Jr. to MM, April 2, 1897, n.d.; Robert Burns Wilson to MM, n.d.; ACM diary, February 17, June 1, 7, August 6, November 16, 1897, all in HCMFP; *Lexington Herald*, April 11, 27, July 1, 4, 15, 24, 25, November 9, 1897; WCPB to SPB, October 3, 10, November 21, 1897, reel 2, SPB Papers, LC; Robert Burns Wilson, *The Shadows of the Trees and Other Poems* (New York, 1898). Letters between Madge and Fox never indicate the title of the book they were promoting for Wilson, but since *The Shadows of the Trees and Other Poems* came out the following year in a very small printing, it appears to be the likely candidate for their subscription project.

2. MM to ACM, May 20, 1897; MM to HCM Sr., May 20, 1897, both in HCMFP.

3. WCPB to SPB, December 19, 1897, January 12, 1898, BFP; Agreement between H.T. Duncan Sr. & Jr., John R. Allen, and DB, January 19, 1898; Agreement between Samuel G. Boyle and DB, January 19, 1898; Attachment, January 19, 1899, DB Papers, Special Collections and Digital Programs, Margaret I. King Library, UK; WCPB to SPB, February 2, 1898, reel 2, SPB Papers, LC.

4. MM to DB, n.d. 1897, BFP.

5. MM to DB, n.d. 1897, BFP (different letter from above).

6. Sophonisba attained the PhD in 1901 and the doctor of jurisprudence three years later from the University of Chicago. *Lexington Herald*, January 23, June 22, 1897; Barr, "A Profession for Women," 173, 179.

7. ACM diary, July 30, August 8, 1897; Henry Watterson to MM, September 11, 1897; HCM Jr. to HCM Sr., February 22, 1897; S. M. DaCosta to W. O. Bullock, August 9, 1897, all in HCMFP.

8. ACM to Nettie Bullock, November 5, 1898, HCMFP; Dodd, Mead & Co. to MM, February 8, 1898; Brentano's to MM, February 11, 1898; American Book Co. to MM, August 8, 1898, all in BFP; *Lexington Herald*, March 29, April 9, 13, 14, 21, 22, 23, 26, 27, 30, May 16, 18, 20, 23, 25, 27, July 31, August 3, 4, 7, September 15, 18, October 30, 28, November 3, 1898; HCM Sr. to Magdalen McDowell, February 20, 1898, HCMFP.

9. WCPB to SPB, May 29, 1898, reel 2, SPB, LC; *Lexington Herald*, May 28, 1898; Stewart Dry Goods to MM, March 30, 1898; Chester Billings & Son Jewelers to DB, December 14, 16, 1897; Loring Andrews to DB, February 4, March 4, April 16, June 20, 1898; Victor Bogaert, Jeweler, to MM, n.d., all in BFP.

10. Klotter, *Breckinridges*, 178; WCPB to SPB, June 29, 1898, vol. 499; Last Will and Testament of Mr. Desha Breckinridge, 1898, both in BFP; *Lexington Herald*, July 20, 22, 1898.

11. DB to WCPB, telegram, August 5, 1898, vol. 499, BFP; DB to HCM, telegrams, August 20, 21, 1898, HCMFP; *Lexington Herald*, September 4, 6, 8, 11, 19, 22, October 1, 23, 26, 27, 1898.

12. HCM Sr. to E. A. Moore, October 3, 1898; HCM Sr. to S. E. Jones, September 23, 1898; HCM Sr. to W. K. Pickens, October 12, 1898, all in HCMFP.

13. WCPB to SPB, September 9, October 30, November 10, 13, 1898; MM to WCPB, November 6, 1898; DB to SPB, November 15, 1898; all in vol. 500, BFP.

14. *Lexington Herald*, November 6, 8, 18, 1898; unidentified newspaper clipping, HCMFP; Mrs. W. O. Bullock Sr. to W. O. Bullock Jr., November 20, 1898, Bullock Family Papers; WCPB to SPB, September 23, 25, October 30, November 13, 15, 1898, all in vol. 500, BFP.

15. DB to WCPB, November 25, 1898; WCPB to DB, November 29, 1898; WCPB to SPB, November 23, 29, December 5, 7, 1898, all in vol. 501, BFP; *Lexington Herald*, December 14, 1898; WCPB to Ella Chalkley, December 26, 1898, Chalkley Family Scrapbooks, Special Collections and Digital Programs, Margaret I. King Library, UK.

16. MMB to SPB, December 7, 1898, vol. 501, BFP.

17. WCPB to SPB, February 1, 1899, vol. 501, BFP; Mrs. W. O. Bullock to Dr. W. O. Bullock Jr., February 1, 1899, Bullock Family Papers; R. A. McDowell to HCM Sr., February 7, 1899; Fayette Hewitt to HCM Sr., January 14, 20, February 6, 1899; HCM Sr. to Fayette Hewitt, January 11, 16, 1899, all in HCMFP; *Lexington Herald*, January 10, February 15, March 18, 1899.

18. HCM Sr. to HCM Jr., March 31, 1899, HCMFP.

19. MMB to HCM Sr., March 17, 1899; MMB to Nettie Bullock, September 25, 1899, both in HCMFP; WCPB to SPB, March 13, 15, April 30, 1899, vol. 502, August 24, 31, 1899, vol. 504; DB to SPB, October 10, 1899, vol. 505, all in BFP; *Lexington Herald*, September 16, 18, 1899.

20. *Lexington Herald*, February 12, 14, 15, 16, 19, 23, April 1, 1899; SPB, "Madeline McDowell Breckinridge," in *Southern Pioneers*, 188. William "Squire" McNamara had killed two men; he was acquitted in one case and pardoned by Governor William Taylor in the other. See *Lexington Herald*, August 17, 1901.

21. SPB, *Breckinridge*, 34. For a discussion of lawlessness in nineteenth-century Kentucky, see Robert M. Ireland, "Homicide in Nineteenth Century

Kentucky," *Register* 81 (1983): 134–53 and "Law and Disorder in Nineteenth Century Kentucky," *Vanderbilt Law Review* 32 (1979): 281–82; also Hambleton Tapp and James C. Klotter, *Kentucky: Decades of Discord, 1865–1900* (Frankfort, 1977).

22. *Lexington Herald*, February 16, 17, 18, 19, 1899.

23. WCPB to SPB, February 19, 26, 1899, vol. 502, BFP.

24. W. O. Bullock Sr. to W. O. Bullock Jr., February 21, 1899, Bullock Family Papers; *Lexington Herald*, February 16, 20, 22, 23, 24, March 2, 8, 9, 31, 1899; "Resolutions of the Mass Meeting of February 21, 1899," BFP; MMB to ACM, n.d. (Sunday), HCMFP. The resolutions for the mass meeting are in Madge's handwriting, indicating that she was probably the chief author.

25. *Lexington Herald*, February 23, 24, March 2, 8, 9, 31, 1899.

26. *Lexington Herald*, March 23, 1899, August 4, 17, September 17, 1901, February 6, 7, 9, 11, 12, 13, 1911, June 15, July 13, 14, 15, 16, 23, 1912. The reward put up at the time of the murder went to Fayette County sheriff Daniel W. Scott, who arrested McNamara. A friend of the sheriff alleged that Scott had been tipped off about McNamara by a female detective named Bettie Foss, who had shadowed McNamara for two years. Foss claimed that Louisville police and some Lexington officials had protected McNamara and enabled him to evade arrest for thirteen years. At the trial, held in July 1912, the jury convicted the defendant of voluntary manslaughter and sentenced him to five years at labor. Because of his health, the *Herald* noted, he would probably be assigned clerical duties. This light sentence aroused much local indignation.

27. *Lexington Herald*, March 11, 12, 18, 23, 1899.

28. SPB, *Breckinridge*, 28–32; WCPB to SPB, May 3, 1899, vol. 503, BFP.

29. WCPB to SPB, May 3, 1899, vol. 503, BFP; *Lexington Herald*, May 15, 28, June 1, 4, 1899, May 21, 1900.

30. SPB, *Breckinridge*, 30–31; WCPB to SPB, July 17, 21, 1899; DB to Curry Breckinridge, July 21, 1899, all in vol. 504, BFP; *Lexington Herald*, May 15, 28, June 1, 4, July 26, 1899; William A. Link, *The Paradox of Southern Progressivism, 1880–1930* (Chapel Hill, NC, 1992), 83; David E. Whisnant, *All That Is Native and Fine: The Politics of Culture in an American Region* (Chapel Hill, NC, 1983), 24–25, 279. Link states that Madeline McDowell Breckinridge and Katherine Pettit founded Camp Cedar Grove settlement on their trip into eastern Kentucky; while Whisnant implies in his text that they both founded the camp, he comments in his notes that there is no evidence that Breckinridge actually took part in Camp Cedar Grove. This author has found no reference to Camp Cedar Grove in the Breckinridge Family Papers or the Henry Clay Memorial Foundation Papers. See also Nancy K. Forderhase, "Eve Returns to the Garden: Women Reformers in Appalachian Kentucky in the Early Twentieth Century," *Register* 85 (1987): 237–61.

31. WCPB to SPB, August 18, September 18, 1899, vol. 504, October 3, 10, 1899, vol. 505, all in BFP; Dr. S. M. DaCosta to Dr. W. O. Bullock Sr., August

17, [1899], Bullock Family Papers; MMB to ACM, March 4, 1899; MMB to Nettie Bullock, September 25, 1899; HCM Sr. to "My dear Cleveland," October 21, 1899; HCM Sr. to Nettie Bullock, October 1, 1899; J. Kennedy Tod to HCM Sr., September 27, 1899, all in HCMFP; *Louisville Times,* November 18, 1899; *Louisville Evening Post,* November 18, 1899; *Lexington Herald,* October 5, November 19, 20, 21, 1899.

32. *Lexington Herald,* November 28, 1920; SPB, *Breckinridge,* 15, 17–18.

33. Last Will and Testament of Henry Clay McDowell, August 14, 1897; ACM to MMB, check stubs, 1900, HCMFP; unidentified newspaper clipping, November 29, 1899, BFP. The buying power of $75 in 1900 would be equivalent to approximately $1,937 in 2008 currency. For calculations on the consumer index, see www.minneapolisfed.org/community_education/teacher/calc/hist1800.cfm.

34. WCPB to SPB, February 1, 1899, vol. 501, February 17, 1900, vol. 506, September 2, 1900, vol. 508, all in BFP; *Lexington Herald,* May 9, 1900; Wright, *Lexington,* 129.

35. *Lexington Herald,* January 3, 8, 1900.

36. Fitzpatrick, *Endless Crusade,* 35–36, 169, 177, 191–92; MMB to ACM, n.d., HCMFP; Allen F. Davis, *Spearheads for Reform: The Social Settlements and the Progressive Movement, 1890–1914* (1967; repr., New Brunswick, NJ, 1994), vii, viii, xii, 20–21, 60, 65; Robyn Muncy, *Creating a Female Dominion in American Reform, 1890–1935* (New York, 1991), 66–78. For more on Hull-House and the settlement house influence on the Progressive movement, see Kathryn Kish Sklar, "Hull House in the 1890s: A Community of Women Reformers," *Signs* 10 (1985): 658–77; John P. Rousmaniere, "Cultural Hybrid in the Slums: The College Woman and the Settlement House, 1889–1894," *American Quarterly* 22 (1970): 45–66; Eleanor J. Stebner, *The Women of Hull House: A Study in Spirituality, Vocation, and Friendship* (Albany, 1997).

37. For discussions of the evolution of social work and charity administration during the Progressive Era, see David B. Danbom, *"The World of Hope": Progressives and the Struggle for an Ethical Public Life* (Philadelphia, 1997), 72–73; Steven J. Diner, *A Very Different Age: Americans of the Progressive Era* (New York, 1998), 195, 199; Ronald C. Federico, *The Social Welfare Institution,* 2nd ed. (Lexington, MA, 1976), 252–55; M. J. Heale, *Twentieth-Century America: Politics and Power in the United States, 1900–2000* (New York, 2004), 30, 33; Philip Klein, *From Philanthropy to Social Welfare: An American Cultural Perspective* (San Francisco, 1968), 149–51, 162; Roy Lubove, *The Professional Altruist: The Emergence of Social Work as a Career, 1880–1930* (Cambridge, MA, 1965), 1–10, 18; Kathleen D. McCarthy, "Parallel Power Structures: Women and Voluntary Spheres," in McCarthy, *Lady Bountiful,* 1; Muncy, *Creating a Female Dominion,* 77, passim; Camilla Stivers, *Bureau Men, Settlement Women: Constructing Public Administration in the Progressive Era* (Lawrence, KS, 2000), 61, 111, 114, 121; Judith Ann Trolander, *Professionalism and Social Change: From the Settlement House Movement to Neighborhood Centers, 1886 to the Present* (New York, 1987), 1–2, 12–19.

38. SPB, *Breckinridge*, 42, 156, 158; Leon Fink, *Progressive Intellectuals and the Dilemmas of Democratic Commitment* (Cambridge, MA, 1997), 24.

39. SPB, *Breckinridge*, 42, 156, 158; *Lexington Herald*, March 28, 30, 1900.

40. *Lexington Herald*, April 15, December 16, 1900.

41. Davis, *Spearheads for Reform*, 21–22. See also Allen F. Davis, *American Heroine: The Life and Legend of Jane Addams* (New York, 1973); Costin, *Two Sisters for Social Justice*, 45, 71; Fitzpatrick, *Endless Crusade*, 10, 56, 80, 175, 190, passim; Louise W. Knight, *Citizen: Jane Addams and the Struggle for Democracy* (Chicago, 2005).

42. *Lexington Herald*, April 29, 1900.

43. *Lexington Herald*, March 25, May 27, June 17, November 25, 1900.

44. *Lexington Herald*, June 18, 1900. Jacob Riis—writer, photojournalist, and reformer—supported the settlement workers in their efforts to alleviate urban poverty. He is best known for his promotion of housing reform. See Alexander Alland, *Jacob Riis: Photographer and Citizen* (Millerton, NY, 1972); Davis, *Spearheads for Reform*, 20, 62, 67.

45. *Lexington Herald*, May 26, 27, June 17, 1900.

46. *Lexington Herald*, February 14, March 4, 9, 11, 1900.

47. *Lexington Herald*, March 4, 1900.

48. Ibid. For more on the Goebel assassination, see James C. Klotter, *William Goebel: The Politics of Wrath* (Lexington, 1977).

49. Nettie Bullock to ACM, June 2, October 5, 1900; ACM to Nettie Bullock, October 31, 1900; Elsie McDowell to Nettie Bullock, May 24, 1900; Eliza Watson McEwan to Nettie Bullock, August 22, 1900, all in HCMFP.

50. SPB, *Breckinridge*, 38–42, 45–46; WCPB to SPB, May 7, July 9, 1900, vol. 507, BFP; *Lexington Herald*, April 7, 15, 18, 25, May 1, 2, 11, 1900.

51. *Lexington Herald*, May 21, 28, June 1, 4, 6, July 23, November 28, 1900; SPB, *Breckinridge*, 31; WCPB to SPB, May 26, 1900, vol. 507, BFP.

52. SPB, *Breckinridge*, 32.

53. Robert H. Wiebe, *The Search for Order, 1877–1920* (New York, 1967), 119, 170; Davis, *Spearheads for Reform*, 54–55; Lubove, *The Professional Altruist*, 38; Link, *Paradox of Southern Progressivism*, 124, 174–75. For an analysis of progressive education reforms promoted by women in one southern state, see Rebecca S. Montgomery, *The Politics of Education in the New South: Women and Reform in Georgia, 1890–1930* (Baton Rouge, 2006).

54. *Lexington Herald*, February 18, 1900.

55. *Lexington Herald*, February 18, October 9, 1900.

56. *Lexington Herald*, October 9, 1900.

57. *Lexington Herald*, November 11, 1900.

58. *Lexington Herald*, December 16, 1900.

59. *Lexington Herald*, July 22, 1900.

60. *Lexington Herald*, July 31, 1900.

61. SPB, *Breckinridge*, 43–44.

62. Heale, *Twentieth-Century America*, 29; Danbom, *"The World of Hope,"* 72.

Chapter 4: Our Hope Lies in the Children

1. SPB, *Breckinridge*, 43.

2. Klotter, "Family Influences on a Progressive," 142–47; Costin, *Two Sisters for Social Justice*, 59–67, 184, 193–94, passim; Fitzpatrick, *Endless Crusade*, 81, 87–88, 166–67, passim; Nancy K. Forderhase, "'Limited Only by Earth and Sky': The Louisville Woman's Club and Progressive Reform," *FCHQ* 59 (1985): 327–43; Victoria Getis, T*he Juvenile Court and the Progressives* (Urbana, IL, 2000), 9; Harrison and Klotter, *New History of Kentucky*, 277–79. As Robert M. Crunden has said in *Ministers of Reform: The Progressives' Achievement in American Civilization, 1889–1920* (New York, 1982), 65–66: "Hull-House was the great catalyst to progressive social science." He further argues that Jane Addams's autobiography, *Twenty Years at Hull-House* (New York, 1910), "concealed beneath the anecdotal style . . . the sort of concepts that provided professional social scientists with organizing hypotheses." Madge embraced many of the ideas coming out of Hull-House, including, for example, the casework method for administering charity. The historiography of the Progressive movement is immense, but for discussions of what the Progressive movement was and who constituted it, see especially Daniel Aaron, *Men of Good Hope: A Story of American Progressives* (New York, 1951), xi, xiii; Edward L. Ayers, *The Promise of the New South: Life after Reconstruction* (New York, 1992), 413–15; John D. Buenker, *Urban Liberalism and Progressive Reform* (New York, 1973); Buenker, John C. Burnham, and Robert M. Cruden, *Progressivism* (Cambridge, MA, 1977), v, 4–18, 22, 31–34, 59–63; Nicholas C. Burckel, "Progressive Governors in the Border States: Reform Governors of Missouri, Kentucky, West Virginia and Maryland, 1900–1918" (PhD diss., University of Wisconsin, 1971); David R. Colburn and George E. Pozzetta, eds., *Reform and Reformers in the Progressive Era* (Westport, CT, 1983), vii, 3, 13, 18; Crunden, *Ministers of Reform*, ix–x, 15; Danbom, *"The World of Hope,"* vii, 113; Diner, *A Very Different Age*, 12–13, 201; Eldon J. Eisenach, *The Lost Promise of Progressivism* (Lawrence, KS, 1994), 72–73, 263; Arthur Ekirch, *Progressivism in America* (New York, 1974), 67, 93; Louis Filler, *Appointment at Armageddon: Muckraking and Progressivism in the American Tradition* (Westport, CT, 1976), 280, 301–2, 350–51; Kenneth Finegold, *Experts and Politicians: Reform Challenges to Machine Politics in New York, Cleveland, and Chicago* (Princeton, NJ, 1995), 3, 178–79; Fink, *Progressive Intellectuals*, 10–13; Noralee Frankel and Nancy Schrom Dye, eds., *Gender, Class, Race and Reform in the Progressive Era* (Lexington, 1991), 1–9, especially Molly Ladd-Taylor, "Hull House Goes to Washington: Women and the Children's Bureau," 110–26; Eric F. Goldman, *Rendezvous with Destiny: A History of Modern American Reform* (New York, 1952), 75, 83; Lynn D. Gordon, *Gender and Higher*

Education in the Progressive Era (New Haven, CT, 1990), 3; Lewis L. Gould, ed., *The Progressive Era* (Syracuse, NY, 1974); Dewey Grantham, *Southern Progressivism: The Reconciliation of Progress and Tradition* (Knoxville, TN, 1983); Heale, *Twentieth-Century America*, 4–5; Richard Hofstadter, *The Age of Reform* (New York, 1955), 5; Morton Keller, *Regulating a New Society: Public Policy and Social Change in America, 1900–1933* (Cambridge, MA, 1994), ix–x, 1–3, 293; Jack T. Kirby, *Darkness at the Dawning* (New York, 1972); Aileen S. Kraditor, *The Ideas of the Woman Suffrage Movement, 1890–1920* (New York, 1965), 56–57; William E. Leuchtenburg, *The Perils of Prosperity, 1914–32* (Chicago, 1958), 3; Peter Levine, *The New Progressive Era: Toward a Fair and Deliberate Democracy* (New York, 2000), xi, 6; Link, *Paradox of Southern Progressivism*, 95, 124–26; Lubove, *The Professional Altruist*, 84, passim; Herbert F. Margulies, "Recent Opinion on the Decline of the Progressive Movement," *Mid-America* 45 (1963): 250–68; Kevin Mattson, *Creating a Democratic Public: The Struggle for Urban Participatory Democracy during the Progressive Era* (University Park, PA, 1998), 4, 7, 13, 129, 131; McCarthy, *Noblesse Oblige*, 101; George Mowry, *The California Progressives* (Los Angeles, 1951) and *The Era of Theodore Roosevelt, 1900–1912* (New York, 1958); David J. Rothman, *Conscience and Convenience: The Asylum and Its Alternatives in Progressive America* (Boston, 1980), 5–7, 43, 46–49, 60, 205; David Sarasohn, *The Party of Reform: Democrats in the Progressive Era* (Jackson, MS, 1989), vii–ix; Stivers, *Bureau Men, Settlement Women*, 4–5; Jack Tager, "Progressives, Conservatives and the Theory of the Status Revolution," *Mid-America* 48 (1966): 167, 174; Thomas, *The New Woman in Alabama*, 2–5; James Weinstein, *The Corporate Ideal in the Liberal State, 1900–1918* (Boston, 1962), x; Wiebe, *Search for Order*, 44.

3. Heale, *Twentieth-Century America*, 29; Hofstadter, *Age of Reform*, 5, passim; Schneider, *American Women in the Progressive Era*, 12, 15, 197; Eisenach, *Lost Promise of Progressivism*, 9; Crunden, *Ministers of Reform*, 56–66; Filler, *Appointment at Armageddon*, 264; Christopher Lasch, *The New Radicalism in America, 1889–1963: The Intellectual as Social Type* (New York, 1965), 11; Tager, "Progressives, Conservatives and the Theory of the Status Revolution," 167, 174.

4. Crunden, *Ministers of Reform*, 19–25, 56–61, 63, 66; Danbom, "*The World of Hope*," 72, 113–15; Lasch, *The New Radicalism in America*, 11–12; Margaret Ripley Wolfe, *Daughters of Canaan: A Saga of Southern Women* (Lexington, 1995), 136–38.

5. *Lexington Herald*, November 18, 1906, May 5, 1907, September 25, 1914; MMB to Alice Lloyd, May 10, 1916, BFP.

6. *Lexington Herald*, January 8, April 14, September 1, December 17, 18, 1901; MMB to ACM, July 9, 1901, HCMFP; Henderson Daingerfield Norman to DB, n.d. [1921], reel 3, SPB Papers, LC.

7. Wright, *Lexington*, 139; SPB, *Breckinridge*, 48–50.

8. Davis, *Spearheads for Reform*, 60–65; Raymond G. Fuller, *Recreation*

and Child Welfare (New York, 1919), 3–11; Link, *Paradox of Southern Progressivism*, 124.

9. SPB, *Breckinridge*, 48–49; MMB to ACM, June 18, 1901, HCMFP; *Lexington Herald*, June 16, 18, July 1, 1901; Cantrill interviews. Betsy Cloud subsequently became principal of the elementary school in Irishtown, a position she held until her death in 1934. Her obituary stated that at Breckinridge's instigation, she had studied the social settlement model at Hull-House and applied it to the Irishtown school. The article also noted that she had always kept Madge's memory alive at the school. *Lexington Herald*, January 14, 1934.

10. SPB, Breckinridge, 54; Klotter, *Breckinridges*, 203.

11. *Lexington Herald*, August 4, 12, 1901.

12. *Lexington Herald*, September 8, 1901.

13. Cantrill interviews.

14. WCPB to SPB, January 12, June 3, 1901, vol. 510, August 17, 26, 31, September 17, 29, 1901, vol. 512, all in BFP; Magdalen McDowell to Nettie Bullock, May 26, 1901; HCM Jr. to Nettie Bullock, November 20, 1901; HCM Jr. to ACM, November 10, 12, 1901; Nathaniel S. Shaler to DB, November 18, 1901, all in HCMFP; WCPB to SPB, August 21, 1901, SPB Papers, LC; *Lexington Herald*, August 2, 5, 15, 27, 24, 28, October 10, November 26, 27, December 6, 20, 1901. Jouett Shouse (1879–1968) was born in Midway, Kentucky. He worked on the staff of the *Lexington Herald* from 1898 to 1904, moved to Kansas in 1911, and was elected to the U.S. House in 1915, serving in the 64th and 65th Congresses. He held the positions of assistant secretary of the U.S. Treasury, 1919–20; chairman of the Democratic National Executive Committee, 1929–32; president of the Association against the Prohibition Amendment, 1932–33; and president of the American Liberty League, 1934–38. See the Jouett Shouse Papers, Special Collections and Digital Programs, Margaret I. King Library, UK.

15. *Lexington Herald*, February 16, November 3, 24, December 8, 15, 1901; SPB, *Breckinridge*, 94–107. Owen Lovejoy, general secretary of the National Child Labor Committee, argued in the *North American Review* in 1910 that industrial education could keep potential dropouts in school for an additional two years, but he noted the danger that such schools would prepare students only for jobs in nearby factories. Nevertheless, he insisted that industrial schools could introduce pupils to a larger variety of vocational opportunities than they might have otherwise. Likewise, John Dewey, famed educator and philosopher, supported the validity of vocational training so long as it was incorporated into the general curriculum but warned of the danger that it could simply emphasize class differences. See Montgomery, *Politics of Education*, 185–230, esp. 316, 319–20. As James L. Leloudis II noted in a 1983 article, education reform in the southern states found its main strength in local groups of women. Reformers were genuinely concerned with the poor and their uplift as well as with social control. Thus, education reform cannot be understood in oppositional terms of either altruism or self-interest—it was both, he argued. Leloudis, "School Reform

in the New South," *Journal of American History* 69 (1983): 886–909.

16. WPB to SPB, November 18, 1901, vol. 512, BFP.

17. *Kentucky Acts* (Louisville, 1830), 272–80, esp. 279; *Kentucky Acts* (Frankfort, 1838), 274–83, esp. 282; *Kentucky Acts* (Frankfort, 1852), 161–69, esp. 166; *Kentucky Acts* (Frankfort, 1894), 234–314, esp. 313; Thomas Woody, *A History of Women's Education in the United States* (New York, 1929), 442; MMB to Magdalen McDowell, n.d. ["Tues."], 1901, HCMFP; Lynn E. Niedermeier, *Eliza Calvert Hall: Kentucky Author and Suffragist* (Lexington, 2007), 84, 113–14.

18. *Lexington Herald*, October 1, 1901; MMB to Nettie Bullock, n.d. ["Wed."], HCMFP.

19. *Lexington Herald*, January 26, March 12, 1902; Claudia Knott, "The Woman Suffrage Movement in Kentucky, 1879–1920" (PhD diss., University of Kentucky, 1989), 194, 213, 224; Clavia Goodman, *Bitter Harvest: Laura Clay's Suffrage Work* (Lexington, 1946), 40; James Duane Bolin, *Bossism and Reform in a Southern City: Lexington, Kentucky, 1880–1940* (Lexington, 2000), 55–57. William Frederick "Billy" Klair served several terms in the Kentucky legislature and became a power in the Democratic Party. He owned the Navare saloon in downtown Lexington, the Leland Hotel, and in 1912 formed the Klair-Scott Insurance Agency. He also worked with the so-called bipartisan combine, comprised of urban Democrats and Republicans who fought to protect the state's railroad, coal mining, liquor, and racetrack interests. His association with the liquor interests in particular put him on a collision course with woman suffragists in the state, who often supported prohibition. Kleber, *Kentucky Encyclopedia*, s.v. "Klair, William Frederick."

20. MMB to SPB, January 14, February 2, 1902, vol. 512, BFP.

21. MMB to Nettie Bullock, n.d. ["Wed."], HCMFP; J. Embry Allen to MMB, January 30, 1902; John L. Whitehead to MMB, February 28, 1902; MMB to SPB, February 2, 1902, vol. 512, all in BFP; *Kentucky Acts* (Louisville, 1902), 44–45. For the background to the Kentucky Equal Rights Association's attempt to get a female appointed to the board of trustees at the State University, see Fuller, *Laura Clay*, 86–88, 186. Fuller notes that the first woman appointed to the board was Mrs. Paul Blazer in 1939. Mary Creegan (Mrs. Ruric Nevel) Roark was an educator at the State University who in 1909 became acting president of Eastern Kentucky State Normal School following the death of her husband, the school's first president. Kleber, *Kentucky Encyclopedia*, s.v. "Eastern Kentucky University."

22. WCPB to SPB, January 13, 1902; MMB to SPB, January 14, 1902, both in vol. 512, BFP.

23. *Lexington Herald*, February 1, 2, 1902; Davis, *Spearheads for Reform*, 60, 62, 67. The National Consumers' League was founded in 1899, and in 1901 Annie Ainslie (Mrs. R. P.) Halleck established the Consumers' League of Kentucky, which was affiliated with the national group. The organization sought to improve wages and working conditions for women and children in industry. John E. Kle-

ber, ed., *The Encyclopedia of Louisville* (Lexington, 2001), s.v. "Halleck, Annie Ainslie"; Heale, *Twentieth-Century America*, 30–31. For more on the women's labor movement, see Nancy Schrom Dye, *As Equals and as Sisters: Feminism, the Labor Movement, and the Women's Trade Union League of New York* (Columbia, MO, 1980).

24. Nettie Bullock to ACM, July 23, 1901, HCMFP; *Lexington Herald*, March 5, April 29, 1902; WCPB to SPB, February 28, April 12, 1902, vol. 512; DB to Magdalen McDowell, April 8, 1902, all in BFP.

25. *Lexington Herald*, May 4, 1902.

26. MMB, *Another Reason for Granting School Suffrage to Kentucky Women* (Lexington, 1910) and "A Mother's Sphere," both in BFP.

27. Wiebe, *Search for Order*, 169, 171.

28. *Lexington Herald*, June 24, 1902.

29. SPB, *Breckinridge*, 241.

30. Ibid., 51; *Lexington Herald*, May 28, 29, July 2, 1902; MMB to ACM, July 9, 1901, HCMFP.

31. *Lexington Herald*, May 29, July 2, 8, 11, 13, 15, 20, 1902.

32. *Lexington Herald*, July 20, 24, August 14, 20, 1902.

33. *Lexington Herald*, August 8, December 5, 1902, May 2, 1903. Rebecca Montgomery has argued in her study of education reform in Georgia that advocacy of the kindergarten movement was not simply about social control, as some historians have maintained. She notes that while a desire for social order was a motivating factor, support for kindergarten education was far more complicated. She states that reformers "believed that the relative deprivation of working-class children gave them a particular need for nurture and guidance, but they regarded early childhood education as appropriate for all classes. . . . They focused as much on the advantages it offered to the individual child as on its social benefits." Montgomery, *Politics of Education*, 195.

34. *Lexington Herald*, August 24, 1902.

35. *Lexington Herald*, July 11, 12, 13, September 8, 1902.

36. Eliza Underwood, interview with author, March 4, 1977.

37. *Lexington Herald*, January 30, May 31, April 1, June 2, 14, 30, August 30, 1903; SPB, *Breckinridge*, 50.

38. *Lexington Herald*, March 19, April 3, 1903.

39. *Lexington Herald*, June 30, July 4, December 5, 1902.

40. WCPB to SPB, June 22, 1902, vol. 512, BFP; *Lexington Herald*, June 22, 24, 1902.

41. *Lexington Herald*, June 28, 1902.

42. MMB to Nettie Bullock, December 26, 1902, HCMFP.

43. *Lexington Herald*, January 31, 1903.

44. *Lexington Herald*, January 13, February 10, 13, 21, March 11, April 2, July 13, 1903.

45. *Lexington Herald*, January 10, 1903; Davis, *Spearheads for Reform*, 18.

46. *Lexington Herald,* March 26, 1903.

47. *Lexington Herald,* April 1, 15, 16, 1903.

48. *Lexington Herald,* January 31, March 31, June 3, July 7, 1903.

49. WCPB to SPB, January 6, 14, 1903, vol. 513, BFP; *Lexington Herald,* March 3, 19, April 25, 1903; Nettie Bullock to ACM, December 7, 1902; Mary ? to Nettie Bullock, February 23, 1903; HCM Jr. to Nettie Bullock, January 20, 1903; ACM to Nettie Bullock, March 26, 1903; MMB to ACM, July 9, 1901, all in HCMFP.

50. ACM to Nettie Bullock, April 18, 1903, HCMFP.

51. *Lexington Herald,* May 12, 1903; WCPB to SPB, May 11, 1903, vol. 513, BFP.

52. *Lexington Herald,* May 12, 13, 1903.

53. Hugh F. Fox, *Some Aspects of Child Labor in the United States* (Atlanta, 1903), 3, in MMB Papers, Special Collections and Digital Programs, Margaret I. King Library, UK; *Lexington Herald,* May 26, June 3, 6, 30, December 15, 1903. For a discussion of Kentucky's education system in the early twentieth century, see James C. Klotter, *Kentucky: Portrait in Paradox, 1900–1950* (Frankfort, 1996), 145–48.

54. Andy B. Ludwig to MMB, June 25, 1903, BFP; *Lexington Herald,* June 30, December 15, 1903.

55. *Lexington Herald,* May 24, 1903.

56. *Lexington Herald,* June 4, July 12, 1903.

57. WCPB to SPB, July 27, 1903, vol. 513, BFP; SPB, *Breckinridge,* 56; *Lexington Herald,* August 4, 1903.

58. *Lexington Herald,* August 30, 1903.

59. WCPB to SPB, October 19, 1903, vol. 513, BFP; HCM Jr. to ACM, January 25, 1904, HCMFP.

60. SPB, *Breckinridge,* 56; *Lexington Herald,* September 27, November 16, December 13, 1903, February 11, 1904.

61. Henderson Daingerfield Norman to DB, n.d. [1921], reel 3, SPB Papers, LC; WCPB to SPB, February 27, 1904, vol. 514, BFP; Edwin A. Weinstein, "Woodrow Wilson's Neurological Illness," *Journal of American History* 57 (1970), 333–36; Weinstein, *Woodrow Wilson: A Medical and Psychological Biography* (Princeton, NJ, 1981), 18, 252. Wilson's condition is also discussed in Bert E. Park, *Ailing, Aging, Addicted: Studies of Compromised Leadership* (Lexington, 1993), 95–117.

62. *Lexington Herald,* March 27, April 10, 24, December 11, 1904. Massachusetts created a probation system for juvenile offenders in 1869, while Illinois enacted a juvenile court law in 1899, due to the lobbying of Hull-House residents. See Elizabeth J. Clapp, *Mothers of All Children: Women Reformers and the Rise of Juvenile Courts in Progressive Era America* (University Park, PA, 1998), 37, 63.

63. *Lexington Herald,* April 10, 1904; Danbom, "*The World of Hope,*" 104;

Keller, *Regulating a New Society*, 169; Rothman, *Conscience and Convenience*, 205, 211, 213–15. For a detailed discussion of Ben Lindsey and the evolution of the Colorado juvenile court system, see Clapp, *Mothers of All Children*, 110–27. Sophonisba Breckinridge and Edith Abbott made a study of the causes of delinquency titled *The Delinquent Child and the Home* (Chicago, 1912). For additional information on the juvenile court system and its implementation in Illinois, see Getis, *Juvenile Court*, 2–4, passim.

64. *Lexington Herald*, August 31, 1904; MMB to Ben B. Lindsey, July 10, 1904, Ben B. Lindsey Papers, LC.

65. *Lexington Herald*, January 11, 31, April 27, June 10, 26, August 31, September 5, 28, November 9, 20, 1904.

66. *Lexington Herald*, July 10, November 18, 1904.

67. *Lexington Herald*, May 1, 25, 29, September 9, 25, October 4, 27, 30, November 6, 8, 13, 1904; marriage announcement for Julia Prather McDowell to William Bass Brock, November 12, 1904, HCMFP.

68. WCPB to SPB, August 11, 1904, vol. 515, BFP.

69. *Lexington Herald*, November 20, 21, December 24, 1904, January 16, 1906; Klotter, *Breckinridges*, 184; DB to SPB, November 26, December 7, 1904, reel 2, SPB Papers, LC.

70. *Lexington Herald*, December 25, 1904.

71. *Lexington Herald*, December 22, 1904; Nettie Bullock to ACM, December 26, 1904, HCMFP.

72. SPB autobiography.

Chapter 5: Whatever a Woman Can Do

1. *Lexington Herald*, March 24, April 2, May 9, August 9, October 12, November 17, 1905, July 4, September 25, 1906, August 13, September 8, 1907; MMB to SPB, June 30, July 1, 1905, reel 2, SPB Papers, LC.

2. MMB to SPB, July 1, 1905, reel 2, SPB Papers, LC; MMB to ACM, ca. February 1905; ACM to Nettie Bullock, August 28, 1906, both in HCMFP; *Lexington Herald*, March 29, 1905.

3. *Lexington Herald*, January 13, 24, February 7, 1905, July 30, 1906. For a discussion of attitudes toward progressive reform in the South, see Link, *Paradox of Southern Progressivism*, xi–xii, 125–26. Link notes that reformers' motives were very diverse and often contradictory, with some oriented toward social control and others toward humanitarianism. Many, he says, were influenced by the national "ideology of child saving and a new fascination with childhood that swept through educational circles after 1890." Furthermore, he believes their rhetoric should often be taken at face value rather than assuming that it masked darker motives, such as social control, racism, or fear of immigrants.

4. *Lexington Herald*, October 16, 17, 1905; "The Seventh Annual Report of the Associated Charities of Lexington and Fayette County," Linda Neville

Papers, Special Collections and Digital Programs, Margaret I. King Library, UK.

5. Anti–Salvation Army books and tracts, BFP; SPB, *Breckinridge*, 170–79; Odum, *Southern Pioneers*, 193.

6. *Lexington Herald*, October 17, 1905.

7. *Lexington Herald*, October 19, 1905.

8. *Lexington Herald*, February 1, 1905, January 9, 14, 1906; Goldman, *Rendezvous with Destiny*, 121–23; Filler, *Appointment at Armageddon*, 274; "Reports of Hon. Ben B. Lindsey, Chairman, Committee on Juvenile Courts," BFP.

9. Ben B. Lindsey to MMB, August 7, 1905, Lindsey Papers; *Lexington Herald*, April 2, 24, November 24, 1905.

10. MMB to ACM, April 2, 14, 1905, HCMFP; MMB to SPB, July 1, 1905, reel 2, SPB Papers, LC.

11. *Lexington Herald*, January 4, 7, 9, 14, 1906; Edward Clopper, *Child Welfare in Kentucky* (New York, 1919), 203.

12. MMB to Ben Lindsey, January 26, 1906, Lindsey Papers; *Lexington Herald*, February 2, 6, March 2, 3, 1906.

13. *Lexington Herald*, March 18, 1906; Clopper, *Child Welfare*, 204; Ben Lindsey to MMB, March 12, 1906, Lindsey Papers.

14. *Lexington Herald*, March 3, 4, 1906.

15. *Lexington Herald*, January 14, February 11, 1906; Fuller, *Laura Clay*, 86–87; Mary E. Oden, *Delinquent Daughters: Protecting and Policing Adolescent Female Sexuality in the United States, 1885–1920* (Chapel Hill, NC, 1995), 185–86.

16. *Lexington Herald*, February 12, 18, 27, 1906.

17. *Lexington Herald*, September 10, December 24, 27, 29, 1905.

18. *Lexington Herald*, December 7, 30, 1906, January 3, 4, 14, 21, 1907.

19. *Lexington Herald*, January 1, 4, February 12, May 5, October 3, 1907.

20. *Lexington Herald*, April 15, 21, 1907.

21. *Lexington Herald*, May 26, June 30, 1907.

22. *Lexington Herald*, May 11, 28, August 27, October 22, 26, November 26, 1905.

23. *Lexington Herald*, October 22, 26, November 1, 5, 1905; M. O. Winfrey to MMB, September 15, 1905; M. A. Cassidy to MMB, October 24, 1904, both in MMB Papers.

24. *Lexington Herald*, August 5, 1906. For the bill creating the normal schools, see *Kentucky Acts* (Frankfort, 1906), 393–404.

25. *Lexington Herald*, March 17, April 9, 21, June 22, July 14, 28, October 5, November 3, 17, 21, 1907; Mrs. R. N. Roark and Mrs. Desha Breckinridge, eds., *Kentucky Federation of Women's Clubs: School Betterment for Kentucky* (Harrodsburg, KY, 1908), 19–31.

26. Klotter, *Portrait in Paradox*, 148–49.

27. *Lexington Herald*, March 18, 1906; "Kentucky Child Labor Association Law," Kentucky Child Labor Association Papers, Louisville Archives and Record

Center, Louisville. For the child labor act of 1906, see *Kentucky Acts* (1906), 296–300.

28. "Kentucky Child Labor Association Law"; "Articles of Incorporation of the Kentucky Child Labor Association"; "Minutes of the Executive Committee of the Kentucky Child Labor Association," December 12, 1906, December 17, 1907, December 6, 1910, all in Kentucky Child Labor Association Papers; *Lexington Leader*, December 24, 1907.

29. Mrs. R. P. Halleck to MMB, January 31, 1907, BFP; *Lexington Herald*, January 10, 24, 1907; Richard W. Knott to MMB, February 14, 1907, MMB Papers.

30. *Lexington Herald*, March 17, 1907; MMB to Nettie Bullock, n.d. [March 1907]; ACM to Nettie Bullock, March 23, 1907, both in HCMFP; Shelley Sallee, *The Whiteness of Child Labor Reform in the New South* (Athens, GA, 2004), 2–5.

31. *Lexington Herald*, March 3, 7, 24, 1907.

32. *Lexington Herald*, March 3, 1905; *Proceedings of the First and Second Session of the Kentucky Conference on Charities and Corrections, 1904–1905* (Louisville, 1905), 1–10.

33. *Lexington Herald*, April 23, November 18, 1906.

34. *Lexington Herald*, May 25, June 3, 1906.

35. *Lexington Herald*, June 10, 1906.

36. *Lexington Herald*, September 30, November 18, December 1, 2, 9, 1906.

37. *Lexington Herald*, April 3, 7, 16, May 14, August 20, 27, September 19, October 4, 1905.

38. *Lexington Herald*, March 11, 20, 27, April 15, June 15, 17, September 18, October 1, 28, November 7, December 23, 1906.

39. MMB to unknown recipient, n.d., HCMFP.

40. *Lexington Herald*, April 8, September 30, October 2, 1906, January 19, 20, April 14, 1907; MMB to SPB, January 8, 1907, reel 2, SPB Papers, LC; Davis, *Spearheads for Reform*, 170; Mattson, *Creating a Democratic Public*, 16–25.

41. *Lexington Herald*, May 12, 13, 16, October 9, 1907. Thomas A. Combs, businessman and politician, owned the Combs Lumber Company in Lexington. He served as mayor of Lexington, 1904–7, and was subsequently elected to the state senate and as a director of the Federal Reserve Board of Cleveland. See Wright, *Lexington*, 129.

42. *Lexington Herald*, August 13, 1905.

43. *Lexington Herald*, February 18, 1906; SPB, *Breckinridge*, 186.

44. *Lexington Herald*, September 30, 1905.

45. *Lexington Herald*, November 11, December 10, 17, 1905; SPB, *Breckinridge*, 188; Cott, *Grounding of Modern Feminism*, 3–5; Stivers, *Bureau Men, Settlement Women*, 61; Blair, *Clubwoman as Feminist*, 7, 117–18; Schneider, *American Women*, 16–17, 94–99; Gwendolyn Mink, "The Lady and the Tramp:

Gender, Race, and the Origins of the American Welfare State," in Gordon, *Women, the State, and Welfare,* 102, 107; Welter, "Cult of True Womanhood," 151–74.

46. Paul Kellogg to MMB, February 15, 1906, BFP; SPB, *Breckinridge,* 187.

47. SPB, *Breckinridge,* 187.

48. Ibid., 186–87; *Lexington Herald,* February 18, April 1, June 24, 1906.

49. *Lexington Herald,* July 15, 1906.

50. *Lexington Herald,* June 3, 1906.

51. *Lexington Herald,* November 18, 1906; MMB to Stites Duvall, October 26, 1915, BFP.

52. *Lexington Herald,* December 2, 1906, April 28, May 19, 1907.

53. *Lexington Herald,* May 12, 1907.

54. *Lexington Herald,* November 11, 1906, March 17, 1907; Lasch, *New Radicalism in America,* 38, 46; Kraditor, *Ideas of the Woman Suffrage Movement,* 66; Wiebe, *Search for Order,* 122.

55. *Lexington Herald,* December 16, 1900, October 1, 1905.

56. *Lexington Herald,* March 18, 25, 1906.

57. *Lexington Herald,* September 10, 1905, August 26, 1906.

58. *Lexington Herald,* September 24, 1905, January 7, August 26, September 30, 1906; clipping, n.d., Neville Papers.

59. *Lexington Herald,* September 24, 1905.

60. HCM Jr. to ACM, December 16, 1906, HCMFP.

61. *Lexington Herald,* January 28, 1907.

62. For a discussion of the racial attitudes of the Breckinridges, see Klotter, *Breckinridges,* 146–48, 179–81, 203–4, 218–21; Klotter, "Family Influences on a Progressive," 123, 141–42.

63. *Lexington Herald,* February 4, April 1, July 22, November 18, 1906; Roark and Breckinridge, *Kentucky Federation of Women's Clubs,* 14. For an account of Laura Clay's experiences in Oregon while working on a state suffrage campaign, see Fuller, *Laura Clay,* 99–101.

64. *Lexington Herald,* October 21, 1906; Klotter, *Portrait in Paradox,* 209–11. For Beckham's career, including his opposition to woman suffrage, see Nicholas C. Burckel, "James B. McCreary" and "J.C.W. Beckham," in *Kentucky's Governors,* 2nd ed., ed. Lowell H. Harrison (Lexington, 2004), 105–10, 137–40; Thomas H. Appleton Jr., "'Like Banquo's Ghost': The Emergence of the Prohibition Issue in Kentucky Politics" (PhD diss., University of Kentucky, 1981), 97–121.

65. *Lexington Herald,* November 10, 22, December 6, 1906, November 7, 1907.

66. *Lexington Herald,* March 1, August 1, 13, November 12, 16, 19, 1905.

67. *Lexington Herald,* November 12, 16, 19, 1905.

68. Typescript, Neville Papers, UK; *Lexington Herald,* November 21, 25, 28, December 3, 5, 13, 17, 1905, February 1, 1906; SPB, *Breckinridge,* 126–27.

69. *Lexington Herald,* February 1, March 17, August 5, 1906, January 12,

20, December 21, 1907; SPB, *Breckinridge,* 125, 127; Kate M. Gordon to Laura Clay, January 31, 1908, Laura Clay Papers, Special Collections and Digital Programs, Margaret I. King Library, UK.

70. Teller, *Tuberculosis Movement,* 1–2, 30–38, 56, 95; Katherine Ott, *Fevered Lives: Tuberculosis in American Culture since 1870* (Cambridge, MA, 1996), 16–17, 19, 111–13, 118–19.

71. SPB, *Breckinridge,* 125.

Chapter 6: Educational Advance and School Suffrage

1. *Lexington Herald,* October 3, November 3, 10, 1907; Augustus E. Willson to MMB, November 2, 1907, Augustus E. Willson Papers, Filson Historical Society, Louisville; Keller, *Regulating a New Society,* 296, 299; Paula Baker, "The Domestication of Politics: Women and American Political Society, 1780–1920," in Gordon, *Women, the State, and Welfare,* 66, 86; Eleanor Clift, *Founding Sisters and the Nineteenth Amendment* (Hoboken, NJ, 2003), 76; Nancy K. Forderhase, "'The Clear Call of Thoroughbred Women': The Kentucky Federation of Women's Clubs and the Crusade for Educational Reform, 1903–1909," *Register* 83 (1985): 19–35. Section 155 of the Kentucky Constitution provided that the General Assembly could regulate school elections, thus exempting these elections from Section 145, which restricted voting to males. Therefore, a simple act of the legislature could confer on women the right to vote in school elections without necessitating a constitutional amendment.

2. MMB to Augustus E. Willson, December 4, 1907, Willson Papers; *Lexington Herald,* February 5, 6, March 24, 1908.

3. *Lexington Herald,* January 1, 5, 6, 8, 9, 12, 20, 1908.

4. *Lexington Herald,* January 21, February 4, 8, 17, 1908; SPB, *Breckinridge,* 190–91; Kate M. Gordon to Laura Clay, January 31, 1908, Clay Papers.

5. Mary C. Roark to Laura Clay, January 22, March 9, 1908, Clay Papers; *Lexington Herald,* July 4, 1909.

6. Carrie Chapman Catt and Nettie Rogers Shuler, *Woman Suffrage and Politics: The Inner Story of the Suffrage Movement* (New York, 1926), 132, 144; Elizabeth Cady Stanton, Susan B. Anthony, Matilda J. Gage, and Ida Husted Harper, eds., *History of Woman Suffrage,* 6 vols. (1881–1922; repr., Salem, NH, 1985), 6:210. For the influence of the prohibition movement in Kentucky, see Appleton, "'Like Banquo's Ghost.'"

7. *Lexington Herald,* August 9, 1908.

8. *Louisville Courier-Journal,* February 23, 1908; *Lexington Herald,* March 10, 19, 24, 25, 1908. For an in-depth discussion of Kentucky's education system and the various bills passed during this session, see Klotter, *Portrait in Paradox,* 147–50.

9. Klotter, *Portrait in Paradox,* 149–50; *Lexington Herald,* July 29, 1908; Harrison and Klotter, *New History of Kentucky,* 382–85; Montgomery, *Politics of Education,* 61–102.

10. SPB, *Breckinridge*, 128–29; *Lexington Herald*, January 12, February 21, March 14, 21, 1908; Sandra Barney, "Gender and Authority in the West Virginia Antituberculosis Campaigns of the Progressive Era," *Southern Historian* 16 (1995): 46–60. On the antituberculosis movement, see also Barbara Bates, *Bargaining for Life: A Social History of Tuberculosis, 1876–1938* (Philadelphia, 1992); Sheila Rothman, *Living in the Shadow of Death: Tuberculosis and the Social Experience of Illness in American History* (New York, 1994); Richard H. Shryock, *National Tuberculosis Association, 1904–1954: A Study of a Voluntary Movement in the United States* (New York, 1957).

11. *Lexington Herald*, February 16, March 10, 19, 24, 25, 1908; ACM to Henry Clay Bullock, March 15, 1909; ACM to Nettie Bullock, March 11, April 1, 1908; MMB to Nettie Bullock, n.d., all in HCMFP.

12. HCM Jr. to ACM, April 19, 26, 1908, HCMFP; Margaret Preston Johnston diary, November 17, 1909, Preston-Johnston Papers.

13. *Lexington Herald*, April 18, 19, 1908.

14. *Lexington Herald*, June 24, 28, 29, 1908; Moses E. Ligon, *A History of Public Education in Kentucky* (Lexington, 1942), 140–41; *Louisville Courier-Journal*, February 23, 1908; *Lexington Leader*, October 5, 1909; Klotter, *Portrait in Paradox*, 149; Montgomery, *Politics of Education*, 74–75. Laura Clay had touted to Louisiana suffragist Kate Gordon the importance of Breckinridge's attending the national Federation of Women's Clubs Convention in Boston, noting that as an editor of the *Herald*, she had "considerable importance" in central Kentucky. Laura Clay to Kate Gordon, May 18, 1908, Clay Papers.

15. MMB, *Some Reasons for Granting School Suffrage to Kentucky Women* (Lexington, 1910) and *Another Reason for Granting School Suffrage to Kentucky Women*; MMB, "Women and the Schools," in Roark and Breckinridge, *Kentucky Federation of Women's Clubs*, 17.

16. MMB, "Women and the Schools," 10–11, 14; MMB, *Some Reasons for Granting School Suffrage to Kentucky Women*.

17. *Lexington Herald*, May 13, August 23, 24, 25, September 16, October 28, November 1, 3, December 15, 1908.

18. *Lexington Herald*, January 31, February 1, 1909.

19. *Lexington Leader*, January 24, June 18, 1909; *Lexington Herald*, January 27, 1909.

20. *Lexington Leader*, May 7, 12, 1909.

21. *Lexington Leader*, June 21, July 2, 1909.

22. *Lexington Herald*, February 18, March 11, April 16, May 2, July 4, 1909; *Lexington Leader*, July 3, 1909.

23. SPB, *Breckinridge*, 92, 113; *Annual Report of the Public Schools of Lexington, Kentucky, June 30, 1908* (Lexington, 1908), 13–14; *Lexington Leader*, May 30, 1909; Davis, *Spearheads for Reform*, 76–77, 81; *The University of Chicago Settlement*, 1908, pamphlet, Kentucky Child Labor Association Papers; Trolan-

der, *Professionalism and Social Change,* 10–13; Mattson, *Creating a Democratic Public,* 48–49, 54.

24. *Lexington Herald,* clipping, n.d.; MMB to Andrew Carnegie, November 3, 1909; Robert W. Woolley to MMB, December 15, 1909, all in BFP; *Lexington Herald,* April 9, 13, May 21, 30, July 1, November 14, 1909; *Lexington Leader,* April 10, 1909; SPB, *Breckinridge,* 92.

25. *Lexington Herald,* May 8, 16, 17, 20, 24, 25, 26, 30, 1909; *Lexington Leader,* May 30, 1909; Margaret Preston Johnston diary, May 25, 1909.

26. *Lexington Herald,* June 17, 19, 1909.

27. *Lexington Herald,* September 29, November 10, 1909; *Lexington Leader,* September 1, 30, November 13, 1909.

28. *Lexington Herald,* November 12, 13, 1909; *Lexington Leader,* January 6, 7, 9, 1910; Laura Clay to Mary C. Roark, December 1, 1909; MMB to Laura Clay, December 30, January 10, 1910; Minutes of the Central Kentucky Woman's Club, December 10, 1909; Laura Clay to Mrs. M. A. Tensley, January 7, 1910, all in Clay Papers.

29. Fuller, *Laura Clay,* 91–93; MMB, "The Relation of the Public Schools to Kentucky's Commercial Development," BFP; Wheeler, *New Women of the New South,* 111; SPB, *Breckinridge,* 217–18.

30. *Lexington Leader,* January 13, 27, February 4, 1910; *Lexington Herald,* January 13, February 4, 1910; *Louisville Courier-Journal,* January 23, 1910; Laura Clay to Emma Roebuck, January 29, 1910; Minutes of Fayette Joint Committee on School Suffrage, January 10, 1910, both in Clay Papers; Preston Johnston to Margaret Preston, January 16, 1910, Preston Johnston Papers.

31. *Lexington Herald,* February 17, 27, March 1, 1910; *Lexington Leader,* February 11, 1910; *Louisville Herald,* February 16, 17, 26, 1910; Margaret Preston Johnston diary, February 10, 1910; *Journal of the Regular Session of the House of Representatives of the Commonwealth of Kentucky* (Louisville, 1910), 690–93; *Journal of the Regular Session of the Senate of the Commonwealth of Kentucky* (Louisville, 1910), 948–50.

32. *Lexington Leader,* May 27, 1910; *Lexington Herald,* March 4, May 27, 1910.

33. *Lexington Herald,* February 17, 20, 26, March 4, May 27, 1910; *Louisville Herald,* February 26, 1910; *Lexington Leader,* May 27, 1910.

34. Laura Clay to Mrs. Nield, November 19, 1910, Clay Papers; *Lexington Leader,* March 15, 1910; MMB, *Some Reasons for Granting School Suffrage to Kentucky Women;* SPB autobiography.

35. *Lexington Herald,* July 5, 1910; SPB, *Breckinridge,* 62–66; MMB to Laura Clay, October 10, 1910, Clay Papers; MMB, "The People Have Spoken," November 1910, Neville Papers. For Linda Neville and her pioneering work on preventing blindness through treatment of trachoma, see Judy Gail Cornett, "Angel for the Blind: The Public Triumphs and Private Tragedy of Linda Neville" (PhD diss., University of Kentucky, 1993); D. Anthony Smith and Arthur H. Kee-

ney, "Linda Neville (1873–1961): Kentucky Pioneer against Blindness," *FCHQ* 64 (1990): 360–76.

36. Augustus E. Willson to MMB, March 6, 1910, BFP.

37. *Lexington Herald*, July 31, 1910, January 17, 18, 24, May 29, 1911; *Louisville Herald*, October 23, 1911.

38. *Lexington Herald*, May 8, 13, 18, July 4, 15, November 10, 1910.

39. *Lexington Herald*, October 5, November 11, 13, 1910; Montgomery, *Politics of Education*, 223. Clinton M. Harbison, one of five children of Shelby T. Harbison, owner of Tattersalls—now a world-famous thoroughbred bloodstock auction house—became active in civic affairs at an early age after receiving a law degree from Harvard. When he died in June 1980 at age ninety-three, he was a senior partner of the Lexington law firm Harbison, Kessinger, Lisle, and Bush. *Lexington Leader*, June 10, 1980.

40. Kate M. Gordon to Laura Clay, January 8, 1910; Laura Clay to Kate M. Gordon, January 17, 1908; Laura Clay to MMB, October 5, 1910; MMB to Laura Clay, October 10, 1910, all in Clay Papers; Reports of the Twenty-first and Twenty-second Annual Meetings of the Kentucky Equal Rights Association, Held at Covington, November 14–15–16, 1910 and Louisville, October 25, 1911, BFP; Knott, "Woman Suffrage Movement," 251.

41. *Lexington Herald*, November 12, 15, 17, 20, 1910; Margaret Preston Johnston diary, November 21, 22, 1910.

42. *Lexington Herald*, November 23, 25, December 1, 2, 1910.

43. *Lexington Herald*, April 16, May 25, July 8, 9, 16, 30, August 26, 27, 1911; *Annual Report of the Lexington Public Schools, 1911* (Lexington, 1911); MMB to Margaret Preston, July 31, 1911, Preston Johnston Papers.

44. Linda Neville to Margaret Preston, September 26, 1911, Preston Johnston Papers; *Lexington Leader*, December 7, 1911; *Lexington Herald*, December 7, 1911; A. B. Woodward to MMB, June 26, 1911, Neville Papers.

45. *Lexington Leader*, December 7, 1911; *Lexington Herald*, December 7, 1911; Mattie Robertson, Dorothy Sutherland, Anne Snowden Praither, eds., "The History of the Lexington Public Schools by the Sixth Grade of Arlington School," typescript, 1931, in possession of Fayette County School System.

46. Memo announcing the Dey Fund gift, n.d.; MMB to Anthony Dey, November 21, 1910, both in BFP; Cantrill interview, March 25, 1976. The late Florence Shelby Cantrill administered the Dey Fund for many years. Robert Milward currently oversees it for the Fayette County Public Schools. The money is "used for prescriptions, heating bills, or any sort of child or family need" for residents of the old Lincoln School district and is "more flexible than funds usually available to schools and resource centers," according to Rodney Jackson, director of financial services, Fayette County Public Schools. The annual gift cash balance is usually around $18,000. Rodney Jackson, e-mail to author, October 3, 2006.

47. *Lexington Herald*, January 20, May 1, June 6, July 3, October 21, 1911;

Lexington Leader, January 10, April 26, May 3, 1911; *New York Evening Post*, April 7, 1911; SPB, *Breckinridge*, 195; Bolin, *Bossism and Reform*, 58.

48. *Lexington Leader*, October 26, 1911. For a discussion of dissensions within NAWSA and Laura Clay's defeat for office in 1911, see Fuller, *Laura Clay*, 116–27. For the voluminous studies in women's history and the suffrage movement, see especially Mildred Adams, *The Right to Be People* (New York, 1967); Jean H. Baker, *Votes for Women: The Struggle for Suffrage Revisited* (New York, 2002); Banner, *Women in Modern America;* Beverly Beeton, *Women Vote in the West: The Woman Suffrage Movement, 1869–1896* (New York, 1986); Mari Jo Buhle and Paul Buhle, *The Concise History of Woman Suffrage: Selections from the Classic Work of Stanton, Anthony, Gage, and Harper* (Urbana, IL, 1978); Catt and Shuler, *Woman Suffrage and Politics;* William H. Chafe, *The Paradox of Change: American Women in the 20th Century* (New York, 1991); Margaret Mary Finnegan, *Selling Suffrage: Consumer Culture and Votes for Women* (New York, 1999); Eleanor Flexner, *Century of Struggle: The Woman's Rights Movement in the United States* (Cambridge, MA, 1959); Friedman and Shade, *Our American Sisters;* Fuller, *Laura Clay;* Michele Gillespie and Catherine Clinton, eds., *Taking Off the White Gloves: Southern Women and Women Historians* (Columbia, MO, 1998); Linda Gordon, *Pitied but Not Entitled: Single Mothers and the History of Welfare, 1890–1925* (New York, 1994); Sara Hunter Graham, *Woman Suffrage and the New Democracy* (New Haven, CT, 1996); Elna C. Green, *Southern Strategies: Southern Women and the Woman Suffrage Question* (Chapel Hill, NC, 1997); Alan P. Grimes, *The Puritan Ethic and Woman Suffrage* (New York, 1967); Carol Guethlein, "Women in Louisville: Moving toward Equal Rights," *FCHQ* 55 (1981): 151–78; Ida Husted Harper, *The Life and Work of Susan B. Anthony*, 3 vols. (Indianapolis, 1878–1908); Nancy Hewitt, *Southern Discomfort: Women's Activism in Tampa, Florida, 1880s–1920s* (Urbana, IL, 2001); Evelyn Brooks Higginbotham, *Righteous Discontent: The Women's Movement in the Black Baptist Church, 1880–1920* (Cambridge, MA, 1993); Helen Deiss Irvin, *Women in Kentucky* (Lexington, 1979); Inez Haynes Irwin, *Angels and Amazons: A Hundred Years of American Women* (New York, 1933); Alana S. Jeydel, *Political Women: The Women's Movement, Political Institutions, the Battle for Women's Suffrage and the ERA* (New York, 2004); Kraditor, *Ideas of the Woman Suffrage Movement;* Ellen C. Lagemann, *A Generation of Women: Education in the Lives of Progressive Reformers* (Cambridge, MA, 1979); Linda J. Lumsden, *Rampant Women: Suffragists and the Right of Assembly* (Knoxville, TN, 1997); Alma Lutz, *Created Equal: A Biography of Elizabeth Cady Stanton* (New York, 1940); Lutz, *Susan B. Anthony: Rebel, Crusader, Humanitarian* (Boston, 1959); Suzanne M. Marilley, *Woman Suffrage and the Origins of Liberal Feminism in the United States, 1820–1920* (Cambridge, MA, 1996); David Morgan, *Suffragists and Democrats: The Politics of Woman Suffrage in America* (East Lansing, MI, 1972); William O'Neill, *Everyone Was Brave: The Rise and Fall of Feminism in America* (Chicago, 1969); Maud Wood Park, *Front Door Lobby*, ed. Edna Lamprey Stan-

tial (Boston, 1960); Martin Pugh, *The March of the Women: A Revisional Analysis of the Campaign for Women's Suffrage, 1866–1914* (Oxford, 2000); Anne Firor Scott and Andrew Scott, *One Half the People: The Fight for Woman Suffrage* (Philadelphia, 1975); Anastatia Sims, *The Power of Femininity in the New South: Women's Organizations and Politics in North Carolina, 1880–1930* (Columbia, SC, 1997); Stanton et al., *History of Woman Suffrage;* A. Elizabeth Taylor, *Citizens at Last: The Woman Suffrage Movement in Texas* (Austin, TX, 1987); Taylor, *The Woman Suffrage Movement in Tennessee* (New York, 1957); Thomas, *New Woman in Alabama;* Elizabeth Hayes Turner, *Women, Culture, and Community: Religion and Reform in Galveston, 1880–1920* (New York, 1997); Wheeler, *New Women of the New South;* Marjorie Spruill Wheeler, ed., *Votes For Women! The Woman Suffrage Movement in Tennessee, the South, and the Nation* (Knoxville, TN, 1995); Margaret Ripley Wolfe, "Fallen Leaves and Missing Pages: Women in Kentucky History," *Register* 90 (1992): 64–89. Also see other works cited throughout these notes.

49. MMB, "The Prospect for Suffrage in the South"; MMB, "A Plea for the Extension of the Right of Suffrage to Women," both in BFP; Mary Winston to MMB, December 12, 1911, Clay Papers; *New York Times*, October 17, 1911; *Louisville Courier-Journal*, October 25, 1911; Wheeler, *New Women of the New South*, 112–20, 127.

50. Fuller, *Laura* Clay, 126–27; *Louisville Courier-Journal*, October 20, 1911; *Lexington Herald*, October 31, 1911.

Chapter 7: Among the Most Brilliant Advocates

1. *Frankfort News-Journal*, January 5, 26, March 9, 10, 1912; *Louisville Herald*, January 22, 28, 1912; *Lexington Herald*, January 26, February 26, March 9, 10, 14, 1912; *Lexington Leader*, March 9, 10, 24, 1912; *Journal of the Regular Session of the House of Representatives of the Commonwealth of Kentucky . . .* (Frankfort, 1912), 414–15; *Journal of the Regular Session of the Senate of the Commonwealth of Kentucky* (Frankfort, 1912), 1671–72; Frank K. Kavanaugh, *Official Manual for the Use of Courts, State and County Officials and General Assembly of the State of Kentucky* (Frankfort, 1912), 206–34. When the right of women to vote for school superintendents under the new law was challenged, the Kentucky Court of Appeals ruled in the case of *J. H. Cook, County Court Clerk v. Bartlett et al.* that the legislature had the power to grant women suffrage in all school elections, including that of superintendent, and that it was the clear intent of the legislature in 1912 to do so. Thus, women were entitled to full school suffrage.

2. *Lexington Leader*, March 21, 24, 1912; Knott, "Woman Suffrage Movement," 252–53.

3. *Louisville Courier-Journal*, January 9, 1912; *Lexington Herald*, June 24, 1911, March 18, 1912; Linda Neville, handwritten note on unidentified newspaper clipping, November 1912, Neville Papers.

4. MMB to ACM, March 6, 1912, HCMFP; SPB, *Breckinridge*, 132–35; *Lexington Herald*, August 22, October 13, 1912, August 29, 1916; Klotter, *Portrait in Paradox*, 218–19; Harrison, *Kentucky's Governors*, 105–10.

5. *Lexington Herald*, February 29, April 12, June 9, 15, August 7, 14, September 21, 1912.

6. SPB, *Breckinridge*, 198; Cott, *Grounding of Modern Feminism*, 29–30; Schneider, *American Women*, 93, 168; Jane Jerome Camhi, *Women against Women: American Anti-suffragism, 1880–1920* (Brooklyn, 1994), 7, 16–19; Kraditor, *Ideas of the Woman Suffrage Movement*, 13–24; Green, *Southern Strategies*, 3–4; Graham, *Woman Suffrage*, 30, 36, 153–54.

7. *St. Louis Republic*, January 14, 1912.

8. *Lexington Herald*, October 21, 1906. For more on the sexual purity campaign, see Oden, *Delinquent Daughters*.

9. SPB, *Breckinridge*, 217–18; *New York Evening Post*, September 16, 1913; *St. Louis Republic*, January 14, 1912; *Owensboro Inquirer*, January 21, 1912; *Lexington Herald*, January 11, February 4, 1912; Glenda E. Gilmore, *Gender and Jim Crow: Women and the Politics of White Supremacy in North Carolina, 1896–1920* (Chapel Hill, NC, 1996), 211; Kraditor, *Ideas of the Woman Suffrage Movement*, 157–61; Wheeler, *New Women of the New South*, 17–19, 21, 25, 103, 111, 127, passim; Green, *Southern Strategies*, 95–97; Link, *Paradox of Southern Progressivism*, 300; Graham, *Woman Suffrage*, 18. In the late nineteenth century Henry Blackwell developed the statistical argument for enfranchising women in the South, pointing out that four million white women would counterbalance four million black men and women, but he failed to account for the distribution of the black population in the region. Unfortunately, instead of giving women the vote, southern legislatures proceeded to disenfranchise black males. See Marilley, *Woman Suffrage*, 162–64, 167–78.

10. *St. Louis Republic*, January 14, 1912; *Owensboro Inquirer*, January 21, 1912; *Lexington Herald*, January 11, February 4, 1912.

11. Note, April 1912, HCMFP; *Lexington Leader*, April 5, 1912; SPB, *Breckinridge*, 205.

12. MMB to ACM, May 7, 1912; MMB to Magdalen McDowell, May 11, 1912, both in HCMFP; *Lexington Herald*, June 4, 1912.

13. MMB to ACM, [n.d. 1912], June 16, 18, 1912; MMB to DB, [n.d. 1912]; MMB to Nettie Bullock, June 27, 1912, all in HCMFP.

14. *Lexington Leader*, August 28, 1912; *Lexington Herald*, August 29, 1912; MMB, "Kentucky," in Stanton et al., *History of Woman Suffrage*, 6:547.

15. *Lexington Herald*, August 2, 3, 4, September 4, October 13, 27, 31, November 1, 2, 4, 6, 1912; Margaret Preston Johnston diary, September 24, 1912.

16. *Lexington Herald*, October 24, 26, 1912; *Lexington Leader*, October 25, 1912; Laura Clay to Harriet Taylor Upton, November n.d., 1912, Clay Papers.

17. *Lexington Herald*, November 17, 30, December 11, 23, 1912; Margaret Preston Johnston diary, November 18, 1912.

18. *Lexington Herald*, March 18, November 21, 1913; *Annual Report of the Lexington Public Schools, 1913* (Lexington, 1913), Neville Papers; Report of the Civic League for the Season 1912–13, BFP; *Lexington Leader*, March 16, 1913.

19. *Lexington Herald*, July 6, 1913.

20. *Annual Report of the Lexington Public Schools, 1913*; Margaret Preston Johnston diary, September 25, 1913; Mary I. Wood to MMB, December 13, 1913; Mabel Zimmerling to MMB, December 16, 1913; MMB to Mary I. Wood, December 18, 1913; Clarence A. Perry to MMB, April 15, 1914, all in BFP; Mary I. Wood, "What Women's Clubs Are Doing," *Ladies Home Journal*, September 1914, 37.

21. Fuller, *Laura Clay*, 131, 302–3; *Lexington Herald*, May 26, August 5, 13, 25, 1913; Laura Clay and MMB to Jennie Quinn, January 21, 1913; Laura Clay to MMB, September 10, 1913, both in Clay Papers; Knott, "Woman Suffrage Movement," 71, 112, 180–82.

22. *Lexington Leader*, April 24, 1913; *Lexington Herald*, April 29, 1913.

23. Fuller, *Laura* Clay, 307–9; SPB, *Breckinridge*, 202; *Lexington Herald*, January 20, 24, February 7, 1913; MMB and Laura Clay to Mrs. Bennett, February 4, 1913; Laura Clay to Mrs. R. N. Roark, February 17, 1913; MMB to Laura Clay, January 24, 1913; MMB to Mrs. Thasp, July 24, 1913, all in Clay Papers.

24. *Lexington Herald*, May 24, 1912, April 11, 12, 1913; SPB, *Breckinridge*, 213. For more on the Pankhursts, see Paula Bartley, *Emmeline Pankhurst* (New York, 2003); June Purvis, *Emmeline Pankhurst: A Biography* (New York, 2002); David Mitchell, *The Fighting Pankhursts: A Study in Tenacity* (New York, 1967); Mary Davis, *Sylvia Pankhurst: A Life in Radical Politics* (Sterling, VA, 1999); Tim Larsen, *Christabel Pankhurst: Fundamentalism and Feminism in Coalition* (Suffolk, UK, 2002).

25. Margaret Preston Johnston diary, April 29, 1913; Max Eastman, *Enjoyment of Living* (New York, 1948), 314; *Lexington Herald*, November 18, 1908, April 11, 12, 30, 1913.

26. Eastman, *Enjoyment of Living*, 306, 314; *Lexington Herald*, November 14, 17, 18, 1913.

27. *Lexington Herald*, March 1, May 22, June 11, December 17, 1913; *Lexington Idea*, May 1, 8, 1913; Mrs. John G. Miller to Laura Clay, March 22, 1913; Mrs. Wilkes Bond to Laura Clay, July 19, 1913, both in Clay Papers; *Lexington Leader*, January 18, February 27, April 11, June 14, 1913.

28. *Louisville Courier-Journal*, May 1, 1913; *Lexington Herald*, April 25, 1913.

29. *Louisville Courier-Journal*, May 1, 14, 1913; *Lexington Herald*, May 4, 1913.

30. Henry Watterson to DB, May 2, 1913; DB to Henry Watterson, May 4, 1913; DB to MMB, May 4, 1913, all in BFP; Klotter, *Breckinridges*, 223–24; Arthur S. Link, *Woodrow Wilson and the Progressive Era, 1910–1917* (New York,

1954), 29; Link, *Wilson: The New Freedom* (Princeton, NJ, 1956), 153–61; Joseph F. Wall, *Henry Watterson: Reconstructed Rebel* (New York, 1956), 266–68, 317–19; Isaac F. Marcosson, *"Marse Henry": A Biography of Henry Watterson* (New York, 1951), 218.

31. Henry Watterson to DB, May 3, 1898, BFP; DB to Henry Watterson, August 5, 1911, vol. 12, Henry Watterson Papers, LC.

32. *Louisville Evening Post*, January 21, 27, 1913.

33. *Lexington Leader*, February 19, March 16, 1913; *Lexington Herald*, February 12, April 10, 1913; MMB to ACM, April 4, 1913, HCMFP.

34. *Lexington Herald*, May 4, July 22, 1913; HCM Jr. to ACM, April 20, 27, 1913; Elsie Clay McDowell to ACM, April 26, 1913; James Nelson to DB, May 4, 1913; MMB to Magdalen McDowell, May 13, 1913, all in HCMFP; SPB, *Breckinridge*, 205; Laura Clay to Mrs. George H. Rudy, May 3, 1913, Clay Papers; *Lexington Leader*, May 8, 1913.

35. Josephine Hunt to MMB, July 3, 1913, BFP; MMB to ACM, September 15, 19, 1913, HCMFP; MMB to Laura Clay, August 19, 1913, Clay Papers. Unfortunately, Dr. Josephine Hunt's papers were not preserved. David Hunt, interview with author, February 22, 1977.

36. MMB to Magdalen McDowell, October 22, 1913, HCMFP; *Lexington Herald*, October 19, 21, November 9, 1913.

37. *Lexington Leader*, November 20, 1913; *Lexington Herald*, November 22, 23, 1913; MMB to Laura Clay, September 3, 1913, Clay Papers; MMB to ACM, October 18, 1913, HCMFP.

38. Wheeler, *New Women of the New South*, 135–45; MMB, "Kentucky," in Stanton et al., *History of Woman Suffrage*, 6:387.

39. Kate M. Gordon to Laura Clay, July 5, September 30, 1913, Clay Papers; Fuller, *Laura Clay*, 141; Thomas, *New Woman in Alabama*, 150–51; Wheeler, *New Women of the New South*, 146–48. Kate Gordon had expressed the belief in 1909 that Negro women as a class were not ready for the ballot and their enfranchisement would mean a "repetition of the original mistake made in the indiscriminate enfranchisement of Negro men." Kate M. Gordon to President William Howard Taft, May 11, 1909, Clay Papers.

40. Wheeler, *New Women of the New South*, 136–37; Fuller, *Laura Clay*, 139–40; Buhle and Buhle, *Concise History of Woman Suffrage*, 413–14; SPB, *Breckinridge*, 213–14; Flexner, *Century of Struggle*, 248–49, 262–63, 265–67; Kraditor, *Ideas of the Woman Suffrage Movement*, 8, 192–96; Anna Howard Shaw, *The Story of a Pioneer* (New York, 1915), 315, 336. For contemporary accounts of the Congressional Union, see Inez Haynes Irwin, *The Story of the Woman's Party* (New York, 1921); and Doris Stevens, *Jailed for Freedom* (New York, 1920).

41. *Lexington Herald*, May 21, December 4, 5, 14, 1913; *Louisville Courier-Journal*, March 16, 1913; SPB, *Breckinridge*, 201, 214–15; Paul Angle, *Crossroads: 1913* (Chicago, 1963), 231; MMB, "Kentucky," in Stanton et al., *History*

of Woman Suffrage, 6:374; Clift, *Founding Sisters*, 99–100; Lexington *Leader*, December 3, 4, 5, 19, 21, 1913.

42. *Lexington Leader*, December 21, 1913.

Chapter 8: An Able Speaker, a Brilliant Woman

1. SPB, Breckinridge, 214.

2. MMB to Lucy Burns, December 18, 1913; James Campbell Cantrill to MMB, December 23, 1914, both in BFP; unidentified newspaper clipping, December 17, 1913, National Woman's Party Papers, LC; MMB to James Campbell Cantrill, February 3, 1914, reel 1, James Campbell Cantrill Papers, Special Collections and Digital Programs, Margaret I. King Library, UK; *Lexington Herald*, January 22, 1914.

3. *Louisville Herald*, January 20, 1914; Mrs. Robert Garrett to James Campbell Cantrill, January 19, 1914, reel 1, Cantrill Papers; MMB to Antoinette Funk, August 14, 1914, BFP; *Lexington Herald*, March 20, 21, 1914.

4. SPB, *Breckinridge*, 206–7; *Lexington Herald*, January 1, 9, 1914.

5. *Lexington Herald*, January 8, 14, 15, 16, 1914; *Lexington Leader*, January 15, 1914.

6. *Lexington Herald*, January 18, 1914; SPB autobiography; Margaret Preston Johnston diary, January 15, 1914.

7. *Lexington Herald*, January 19, 22, 23, February 5, 20, March 13, 18, 1914; Robert Woolley to MMB, February 5, 18, 1914; Robert Woolley to DB, February 17, 1914; DB to Robert Woolley, February 12, 16, 18, 26, 1914; MMB to Robert Woolley, February 18, 26, 1914, all in Robert Woolley Papers, LC.

8. "Suffrage," typescript itinerary, BFP; *Boston Herald*, April 2, 1914; SPB, *Breckinridge*, 207; *Lexington Herald*, March 16, April 8, 30, May 1, 3, 10, 22, June 7, 1914; MMB to Ida Earle Fowler, June 9, 1914, MMB Papers; MMB to W. K. Tate, March 16, 1914; MMB to Rabbi Stephen S. Wise, March 21, 1914; MMB to Mrs. E. C. McDougald, May 8, 1914; MMB to Mary I. Wood, May 15, 1914; MMB to SPB, June 2, 1914, all in BFP; MMB to ACM, May 10, 1914; MMB to DB, May 10, 1914; MMB to ACM, June 24, 1914, all in HCMFP; SPB to MMB, July 25, 1915; MMB to SPB, July 27, 1914, reel 3, SPB Papers, LC.

9. *Lexington Herald*, July 16, September 6, 11, 25, October 23, 24, 1914; *Aurora (NE) Hamilton County Advocate*, September 22, 1914, clipping, HCMFP; MMB to Eliza Kennedy, October 20, 1914; MMB to J. L. Kennedy, September 24, 1914; J. L. Kennedy to MMB, October 3, 1914, all in BFP.

10. *Lexington Herald*, July 18, 19, August 1, 5, November 1, 8, 1914; MMB to Mrs. L. S. Petit, October 3, 1914; MMB to Mrs. George H. Rudy, October 3, 1914; Mrs. George H. Rudy to MMB, October 5, 1914; MMB to Laura Clay, October 5, 1914, all in Clay Papers; SPB, *Breckinridge*, 215; Kate Gordon to MMB, October 12, 1914; MMB to Kate Gordon, November 27, 1914, both in BFP.

11. Fuller, *Laura Clay*, 198; MMB to Mrs. B. B. Valentine, August 20, 1914;

Kate Gordon to MMB, September 21, 1915, both in BFP; *Lexington Herald*, November 8, 1914.

12. Mrs. Medill (Ruth Hanna) McCormick to presidents of state organizations, March 24, 1914, BFP; *Lexington Herald*, January 16, 1914; Wheeler, *New Women of the New South*, 137, 148; Fuller, *Laura Clay*, 144, 198; Buhle and Buhle, *Concise History of Woman Suffrage*, 413.

13. MMB to Mrs. Medill McCormick, May 31, 1915, BFP; SPB, *Breckinridge*, 221.

14. Harriet Taylor Upton to MMB, February 11, 1914; MMB to Lila Valentine, August 20, 1914; MMB to Florence Kelly, September 26, 1914, all in BFP; MMB to Mrs. Medill McCormick, October 10, 1914; MMB to Jouett Shouse, October 10, 1914, National American Woman Suffrage Association Papers, LC; Clift, *Founding Sisters*, 85–111. For more on Alice Paul, see Christine A. Lunardini, *From Equal Suffrage to Equal Rights: Alice Paul and the National Woman's Party, 1910–1928* (New York, 1986). It should be noted that the pressure placed on the Democratic Party by the Congressional Union holding them responsible for failure to pass a woman suffrage amendment proved to be effective in a number of elections. For example, the CU helped defeat twenty-three of forty-three Democratic congressional candidates in several western states in the 1914 election. See Lumsden, *Rampant Women*, 170.

15. *New York Times*, November 13, 14, 17, 1914; SPB, *Breckinridge*, 221.

16. MMB to Mrs. Joseph Tilton, May 25, 1914; SPB to MMB, July 13, 1914, both in BFP.

17. Gertrude H. Leonard to MMB, November 2, 7, 1914; SPB to MMB, n.d.; MMB to SPB, November 3, 1914, all in BFP; MMB to SPB, July 21, 1914, SPB Papers, LC; *Lexington Herald*, November 12, 13, 1914; Laura Clay to Miss Yates, December 1, 1914, Clay Papers; *Lexington Leader*, November 13, 15, 1914.

18. R. A. McDowell to Magdalen McDowell, November 20, 1914; Jane Addams to MMB, November 23, 1914; SPB to MMB, November 14, 1914, all in BFP.

19. MMB to Jane Addams, November 18, December 30, 1914; Jane Addams to MMB, November 23, 30, 1914; SPB to MMB, November 22, 1914; MMB to Mrs. Henry Wade Rogers, February 22, 1915, all in BFP.

20. MMB to Dr. Anna Howard Shaw, May 16, 1915; MMB to Lila Valentine, May 31, 1915; Harriet T. Upton to MMB, June 21, 1915; MMB to Harriet T. Upton, June 28, 1915; Nellie Sawyer Clark to MMB, June 12, 1915; MMB to Kate Gordon, June 11, 1915, all in BFP; *Lexington Herald*, June 8, 1915.

21. *Houston Chronicle*, December 4, 1914; *Houston Post*, December 3, 1914; *New Orleans Times-Picayune*, December 3, 1914; Emily C. McDougal to MMB, December 4, 1914; MMB to ACM, December 5, 10, 1914; MMB to Nettie Bullock, December 7, 1914; MMB to DB, December 7, 9, 10, 1914; unidentified newspaper clipping, marked "Atlanta," all in HCMFP; *Atlanta Constitution*, December 15, 1914; *Savannah Morning News*, December 16, 1914;

MMB to Caroline Lamar Woodbridge, December 22, 1914, BFP; DB to Curry Breckinridge, December 20, 1914, Lyman Chalkley Papers, Special Collections and Digital Programs, Margaret I. King Library, UK.

22. *Houston Post*, December 3, 1914; unidentified newspaper clipping, marked "Atlanta"; MMB to ACM, December [17?], 1914, both in HCMFP.

23. MMB to Nettie Bullock, December 7, 1914; MMB to ACM, December 5, 1914; MMB to DB, December 6, 7, 9, 1914; MMB to ACM, December 10, 1914; DB to ACM, December 10, 1914, all in HCMFP; DB to SPB, December 9, 1914; DB to Curry Breckinridge, December 20, 1914, both in Chalkley Papers; MMB to Caroline Lamar Woodbridge, December 22, 1914, BFP.

24. MMB to Janet Simons Harris, November 20, 1914; Mary Haydon to MMB, November 5, 1914; MMB to Robert Lincoln, November 26, 1914; MMB to Caroline Ruutz-Rees, May 29, 1914, all in BFP; *Lexington Herald*, December 23, 1914, September 22, 2004, June 28, 2006. The Baby Health Service celebrated its ninetieth anniversary in 2004. It currently provides free health care, medicine, immunizations, and referrals to children of families who do not have a medical card and who cannot afford insurance.

25. *Lexington Herald*, January 1, 1915; DB to Robert Woolley, July 20, 1915, Woolley Papers; *Lexington Herald*, August 15, 1915; DB to Curry Breckinridge, February 23, 1915, Chalkley Papers; MMB to Mrs. Samuel T. Castleman, June 3, 1915, BFP; MMB to Nettie Bullock, January 27, 1915; MMB to ACM, n.d., both in HCMFP.

26. MMB to Harriet Taylor Upton, February 13, 1915; MMB to Susan P. Frost, February 22, 1915, both in BFP; MMB to Nettie Bullock, March 5, 1915, HCMFP; Henry Breckinridge to DB, March 18, 1915, Henry Breckinridge Papers, LC.

27. MMB to Nettie Bullock, March 25, 1915, HCMFP; SPB, *Breckinridge*, 210. As noted in Scott, *The Southern Lady*, the concept of the southern lady was so deeply inculcated that suffragists in that region tried to conform to the stereotype.

28. SPB, *Breckinridge*, 212–13; MMB to Mrs. J. B. Judah, May 29, 1915; Dr. Irene B. Bullard to MMB, June 24, 1915, both in BFP; *Lexington Herald*, August 8, 1915.

29. *Lexington Herald*, July 9, 18, 19, 24, September 5, 23, 1915; Susan Fitzgerald, ed., *Annual Report at the 47th Convention of the National American Woman Suffrage Association* (n.p., 1915), 114; Fuller, *Laura Clay*, 135; MMB to Mrs. John M. Thomas, February 4, 1915; MMB to Mrs. R. H. Cunningham, October 18, 1915, both in BFP.

30. *Lexington Herald*, January 13, November 15, 1913; MMB to Mrs. Murray Hubbard, August 30, 1915; MMB to Governor James B. McCreary, November 19, 1915, both in BFP; SPB, *Breckinridge*, 244–45. For Desha Breckinridge's position on American entry into World War I, see Klotter, *Breckinridges*, 225–27.

31. Margaret Preston Johnston diary, March 16, April 7, 1915; *Lexington Herald*, April 1, 4, 8, 1915.

32. *Lexington Herald*, April 28, 30, May 1, 2, 3, 4, 19, 20, 21, 1915; Blair, *Clubwoman as Feminist*, 117–19.

33. *Lexington Herald*, May 23, September 26, November 7, 8, 9, 10, 11, 1915; *Lexington Leader*, October 17, 1915; MMB to Charles H. Berryman, September 11, 1915; MMB to Mrs. Edward McDowell, September 24, 1915; MMB to R. A. McDowell, October 26, 1915; MMB to Kate Gordon, November 16, 1915; Elise Smith to MMB, November 16, 1915; Mrs. John M. S. Graham, December ?, 1915, all in BFP; MMB to Elizabeth King Smith, October 29, 1915; Laura Clay to MMB, November 24, 1915, both in Clay Papers.

34. MMB to Mrs. Johnson N. Camden, January 20, 1915; Mrs. Johnson N. Camden to MMB, January 22, 1915, both in BFP.

35. MMB to Mrs. J. D. Haggin, February 23, 1915; MMB to Mrs. B. L. Hodge, November 22, 1915; "The Public Health Nursing Association," November 1915, typescript, all in BFP; *Lexington Herald*, October 15, 1915; *Annual Report of the Lexington Public Schools* (Lexington, 1915), Neville Papers.

36. Stivers, *Bureau Men, Settlement Women*, 57; Arthur Leland to MMB, January 13, 1915; C. L. Williamson to MMB, March 31, April 2, 1915; MMB to Frances Jewell, April 12, 1915; MMB to Jouett Shouse, August 20, 1915; MMB to Mrs. J. R. Morton, August 20, 1915; MMB to C. L. Williamson, September 2, 1915, all in BFP.

37. MMB to C. L. Williamson, September 2, 1915; MMB to Elise Smith, June 30, 1916; MMB to Dr. James H. Dillard, March 25, 1916; MMB to F. J. Werking, May 25, 1916, all in BFP; *Lexington Herald*, July 23, 1916; MMB to ACM, August 5, 1916, HCMFP.

38. MMB to Mrs. Joseph B. Russell, July 18, 1916; MMB to Edwin S. Harkness, July 22, 1916; MMB to Milton H. Smith, October 7, 1916; MMB to C. L. Williamson, October 27, 1916, all in BFP; *Lexington Herald*, July 23, 1916.

39. Margaret Preston Johnston diary, February 22, 1915; Minutes of Civic League Meeting, February 22, 1915; MMB to Mrs. Clarence LeBus, April 1, 8, 1916, all in BFP; *Lexington Herald*, January 18, February 23, April 11, 1915.

40. SPB, *Breckinridge*, 130–35; *Lexington Herald*, December 21, 1913; "The Public Health Nursing Association," typescript, 1915; MMB to N. Josephine Smith, July 2, 1915, both in BFP.

41. MMB to Rudolph Tietig of Tietig & Lee Architects, Cincinnati, April 13, May 26, December 29, 1915; Rudolph Tietig to MMB, April 14, 1915; MMB to William Worthington, December 29, 1915, all in BFP; SPB, *Breckinridge*, 135–36; *Lexington Herald*, December 13, 1915.

42. SPB, *Breckinridge*, 140–42; MMB to Dr. H. S. Keller, July 7, 1916; MMB, "Statement of Some Members of the State Tuberculosis Commission during the Last Gubernatorial Term," typescript, both in BFP.

43. H. H. Cherry to MMB, June 4, 1915; MMB to Jessie O. Yancey, June 23, August 19, 1915; Dr. U. V. Williams to MMB, June 10, 1915; MMB to Dr. Ar-

chibald Dixon, June 15, 1916, all in BFP; *Lexington Herald*, February 19, August 15, September 10, 1915.

Chapter 9: I Cannot Keep Her from Doing More

1. *Frankfort State Journal*, January 2, 5, 1916.

2. *Frankfort State Journal*, January 2, 5, 9, 18, 26, 1916; *Lexington Herald*, January 12, 15, 19, 26, March 9, 1916; *Lexington Leader*, January 13, 18, 26, 28, 1916; MMB, "Kentucky," in Stanton et al., *History of Woman Suffrage*, 6:210–11; MMB to Mrs. Green Garrett, January 15, 1916; Frances Beauchamp to MMB, January 12, 19, 1916, all in BFP; MMB to Laura Clay, November 20, 1915, Clay Papers; *Louisville Courier-Journal*, March 9, 1916.

3. Klotter, *Portrait in Paradox*, 226–32; MMB to Mrs. Murray Hubbard, January 15, 1916, BFP; MMB, "Kentucky," in Stanton et al., *History of Woman Suffrage*, 6:210–11; *Frankfort State Journal*, February 1, 2, 1916; *Lexington Herald*, February 1, 3, 11, 24, 27, 1916; Appleton, "'Like Banquo's Ghost,'" 217–21.

4. *Lexington Leader*, February 26, 1916; *Lexington Herald*, March 3, 1916; MMB to Mrs. R. A. McDowell, March 9, 1916, BFP; *Louisville Courier-Journal*, March 3, 1916.

5. *Lexington Herald*, March 7, 9, 11, 1916; Claude D. Minor to MMB, March 17, 1916, BFP.

6. *Lexington Herald*, March 17, 21, 1916; MMB, "Kentucky," in Stanton et al., *History of Woman Suffrage*, 6:211; MMB to Alben W. Barkley, March 12, 1916; DB to Alben Barkley, March 14, 1916, both in Alben Barkley Papers, Special Collections and Digital Programs, Margaret I. King Library, UK; Fuller, *Laura Clay*, 340; SPB, *Breckinridge*, 222–28.

7. *Lexington Herald*, March 17, April 10, 1916; Alben Barkley to MMB, March 25, 1916; Alben Barkley to DB, May 25, 1916; J. C. W. Beckham to DB, March 16, 1916; William J. Fields to MMB, April 17, 1916; Ollie James to MMB, December 13, 1917; DB to Ollie James, December 17, 1917, all in BFP; Alben Barkley, *That Reminds Me* (New York, 1954), 103–4; Ella Lewis, *Constitution of Kentucky* (Frankfort, 1928), 54, 62.

8. MMB to Mrs. L. B. Leigh, January 29, 1916; MMB to Anne Martin, January 25, 1916; MMB to Mrs. Harrison Munro Brown, May 23, 1916; DB to Curry Breckinridge, June 24, 1916, all in BFP; *Lexington Herald*, March 12, 19, 23, 29, April 13, 14, 20, May 6, 7, 19, 20, 1916; *Lexington Leader*, May 1, 1916. For more on Catt, see Mary G. Peck, *Carrie Chapman Catt: A Biography* (New York, 1944).

9. MMB to Mrs. W. A. McDowell, January 28, 1916; MMB to Mrs. J. B. Judah, March 25, 1916, both in BFP; *Lexington Herald*, January 23, 1916; HCM Jr. to ACM, March 5, 1916, HCMFP; Margaret Preston Johnston diary, January 13, February 1, 1916.

10. MMB to Mrs. Henry Wade Rogers, October 16, 1915; MMB to SPB,

March 31, 1916; MMB to Mrs. J. B. Judah, March 25, June 21, October 13, November 4, 1916; Mrs. J. B. Judah to MMB, October 10, 1916; MMB to Elise Smith, November 6, 1916, all in BFP; Mrs. J. B. Judah, *Report of Treasurer, Kentucky Equal Rights Association* (n.p., 1919). Rebecca Judah was the wife of Jacob B. Judah, general manager of Kaufman-Straus Co., in Louisville. See *Caron's Directory of the City of Louisville for 1916* (Louisville, 1916), 778.

11. SPB, *Breckinridge*, 135–37; MMB to Rudolph Tietig, December 29, 1915, February 8, 1916; MMB to William Worthington, December 29, 1915, all in BFP; *Lexington Herald*, June 22, 1916.

12. *Frankfort State Journal*, January 30, February 10, 11, 1916; *First Annual Tuberculosis Conference of Kentucky* (pamphlet); Jessie O. Yancey to MMB, June 22, 1916; MMB to Mrs. Helm Bruce, July 4, 1916; MMB to A. O. Stanley, August 21, 1916, all in BFP; *Lexington Herald*, August 29, September 19, 1916.

13. *Lexington Herald*, July 23, 1916; MMB to Margaret Preston, June 24, 1916; MMB to Harrison Simrall, June 21, 1916, all in BFP; Cantrill interviews; Underwood interview.

14. DB to Curry Breckinridge, July 6, 17, 22, 1916, BFP.

15. Ibid.; Ellison, *Healing Tuberculosis in the Woods*, 38, 65, 173; Ott, *Fevered Lives*, 157–61. Today the words "sanatorium" and "sanitarium" are used interchangeably, but Trudeau used sanitarium, which comes from the Latin word meaning health. After his death, the facility's name was changed to the Trudeau Sanatorium in 1917, as sanatorium came to mean a place for treatment of invalids, especially consumptives. Today the Trudeau Institute is a center for research in immunology. See http://www.TrudeauInstitute.org.

16. DB to Curry Breckinridge, July 17, 1916; brochure for Santanoni Apartments, both in BFP; MMB to Nettie Bullock, August 4, 1916; MMB to ACM, August 5, 1916, both in HCMFP; Ellison, *Healing Tuberculosis in the Woods*, 151–54, 179; Teller, *Tuberculosis Movement*, 25–26; Ott, *Fevered Lives*, 64, 69, 74; Fred. H. Heise, *Thirteenth Medical Supplement of the Thirty-third Annual Report of the Trudeau Sanatorium for the Year Ending October 31, 1917*, photocopy provided author by Linda Auclair, Trudeau Institute. For monetary conversions, see www.minneapolisfed.org/community_education/teacher/calc/hist1800.cfm.

17. MMB to A. T. Hert, July 14, 1916, BFP; MMB to ACM, August 5, 15, 1916; MMB to Nettie Bullock, August 16, 21, September 13, 1916, all in HCMFP; Dr. Joe T. Petty, interview with author, December 18, 1976.

18. MMB to Nettie Bullock, August 27, September 26, 1916, HCMFP; DB to SPB, October 24, 1916, reel 2, SPB Papers, LC; DB to Curry Breckinridge, September 18, October 16, December 27, 1916, BFP; Margaret Preston Johnston diary, October 9, 1916.

19. *Lexington Herald*, September 4, 29, 1916; DB to Curry Breckinridge, November 23, 1916, SPB Papers, LC.

20. DB to Curry Breckinridge, November 17, 1916, BFP; *Lexington Herald*,

November 16, 1916; Margaret Preston Johnston diary, November 15, 1916; SPB, *Breckinridge*, 136–37.

21. *Lexington Herald*, November 15, 16, 17, 1916; *Louisville Courier-Journal*, November 16, 1916; *Lexington Leader*, November 16, 1916; MMB to Mrs. J. B. Judah, November 4, 1916; MMB to KERA president and board, November 13, 1916; MMB to Christine Bradley South, November 24, 1916; Report of the Campaign Chairman of the Kentucky Equal Rights Ass'n. for the Year November 1915—November 1916; Report of the 27th Annual Convention of the Kentucky Equal Rights Association Held at Louisville, Ky., November 15 and 16, 1916, all in BFP.

22. DB to Curry Breckinridge, December 27, 1916; MMB to Mrs. Edward McDowell, September 24, 1915; MMB to Stites Duvall, October 26, 1915; MMB to Christine South, January 20, 1917; DB to Henry Breckinridge, February 6, 1917; MMB to HCM Jr., April 18, 1916, all in BFP; DB to Robert Woolley, December 4, 1912, Woolley Papers; DB to Curry Breckinridge, February 6, 1917, SPB Papers, LC; Henry Breckinridge to DB, February 13, 1917, Henry Breckinridge Papers; Laura Cravens to MMB, February 10, 1917; Margaret Preston to MMB, February 12, 1917; Bessie Wells Angus to MMB, February 2, 1917; Sally ? to MMB, February 15, 1917, all in HCMFP; *Lexington Herald*, February 4, 5, 1917.

23. SPB, *Breckinridge*, 176–78; *Lexington Herald*, January 11, 17, 18, 22, 25, 26, 29, 30, August 1, 3, 1917.

24. *Lexington Herald*, January 29, 30, July 26, 1917; *Lexington Leader*, July 25, 1917; James G. Denny to DB, February 26, 1917, BFP.

25. *Lexington Leader*, July 25, 28, 31, 1917.

26. *Lexington Herald*, August 16, 17, 24, September 1, 1917; J. M. Hanson to MMB, March 6, 1917; J. Byron Deacon to MMB, February 19, 1917, both in BFP; John Manson, *The Salvation Army and the Public* (New York, 1908); N. P. Hulst, *Report to the Merchants and Manufacturers Association of Milwaukee on Unworthy Charities* (Milwaukee, 1911).

27. *Lexington Herald*, June 5, 8, 15, 1917.

28. *Lexington Herald*, October 16, 20, 1917; SPB, *Breckinridge*, 176.

29. *Lexington Herald*, March 7, April 15, May 9, July 1, 12, December 23, 1917; SPB, *Breckinridge*, 137–40; DB to SPB, May 28, 1917, SPB Papers, LC.

30. MMB to Margaret Preston, April 12, 14, 30, August 2, 1917, Preston Johnston Papers; *Lexington Herald*, June 6, July 16, November 25, 1917.

31. MMB to Ella Chalkley, August 31, 1917, reel 3, SPB Papers, LC; MMB to Thomas Bullock, August 28, 1917; MMB to Nettie Bullock, September ? 1917; DB to HCM Jr., November 21, 1917; MMB to Nettie Bullock, December 25, n.d., 1917, all in HCMFP; *Lexington Herald*, December 1, 1917.

32. MMB to Mrs. J. B. Judah, December 4, 12, 24, 1917, Clay Papers.

33. DB to MMB, May 4, 1913; Mrs. Thruston Ballard to MMB, n.d. [1913–14]; MMB to Mrs. Henry Wade Rogers, October 16, 1915; MMB to SPB, March 31, 1916, all in BFP; MMB to DB, n.d. [1912], HCMFP; *Lexington Herald*, No-

vember 8, 28, 1908, July 25, September 2, 1909, August 18, December 18, 1910, May 31, 1911, July 17, 1913, January 1, October 7, 1915; *Lexington Leader*, April 24, 1913; Margaret Preston Johnston diary, April 15, 1910; Cantrill interviews; Helen Nesbit, interview with author, September 30, 1977; Joseph Robinson, interview with Thomas H. Appleton Jr., July 2, 1976.

34. Mrs. Florence Shelby Cantrill, interview with James C. Klotter, January 31, 1975, notes in possession of Klotter.

35. Fuller, *Clay*, 145–52; Glen Finch, "The Election of United States Senators in Kentucky—The Beckham Period," *FCHQ* 44 (1970): 41; Link, *Wilson: The New Freedom*, 257–58; *New York Times*, January 7, 1918. For a discussion of World War I's effect on Kentucky and the woman suffrage movement therein, see Harrison and Klotter, *New History of Kentucky*, 286–91. For more on the political situation in Kentucky during this period, see Nicholas C. Burckel, "From Beckham to McCreary: The Progressive Record of Kentucky Governors," *Register* 76 (1978): 285–306; Thomas W. Ramage, "Augustus Owsley Stanley: Early Twentieth Century Kentucky Democrat" (PhD diss., University of Kentucky, 1968); Klotter, *Portrait in Paradox*, 203–33; Wheeler, *New Women of the New South*, 29–30, 34, 36, 165–67; Lumsden, *Rampant Women*, 135, 139.

36. Fuller, *Clay*, 146–48; MMB to Christine Bradley South, January 3, 1918, Clay Papers; Graham, *Woman Suffrage*, 99–127; Clift, *Founding Sisters*, 110, 158; Buhle and Buhle, *Concise History of Woman Suffrage*, 413, 421; Marilley, *Woman Suffrage*, 211–16.

37. Fuller, *Clay*, 148–52; Laura Clay to Kate Gordon, January 26, 1918; Laura Clay to MMB, January 31, October 9, 1918; DB to Laura Clay, June 7, 1918; MMB to Laura Clay, January 4, October 8, 1918; A. O. Stanley to Christine Bradley South, October 10, 1918, all in Clay Papers; MMB, "Kentucky," in Stanton et al., *History of Woman Suffrage*, 6:212; Wheeler, *New Women of the New South*, 136, 139–40, 145–46, 160–61, 165–66, 175–76.

38. Klotter, *Breckinridges*, 229; *Lexington Herald*, May 21, 31, June 24, 25, 1918; DB to SPB, August 5, 1918, reel 3, SPB Papers, LC.

39. SPB, *Breckinridge*, 230–31; MMB to Margaret Preston Johnston, January 9, February 5, n.d., August 20, September 21, October 16, 1918, Preston Johnston Papers; *Lexington Herald*, March 11, May 26, June 22, 1918; Minutes of the Civic League, October 4, 1918, BFP.

40. Petition in Equity, *H. C. McDowell Jr. v. Nannette Bullock, W. A. McDowell, T. C. McDowell, Julia Brock, and Madeline McDowell Breckinridge*, January 1, 1918; HCM Jr. to Messrs. Allen & Duncan, February 26, 1918; HCM Jr. to W. A. McDowell, December 28, 1918, all in HCMFP. Part of the Ashland estate had already been subdivided. See Plans for the Sale of Certain Lots on the West Side of Hanover Avenue, Ashland Addition: April 15, 1916, HCMFP; www.minneapolisfed.org/community_education/teacher/calc/hist1800.cfm.

Chapter 10: Kentucky's Most Distinguished Woman Citizen

1. *Lexington Herald*, February 11, 1919; "Last Annual Report of the Kentucky Equal Rights Association to the National American Woman Suffrage Association," BFP; Finch, "Election of United States Senators," 41; Gilmore, *Gender and Jim Crow*, 208–10; Green, *Southern Strategies*, 93–97; Thomas, *New Woman in Alabama*, 174–203; Kraditor, *Ideas of the Woman Suffrage Movement*, 7, 192–95; Wheeler, *New Women of the New South*, 29, 162–71; Flexner, *Century of Struggle*, 273–88; Lumsden, *Rampant Women*, 3, 140–53; Graham, *Woman Suffrage*, 52–55, 82–84, 117, 122; Stevens, *Jailed for Freedom*, 63, 91, 109–11, 158; Irwin, *Story of the Woman's Party*, 260, 284; Carrie Chapman Catt, *Woman Suffrage by Federal Constitutional Amendment* (New York, 1917), 1, 60, 69; Park, *Front Door Lobby*, 11–27; Olivia Coolidge, *Women's Rights: The Suffrage Movement in America, 1848–1920* (New York, 1966), 129; Link, *Wilson: The New Freedom*, 257–58.

2. Fuller, *Clay*, 150–55; SPB, *Breckinridge*, 215–18; Harrison and Klotter, *New History of Kentucky*, 287–89, 348; Klotter, *Portrait in Paradox*, 115–17; Kraditor, *Ideas of the Woman Suffrage Movement*, 157, 170–71.

3. *Lexington Herald*, February 16, 1919; Fuller, *Clay*, 153.

4. Klotter, *Breckinridges*, 161; *Lexington Herald*, February 14, 15, 18, 1919.

5. *Lexington Herald*, February 22, 1919.

6. Ibid.

7. *Lexington Herald*, February 25, 1919.

8. Fuller, *Clay*, 153–54; "M.M. Breckinridge Suffrage—Ky—Equal Rights Association," original notes on the debate with Laura Clay, BFP; Kenneth R. Johnson, "Kate Gordon and the Woman Suffrage Movement," *Journal of Southern History* 38 (1972): 365–92; Wheeler, *New Women of the New South*, 104, 138–39.

9. *Lexington Herald*, March 13, 1919; Minutes Executive Board K.E.R.A., March 31, 1919; Laura Clay to MMB, May 7, 1919, both in BFP; Fuller, *Clay*, 152–53; Goodman, *Bitter Harvest*, 60.

10. *Lexington Herald*, March 14, 25, 1919; *Lexington Leader*, March 14, 16, 1919; MMB to Board Member, May 1, 1919, BFP; Fuller, *Clay*, 153.

11. Finch, "Election of United States Senators," 40–41; Park, *Front Door Lobby*, 90; Barkley, *That Reminds Me*, 103; DB to Alben Barkley, September 2, 1919; MMB to Alben Barkley, September 2, 17, 1919, all in Barkley Papers; Alben Barkley to MMB, December 17, 1919, BFP; *Lexington Herald*, May 22, June 5, July 4, September 3, 1919.

12. Laura Clay to MMB, June 5, 1919, BFP; *Lexington Herald*, June 6, 8, 9, 1919; *Lexington Leader*, June 29, 1919; Fuller, *Clay*, 154; Goodman, *Bitter Harvest*, 60–62.

13. Christine Bradley South to MMB, June 23, 1919, BFP; Fuller, *Clay*, 155–57.

14. MMB to Antoinette Funk, May 31, 1915; MMB to Mrs. J. B. Judah, November 17, 1919, both in BFP; *Lexington Herald,* September 4, 1919; *Lexington Leader,* June 12, 1919; Goodman, *Bitter Harvest,* 61; Fuller, *Clay,* 155–57; MMB, "Kentucky," in Stanton et al., *History of Woman Suffrage,* 6:212.

15. *Lexington Herald,* July 3, 4, 9, October 14, 1919; *Lexington Leader,* June 29, 1919; SPB, *Breckinridge,* 235; Charles M. Harriss to MMB, July 4, 1919; Dr. H. T. Morris to MMB, July 29, 1919; Dr. J. L. Early to MMB, August 6, 1919; Brig H. Harris to MMB, August 2, 1919, all in BFP.

16. *Lexington Herald,* February 14, April 10, 18, August 29, 1919; MMB check for automobile driving instruction; clipping as vice president of Kentucky Tuberculosis Association, October 15, 1919; MMB to Southern Tuberculosis Society, October 20, 1919; "Superintendent's Report for the Blue Grass Sanatorium, November 1919," all in BFP.

17. *Lexington Herald,* January 10, August 3, 1919; notation on sale of portion of Ashland, BFP; DB to HCM Jr., June 30, 1919; MMB to H.C. Bullock, August 17, September 6, 1919, all in HCMFP.

18. MMB to Nettie Bullock, August 13, 21, 28, September 15, 1919, all in HCMFP; Cantrill interviews; Nesbit interview. Although one of Desha's relatives claimed there had not been an affair (Scott Breckinridge, interview with James C. Klotter, May 22, 1980, notes in possession of Klotter), several people who had known them remembered, and most believed, the gossip: Florence Cantrill, Clinton Harbison, Helen Nesbit, Elizabeth Gatten, and Joseph M. Robinson. Even Eliza Underwood, wife of the man who succeeded Desha at the *Herald,* admitted having heard the gossip, though she replied as to its veracity: "I really couldn't say." Cantrill interviews; Elizabeth Gatten, interview with author, April 13, 1979; Clinton M. Harbison, interview with author, July 21, 1976; Nesbit interview; Underwood interview.

19. *Lexington Herald,* June 29, October 14, 1919; *Lexington Leader,* June 29, 1919.

20. Thomas Combs to DB, September 3, 1919, DB Papers; Harrison, *Kentucky's Governors,* 152–55; *Lexington Herald,* April 19, 1903, October 14, 1919; Emmeline Pankhurst to MMB, September 23, 1919; Carrie Chapman Catt to MMB, September 23, December 15, 1919; Christine South to MMB, November 25, 1919; MMB to Christine South, November 17, 1919; MMB to Mrs. J. B. Judah, November 4, December 19, 24, 1919; MMB to Carrie Chapman Catt, December 20, 1919; typescript by DB, n.d., all in BFP; SPB, *Breckinridge,* 235–36.

21. *Lexington Herald,* November 9, 1919; MMB to Mrs. J. N. Forgy, December 2, 1919; MMB to Elise Smith, December 26, 1919; MMB to Carrie Chapman Catt, December 20, 1919, all in BFP.

22. Carrie Chapman Catt to MMB, June 27, July 2, December 11, 1919, all in BFP.

23. MMB to Carrie Chapman Catt, December 15, 1919, BFP.

24. SPB, *Breckinridge*, 235; typescript by DB, BFP; *Frankfort State Journal*, January 2, 1920; *Lexington Herald*, January 4, 1920; *Louisville Courier-Journal*, January 4, 1920.

25. "Biennial Message of Governor Edwin P. Morrow Before the General Assembly of Kentucky . . . January 6, 1920," Edwin P. Morrow Papers, microfilm, Special Collections and Digital Programs, Margaret I. King Library, UK; *Lexington Herald*, January 7, 1920; *Frankfort State Journal*, January 7, 1920; *New York Times*, January 7, 1920; MMB, "Kentucky," in Stanton et al., *History of Woman Suffrage*, 6:214.

26. *Lexington Herald*, January 7, 8, 9, 1920; *New York Times*, January 10, 1920; *Frankfort State Journal*, January 9, 1920; Scott, *Southern Lady*, 184; typescript by DB, BFP; MMB, "Kentucky," in Stanton et al., *History of Woman Suffrage*, 6:214–15; SPB, *Breckinridge*, 236. KERA paid $300 for Pankhurst's fee. See MMB to Coit Lyceum Bureau, January 9, 1920, BFP. For Katrina Ely Tiffany, see Lois K. M. Rosenberry, "Katrina Ely Tiffany," in *Dictionary of American Biography*, ed. Dumas Malone et al. (New York, 1936), 18:533–34.

27. *Lexington Herald*, January 20, 23, March 16, 1920; Sarah Clay Bennett to MMB, January 3, January n.d., February 2, 1920; MMB to Carrie Chapman Catt, February 7, 1920; MMB to Sarah Clay Bennett, January 20, 31, 1920; MMB to J. Pelham Johnston, March 13, 1920, all in BFP.

28. *Louisville Times*, January 6, 1970; SPB, *Breckinridge*, 236–37.

29. MMB to Laura Clay, March 1, 16, 1920, Clay Papers; Laura Clay to MMB, March 3, 17, 1920; MMB to Carrie Chapman Catt, October 4, 1919; manuscript for "Kentucky" chapter in Stanton et al., *History of Woman Suffrage*, all in BFP.

30. DB to SPB, January 19, 1920; Codicil to Will of Desha Breckinridge, April 1920, both in SPB Papers, LC; SPB, *Breckinridge*, 121, 236, portrait is shown between 236 and 237; MMB to Mrs. J. B. Judah, January 30, 1920, BFP. The portrait now hangs in the Madeline McDowell Breckinridge Elementary School in Lexington.

31. *Lexington Herald*, April 18, 1919; MMB to C. L. Adler, January 27, 1920, BFP; Eberson, "Madeline McDowell Breckinridge, 1872–1920," in *Portraits*, 10–12.

32. MMB to C. L. Adler, January 27, 1920; MMB to Edwin P. Morrow, January 31, February 25, 1920; MMB to Members of the Legislature, February 2, 1920; MMB to Members of Kentucky Tuberculosis Society, March 6, 1920, all in BFP; *Lexington Herald*, February 2, 1920; SPB, *Breckinridge*, 154–55.

33. DB to SPB, January 19, 1920, March 21, 1920; Codicil to Will of Desha Breckinridge, April 1920, all in SPB Papers, LC; SPB, *Breckinridge*, 237; *Lexington Herald*, February 29, April 4, 1920.

34. MMB to Mrs. Herbert Mengel, April 16, 1920, BFP; *Lexington Herald*, April 18, 1920; DB to SPB, May 3, 1920, SPB Papers, LC; MMB to Nettie Bullock, May 7, 1920, HCMFP.

35. MMB to Nettie Bullock, May 14, 26, 1920; MMB to DB, June 29, 1920, all in HCMFP; Cantrill interviews; *Lexington Herald,* May 20, 1920.

36. MMB to Nettie Bullock, June 4, 1920; MMB to DB, June 8, 1920; MMB to Julia Brock, July 16, 1920, all in HCMFP; Thomas Feltner to Milton H. Smith, August 27, 1908, Milton Hannibal Smith Family Collection. The Feltners had lived in Paris at least since 1908. See Thomas Feltner to Milton H. Smith, August 27, 1908, Milton Hannibal Smith Family Collection.

37. MMB to DB, June 6, 8, 14, 17, July 5, 9, n.d., 1920; MMB to Nettie Bullock, June 28, 1920, all in HCMFP.

38. MMB to Nettie Bullock, June 10, 1920; MMB to DB, June 10, 13, 20, July 12, 26–27, August 12, 20, 1920, all in HCMFP.

39. MMB to DB, June 10, 13, 17, 19, 20, 24, 29, July 2, 3, 4, 5, 14, 20, 22, 27, 29, 31, August 7, 20, 1920; MMB to Nettie Bullock, July 31, 1920, all in HCMFP.

40. MMB to DB, July 9, 1920; DB to Nettie Bullock, September 14, 1920, both in HCMFP; *Lexington Herald,* September 10, 12, 21, 25, 1920.

41. Rebel Withers to Nettie Bullock, December 5, 1920; MMB to DB, October 1920 (two letters written from Missouri), all in HCMFP; A. Elizabeth Taylor, "Tennessee: The Thirty-sixth State," in Wheeler, *Votes for Women!* 53–70; *Lexington Herald,* February 27, April 10, September 28, October 8, 12, 13, 14, 15, 18, November 1, 1920; Gertrude Duncan to MMB, October 11, 1920, BFP; SPB, *Breckinridge,* 246–47.

42. *Lexington Herald,* April 18, May 2, November 3, 10, 12, 21, 24, December 5, 1920; MMB to Mrs. M. S. McLaughlin, April 16, 1920; MMB to H. Rogers, January 10, 1920; H. Rogers to MMB, December 13, 1919, January 7, 1920; MMB to Wood G. Dunlap, April 16, 1920; "Report of Community Organizer to the Community Service League of Fayette County, Oct. 8th, 1920," all in BFP; Harrison and Klotter, *New History of Kentucky,* 289; Klotter, *Portrait in Paradox,* 267. For a discussion of the importance of studying the history of woman suffrage, see Jean H. Baker, "Getting Right with Women's Suffrage," *Journal of the Gilded Age and the Progressive Era* 5 (2006): 7–17.

43. *Lexington Herald,* October 17, November 12, 26, 1920; MMB to HCM Jr., October 5, 1920; Fanny Ballard to Nettie Bullock, November 26, 1920, both in HCMFP; *New York Times,* November 25, 26, 1920; *Lexington Leader,* November 24, 25, 26, 1920; DB to SPB, November 24, 1920, reel 3, SPB Papers, LC.

44. *Lexington Herald,* November 26, 27, 28, 1920; SPB, *Breckinridge,* 265–67.

Epilogue: She Belonged to Kentucky

1. *Lexington Herald,* November 26, December 5, 1920; SPB, *Breckinridge,* 249–64; D.A.H. to Cora Wilson Stewart, December 13, 1920, Cora Wilson Stewart Papers, Special Collections and Digital Programs, Margaret I. King Library,

UK; Marion Houston Smith to Nettie Bullock, December 15, 1920; Linda Neville to Nettie Bullock, December 2, 1920; handmade card, all in HCMFP; Jane Addams, "Madeline McDowell Breckinridge," *Survey*, December 25, 1920, 469; "Mrs. Desha Breckinridge," *Register* 19 (1921): 35–37. For Cora Wilson Stewart, see Yvonne Honeycutt Baldwin, *Cora Wilson Stewart and Kentucky's Moonlight Schools: Fighting for Literacy in America* (Lexington, 2006); and Willie Nelms, *Cora Wilson Stewart: Crusader against Illiteracy* (Jefferson, NC, 1997).

2. Ida W. Harrison, "Program of Fortnightly Club, 1894–96," BFP; Henderson Daingerfield Norman to DB, n.d. [1921], reel 3, SPB Papers, LC; Klotter, *Breckinridges*, 230; *Lexington Herald*, January 1, 1922.

3. Dr. John W. Scott, Medical Report on DB, March 1, 1929, DB Papers.

4. *Lexington Herald*, January 1, 17, 1922. Allen Lee Swisher painted the portrait; information supplied by Lynne Hollingsworth of the Kentucky Historical Society.

5. *Lexington Herald*, November 27, December 15, 16, 1920; *Lexington Leader*, November 28, 1920; DB to SPB, December 9, 1920, SPB Papers, LC; Baker, "Getting Right with Women's Suffrage," 7, 9.

6. Marian Williamson to Linda Neville, December 8, 1920, Neville Papers; *Lexington Herald*, December 3, 4, 5, 12, 1920.

7. *Lexington Herald*, December 18, 23, 24, 1920.

8. DB to SPB, May 12, 18, 1921, reel 3, SPB Papers, LC; DB to Henry Breckinridge, May 19, 1925, Henry Breckinridge Papers; DB to Breckinridge Long, May 12, 1928, Breckinridge Long Papers, LC.

9. HCM Jr. to Nettie Bullock, April 17, 1922; Last Will and Testament of Nannette McDowell Bullock, probated July 12, 1948; Clinton M. Harbison to Raymond F. McLain, October 26, 1948, all in HCMFP.

10. *Lexington Herald*, December 14, 1920, April 24, 1921; Cantrill interviews. For more on Cantrill, see *Lexington Herald Leader*, November 3, 1981; "Among My Souvenirs," autobiography of Florence Cantrill (manuscript), Florence McDowell (Shelby) Cantrill–Mary B. Bryan Papers, Special Collections and Digital Programs, Margaret I. King Library, UK.

11. DB to SPB, March 28, 29, May 2 (two letters), 1921; Oswald Garrison Villard to SPB, March 22, 1921; M.A. Cassidy to SPB, March 23, 1921; Henderson Daingerfield Norman, June 10, n.d., 1921, all in reel 3, SPB Papers, LC; SPB to Nettie Bullock, July 2, 1921; Elsie McDowell to Nettie Bullock, postmarked October 30, 1921; Nannie F. Maclean to Nettie Bullock, February 27, 1922, all in HCMFP; Librarian of Congress to SPB, February 28, 1921, BFP.

12. *Lexington Herald*, June 29, 1924, November 5, 1972; "Madeline McDowell Breckinridge Fresh Air Camp," typescript in possession of author, dated January 3, 1989; Biff Starr, YMCA, interview with author, February 26, 1977; *Lexington Leader*, June 29, 1924; Mrs. Graham Lawrence to DB, December 12, 1925; DB to Mrs. Graham Lawrence, December 14, 26, 1925; DB to Nettie Bullock, December 18, 1925, all in DB Papers. For a discussion of how Desha

Breckinridge's progressivism changed in the years between Madge's death and his own, see Klotter, *Breckinridges*, 230–43.

13. DB to SPB, March 22, 1933, DB Papers; SPB to Nettie Bullock, August 11, 1929; DB to Nettie and Tom Bullock, telegram, July 27, 1928, both in HCMFP; Breckinridge interview; Klotter, *Breckinridges*, 326; Cantrill interviews.

14. SPB to DB, January 21, 1932, April 29, May 3, 6, July 5, August 2, 4, 1933; Scott, Medical Report on DB, March 1, 1929, all in DB Papers; *Lexington Herald*, February 19, 1935; *Lexington Leader*, February 18, 1935; *New York Times*, February 19, 1935.

15. John G. Cramer to MMB, July 24, 1914; MMB to Mrs. Charles T. Hallinan, September 26, 1914; DB to SPB, June 18, 1921, all in BFP; SPB, *Breckinridge*, 8–9, 235; MMB to ACM, September 15, 1919, HCMFP; Wheeler, *New Women of the New South*, 46; Lindsey Apple, *Cautious Rebel: A Biography of Susan Clay Sawitzky* (Kent, OH, 1997), 9. Apple concludes of Madge's cousin that "loyalty to family in its many forms may have been the major deterrent to Susan Clay Sawitzky's achieving success" as an independent woman in her chosen field of poetry.

16. MMB, *Another Reason for Granting School Suffrage to Kentucky Women*, and "A Mother's Sphere"; Lorraine Seay, interview with author, September 23, 1976.

17. MMB to C. F. Brower and Co., August 15, 1914; John G. Cramer to MMB, July 24, 1914, both in BFP; Marjie ? to Margaret Preston Johnston, May 29, 1918, Preston Johnston Papers; Cantrill interviews; Underwood interview.

18. *Lexington Herald*, December 5, 1920.

19. *Lexington Herald*, June 13, 24, 1902; SPB, *Breckinridge*, 241; Cantrill interviews.

20. Thomas A. Combs to MMB, April 8, 1920, BFP; SPB, *Breckinridge*, 181.

21. SPB, *Breckinridge*, 8; Wheeler, *New Women of the New South*, 39; Eisenach, *Lost Promise of Progressivism*, 5, 9, 72–73, 263; Danbom, "*The World of Hope*," 104, 113–15; Wolfe, *Daughters of Canaan*, 141–42.

Bibliography

Manuscript Collections

Filson Historical Society, Louisville

Bessie Taul Conkwright Clippings
Augustus E. Willson Papers

Kentucky Historical Society, Thomas D. Clark Center for Kentucky History, Frankfort

Ephraim McDowell Folder
Milton Hannibal Smith Family Collection

Library of Congress Manuscripts Division, Washington, DC

Breckinridge Family Papers
Henry Breckinridge Papers
Sophonisba P. Breckinridge Papers
Ben B. Lindsey Papers
Breckinridge Long Papers
National American Woman Suffrage Association Papers
National Woman's Party Papers
Henry Watterson Papers
Robert Woolley Papers

University of Chicago, Special Collections Research Center, Joseph Regenstein Library

Sophonisba P. Breckinridge Papers

University of Kentucky, Special Collections and Digital Programs, Margaret I. King Library, Lexington

Alben Barkley Papers
Desha Breckinridge Papers
Madeline McDowell Breckinridge Papers
Bullock Family Papers

Florence McDowell (Shelby) Cantrill–Mary B. Bryan Papers
James Campbell Cantrill Papers
Chalkley Family Scrapbooks
Lyman Chalkley Papers
Henry Clay Memorial Foundation Papers
Laura Clay Papers
Thomas Clay Papers
Mary Elliott Flannery Papers
Ollie M. James Papers
Lexington Civic League Papers
Lexington Parks and Recreation Department Papers
Edwin P. Morrow Papers
Linda Neville Papers
Preston Johnston Papers
Jouett Shouse Papers
Augustus Owsley Stanley Papers
Cora Wilson Stewart Papers

University of Louisville Archives and Records Center

Kentucky Child Labor Association Papers

Secondary Sources

Aaron, Daniel. *Men of Good Hope: A Story of American Progressives.* New York: Oxford University Press, 1951.
Adams, Mildred. *The Right to Be People.* New York: Lippincott, 1967.
Addams, Jane. "Madeline McDowell Breckinridge." *Survey,* December 25, 1920.
———. *Twenty Years at Hull-House.* New York: Macmillan, 1910.
Alland, Alexander. *Jacob Riis: Photographer and Citizen.* Millerton, NY: Aperture Foundation, 1972.
Allen, James Lane. *The Blue-Grass Region of Kentucky.* New York: Harper & Brothers, 1892.
Angle, Paul. *Crossroads: 1913.* Chicago: Rand McNally, 1963.
Annual Register of the State College of Kentucky, 1890–91. Lexington: The College, 1891.
Annual Register of the State College of Kentucky, 1891–92. Lexington: The College, 1892.
Annual Register of the State College of Kentucky, 1892–93. Lexington: The College, 1893.
Annual Report of the Lexington Public Schools. Lexington: Board of Education, 1915.
Annual Report of the Lexington Public Schools, 1911. Lexington: Board of Education, 1911.

Annual Report of the Lexington Public Schools, 1913. Lexington: Board of Education, 1913.

Annual Report of the Public Schools of Lexington, Kentucky, June 30, 1908. Lexington: Board of Education, 1908.

Apple, Lindsey. *Cautious Rebel: A Biography of Susan Clay Sawitzky*. Kent, OH: Kent State University Press, 1997.

Appleton, Thomas H., Jr. "'Like Banquo's Ghost': The Emergence of the Prohibition Issue in Kentucky Politics." PhD diss., University of Kentucky, 1981.

Ashland Catalogue of Trotting Stock for 1883, Belonging to H. C. McDowell. Frankfort: privately printed, 1883.

Ayers, Edward L. *The Promise of the New South: Life after Reconstruction*. New York: Oxford University Press, 1992.

Baker, Jean H. "Getting Right with Women's Suffrage." *Journal of the Gilded Age and the Progressive Era* 5 (2006): 7–17.

———. *Votes for Women: The Struggle for Suffrage Revisited*. New York: Oxford University Press, 2002.

Baldwin, Yvonne Honeycutt. *Cora Wilson Stewart and Kentucky's Moonlight Schools: Fighting for Literacy in America*. Lexington: University Press of Kentucky, 2006.

Banner, Lois W. *Women in Modern America: A Brief History*. New York: Harcourt Brace Jovanovich, 1974.

Barkley, Alben. *That Reminds Me*. New York: Doubleday, 1954.

Barney, Sandra. "Gender and Authority in the West Virginia Antituberculosis Campaigns of the Progressive Era." *Southern Historian* 16 (1995): 46–60.

Barr, Nancy Ellen. "A Profession for Women: Education, Social Service Administration, and Feminism in the Life of Sophonisba P. Breckinridge." PhD diss., Emory University, 1993.

Bartley, Paula. *Emmeline Pankhurst*. New York: Routledge, 2003.

Bates, Barbara. *Bargaining for Life: A Social History of Tuberculosis, 1876–1938*. Philadelphia: University of Pennsylvania Press, 1992.

Beeton, Beverly. *Women Vote in the West: The Woman Suffrage Movement, 1869–1896*. New York: Garland, 1986.

Blair, Karen J. *The Clubwoman as Feminist: True Womanhood Redefined, 1868–1914*. New York: Holmes & Meier, 1980.

Blatch, Harriot S., and Alma Lutz. *Challenging Years*. New York: G. P. Putnam & Sons, 1940.

Blatch, Harriot S., and Theodore Stanton, eds. *Elizabeth Cady Stanton as Revealed in Her Letters and Reminiscences*. New York: Harper & Brothers, 1922.

Bolin, James Duane. *Bossism and Reform in a Southern City: Lexington, Kentucky, 1880–1940*. Lexington: University Press of Kentucky, 2000.

Breckinridge, Madeline McDowell. *Another Reason for Granting School Suffrage to Kentucky Women*. Lexington: Kentucky Federation of Women's Clubs, 1910.

———. "Building a Public School to Be a Recreation Center." *American City,* June 1913, 659–61.

———. *Some Reasons for Granting School Suffrage to Kentucky Women.* Lexington: Kentucky Federation of Women's Clubs, 1910.

Breckinridge, Scott. Interview with James C. Klotter, May 22, 1980. Notes in possession of Klotter.

Breckinridge, Sophonisba P. *The Child in the City.* Chicago: Hollister, 1912.

———. "Madeline McDowell Breckinridge." In *Southern Pioneers in Social Interpretation,* edited by Howard W. Odum. Chapel Hill: University of North Carolina Press, 1925.

———. *Madeline McDowell Breckinridge: A Leader in the New South.* Chicago: University of Chicago Press, 1921.

Breckinridge, Sophonisba P., and Edith Abbott. *The Delinquent Child and the Home.* Chicago: Survey Associates, 1912.

Brooks, Eric. *Ashland: The Henry Clay Estate.* Charleston, SC: Arcadia, 2007.

Brown, Alexander. *The Cabells and Their Kin.* New York: Garrett & Massie, 1895.

Brown, John M. *Memoranda of the Preston Family.* 1842. Reprint, Frankfort: S. I. M. Major Printer, 1870.

Buenker, John D. *Urban Liberalism and Progressive Reform.* New York: Scribner, 1973.

Buenker, John D., John C. Burnham, and Robert M. Crunden. *Progressivism.* Cambridge, MA: Schenkman, 1977.

Buhle, Mari Jo, and Paul Buhle. *The Concise History of Woman Suffrage: Selections from the Classic Work of Stanton, Anthony, Gage, and Harper.* Urbana: University of Illinois Press, 1978.

Burckel, Nicholas C. "From Beckham to McCreary: The Progressive Record of Kentucky Governors." *Register of the Kentucky Historical Society* 76 (1978): 285–306.

———. "Progressive Governors in the Border States: Reform Governors of Missouri, Kentucky, West Virginia and Maryland, 1900–1918." PhD diss., University of Wisconsin, 1971.

Byington, Margaret F. *Report on the Charities of Lexington, Kentucky.* Lexington: The City, 1918.

Camhi, Jane Jerome. *Women against Women: American Anti-suffragism, 1880–1920.* Brooklyn: Carlson, 1994.

Cantrill, Florence Shelby. Interview with author, March 25 and October 25, 1976.

———. Interview with James C. Klotter, January 31, 1975. Notes in possession of Klotter.

Caron's Directory of the City of Louisville for 1916. Louisville: Caron Directory, 1916.

Castleman, John B., ed. *In Memoriam, Breckinridge Castleman.* Louisville: no publisher, 1913.

Catalogue of the State College of Kentucky, 1893–94. Lexington: The College, 1894.

Catalogue of Trotting Stock Belonging to H. C. McDowell of Woodlake. Frankfort: privately printed, 1876.

Catt, Carrie Chapman. *Woman Suffrage by Federal Constitutional Amendment.* New York: National Woman Suffrage Pub. Co., 1917.

Catt, Carrie Chapman, and Nettie Rogers Shuler. *Woman Suffrage and Politics: The Inner Story of the Suffrage Movement.* New York: Charles Scribner's Sons, 1926.

Chafe, William H. *The Paradox of Change: American Women in the 20th Century.* New York: Oxford University Press, 1991.

Clapp, Elizabeth J. *Mothers of All Children: Women Reformers and the Rise of Juvenile Courts in Progressive Era America.* University Park: Pennsylvania State University Press, 1998.

Clift, Eleanor. *Founding Sisters and the Nineteenth Amendment.* Hoboken, NJ: John Wiley & Sons, 2003.

Clopper, Edward. *Child Welfare in Kentucky.* New York: National Child Labor Committee, 1919.

Coghlan, Cathy. "An Examination of the Contributions of Sophonisba Preston Breckinridge (1866–1948) to the Discipline of Sociology." PhD diss., Texas Woman's University, 2002.

Colburn, David R., and George E. Pozzetta, eds. *Reform and Reformers in the Progressive Era.* Westport, CT: Greenwood, 1983.

Coleman, J. Winston, Jr. *Robert Burns Wilson: Kentucky Painter, Novelist and Poet.* Lexington: Winburn, 1956.

Connelley, William Elsey, and E. Merton Coulter. *History of Kentucky.* 5 vols. Edited by Charles Kerr. Chicago: American Historical Society, 1922.

Cook, Mary E., Ann Lenroot, et al. "Sophonisba P. Breckinridge, 1866–1948." *Social Science Review* 23 (1949): 131–35.

Coolidge, Olivia. *Women's Rights: The Suffrage Movement in America, 1848–1920.* New York: E. P. Dutton, 1966.

Cornett, Judy Gail. "Angel for the Blind: The Public Triumphs and Private Tragedy of Linda Neville." PhD diss., University of Kentucky, 1993.

Costin, Lela B. *Two Sisters for Social Justice: A Biography of Grace and Edith Abbott.* Urbana: University of Illinois Press, 1983.

Cott, Nancy F. *The Grounding of Modern Feminism.* New Haven, CT: Yale University Press, 1997.

———. *Root of Bitterness: Documents of the Social History of American Women.* New York: E. P. Dutton, 1972.

Cott, Nancy F., and Elizabeth H. Pleck. A *Heritage of Her Own: Toward a New Social History of American Women.* New York: Simon & Schuster, 1979.

Counts, George S. *School and Society in Chicago.* New York: Harcourt, Brace, 1928.

Craig, Berry. "Charting the Evolution of the Hospital for Special Surgery." *O & P Business News*, September 15, 2002.

Crunden, Robert M. *Ministers of Reform: The Progressives' Achievement in American Civilization, 1889–1920*. New York: Basic, 1982.

Danbom, David B. *"The World of Hope": Progressives and the Struggle for an Ethical Public Life*. Philadelphia: Temple University Press, 1997.

Davis, Allen F. *American Heroine: The Life and Legend of Jane Addams*. New York: Oxford University Press, 1973.

———. *Spearheads for Reform: The Social Settlements and the Progressive Movement, 1890–1914*. 1967. Reprint, New Brunswick, NJ: Rutgers University Press, 1994.

Davis, Mary. *Sylvia Pankhurst: A Life in Radical Politics*. Sterling, VA: Pluto, 1999.

Davis, William C. *Breckinridge: Statesman, Soldier, Symbol*. Baton Rouge: Louisiana State University Press, 1974.

Diner, Steven J. *A Very Different Age: Americans of the Progressive Era*. New York: Hill & Wang, 1998.

Dye, Nancy Schrom. *As Equals and as Sisters: Feminism, the Labor Movement, and the Women's Trade Union League of New York*. Columbia: University of Missouri Press, 1980.

———. "The Louisville Woolen Mills Strike of 1887: A Case Study of Working Women, the Knights of Labor, and Union Organization in the New South." *Register of the Kentucky Historical Society* 82 (1984): 136–50.

Eastman, Max. *Enjoyment of Living*. New York: Harper & Brothers, 1948.

Eberson, Frederick. *Portraits: Kentucky Pioneers in Community Health and Medicine*. Lexington: University of Kentucky Medical Center, 1968.

Eisenach, Eldon J. *The Lost Promise of Progressivism*. Lawrence: University Press of Kansas, 1994.

Ekirch, Arthur. *Progressivism in America*. New York: New Viewpoints, 1974.

Eller, Ronald D. "The Coal Barons of the Appalachian South, 1880–1930." *Appalachian Journal* 4 (1977): 195–207.

Ellison, David L. *Healing Tuberculosis in the Woods: Medicine and Science at the End of the Nineteenth Century*. Westport, CT: Greenwood, 1994.

Evans, Sara M. *Born for Liberty: A History of Women in America*. New York: Free Press, 1991.

Federico, Ronald C. *The Social Welfare Institution*. 2nd ed. Lexington, MA: Heath, 1976.

Filler, Louis. *Appointment at Armageddon: Muckraking and Progressivism in the American Tradition*. Westport, CT: Greenwood, 1976.

Finch, Glen. "The Election of United States Senators in Kentucky—The Beckham Period." *Filson Club History Quarterly* 44 (1970): 38–50.

Finegold, Kenneth. *Experts and Politicians: Reform Challenges to Machine Politics in New York, Cleveland, and Chicago*. Princeton, NJ: Princeton University Press, 1995.

Fink, Leon. *Progressive Intellectuals and the Dilemmas of Democratic Commitment.* Cambridge, MA: Harvard University Press, 1997.

Finnegan, Margaret Mary. *Selling Suffrage: Consumer Culture and Votes for Women.* New York: Columbia University Press, 1999.

Fitzgerald, Susan, ed. *Annual Report at the 47th Convention of the National American Woman Suffrage Association.* N.p., 1915.

Fitzpatrick, Ellen. *Endless Crusade: Women Social Scientists and Progressive Reform.* New York: Oxford University Press, 1990.

Flexner, Eleanor. *Century of Struggle: The Woman's Rights Movement in the United States.* Cambridge, MA: Belknap Press of Harvard University Press, 1959.

Forderhase, Nancy K. "'The Clear Call of Thoroughbred Women': The Kentucky Federation of Women's Clubs and the Crusade for Educational Reform, 1903–1909." *Register of the Kentucky Historical Society* 83 (1985): 19–35.

———. "Eve Returns to the Garden: Women Reformers in Appalachian Kentucky in the Early Twentieth Century." *Register of the Kentucky Historical Society* 85 (1987): 237–61.

———. "'Limited Only by Earth and Sky': The Louisville Woman's Club and Progressive Reform." *Filson Club History Quarterly* 59 (1985): 327–43.

Fox, Hugh F. *Some Aspects of Child Labor in the United States.* Atlanta: National Child Labor Commission, 1903.

Frankel, Noralee, and Nancy Schrom Dye, eds. *Gender, Class, Race and Reform in the Progressive Era.* Lexington: University Press of Kentucky, 1991.

Friedman, Jean E., and William G. Shade, eds. *Our American Sisters.* 2nd ed. Boston: Allyn & Bacon, 1976.

Fuller, Paul E. "Congressman Breckinridge and the Ladies; or, Sex, Politics and Morality in the Gilded Age." *Adena* 2 (1977): 1–13.

———. "An Early Venture of Kentucky Women in Politics: The Breckinridge Congressional Campaign of 1894." *Filson Club History Quarterly* 63 (1989): 224–42.

———. *Laura Clay and the Woman's Rights Movement.* Lexington: University Press of Kentucky, 1975.

Fuller, Raymond G. *Recreation and Child Welfare.* New York: The City, 1919.

Garraty, John A. "The Interrelation of Psychology and Biography." *Psychological Bulletin* 51 (1954): 569–82.

———. *The Nature of Biography.* London: J. Cape, 1957.

Gatten, Elizabeth. Interview with author, April 13, 1979.

Gere, Anne Ruggles. *Intimate Practices: Literacy and Cultural Work in U.S. Women's Clubs, 1880–1920.* Urbana: University of Illinois Press, 1997.

Getis, Victoria. *The Juvenile Court and the Progressives.* Urbana: University of Illinois Press, 2000.

Gibbons, Charles E. *Enforcement of the Child Labor Law in Kentucky.* New York: National Child Labor Commission, 1925.

Gillespie, Michele, and Catherine Clinton, eds. *Taking Off the White Gloves: Southern Women and Women Historians*. Columbia: University of Missouri Press, 1998.

Gilmore, Glenda E. *Gender and Jim Crow: Women and the Politics of White Supremacy in North Carolina, 1896–1920*. Chapel Hill: University of North Carolina Press, 1996.

Goldman, Eric F. *Rendezvous with Destiny: A History of Modern American Reform*. New York: Alfred A. Knopf, 1952.

Goodman, Clavia. *Bitter Harvest: Laura Clay's Suffrage Work*. Lexington: Bur, 1946.

Gordon, Linda. *Pitied but Not Entitled: Single Mothers and the History of Welfare, 1890–1925*. New York: Free Press, 1994.

———, ed. *Women, the State, and Welfare*. Madison: University of Wisconsin Press, 1990.

Gordon, Lynn D. *Gender and Higher Education in the Progressive Era*. New Haven, CT: Yale University Press, 1990.

Gould, Lewis L., ed. *The Progressive Era*. Syracuse, NY: Syracuse University Press, 1974.

Graham, Sara Hunter. *Woman Suffrage and the New Democracy*. New Haven, CT: Yale University Press, 1996.

Grantham, Dewey. *Southern Progressivism: The Reconciliation of Progress and Tradition*. Knoxville: University of Tennessee Press, 1983.

Gray, Laman A. "Ephraim McDowell, Father of Abdominal Surgery, Biographical Data." *Filson Club History Quarterly* 43 (1969): 216–29.

Green, Elna C. *Southern Strategies: Southern Women and the Woman Suffrage Question*. Chapel Hill: University of North Carolina Press, 1997.

Green, Thomas Marshall. *Historic Families of Kentucky*. 1889. Reprint, Baltimore: Clearfield, 1996.

Grimes, Alan P. *The Puritan Ethic and Woman Suffrage*. New York: Oxford University Press, 1967.

Guethlein, Carol. "Women in Louisville: Moving toward Equal Rights." *Filson Club History Quarterly* 55 (1981): 151–78.

Harbison, Clinton M. Interview with author, July 21, 1976.

Harper, Ida Husted. *The Life and Work of Susan B. Anthony*. 3 vols. Indianapolis: Bowen-Merrill, 1878–1908.

Harrison, Lowell H. "Attorney General John Breckinridge." *Filson Club History Quarterly* 36 (1962): 319–28.

———. *John Breckinridge: Jeffersonian Republican*. Louisville: Filson Club, 1969.

———. "John Breckinridge: Kentucky Planter, Speculator and Businessman." *Filson Club History Quarterly* 34 (1960): 205–27.

———. "John Breckinridge's Bluegrass Plantation Agreement to Operate, 1806." *Filson Club History Quarterly* 31 (1957): 104–14.

———. *Kentucky's Governors.* 2nd ed. Lexington: University Press of Kentucky, 2004.

Harrison, Lowell H., and James C. Klotter. *A New History of Kentucky.* Lexington: University Press of Kentucky, 1997.

Heale, M. J. *Twentieth-Century America: Politics and Power in the United States, 1900–2000.* New York: Oxford University Press, 2004.

Hecker, Eugene A. *A Short History of Women's Rights.* New York: G. P. Putnam's Sons, 1914.

Heise, Fred. H. *Thirteenth Medical Supplement of the Thirty-third Annual Report of the Trudeau Sanatorium for the Year Ending October 31, 1917.* Photocopy provided author by Linda Auclair, Trudeau Institute.

Hewitt, Nancy. *Southern Discomfort: Women's Activism in Tampa, Florida, 1880s–1920s.* Urbana: University of Illinois Press, 2001.

Higginbotham, Evelyn Brooks. *Righteous Discontent: The Women's Movement in the Black Baptist Church, 1880–1920.* Cambridge, MA: Harvard University Press, 1993.

Hofstadter, Richard. *The Age of Reform.* New York: Vintage, 1955.

Holman, Harriet R., ed. "The Kentucky Journal of Thomas Nelson Page." *Register of the Kentucky Historical Society* 68 (1970): 1–16.

Hopkins, James F., Mary W. M. Hargreaves, Robert Seager II, and Melba Porter Hay, eds. *The Papers of Henry Clay.* 11 vols. Lexington: University Press of Kentucky, 1959–92.

Hulst, N. P. *Report To the Merchants and Manufacturers Association of Milwaukee on Unworthy Charities.* Milwaukee: no publisher, 1911.

Hunt, David. Interview with author, February 22, 1977.

Ireland, Robert M. "Homicide in Nineteenth Century Kentucky." *Register of the Kentucky Historical Society* 81 (1983): 134–53.

———. "Law and Disorder in Nineteenth Century Kentucky." *Vanderbilt Law Review* 32 (1979): 281–82.

Irvin, Helen Deiss. *Women in Kentucky.* Lexington: University Press of Kentucky, 1979.

Irwin, Inez Haynes. *Angels and Amazons: A Hundred Years of American Women.* New York: Doubleday, Doren, 1933.

———. *The Story of the Woman's Party.* New York: Harcourt, Brace, 1921.

Jackson, Rodney. E-mail to author, October 3, 2006.

Jeydel, Alana S. *Political Women: The Women's Movement, Political Institutions, the Battle for Women's Suffrage and the ERA.* New York: Routledge, 2004.

Jillson, Willard Rouse. "Flamma Clara Maturae Medicinae Kentuckiensis." *Filson Club History Quarterly* 21 (1947): 103–29.

Johnson, Kenneth R. "Kate Gordon and the Woman Suffrage Movement." *Journal of Southern History* 38 (1972): 365–92.

Journal of the Regular Session of the House of Representatives of the Commonwealth of Kentucky. Louisville: Continental, 1910.

Journal of the Regular Session of the House of Representatives of the Commonwealth of Kentucky. Frankfort: Kentucky State Journal, 1912.

Journal of the Regular Session of the Senate of the Commonwealth of Kentucky. Louisville: Continental, 1910.

Journal of the Regular Session of the Senate of the Commonwealth of Kentucky. Frankfort: Kentucky State Journal, 1912.

Judah, Mrs. J. B. *Report of Treasurer, Kentucky Equal Rights Association*. N.p.: Kentucky Equal Rights Association, 1919.

Kavanaugh, Frank K. *Official Manual for the Use of Courts, State and County Officials and General Assembly of the State of Kentucky*. Frankfort: State Journal, 1912.

Keller, Morton. *Regulating a New Society: Public Policy and Social Change in America, 1900–1933*. Cambridge, MA: Harvard University Press, 1994.

Kennedy, Evelyn. "Some Kentucky Women." *Leslie's Monthly Magazine*, October 1897, 394–95.

Kentucky Acts. Louisville: J. G. Dana & A. G. Hodges, 1830.

Kentucky Acts. Frankfort: A. G. Hodges, 1838.

Kentucky Acts. Frankfort: A. G. Hodges, 1852.

Kentucky Acts. Frankfort: Capital, 1894.

Kentucky Acts. Louisville: Geo. G. Fetter, 1902.

Kentucky Acts. Louisville: Geo. G. Fetter, 1906.

Kerber, Linda K. *No Constitutional Right to Be Ladies: Women and the Obligations of Citizenship*. New York: Hill & Wang, 1998.

———. *Toward an Intellectual History of Women: Essays*. Chapel Hill: University of North Carolina Press, 1997.

Kerber, Linda K., Alice Kessler-Harris, and Kathryn Kish Sklar, eds. *U.S. History as Women's History: New Feminist Essays*. Chapel Hill: University of North Carolina Press, 1995.

Kirby, Jack T. *Darkness at the Dawning: Race and Reform in the Progressive South*. Philadelphia: Lippincott, 1972.

Kleber, John E., ed. *The Encyclopedia of Louisville*. Lexington: University Press of Kentucky, 2001.

———, ed. *The Kentucky Encyclopedia*. Lexington: University Press of Kentucky, 1992.

Klein, Maury. *History of the Louisville & Nashville Railroad*. Lexington: University Press of Kentucky, 2003.

Klein, Philip. *From Philanthropy to Social Welfare: An American Cultural Perspective*. San Francisco: Jossey-Bass, 1968.

Klotter, James C. *The Breckinridges of Kentucky, 1760–1981*. Lexington: University Press of Kentucky, 1986.

———. "The Breckinridges of Kentucky: Two Centuries of Leadership." PhD diss., University of Kentucky, 1975.

———. "Family Influences on a Progressive: The Early Years of Sophonisba P. Breckinridge." In *Kentucky Profiles: Biographical Essays in Honor of Holman Hamilton*, edited by James C. Klotter and Peter J. Sehlinger. Frankfort: Kentucky Historical Society, 1982.

———. *Kentucky: Portrait in Paradox, 1900–1950.* Frankfort: Kentucky Historical Society, 1996.

———. "Sex, Scandal, and Suffrage in the Gilded Age." *Historian* 42 (1980): 225–43.

———. *William Goebel: The Politics of Wrath.* Lexington: University Press of Kentucky, 1977.

Knight, Louise W. *Citizen: Jane Addams and the Struggle for Democracy.* Chicago: University of Chicago Press, 2005.

Knott, Claudia. "The Woman Suffrage Movement in Kentucky, 1879–1920." PhD diss., University of Kentucky, 1989.

Kraditor, Aileen S. *The Ideas of the Woman Suffrage Movement, 1890–1920.* New York: Columbia University Press, 1965.

Lagemann, Ellen C. *A Generation of Women: Education in the Lives of Progressive Reformers.* Cambridge, MA: Harvard University Press, 1979.

Larsen, Tim. *Christabel Pankhurst: Fundamentalism and Feminism in Coalition.* Woodbridge, UK: Boydell, 2002.

Lasch, Christopher. *The New Radicalism in America, 1889–1963: The Intellectual as Social Type.* New York: Alfred A. Knopf, 1965.

Leloudis, James L., II. "School Reform in the New South." *Journal of American History* 69 (1983): 886–909.

Lerner, Gerda. *The Majority Finds Its Past: Placing Women in History.* New York: Oxford University Press, 1979.

Leuchtenburg, William E. *The Perils of Prosperity, 1914–32.* Chicago: University of Chicago Press, 1958.

Levine, Peter. *The New Progressive Era: Toward a Fair and Deliberate Democracy.* New York: Rowman & Littlefield, 2000.

Lewis, Ella. *Constitution of Kentucky.* Frankfort: no publisher, 1928.

Ligon, Moses E. *A History of Public Education in Kentucky.* Lexington: University of Kentucky, 1942.

Link, Arthur S. *Wilson: The New Freedom.* Princeton, NJ: Princeton University Press, 1956.

———. *Woodrow Wilson and the Progressive Era, 1910–1917.* New York: Harper & Brothers, 1954.

Link, William A. *The Paradox of Southern Progressivism, 1880–1930.* Chapel Hill: University of North Carolina Press, 1992.

Lubove, Roy. *The Professional Altruist: The Emergence of Social Work as a Career, 1880–1930.* Cambridge, MA: Harvard University Press, 1965.

Lumsden, Linda J. *Rampant Women: Suffragists and the Right of Assembly.* Knoxville: University of Tennessee Press, 1997.

Lunardini, Christine A. *From Equal Suffrage to Equal Rights: Alice Paul and the National Woman's Party, 1910–1928.* New York: New York University Press, 1986.

Lutz, Alma. *Created Equal: A Biography of Elizabeth Cady Stanton.* New York: John Day, 1940.

———. *Susan B. Anthony: Rebel, Crusader, Humanitarian.* Boston: Beacon, 1959.

Manson, John. *The Salvation Army and the Public.* New York: E. P. Dutton, 1908.

Marcosson, Isaac F. *"Marse Henry": A Biography of Henry Watterson.* New York: Dodd, Mead, 1951.

Margulies, Herbert F. "Recent Opinion on the Decline of the Progressive Movement." *Mid-America* 45 (1963): 250–68.

Marilley, Suzanne M. *Woman Suffrage and the Origins of Liberal Feminism in the United States, 1820–1920.* Cambridge, MA: Harvard University Press, 1996.

Mattson, Kevin. *Creating a Democratic Public: The Struggle for Urban Participatory Democracy during the Progressive Era.* University Park: Pennsylvania State University Press, 1998.

McCarthy, Kathleen D., ed. *Lady Bountiful Revisited: Women, Philanthropy, and Power.* New Brunswick, NJ: Rutgers University Press, 1990.

———. *Noblesse Oblige: Charity and Cultural Philanthropy in Chicago, 1849–1929.* Chicago: University of Chicago Press, 1982.

McDowell, Madeline. "Recollections of Henry Clay." *Century Magazine*, May 1895, 765–70.

The Merck Manual of Diagnosis and Therapy. Rahway, NJ: Merck, 1950.

Mitchell, David. *The Fighting Pankhursts: A Study in Tenacity.* New York: Macmillan, 1967.

Montgomery, Rebecca S. *The Politics of Education in the New South: Women and Reform in Georgia, 1890–1930.* Baton Rouge: Louisiana State University Press, 2006.

Moon, Anna Mary. *Sketches of the Shelby, McDowell, Deaderick, and Anderson Families.* Chattanooga: no publisher, 1933.

Morgan, David. *Suffragists and Democrats: The Politics of Woman Suffrage in America.* East Lansing: Michigan State University Press, 1972.

Mowry, George. *The California Progressives.* Los Angeles: University of California Press, 1951.

———. *The Era of Theodore Roosevelt, 1900–1912.* New York: Harper & Brothers, 1958.

"Mrs. Desha Breckinridge." *Register of the Kentucky Historical Society* 19 (1921): 35–37.

Muncy, Robyn. *Creating a Female Dominion in American Reform, 1890–1935.* New York: Oxford University Press, 1991.

Nelms, Willie. *Cora Wilson Stewart: Crusader against Illiteracy.* Jefferson, NC: McFarland, 1997.

Nesbit, Helen. Interview with author, September 30, 1977.

Niedermeier, Lynn E. *Eliza Calvert Hall: Kentucky Author and Suffragist.* Lexington: University Press of Kentucky, 2007.

Oden, Mary E. *Delinquent Daughters: Protecting and Policing Adolescent Female Sexuality in the United States, 1885–1920.* Chapel Hill: University of North Carolina Press, 1995.

O'Neill, William. *Everyone Was Brave: The Rise and Fall of Feminism in America.* Chicago: Quadrangle, 1969.

Ott, Katherine. *Fevered Lives: Tuberculosis in American Culture since 1870.* Cambridge, MA: Harvard University Press, 1996.

Owens, W. T., ed. *Who's Who in Louisville . . . 1926.* Louisville: Standard, 1926.

Park, Bert E. *Ailing, Aging, Addicted: Studies of Compromised Leadership.* Lexington: University Press of Kentucky, 1993.

Park, Maud Wood. *Front Door Lobby.* Edited by Edna Lamprey Stantial. Boston: Beacon, 1960.

Peck, Mary G. *Carrie Chapman Catt: A Biography.* New York: H. W. Wilson, 1944.

Petty, Joe T., MD. Interview with author, December 18, 1976.

Proceedings of the First and Second Session of the Kentucky Conference on Charities and Corrections, 1904–1905. Louisville: Kentucky Conference on Charities and Corrections, 1905.

Pugh, Martin. *The March of the Women: A Revisional Analysis of the Campaign for Women's Suffrage, 1866–1914.* New York: Oxford University Press, 2000.

Purvis, June. *Emmeline Pankhurst: A Biography.* New York: Routledge, 2002.

Ramage, James A. *Rebel Raider: The Life of General John Hunt Morgan.* Lexington: University Press of Kentucky, 1986.

Ramage, Thomas W. "Augustus Owsley Stanley: Early Twentieth Century Kentucky Democrat." PhD diss., University of Kentucky, 1968.

Roark, Mrs. R. N., and Mrs. Desha Breckinridge, eds. *Kentucky Federation of Women's Clubs: School Betterment for Kentucky.* Harrodsburg: Kentucky Federation of Women's Clubs, 1908.

Robertson, Mattie, Dorothy Sutherland, and Anne Snowden Praither, eds. "The History of the Lexington Public Schools by the Sixth Grade of Arlington School." Typescript, 1931. In possession of Fayette County School System.

Robinson, Joseph. Interview with Thomas H. Appleton Jr., July 2, 1976.

Rosenberry, Lois K. M. "Katrina Ely Tiffany." In *Dictionary of American Biography,* vol. 18, edited by Dumas Malone et al. New York: Charles Scribner's Sons, 1936.

Rothman, David J. *Conscience and Convenience: The Asylum and Its Alternatives in Progressive America.* Boston: Little, Brown, 1980.

Rothman, Sheila. *Living in the Shadow of Death: Tuberculosis and the Social Experience of Illness in American History*. New York: Basic, 1994.

Rousmaniere, John P. "Cultural Hybrid in the Slums: The College Woman and the Settlement House, 1889–1894." *American Quarterly* 22 (1970): 45–66.

Ryan, Mary P. *Womanhood in America from Colonial Times to the Present*. New York: New Viewpoints, 1975.

Sallee, Shelley. *The Whiteness of Child Labor Reform in the New South*. Athens: University of Georgia Press, 2004.

Sarasohn, David. *The Party of Reform: Democrats in the Progressive Era*. Jackson: University Press of Mississippi, 1989.

Schneider, Dorothy, and Carl J. Schneider. *American Women in the Progressive Era, 1900–1920*. New York: Facts on File, 1993.

Scott, Anne Firor, ed. *The American Woman: Who Was She?* Englewood Cliffs, NJ: Prentice-Hall, 1971.

———. *Making the Invisible Women Visible*. Urbana: University of Illinois Press, 1984.

———. *Natural Allies: Women's Associations in American History*. Urbana: University of Illinois Press, 1991.

———. "The 'New Woman' in the New South." *South Atlantic Quarterly* 6 (1962): 473–83.

———. *The Southern Lady: From Pedestal to Politics, 1830–1930*. Chicago: University of Chicago Press, 1970.

Scott, Anne Firor, and Andrew Scott. *One Half the People: The Fight for Woman Suffrage*. Philadelphia: Lippincott, 1975.

Scott, Caroline, MD. Interview with author, February 24, 1977.

Seay, Lorraine. Interview with author, September 23, 1976.

Shaw, Anna Howard. *The Story of a Pioneer*. New York: Harper & Brothers, 1915.

Shryock, Richard H. *National Tuberculosis Association, 1904–1954: A Study of a Voluntary Movement in the United States*. New York: National Tuberculosis Association, 1957.

Simpson, Henry Clay. *Josephine Clay: Pioneer Horsewoman of the Bluegrass*. Louisville: Harmony House, 2005.

Sims, Anastatia. *The Power of Femininity in the New South: Women's Organizations and Politics in North Carolina, 1880–1930*. Columbia: University of South Carolina Press, 1997.

Sklar, Kathryn Kish. "Hull House in the 1890s: A Community of Women Reformers." *Signs* 10 (1985): 658–77.

Smith, D. Anthony, and Arthur H. Keeney. "Linda Neville (1873–1961): Kentucky Pioneer against Blindness." *Filson Club History Quarterly* 64 (1990): 360–76.

Sprague, Stuart Seely. "The Great Appalachian Iron and Coal Town Boom of 1889–1893." *Appalachian Journal* 4 (1977): 216–23.

Stanton, Elizabeth Cady. *Eighty Years and More (1815–1897): Reminiscences of Elizabeth Cady Stanton*. New York: European, 1898.

Stanton, Elizabeth Cady, Susan B. Anthony, Matilda J. Gage, and Ida Husted Harper, eds. *History of Woman Suffrage*. 6 vols. 1881–1922. Reprint, Salem, NH: Ayer, 1985.

Starr, Biff. Interview with author, February 26, 1977.

Stebner, Eleanor J. *The Women of Hull House: A Study in Spirituality, Vocation, and Friendship*. Albany: State University of New York Press, 1997.

Stevens, Doris. *Jailed for Freedom*. New York: Boni & Liveright, 1920.

Stivers, Camilla. *Bureau Men, Settlement Women: Constructing Public Administration in the Progressive Era*. Lawrence: University Press of Kansas, 2000.

Tager, Jack. "Progressives, Conservatives and the Theory of the Status Revolution." *Mid-America* 48 (1966): 162–75.

Talbot, Marion. *The Education of Women*. Chicago: University of Chicago Press, 1910.

Tapp, Hambleton. "Rogers Clark Ballard Thruston, Good Kentuckian, November 6, 1858–December 30, 1946." *Filson Club History Quarterly* 21 (1947): 103–29.

———. "Rogers Clark Ballard Thruston (1858–1946), Good Kentuckian." *Register of the Kentucky Historical Society* 45 (1947): 107–28.

Tapp, Hambleton, and James C. Klotter. *Kentucky: Decades of Discord, 1865–1900*. Frankfort: Kentucky Historical Society, 1977.

Taylor, A. Elizabeth. *Citizens at Last: The Woman Suffrage Movement in Texas*. Austin, TX: Ellen C. Temple, 1987.

———. *The Woman Suffrage Movement in Tennessee*. New York: Bookman, 1957.

Teller, Michael E. *The Tuberculosis Movement: A Public Health Campaign in the Progressive Era*. Westport, CT: Greenwood, 1988.

Thomas, Mary Martha. *The New Woman in Alabama: Social Reforms and Suffrage, 1890–1920*. Tuscaloosa: University of Alabama Press, 1993.

Travis, Anthony R. "Sophonisba Breckinridge, Militant Feminist." *Mid-America* 58 (1976): 111–18.

Trolander, Judith Ann. *Professionalism and Social Change: From the Settlement House Movement to Neighborhood Centers, 1886 to the Present*. New York: Columbia University Press, 1987.

Troutman, Richard. "Henry Clay and His 'Ashland' Estate." *Filson Club History Quarterly* 30 (1956): 159–74.

Turner, Elizabeth Hayes. *Women, Culture, and Community: Religion and Reform in Galveston, 1880–1920*. New York: Oxford University Press, 1997.

Underwood, Eliza. Interview with author, March 4, 1977.

University of Chicago Settlement, 1908. Chicago: University of Chicago Press, 1908.

Van Rie, Annelies, and Donald Enarson. "XDR Tuberculosis: An Indicator of Public Health Negligence." *Lancet*, November 4–10, 2006, 1554–55.

Wall, Joseph F. *Henry Watterson: Reconstructed Rebel*. New York: Oxford University Press, 1956.

Weinstein, Edwin A. *Woodrow Wilson: A Medical and Psychological Biography*. Princeton, NJ: Princeton University Press, 1981.

———. "Woodrow Wilson's Neurological Illness." *Journal of American History* 57 (1970): 324–51.

Weinstein, James. *The Corporate Ideal in the Liberal State, 1900–1918*. Boston: Beacon, 1968.

Welter, Barbara. "The Cult of True Womanhood, 1820–1860." *American Quarterly* 18 (1966): 151–74.

———. *Dimity Convictions: The American Woman in the Nineteenth Century*. Athens: Ohio University Press, 1976.

Wheeler, Marjorie Spruill. *New Women of the New South: The Leaders of the Woman Suffrage Movement in the Southern States*. New York: Oxford University Press, 1993.

———, ed. *Votes for Women! The Woman Suffrage Movement in Tennessee, the South, and the Nation*. Knoxville: University of Tennessee Press, 1995.

Whisnant, David E. *All That Is Native and Fine: The Politics of Culture in an American Region*. Chapel Hill: University of North Carolina Press, 1983.

Wiebe, Robert H. *The Search for Order, 1877–1920*. New York: Hill & Wang, 1967.

Wilson, Robert Burns. *The Shadows of the Trees and Other Poems*. New York: R. H. Russell, 1898.

Wolfe, Margaret Ripley. *Daughters of Canaan: A Saga of Southern Women*. Lexington: University Press of Kentucky, 1995.

———. "Fallen Leaves and Missing Pages: Women in Kentucky History." *Register of the Kentucky Historical Society* 90 (1992): 64–89.

Wood, Mary I. "What Women's Clubs Are Doing." *Ladies Home Journal*, September 1914, 37.

Woody, Thomas. *A History of Women's Education in the United States*. New York: Science Press, 1929.

Wright, John D., Jr. *Lexington, Heart of the Bluegrass*. Lexington: Lexington-Fayette County Historic Commission, 1982.

Index